Aspect-Oriented Requirements Engineering

Ana Moreira • Ruzanna Chitchyan • João Araújo
Awais Rashid
Editors

Aspect-Oriented Requirements Engineering

Editors
Ana Moreira
João Araújo
Universidade Nova de Lisboa
Caparica, Portugal

Ruzanna Chitchyan
University of Leicester
Leicester, United Kingdom

Awais Rashid
University of Lancaster
Lancaster, United Kingdom

ISBN 978-3-662-52153-3 ISBN 978-3-642-38640-4 (eBook)
DOI 10.1007/978-3-642-38640-4
Springer Heidelberg New York Dordrecht London

ACM Computing Classification (1998): D.2, K.6

Printed on acid-free paper

Springer is part of Springer Science+Business Media (www.springer.com)

Preface

Introduction

Aspect-oriented requirements-engineering (AORE) approaches aim to facilitate identification and analysis of *crosscutting concerns* (also termed as *aspects*) during requirements engineering to understand their potential effects and trade-offs with respect to other stakeholder requirements.

Often AORE approaches extend existing requirements-engineering techniques with additional support for identification, modularisation, composition, and analysis of crosscutting concerns. Such support is missing in most contemporary requirements-engineering techniques. For instance, in the classical use cases approach [1], non-functional requirements (NFR) cannot be readily modelled. Although techniques such as goal-based approaches [2, 3] support modularisation and analysis of such NFRs, they lack effective composition mechanisms to reflect and explore the complex dependencies and interactions (between NFRs themselves as well as NFRs and functional concerns) fully. Thus, AORE focuses on providing systematic means for modularisation, composition, and analysis of crosscutting concerns in requirements.

In the recent years significant work has been carried out in aspect-oriented requirements engineering. The aim of this book is to serve as a consolidation medium. The message given here is that whatever requirements engineering approach one uses, there will be a problem of treatment of broadly scoped concerns, which repeatedly appear, often have system-wide effects, and interact (e.g. conflict or supplement) with other requirements as well as influence the architectural decisions for the system-to-be. In this book we discuss how such *aspects* can be identified, represented, composed, and reasoned about, as well as used in specific domains and in industry. Thus, the book does not aim to present or promote a particular aspect-oriented requirements engineering approach but aims to provide an understanding of the aspect-oriented perspective on requirements engineering: what challenges does it tackle that supplement the more established requirements engineering work, what tasks and processes does it use, and how does it benefit its adopting community.

Use of the Crisis Management [4] case study has been advised throughout the book as the common medium for demonstration of the work presented in each chapter. This is to shelter the reader from having to understand a potentially large set of different examples and instead focus on the essence of each presented approach. However, in some chapters, where the application of AORE to a specific domain is of significance by itself (e.g. in chapters discussing use of AORE in industrial setting), the common case study has been omitted.

1 Getting Started: AORE Main Concepts

In AORE a *concern* is defined as a unit encapsulating (one or more) requirements related to a certain matter of interest. For instance, a use case or a viewpoint with its requirements is an example of a concern.

An *aspect* (or *crosscutting concern*) is a modularisation unit for those requirements that do not align well into the established single-type decomposition modularisation units. For example, while use case units are ideal for functionality modularisation, non-functional requirements do not fit into the use case structure, but normally crosscut several use cases. Therefore, an aspect at the requirements level is a broadly scoped property (represented by a single requirement or a coherent set of requirements), which affects multiple other requirements in the system so that it may constrain the specified behaviour of the affected requirements or influence the affected requirements to alter their specified behaviour.

As illustrative example, consider a security requirement that constrains a requirement providing access to certain types of data in the system so that only a certified set of users may access that data. Similarly, another security requirement may influence communication requirements by altering their behaviour to impose encryption constraints. The requirements affected by a requirements-level aspect may already have been partitioned using abstractions such as viewpoints, use cases, and themes. Figure 1 shows a requirements-level aspect affecting multiple requirements in such a partitioning. Composition specification is used to relate requirements-level aspects with the non-crosscutting requirements.

Some awareness of the crosscutting concerns existed in the Requirements Engineering community before AORE, for instance, in works on NFR/softgoals [5] and viewpoints [6]. However, this was a segmented perspective, with crosscutting concerns considered as a "special" type of concerns, with "unusual" properties. AORE, on the other hand, provides a general unified framework explaining the properties of the crosscutting requirements as the natural result of (the traditional) modelling of the multi-perspective world with a single type of modularisation unit (such as use cases and goals). Also, AORE underlines the need for composition of concerns and aims to provide an extensive support for it. Compositions are used for understanding and analysis of concern interdependencies—for detection of potential

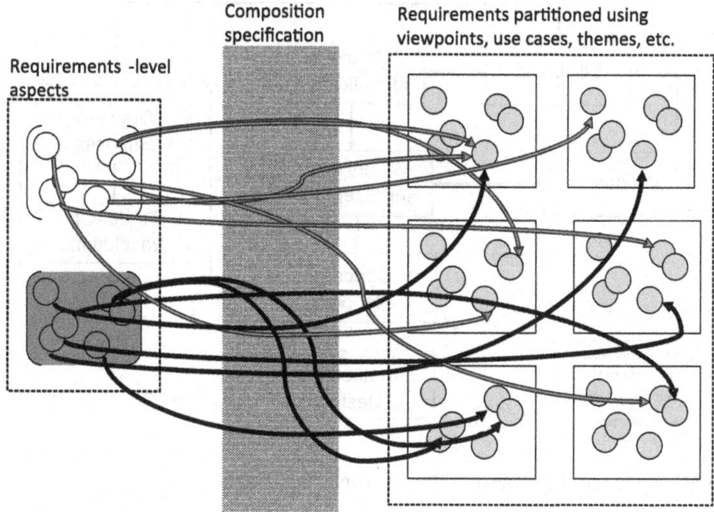

Fig. 1 Requirements-level aspects constraining and influencing (via a composition specification) other requirements

conflicts between various concerns/requirements very early on in order to either take corrective measures or make appropriate decisions for the next development step. The composed requirements also become valuable sources of validation for the complete system, as well as potential artefacts for requirement reuse.

Therefore, if requirements aspects are not effectively modularised, it is not possible to reason about their effect on the system or on each other, and the lack of modularisation of such properties can result in a large ripple effect on other requirements or architectural components upon evolution. The provision of effective means for handling aspects in requirements makes it possible to establish critical trade-offs early on in the software lifecycle.

Figure 2 depicts a general AORE framework, highlighting in grey the activities where AORE makes its major contribution.

One other issue noted by the AORE work is the need to trace crosscutting properties across the lifecycle of a software system. It is not sufficient to identify and reason about crosscutting concerns during requirements engineering. Once these concerns and their associated trade-offs have been established, it is essential that the software engineers can trace them to architecture (illustrated in Fig. 2 by the concern mapping activity), design, implementation and subsequent maintenance and evolution. Modularisation of crosscutting properties at the requirements level is the first step towards establishing such traceability.

As in other AO software lifecycle stages, AORE uses the concepts of joinpoints, pointcuts, advice, intertype declarations, and composition (or weaving) [7]. These concepts are normally interpreted somewhat differently for each individual AORE approach and the full or partial set of these concepts may be utilised by each given

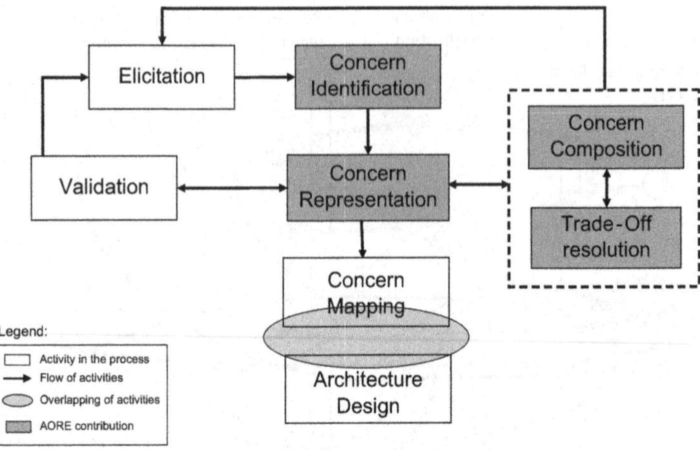

Fig. 2 AORE in the broader context of Requirements Engineering

work. However, presence of (any of) these notions in an RE approach will generally indicate presence of an AO perspective in it. These notions are generically defined below:

- Aspects can only be invoked, or composed with other modules, at some well-defined and principled points within the software artefacts. These points are referred to as *joinpoints*. As stated in [8]: "A joinpoint is a point of interest in some artifact in the software lifecycle through which two or more concerns may be composed. A *joinpoint model* defines the kinds of joinpoints available and how they are accessed and used". Examples of such well-defined, principled points in AORE are, for instance, goal notes, or tasks in goal graphs, or identifiable (e.g. via ID or name) requirements and concerns encapsulating those requirements, identifiable (e.g. via their grammatical role or meaning) parts of text, etc.
- *Pointcuts* specify a set of joinpoints at which a given aspect should interact with some other modules. Pointcuts can be defined *by extension*, i.e. by enumerating each joinpoint relevant for the given aspect application, or *by intension*, i.e. via a more abstract selection criteria, such as regular expressions, or semantic-matching queries. Because aspects normally broadly affect a number of other concerns, defining their interactions by extension is rather inefficient. Consequently, in AOSD, pointcuts are normally defined by intension [7]. Thus, a *pointcut* normally is a predicate that matches joinpoints.
- As noted above, an aspect affects a set of other concerns at the joinpoints. In AOSD terminology, it is said that aspects *advise* other concerns. An *advice* represents the particular part of aspect that will manifest itself (e.g. by adding or changing behaviour) at a given joinpoint of the affected concern. Traditionally, an advice in AOSD implies a *behaviour-related interaction* between aspectual

and non-aspectual artefacts. Such an interaction is also defined in respect with some temporal, conditional, or unconditional order.

- *Intertype declarations* (also called *introductions*) are an additional mechanism for directly modifying the *structure* of the original artefacts. For instance, an intertype declaration may insert a new requirement into a viewpoint or even change subtype structure, etc.
- *Composition* (also called *weaving*) is the integration of the separated crosscutting elements back into the modules crosscut by them. However, in AORE, it is not always necessary to physically integrate the aspectual elements into other modules [7]. Often a *composition specification* is sufficient for reasoning about aspectual and non-aspectual module interactions. Thus, composition here can often imply projecting the constraints and influences of individual requirements-level aspects on other system requirements, based on the knowledge inherent in the composition specification.

The composition specification define which aspectual elements (advice, intertype declarations, and so forth.) affect which joinpoints (selected by pointcuts) of which other modules, in what way, and defines what are the temporal, conditional, or unconditional circumstances of aspect invocation.

In summary, AORE uses the above outlined concepts to provide improved separation of concerns and composition at the requirements level. The composition definitions are often used as an analysis tool for conflict-point identification and interaction understanding, and, in some cases [9], transformational compositions are also realised.

It is also essential to note that not all aspectual artefacts identified at the requirements level will subsequently be represented as code-level aspects. On the contrary, some may well transform into other software artefacts (e.g. architectural topology) or business-related decisions (e.g. procedures for security policy used by the business) before an application is implemented. In addition, new aspects, often related to the selected development technology, will emerge at the other stages of software development, but these will not be visible in requirements.

2 *Structure of the Book*

This book is largely alighted with the main AORE-related activities depicted in Fig. 2: concern identification-related issues are discussed in the similarly titled Part I; topics on concern representation and composition are discussed in Part II titled Concern Modelling and Composition; topics of concern mapping (e.g. architectural implications of requirements level aspects and aspects in particular domains) are presented in Part III titled Domain-Specific Use of AORE; the issues of trade-off, conflicts, and validity are discussed in Part IV, under the title of Interaction Analysis; finally, under the title AORE Evaluation Part V presents two perspectives on how AORE is used in industry and an overview chapter on evaluation work in AORE so far.

The **Concern Identification** section discusses crosscutting concern identification in textual as well as model-based requirements. The aim of concern identification is to, first of all, facilitate building the knowledge on what crosscutting occurs in requirements and why. Along with such knowledge collection, identification should be accompanied with modularisation support, which, ideally, can propagate the modularity to later stages of software development. In this section, Chap. 1 describes the EA-Miner tool-based approach, which offers automated support for identifying crosscutting in such requirements artefacts as viewpoints or use cases, which consist of natural language text. The main characteristic of this approach is the use of natural language processing (NLP) for concern identification. Chapter 2 presents a goal-based approach that uses a list of adaptation rules for the requirements aspects to be managed at runtime. It explains how different concepts in requirements aspects are formulated and reasoned about. The basic adaptation rules are classified according to the roles played in the runtime changes.

The **Concern Modelling and Composition** section, which includes Chaps. 3–7, is focused on modelling and composition definition in AORE. Since AORE defines an aspect as a new type of module with its particular rules of interacting with other modules, it is essential to deliver a good modelling support for representation of these new modules and their interrelationships with each other as well as non-aspectual modules. There are the challenges tackled in the present section.

Chapter 3 introduces an aspectual scenario-based approach where sequence diagram and state machines are modelled using a technique for modelling and composition of patterns based on graph transformations called MATA (Modelling Aspects Using a Transformation Approach).

Chapter 4 describes a semantics-based composition approach applied to textual requirements. Here the composition specifications are based on the semantics of the natural language. This is achieved by annotating the natural language requirements with information on their grammatical and semantic properties, and using these annotations as well as natural language semantics as a joinpoint model for composition specification.

Chapter 5 presents the composition mechanism for aspect-oriented user requirements notations (AoURN). The focus is on interleaving and enhanced matching based on semantics composition rules. Interleaved composition allows two scenarios to be combined keeping the overall behaviour of the original scenarios. Semantics-based matching allows for a class of refactoring operations to be performed on an AoURN model without breaking the matches of an aspect's pattern.

Chapter 6 presents AOV-graph, an approach that deals with the crosscutting problems arising from interactions in goal models. This approach helps in defining a crosscutting relationship which modularises interactions and provides composition and visualisation mechanisms to analyse and model the goal-based requirements.

Chapter 7 shows how to identify and model crosscutting concerns in Problem Frames. This is particularly relevant as in problem frames some requirements appear in several (sub) problems diagrams, resulting in scattering effect. This work shows how to compose such concerns with the elements they crosscut via a textual composition language.

The **Domain-specific use of AORE** section discusses specific uses of requirements-level aspects, like architecture derivation from requirements, modelling security requirements with aspects, and volatile requirements modelling. This section demonstrates how effectively AORE can be used in more specific contexts. This part consists of Chaps. 8–10.

Chapter 8 offers a strategy to derive architectural component-based model from an aspect-oriented requirements specification. It uses model-driven development where meta-models and transformations are specified and implemented.

Chapter 9 presents an approach for handling changes made to security-critical programmes. The authors observe that when a change happens (in any part of a system), the validation procedure for the security requirements may need to be updated even if the security requirements have not changed.

Chapter 10 demonstrates how can help to deal with volatile (i.e. highly unstable) requirements. Here it is noted, that although volatile concerns are not always crosscutting, they have the same issues of independency, modular representation and composition that are required for aspects. Thus, AO perspective is particularly fruitful in this context. Moreover, the chapter discusses how evolution, constrained by volatile requirements, is facilitated via adoption of an aspect-oriented approach.

Aspects bring with themselves a new set of challenges of handling independencies and interactions. These challenges are discussed in the **Interaction Analysis** section. Aspects composition may result in undesirable behaviour that violates the overall systems requirements. These interactions happen due to side effects introduced by aspect composition, such as interference or negative contributions. These are discussed in Chaps. 11–14.

Chapter 11 shows an approach and tool called EA-Analyzer that automates the process of detecting conflicts within textual AO requirements specifications. The aim is to facilitate the requirements engineers' work with large natural language specifications, which may contain numerous interdependencies. An empirical evaluation of the tool is also discussed, showing that conflicts within AO textual requirements specifications can be detected with a good accuracy.

Chapter 12 presents a tool-supported approach for conflict management at the AORE level. It uses a hybrid multi-criteria analysis technique to perform trade-offs analysis and obtain a ranking of concerns. This technique can be used to support architectural choices during the software architecture design and "what-if" scenario analysis.

Chapter 13 presents a use case-driven approach and tool for analysing consistency at the level of requirements modelling. Activities are used to refine use cases and are combined with a specification of pre-and post-conditions into an integrated behaviour model. This is formalised using the graph transformation theory and used for reason about consistency.

Chapter 14 shows an approach where features are treated as aspects and feature composition as aspect composition. They use Composition Frames to compose aspects and resolve aspect interactions at runtime.

The **AORE evaluation** section describes experiences of use of AORE in industry and presents an overview of AORE evaluation work so far. The first part consists of Chaps. 15 and 16. Chapter 15 discusses how the technique called Requirements Composition Table (RCT) is used in two financial applications. The RCT technique has been implemented for a number of Wall Street applications at various investment banks. This chapter illustrates how RCT can help perform change impact analysis for releases and assess test coverage of existing regression test suites.

Chapter 16 discusses the application and evaluation of two AORE approaches (Theme/Doc and MDSOCRE) in the slot machines domain. This application involved several large requirement documents that have ambiguity issues and aspectual interactions.

Finally, Chap. 17, which also concludes the book, draws upon experience from evaluation performed in other phases of development and also the problems that can be experienced when evaluating AORE approaches to establish a series of guidelines to assist software developers.

3 *Crisis Management System Case Study*

In order to observe how the same problem is addressed by different approaches, we adopt a common case study to be used throughout the chapters of this book. The case study domain is crisis management systems, i.e. systems that manage the relevant parties, activities and information involved in solving a crisis. This case study was proposed as an exemplar to evaluate aspect-oriented modelling approaches in 2010 [4] and has since been used by the AOSD community for the evaluation and comparison of aspect-oriented approaches (e.g. CMA workshop series). The requirements used to create this exemplar were based on the real requirements document for crisis management systems created by Optimal Security [10].

The general objectives of a Crisis Management System (CMS) is to assist in the coordination of a crisis; to guarantee that a catastrophic situation is under control; to mitigate the crisis effects by allocating and managing the available resources in an effective manner; to identify, create, and execute missions in order to manage the crisis; and to recover the crisis information to allow future analysis [4]. A crisis can range from natural disasters (e.g. earthquakes, fire, floods), terrorist attacks or sabotage (e.g. explosions, kidnapping), accidents (e.g. car crash plant explosion, plane crash) and technological disruptions. All these are examples of emergency situations that are unpredictable and can lead to severe after-effects unless handled immediately.

A crisis management system facilitates the communication and interoperation between all stakeholders involved in handling the crisis (e.g. government, police systems, medical services, military systems). A CMS allocates and manages resources, and facilitates access to relevant information to authorised users of the CMS.

Finally, several non-functional properties are related to CMS, e.g. availability, response time, security, safety, mobility, persistence and multi-access. They are broadly scope and potentially crosscutting. The full case study documents are provided in the Appendix A of this book.

4 *Intended Audience*

This book is intended for software developers, software engineers, industrial trainees, and undergraduate and postgraduate students.

5 *Acknowledgements*

We are grateful to many people and several institutions for their contributions on the development of AORE.

To our co-organisers of Early Aspects workshop series. Sixteen editions have been organised since 2002. Thank you to Paul Clements, Bedir Tekinerdogan, and Elisa Baniassad for helping with the steering of the workshop, and to Alberto Sardinha, Alessandro Garcia, Carla Silva, Christa Schwanninger, Gunter Mussbacher, Jan Gerben Wijnstra, Jeff Gray, Jon Whittle, John Grundy, Mónica Pinto, Nan Niu, Pablo Sanchez, Paulo Merson, Uirá Kulesza, and Vander Alves, for taking the lead of the organisation in different editions. We are grateful for the interest demonstrated by all the authors who submitted their work and helped so much in creating the Early Aspects community, to the Program Committee members for offering their time to review the papers, to the participants that helped keeping discussions alive, to everyone that contributed to the increase of the number of postgraduate students that accomplished their dissertations in the field of Early Aspects, and to all the reviewers of the chapters included in this book.

A special word of thanks goes to Pete Sawyer for the discussions we had with him from the time the idea born in our minds. He contributed with the first vision paper on AORE, and his expertise and extensive experience on Requirements Engineering helped us finding an integrated view for RE with aspects.

During these 15 years of work, several people contributed to the development of Early Aspects through several projects funded by European Union, EPSRC, Fundação para a Ciência e Tecnologia (FCT), Conselho de Reitores das Universidades Portuguesas (CRUP) (bilateral projects with France and Spain), and CAPES/GRICES (bilateral projects between Brazil and Portugal). A special thanks to the European AMPLE and AOSD-Europe projects.

Finally, we thank to CITI research centre at Universidade de Nova Lisboa for funding several visits of Awais to Lisbon.

6 *Concluding Remarks*

Aspect-Oriented Requirement Engineering (AORE) has focused on the problem of treatment of crosscutting concerns in requirements. AORE includes developing techniques for modularising such concerns, identifying their influence on other requirements in the system, establishing critical trade-offs between aspectual requirements before the architecture is derived, and determining their mapping and influence on artefacts at later software development stages.

Each section of this book addresses a particular field of interest for AORE. While Part I is dedicated to the identification and representation of requirements aspects, Part II discusses concern modelling and the value of composition as a means to reason about the requirements specifications. Part III covers specific uses of AORE while offering some support for traceability. Part IV is dedicated to aspect interactions, including conflict resolution and trade-off analysis techniques. Finally, Part V discusses the use of AORE in industry.

References

1. I. Jacobson, M. Chirsterson, P. Jonsson, G. Overgaard, *Object-Oriented Software Engineering: A Use Case Driven Approach* (Addison-Wesley Professional, 1992)
2. A. Dardenne, A. van Lamsweerde, S. Fickas, Goal-directed requirements acquisition. Sci. Comput. Programm. **20**(1–2), 3–50 (1993). doi:10.1016/0167-6423(93)90021-G. http://dx.doi.org/10.1016/0167-6423(93)90021-G
3. A. van Lamsweerde, Goal-oriented requirements engineering: a guided tour, in *Proceedings of the Fifth IEEE International Symposium on Requirements Engineering (RE '01)*. IEEE Computer Society, Washington, DC, 2001, p. 249
4. J. Kienzle, N. Guelfi, S. Mustafiz, Crisis management systems: a case study for aspect-oriented modeling, in *Transactions on Aspect-Oriented Software Development 7*, ed. by S. Katz, M. Mezini, J. Kienzle. LNCS, vol. 6210 (2010), pp. 1–22
5. L. Chung, B. Nixon, E. Yu, J. Mylopoulos, *Non-functional Requirements in Software Engineering* (Kluwer Academic, 2000)
6. A. Finkelstein, I. Sommerville, The viewpoints FAQ. BCS/IEE Softw. Eng. J. **11**(1), (1996)
7. J. Brichau, R. Chitchyan, A. Rashid, T. D'Hondt, *Aspect-Oriented Software Development: An Introduction*. Article in "Wiley Encyclopaedia of Computer Science and Engineering", ed. by B.W. Wah, vol. 1. ISBN 978-0-471-38393-2 (Wiley, 2008), pp. 188–199
8. K. van de Berg, J.-M. Conejero, R. Chitchyan, AOSD ontology 1.0: public ontology of aspect orientation, in *Report of the EU Network of Excellence on AOSD*, 2005

9. R. Chitchyan, M. Pinto, A. Rashid, L. Fuentes, COMPASS: composition-centric mapping of aspectual requirements to architecture. T. Aspect Oriented Softw. Dev. **4**, 3–53 (2007)
10. Optimal Security: Requirements document: Version 0.8., http://www.cs.colostate.edu/remodd/v1/sites/default/files/cms_case_study.pdf. Accessed 15 Jan 2013

Caparica, Portugal — Ana Moreira
Leicester, UK — Ruzanna Chitchyan
Caparica, Portugal — João Araújo
Lancaster, UK — Awais Rashid

Contents

Part III Domain-Specific Use of AORE

Part IV Aspect Interactions

Part V AORE in Industry

Part I
Concern Identification in Requirements

Chapter 1
Aspect Identification in Textual Requirements with EA-Miner

Nathan Weston, Ruzanna Chitchyan, Americo Sampaio, Awais Rashid, and Phil Greenwood

Abstract This chapter presents a methodology for identification of crosscutting concerns in textual requirements along with its supporting tool EA-Miner. This chapter discusses how EA-Miner uses natural language processing techniques in aspect identification and structuring using a requirements level feature model as an example. The process is illustrated using the Car Crash case study.

1.1 Introduction

As most documents used in the Requirements Engineering (RE) are still written in natural language, it is not surprising that a notable body of work has studied automation support for RE tasks using [9, 10, 12, 13, 15, 16, 24] natural language processing (NLP) techniques over requirements-related documents. The aspect identification approach presented in this chapter also follows a similar line of work.

Nevertheless, since natural language is quite imprecise and full of ambiguities, use of NLP for aspectual model extraction is not a straightforward activity. However, since structuring of requirements into crosscutting and non-crosscutting modules has been shown [2, 20, 21, 27] to provide such benefits as facilitated conflict detection, simplified analysis of aspect-to-aspect interactions and assisted derivation of architecture form requirements models, researching into NLP-based automation

N. Weston · A. Rashid · P. Greenwood
Lancaster University, Lancaster, UK
e-mail: westonn@comp.lancs.ac.uk; greenwop@comp.lancs.ac.uk; marash@comp.lancs.ac.uk

R. Chitchyan (✉)
University of Leicester, Leicester, UK
e-mail: rc256@le.ac.uk

A. Sampaio
Universidade de Fortaleza, Fortaleza, Brasil
e-mail: americo.sampaio@unifor.br

A. Moreira et al. (eds.), *Aspect-Oriented Requirements Engineering*,
DOI 10.1007/978-3-642-38640-4_1, © Springer-Verlag Berlin Heidelberg 2013

for such aspect identification is a well-worth endeavour. Yet, most of the current AORE approaches [19–21, 26, 27] (with exception of Theme/Doc [2]) have not addressed the automation problem.

This is where the EA-Miner tool-based approach comes into play by offering automation support for identifying the abstractions of different AORE techniques (e.g. viewpoints [11] based, use-case [14] based) and helping to build the respective requirements models. The tool facilitate the tasks of:

- *Identification of model abstractions*: For example, concepts such as use cases, viewpoints and early aspects that belong to a specific requirements technique (e.g. Viewpoints-based AORE [20, 21]) can be automatically mined from different elicitation documents;
- *Structuring abstractions into various models*: The tool offers features to edit the identified abstractions (add, remove, filter) as well as to map them into a chosen model (e.g. a structured AORE specification based on viewpoints or feature models).

It should be noted that EA-Miner does not fully replace the work of a requirements engineer but only promotes the efficiency of his/her work by pinpointing the key crosscutting information. The use of EA-Miner in an AORE process is discussed in Sect. 1.2 below. In Sect. 1.3 we show how EA-Miner uses NLP techniques to automate the identification of concepts and mapping of models. Section 1.4 demonstrates use of EA-Miner for identification of aspects and variability in a feature model built from the requirements of the Car Crash Management system. Section 1.5 presents related work with Sect. 1.6 concluding the chapter.

1.2 EA-Miner and (AO)RE Process

The common goal of all (AO)RE approaches (e.g. [3, 19–21, 26, 27]) is to provide an appropriate separation of concerns at the requirements level, encapsulating crosscutting properties in early aspects. With this in mind, the present work offers a framework (consisting of the EA-Miner tool and guidelines) that can be used with any text-based (AO)RE approach. This is demonstrated in Fig. 1.1 with a viewpoint-based RE model as an example.

The top of Fig. 1.1 shows the general activities (1–4) common to most AORE processes, while the bottom shows an adaptation of activities 2 and 3 based on viewpoint-based AORE. Depending on the AORE approach used, each activity is adapted accordingly (e.g. had we considered a feature-based RE approach we would identify features instead of viewpoints in activity 2.1).

The reason we highlighted activities 2 and 3 is that these are the ones that represent the core focus of EA-Miner and also where it significantly contributes to existing (AO)RE approaches by identifying crosscutting concepts from requirement elicitation documents and mapping into an AORE model. The overview of these two activities, the artefacts involved and the role of EA-Miner is discussed below.

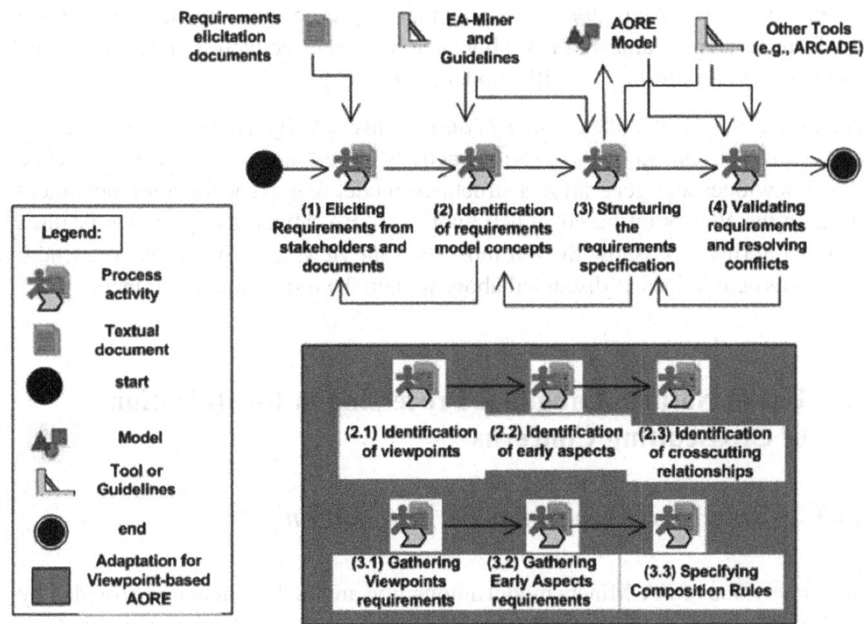

Fig. 1.1 General AORE process with detailed adaptation for viewpoint-based AORE

Identification of requirements model concepts[1]: EA-Miner helps in automating activity 2, using the documents produced in activity 1 (i.e. any requirements elicitation process) as input, of identifying model concepts (e.g. viewpoints, early aspects, features and others) and presenting them to the user. Some characteristics about the identification are:

- *Rule based and NLP based*: For each AORE model considered, the mining technique utilised can be different. For example, for the Viewpoint model, part-of-speech (POS) NLP technique is used to identify nouns as viewpoint candidates, while for a feature-based approach we can consider action verbs as candidate features and nouns as candidate entities.
- *Every concept identified is a candidate*: EA-Miner identifies the model concepts and considers them to be candidates. The tool offers several features to show information about the candidates (e.g. their frequency of occurrence in the text, their meaning) as well as process guidelines to help the requirements engineer accept or reject that concept.
- *Process Guidelines can be used*: We underline that EA-Miner does not replace the work of the requirements engineer and is not aimed at 100 % automation. For this reason, guidelines documenting previous experience and best practices can

[1]The details on concept identification are presented in [23].

be used to assist the requirements engineer by prescribing some tips on how the information and features of EA-Miner can be used effectively. Guidelines can be customised according to AORE model used.

Structuring the Requirements specification: This activity constitutes editing the initial model produced in the previous activity by discarding irrelevant concepts, adding new ones and generating a structured model (e.g. a specification document based on the Viewpoint-based AORE approach). EA-Miner also provides features such as filtering (e.g. show the ten most relevant viewpoints based on frequency) and process guidelines as discussed above to help the requirements engineer.

1.3 Use of Natural Language Processing in Identification of Crosscutting Concerns

1.3.1 Using NLP Techniques for Automation

The cornerstone of EA-Miners model automation are the NLP features provided by the WMatrix NLP tool suite which have been shown to be effective in early phase requirements engineering [22, 24]. WMatrix implements NLP techniques such as frequency analysis, POS (with a precision of 97 %), and semantic tagging (with a precision of 91 %) that provide relevant information about the properties and semantics of a text in natural language. Frequency analysis shows statistical data about frequencies of words that help to find out which words are more significant in the text. WMatrix takes a corpus-based NLP approach. Corpus Linguistics [18] can be understood as the study of language based on real-life language use. A corpus is a collection of texts from different sources (e.g. newspapers, magazines, books, journals) that can be collected over several years and made available for researchers. For example, the British National Corpus (BNC) [4], on which WMatrix draws, is a 100 million word reference collection of samples of written and spoken English from a wide range of sources. POS tagging [22, 24] assigns to each word its grammatical function (POS) such as singular common noun, comparative adjective, infinitive verb and other categories such as the ones in Table 1.1. The tagging process in WMatrix is based on a language model derived from the large reference corpus and uses surrounding context to decide the most likely tag for each word.

Semantic tagging [22, 24] assigns a word or multiword expression to a specific class of meaning. The semantic tags are represented in a tagset arranged in 21 top-level categories (e.g. M and S in Table 1.1) that expand into 232 sub-categories (e.g. M3 and S7.4) [22]. Each of these categories groups words that are related via a specific meaning (e.g. M3 contains vehicle, car, bus, truck, automobile). The taxonomy originates from a corpus-based dictionary and has been comparatively evaluated against publicly available semantic hierarchies. Moreover, the same word (e.g. performance) can contain different meanings (e.g. act of a dancer or artist,

Table 1.1 Examples of POS and semantic tags from [22, 24]

POS tag	What it represents
VVI	Infinitive (e.g. to give... It will work...)
NN1	Singular common noun (e.g. book, girl)
SEM tag	What it represents
M	Movement, location, travel and transport
S	Social actions, states and processes
M3	Vehicles and transport on land
S7.4	Permission

processing power of the computer) and thus be present in more than one semantic category. The semantic tagger deals with this by analysing the context of the phrase in which the word is used and also by using POS tags for disambiguation in order to attribute the correct tag. It is important to highlight that both tasks of POS and semantic tagging are completely handled by WMatrix and do not require any input from the requirements engineer. The semantic tagger makes its decisions based on a large coverage dictionary of single words and multiword expressions, currently containing 73,894 words and multiwords. These resources have been constructed manually by linguists for other corpus-based projects over a number of years. EA-Miner utilises WMatrix to pre-process a requirements document provided as input. WMatrix returns another file which consists of the same content as the input file but tagged with POS and SEM tags. For instance, WMatrix will take an input of "road traffic" and returned the tagged output where the word road has POS tag = NN1 which represents a singular noun and traffic has the SEM tag = M3 which represents the vehicles and transport on land semantic class. Another important concept that is utilised in EA-Miner is Stemming [22, 24] which is the process of reducing similar words to the same canonical form. For example the words availability and available will be stemmed to avail. This makes it possible to recognise words that are not exactly equal and treat them as the same concept (e.g. for a requirements engineer the words driver and drivers are the same).

1.3.2 Aspect Identification

The identification of early aspects in EA-Miner can be broken into two categories: non-functional and functional. Non-functional requirements (NFR) (e.g. security, concurrency, persistence, parallelism and so forth) are generally natural candidates for crosscutting concerns at the RE level since they are broadly scoped properties that tend to constrain many other requirements [20, 21]. One important NLP feature that EA-Miner uses to identify these early aspects is the SEM tags produced by WMatrix. For example, the word authorised will have the semantic tag SEM = S7.4+ which means permission that is a natural candidate for a security early aspect (See Table 1.1: The + sign is just an extra annotation to mean that it is a positive type of permission; unauthorised would be tagged as S7.4-). The identification of these broadly scoped non-functional early aspects (e.g. security, performance, concurrency, usability) in a viewpoint-based, feature-based or other models uses the NLP semantic tagging. These broadly scoped concerns represent restrictions applied to their requirements and functionalities (the base abstractions such as viewpoints and features) and therefore are similar in nature and can be identified in a similar fashion. Once the relevant annotated corpus elements are identified and confirmed by a requirements engineer as relevant to a particular crosscutting concern (such as authorised with tam S7.4 to security), EA-Miner supports aggregation of such entries into concern-related lexicons. Such a lexicon is a vocabulary describing a particular concern. The more entries are collected in a lexicon, the more detailed knowledge is built and subsequently utilised in identification of a given concern. The details on how NFR automation is handled in the context of EA-Miner is presented in [23].

Regarding the analysis of functional early aspects, an adaptation of the Fan-in-based aspect mining code analysis technique [17] is be used. Fan-in analysis considers the fan-in of a node n in a method call graph as the number of incoming edges (represented by direct callers of *n*). To clarify, suppose, e.g. that in some system there is a log method of the Logger class which is called by 5 other methods in different classes (the fan-in of the log method is 5). Methods with a high fan-in (such as log) represent behaviour that is likely to be crosscutting (as it is called from several places) and is a strong candidate for a functional aspect [17].

Having identified the presence of potentially crosscutting concerns, it is then necessary to verify that these concerns are in fact crosscutting and affects multiple requirements. EA-Miner achieves this by treating each requirement sentence as a potential joinpoint and the collection of requirements (both crosscutting and non-crosscutting) are compared based on a set intersection operation. If the resulting set is empty, it means that there is no crosscutting relationship between the base requirements and the potential early aspect. If the resulting set is non-empty, then there is a crosscutting relationship between the viewpoint and the early aspect and the overlapping sentence-join-points are the resulting set.

1.3.3 Commonality and Variability Identification with EA-Miner

It has long been reported that commonality and variability in feature models can often manifest as a crosscutting concern, as a given element can be repeated as a child of several independent features.

Where requirements-level feature models are built on basis of textual input, EA-Miner can also support identification of variability and commonality elements [25]. This is achieved using the above discussed EA-Miner principle of lexicon-based concern identification. In this case a lexicon will pinpoint potential presence of variable elements (e.g. when detecting such words as *different*, *like*, *such as*) or mandatory ones (e.g. denoted by such words as *only*, *unless*, *each*). This lexicon again relies on the semantic and part of speech tagging applied by WMatrix to disambiguate the meaning of certain words in the lexicon. For instance, if in a given text "like" refers to similarity, it is relevant for variability identification; on the other hand, if it is used to denote a verb for preference, it is irrelevant and will not be marked for variability. This characteristic of EA-Miner is demonstrated in Sect. 1.4.2.

1.4 Using EA-Miner for Feature Model Refinement

Having discussed the main principles on which the EA-Miner tool is built, we now turn to demonstration of its use. In this study we apply EA-Miner to a feature model representation of the Car Crash case study, as shown in Fig. 1.2. This model has been derived[2] from the text of the given case study, with each feature containing text relevant to it. Thus EA-Miner can be applied to this model.

We discuss how the feature model could be complemented with the new concerns identified via EA-Miner by presenting the potential improvements as well as potential structure degradation to the given model due to the new concern addition.

1.4.1 Finding Crosscutting Concerns with EA-Miner

When used with the initial feature model (see Fig. 1.2) for potential aspect identification, EA-Miner was able to identify the following crosscutting concerns:

- Database (Persistence)
- Profiles (Access Control)
- Surveillance (Security)

These concerns represent non-functional properties of the CMS system which affect several features (i.e. are early aspects that need a better modularisation). For these concerns to be successfully modelled in a feature diagram, it is necessary to identify which features they affect. Table 1.2 shows the results of this analysis by detailing the crosscutting concerns and which features they affect; these concerns are represented in the refined feature model in Fig. 1.3.

Structure Improvements. Thus, for the given feature model, EA-Miner has identified three crosscutting concerns: Persistence, Access Control and Security.

[2]The model is derived using the ArborCraft tool. Any other way of model construction that has text related to the respective features would be equally suitable. Although the process of this specific model derivation is irrelevant to the present chapter, the interested reader is referred to [25] for more detail on ArborCraft and its use.

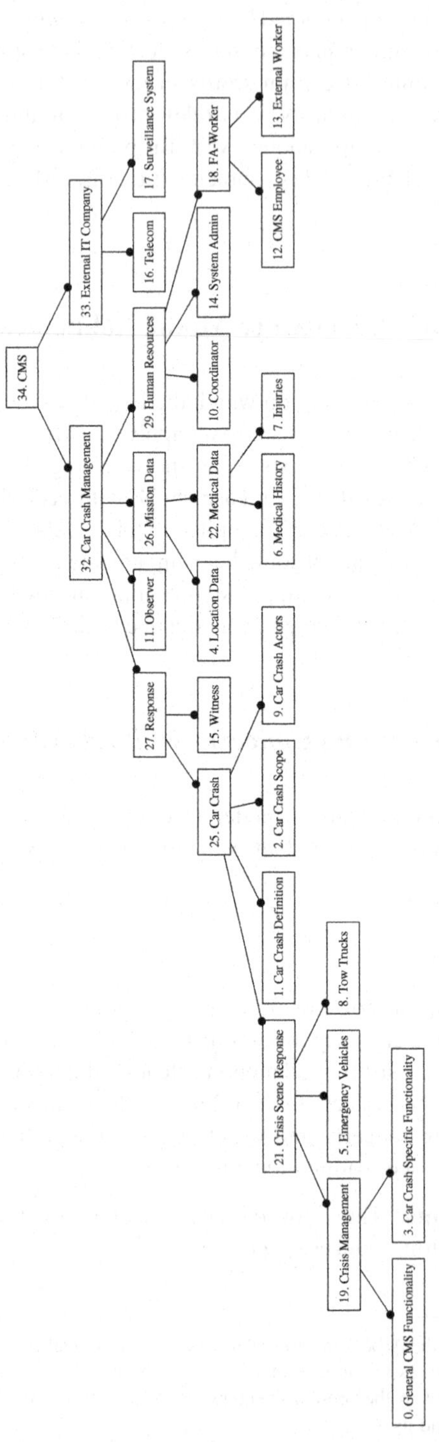

Fig. 1.2 Initial feature model for the CMS study

Table 1.2 Non-functional crosscutting concerns and the features they affect

Concern name	Requirements	Affects
Database (Persistence)	– (10) facilitating the first-aid missions by providing relevant medical history of identified victims to the first-aid workers by querying databases of local hospitals. – (18) System Admin is the specialist who maintains the system and creates all profiles of workers and resources to feed the crisis management database.	System admin, medical history
Profile (Access control)	– (18) System Admin is the specialist who maintains the system and creates all profiles of workers and resources to feed the crisis management database.	System admin, human resource, database
Surveillance (Type of NFR: Security)	– (21) Surveillance System is an external entity which monitors traffic in highways and cities with the use of cameras.	Surveillance system

By identifying these concerns which affect others, the modularity of the feature model is improved. Interestingly, the persistence (database), surveillance system (security) and access control (authentication system) concerns are present as features in the reference feature model under the *IT-Option* feature, although they are not modelled as crosscutting concerns; i.e. the features affected by these concerns are not explicitly identified. Modelling such *crosscutting relationships* is just as critical as early aspect identification, so that feature implementations are treated accordingly.

Interestingly, EA-Miner identifies Surveillance (Security) as a crosscutting concern. Typically, this would be a correct assignment of Security. However, in this instance surveillance refers to a network of cameras and other devices to monitor traffic conditions. Though this network is in place to monitor and ensure security, in this case the surveillance system is already well modularised and is not a crosscutting concern. This issue is to some degree reflected by the fact that the Security concern identified by EA-Miner only affects one feature in the ArborCraft model—the actual surveillance sub-system.

Structure Degeneration. Use of EA-Miner for crosscutting concern identification has not led to any structure degradation in initial feature model. This is mainly due to the fact that such crosscutting concern identification was absent in the given feature model (which is a symptomatic characteristic of feature models in general) and, consequently, it complements the initial model.

One problem associated with using EA-Miner is that a lot of candidate crosscutting concerns can be suggested with many being false-positives. This is particularly the case when dealing with a large document. On the other hand, EA-Miner provides tool support to prune the list of suggestions to arrive at a set of good candidates.

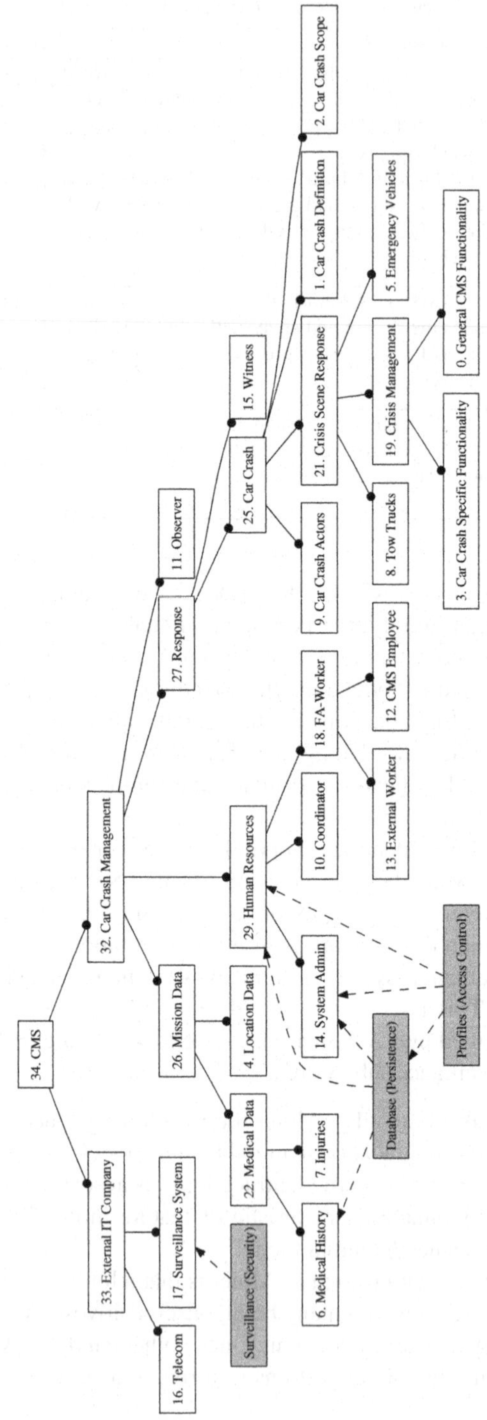

Fig. 1.3 Initial Feature Model refined by EA-Miner. Crosscutting concerns are shown in *grey*

Furthermore, filters can be applied to reduce the list including: thresholds to get only the N most significant concepts, stemmers to recognise similar words (e.g. "resources" and "resource") and synonym lists.

There is also the problem that EA-Miner may miss certain concerns that are in fact crosscutting. This may occur when a certain crosscutting concern is implied, but not explicitly mentioned in the text of the features to-be-crosscut by it. If there is no text referring to such a "silently implied" concern, it cannot be identified by EA-Miner and will, subsequently, not be modelled in the feature diagram. However, this limitation cannot be addressed by a tool that works over a given text, as EA-Miner does. This is one reason why we have underlined that EA-Miner is not a substitute for the requirements engineer; instead its purpose is to provide a guide to the engineer, facilitating the development process.

1.4.2 Refining Features with EA-Miner for Variability

As discussed in Sect. 1.3.3, our initial feature model has not taken into consideration variability and commonality potentially present within individual requirements (i.e. the intra-requirement[3] commonality and variability). This is not unusual in requirements level feature model construction, when the main features are identified and modelled, leaving more detailed commonality and variability analysis for later refinements. Such intra-requirement variability and commonality identification can be supported by EA-Miner's dedicated lexicon, a requirement will be a variability/commonality candidate if it contains a word that belongs to the "Variability" (or "Commonality") semantic tag (determined via the Variability and Commonality lexicon).

At this stage the identification of commonality and variability relates to finer-grained—often leaf-level—characteristics of a system, such as listing a set of ways to carry out a task or detailing specific functions expected of a feature. However, in some cases, such finer characteristics may indicate variability/commonality that needs to be modelled at the higher levels of the feature tree.

Figure 1.4 depicts the CMS feature tree refined with intra-requirement variability. This tree is produced by providing EA-Miner the input of the text structured into features of the initial feature model (see Fig. 1.2), EA-Miner then treats variability as a crosscutting concern and attempts to discover this concern and its joinpoints within the features. The EA-Miner's lexicon-based variability identification is used to help analyse the additional variant/commonality features. Each feature is selected in turn and examined for the presence of the lexicon terms. For instance, in our example the following terms are detected: *or*, *for example*, *all*, *and*, *include*, *following*.

Having detected the variability/commonality terms, we need to consider each term and decide if (and then how) it is relevant to the feature refinement.

[3]This has been referred to as "in-text" variability in [25].

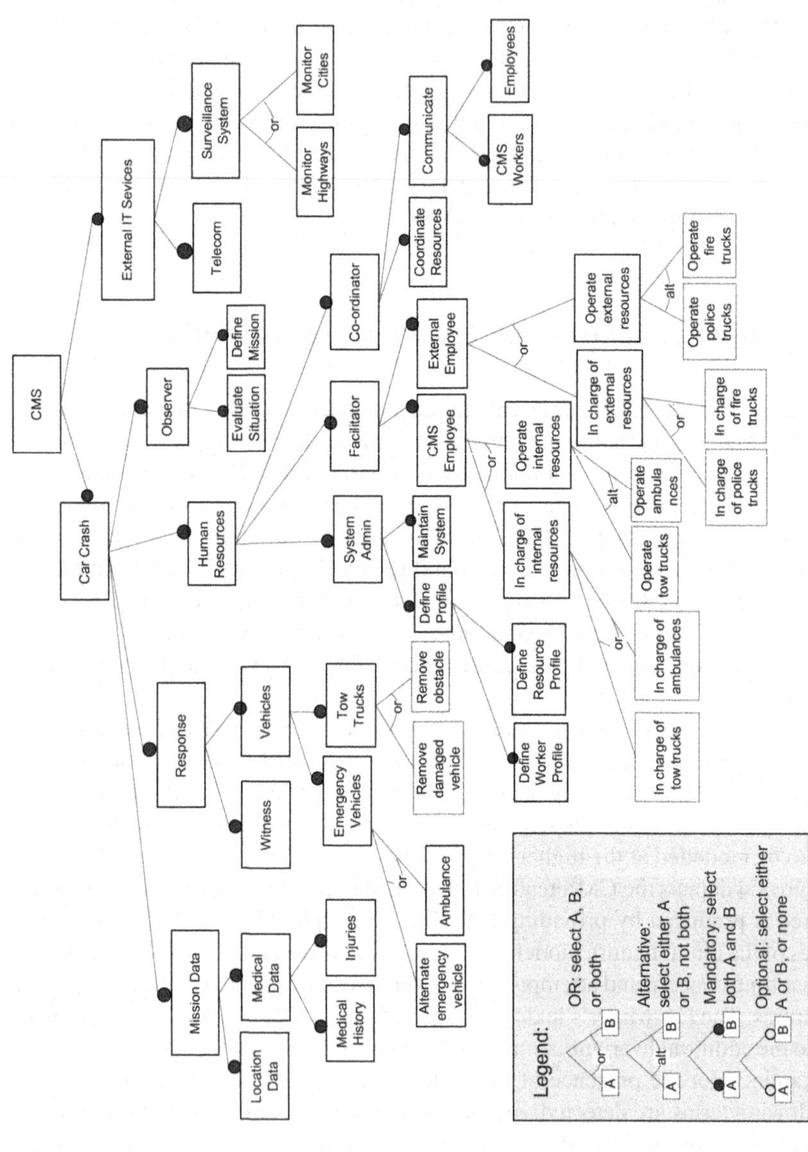

Fig. 1.4 Feature tree after initial refinement with extended EA-Miner

For example, both *CMS Employee* and *External Employee* can be "in charge of or operating" resources. Thus, the *CMS Employee* and *External Employee* features are both refined into "In Charge Of Internal/External Resource" and "Operate Internal/External Resource" sub-features. This refinement is of type "or", meaning that at least one of the sub-features is required, but both may be selected at the same time.

In the case of *External Employee*, the relevant resources are listed as *"for example, police trucks or fire trucks"*, and for *CMS Employee* they are listed as *"for example, tow trucks or ambulances"*. A consequence of this is that *In Charge Of Internal Resource* and *Operate Internal Resource* are further refined into *In Charge of Tow Trucks* and *In Charge of Ambulances*, and *Operate Tow Truck* and *Operate Ambulances* sub-features, respectively. Both subsets are identified from the same "or" variability term. However, the *In Charge of Tow Trucks* and *In Charge of Ambulances* set is modelled as an OR set in Fig. 1.4, while *Operate Tow Truck* and *Operate Ambulances* is modelled as an alternative set. This is because one can be in charge of a truck and ambulance at the same time but can only operate one of them at a time.

All other variability/commonality terms identified by the EA-Miner are processed in the similar manner, refining the feature model into a set of OR, Mandatory, Optional and Alternative subsets. In total, this activity took 16 min, whereby each of the terms was considered and a feature model was annotated with the appropriate refinements. The result is presented in Fig. 1.4.

Once the initial refinement of the feature tree is completed, the analyst then needs to review the tree. The revision is necessary in order to decide to what level of the feature model the identified refinements should be propagated. In the given model, initially, all intra-requirement variability/commonality will be identified at the leaf-level nodes. This is due to the hierarchical nature of this particular feature model construction process.[4] However, it may be necessary to propagate this variability up (or, in case of other models, also down) the tree. Such an example occurs in the car crash case study.

Having reviewed the initial refinement of the feature model in Fig. 1.4, we decided that a set of resources, such as tow trucks, police and fire trucks, and ambulances together constitute a new high level feature, which we have called *Non-human Resources* feature (see Fig. 1.5).

Thus, we have defined the *Non-human Resources* feature and its two sub-features—*Internal* and *External Resources*, which are in turn refined into *Ambulances*, *Tow trucks*, *Police trucks* and *Fire trucks* sub-features. The original definition of these features were removed. All the revision activity took 6 min, whereby the refined tree was considered for each refinement, and a decision on aggregation and removal was made with the feature tree annotated accordingly.

[4]This is a peculiarity of the ArborCraft tool used for the generation of the initial feature model. In this tool all text of the higher level features is also considered within the lower level ones.

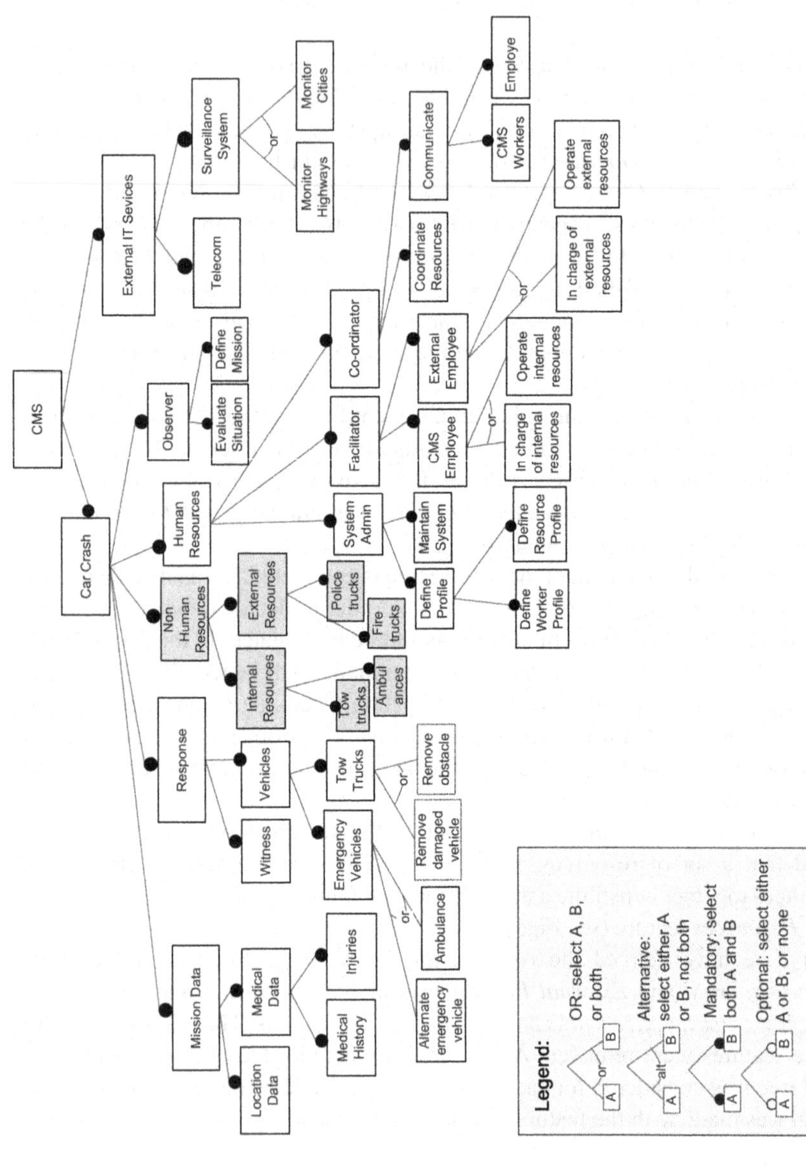

Fig. 1.5 Revised feature tree after initial refinement

Structure Improvements. One of the immediate effects which this process has on the generated feature model is the inclusion of new features. Each of these new features simply decomposes previous leaf-nodes into new sub-features. For example, the previous leaf feature *System Admin* is decomposed further by an additional two levels. Other features are decomposed in a similar manner such as *Emergency Vehicles*, *Tow Trucks* and *Surveillance System*. As with the System Admin feature, the additional decomposition of these features does not cause any additional effects through the rest of the feature model (i.e. no additional refactoring needs to occur).

Structure Degeneration. As shown in Fig. 1.4, the modularity of the feature model after applying the EA-Miner's variability lexicon is poor. The sub-features of *CMS Employee* are repeated across *External Employee*, with features pertaining to operating and managing resources present in both. The only differentiating factor between the two is whether the resources are external or internal. This problem was rectified by refactoring the feature model (see Fig. 1.5). The refactoring involved introducing a new high-level feature (*Non-Human Resources*) that allowed external and internal resources to be modelled. Notice that this refactoring did not remove the need to identify the tasks of CMS or External Employees and resources to which these tasks apply. Instead this reduces the number of leaf-nodes as each explicit resource type (i.e. tow truck, ambulances, etc.) no longer has to be stated for each task.

However, this refactoring introduces additional issues with certain other features being duplicated throughout the feature model. For instance *Tow Trucks* is repeated as a sub-feature of both *Internal Resources* and *Vehicles*. Thus, a new crosscutting feature is introduced due to certain commonality elements. Thus, for the *Tow Trucks* feature to be fully understood, all instances where this feature appears need to be analysed. Consequently, from the perspective of Tow Trucks, model has poor modularity. On the other hand, from the perspective of Non-Human Resources the modularity is superior as all related features are contained within this single subtree. Similarly, from the perspective of the Response, all elements related to this feature are localised. Although having un-contained crosscutting and poor modularity from any perspective is undesirable, in certain cases it cannot be avoided. In such cases, it is important that good modularity is achieved for the key perspectives that developers will use to understand and decompose the system. In the given case, we consider that the top-down perspective, that achieves good modularity, will be initially more useful to developers and provide this understanding.

1.5 Related Work

The work related to EA-Miner that addresses crosscutting in requirements can be represented by Viewpoint-based AORE [20, 21], scenario-based AORE [26] as well as work on goals and aspects [27], Theme/Doc [2] and multidimensional separation of concerns [19]. Among these approaches the only one that supports automation for identification of requirements concepts is Theme/Doc that provides a tool for semi-automatic identification of crosscutting behaviors from requirements specification. In this approach the developer has to read through input documentation and manually provide a list of action words and their related entities as input to the Theme/Doc tool.

The advantage of EA-Miner over the above AORE-mentioned approaches is the use of precise POS and semantic tagging that helps to improve the identification of concepts at the requirements level. Moreover, EA-Miner offers mining capabilities for different AORE models as well as handles requirements documents of varied structure (e.g. user manuals, interviews and others). Therefore, EA-Miner can be seen as complementary to current AORE approaches offering automation for their costly activities. For instance, we could implement a plug-in that facilitates mining for themes which are subsequently modelled and analysed using Theme/Doc.

Regarding code level aspect mining approaches such as [17], what is important to consider is how some techniques such as Fan-in analysis can be adapted to be used at the requirements level. Aspect mining at RE level helps to achieve earlier separation of concerns that can minimise refactorings at later stages such as code. However, some crosscutting concerns (e.g. the code of a design pattern) can only be detected at code level since they don't make sense at the requirements level. Therefore, requirements and code aspect mining are complementary approaches that can be applied whenever it suits best the problem at hand.

Moreover, it is also important to mention work related to the issue of cataloguing and reusing NFR knowledge in case tools as we use this in our lexicon-based approach for identifying NFRs. Cysneiros et al. [7] proposes ways for structuring and cataloguing NFR framework [6] knowledge with the intention of reusing and querying this knowledge. [8] describes in detail an approach for eliciting and building NFR models as well as integrating the non-functional perspective with the functional one in scenarios as well as in class diagrams. This approach utilises a lexicon (language extended lexicon—LEL) that contains information about the entities of the system as well as the NFR. We believe that our NLP-based approach could benefit [8] by enabling to automatically identify the entities and NFRs and suggest a list of candidates that could be added by the user in the LEL lexicon.

Other work that uses NLP techniques in automation of some tasks in RE has been discussed in [1, 5, 12, 13, 15, 16]. These papers also focus on using NLP at the requirements level to identify concepts and build models.

The Color-X approach [5] offers NLP to semiautomatically parse the input (e.g. a document in natural language) into an intermediate formal model based on the common representation language (CPL) [5]. The transformation is not a fully automated step and requires manual structuring from the user (some guidelines are offered) and some words need to be entered in a lexicon. After the CPL representation is built two models can be generated: One static object model, called CSOM, similar to a UML class diagram, and an event-based model, called CEM, similar to a state machine. The Circe [1, 12] environment provides a tool that processes natural language text as input and generates an intermediate

Table 1.3 Summary of techniques

Technique	Effort	Benefits	Drawbacks
EA-Miner	35 min	Crosscutting concern identification	No guidance provided
EA-Miner extended	22 min	Increased detail	Potential duplication

model based on some rules called model, action and substitution rules. After the intermediate model is created, different analysis models can be generated such as entity relationship (E-R) models, data flow diagrams (DFDs) or OO models. Similar to what happens with Color-X, the user has to input some elements in the glossary along with some tags that refer to the semantics of the rules. This characteristic is a bit different from our approach since our NLP processor does not require any input from the user (apart from the natural language documents). Nor does it require that the user has detailed knowledge on how it works.

The Abstfinder [13] approach offers automation for the identification of abstractions in requirements documents described in natural language. Abstractions are considered to be relevant concepts that can be understood without having to know their details such as booking and flight in a reservation system. The process of concept identification is based on pattern matching between sentences in the text. The output of the tool is a list of abstractions and the knowledge on what to do with this information is left to the requirements engineer.

Thus, the previous work on use of NLP in requirements has shown that NLP and information retrieval techniques can provide a great deal of contribution on automating requirements engineering. EA-Miner is one of the first tools that applied these techniques to the problem of identification and representation of crosscutting concerns at the requirements level.

1.6 Conclusion

In this chapter we have presented EA-Miner—a tool for aspect identification in textual requirements. We also used EA-Miner to refine the initial given feature model for variability. Using the car crash case study, we observed that the structure of a given requirements-level feature models can be improved by using EA-Miner, as summarised in Table 1.3 below. We note that in this case study it was possible to identify potentially crosscutting concerns and their points of interaction with already present features without degrading the feature model structure.

However, when using EA-Miner to identify intra-requirements variability, we obtained both a positive and negative influence on the overall structure of the feature model. Extra details were added which can lead to a better detailing of certain crosscutting features and understanding of the overall system. However, these extra details can, in turn, cause duplication and scattering of features which requires extra refactoring to resolve. Yet, with some extra refactoring, the structure of the model and the granularity of the features and (in this example at least) can be improved.

This, of course, requires the skilled eye of an experienced product line engineer. But, as we have already mentioned before, EA-Miner is not intended to be fully automatic, but rather guide and ease the arduous task of producing well-structured aspect-enriched models from textual requirements documents. In this, we believe, the tool has succeeded.

References

1. V. Ambriola, V. Gervasi, Processing natural language requirements, in *Proceedings of International Conference on Automated Software Engineering* (IEEE Computer Society Press, Los Alamitos, 1997)
2. E. Baniassad, S. Clarke, Theme: An approach for aspect-oriented analysis and design, in *Proceedings of the ICSE*, Edinburgh, Scotland, 2004
3. E. Baniassad, S. Clarke, Theme: An approach for aspect-oriented analysis and design, in *ICSE '04: Proceedings of the 26th International Conference on Software Engineering* (IEEE Computer Society, Washington, DC, 2004), pp. 158–167
4. BNC (British national corpus), http://www.natcorp.ox.ac.uk/. Accessed 15 Dec 2012
5. F.M. Burg, *Linguistic Instruments in Requirements Engineering* (IOS, Amsterdam, 1997)
6. L. Chung, B.A. Nixon, E. Yu, J. Mylopoulos, *Non-Functional Requirements in Software Engineering* (Kluwer, Boston, 2000)
7. L.M. Cysneiros, E. Yu, J.C.S.P. Leite, Cataloguing non-functional requirements as softgoals networks, in *Workshop on Requirements Engineering for Adaptable Architectures at the International Requirements Engineering Conference (RE'03)* (Monterey Bay, California, 2003), pp. 13–20
8. L.M. Cysneiros, J.C.S.P. Leite, Nonfunctional requirements: From elicitation to conceptual models. IEEE Trans. Software Eng. **30**(5), 328–350 (2004)
9. J.N.O. Dag, B. Regnell, P. Carlshamre, M. Andersson, J. Karlsson, A feasibility study of automated natural language requirements analysis in market-driven development. Requir. Eng. **7**(1), 20–33 (2002)
10. J.N.O. Dag et al., Speeding up requirements management in a product software company: Linking customerwishes to product requirements through linguistic engineering, in *RE '04: Proceedings of the Requirements Engineering Conference, 12th IEEE International (RE'04)* (IEEE Computer Society, Washington, DC, 2004), pp. 283–294
11. A. Finkelstein, J. Kramer, B. Nuseibeh, L. Finkelstein, M. Goedicke, Viewpoints: A framework for integrating multiple perspectives in system development. Int. J. Software Eng. Knowl. Eng. **2**(1), 31–57 (1992)
12. V. Gervasi, *Environment Support for Requirements Writing and Analysis.* PhD thesis, Universita Degli Studi de Pisa, 1999
13. L. Goldin, D.M. Berry, Abstfinder: A prototype natural language text abstraction finder for use in requirements elicitation. Automat. Software Eng. **4**, 375–412 (1997)
14. I. Jacobson, M. Christerson, P. Jonsson, G. Övergaard, *Object-oriented Software Engineering: A Use Case Driven Approach* (Addison-Wesley, Reading, MA, 1992)
15. M. Luisa, F. Mariangela, I. Pierluigi, Market research for requirements analysis using linguistic tools. Requir. Eng. **9**(1), 40–56 (2004)
16. M. Luisa, G. Roberto, Nl-oops: A requirements analysis tool based on natural language processing, in *Proceedings of the 3rd International Conference on Data Mining*, Bologna, 2002
17. M. Marin, A. Deursen, L. Moonen, Identifying aspects using fan-in analysis, in *WCRE '04: Proceedings of the 11th Working Conference on Reverse Engineering* (IEEE Computer Society, Washington, DC, 2004), pp. 132–141

18. T. McEnery, A. Wilson, *Corpus Linguistics* (Edinburgh University Press, Edinburgh, 1996)
19. A. Moreira, A. Rashid, J. Araujo, Multi-dimensional separation of concerns in requirements engineering, in *RE '05: Proceedings of the 13th IEEE International Conference on Requirements Engineering (RE'05)* (IEEE Computer Society, Washington, DC, 2005), pp. 285–296
20. A. Rashid, A. Moreira, J. Araujo, Modularisation and composition of aspectual requirements, in *Proceedings of the 2nd International Conference on Aspect-Oriented Software Development* (ACM, Boston, MA, 2003), pp. 11–20
21. A. Rashid, P. Sawyer, A. Moreira, J. Arajo, Early aspects: A model for aspect-oriented requirements engineering, in *Proceedings of the International Conference on Aspect-Oriented Software Engineering* (IEEE Computer Society Press, Los Alamitos, 2002), pp. 199–202
22. P. Rayson, Ucrel semantic analysis system (USAS), 2005, http://www.comp.lancs.ac.uk/ucrel/usas/. Accessed 15 Dec 2012
23. A. Sampaio, A. Rashid, R. Chitchyan, P. Rayson, Ea-miner: Towards automation in aspect-oriented requirements engineering. Trans. AOSD **4620**(3), 4–39 (2007)
24. P. Sawyer et al., Revere: Support for requirements synthesis from documents. Inform. Syst. Front. **4**(3), 343–353 (2002)
25. N. Weston, R. Chitchyan, A. Rashid, A framework for constructing semantically composable feature models from natural language requirements, in *SPLC'09: Proceedings of the 13th International Software Product Line Conference*, San Francisco, 2009, pp. 211–220
26. J. Whittle, J. Araujo, Scenario modeling with aspects. IEE Proc. Software **151**(4), 157–172 (2004)
27. Y. Yu, J.C.S.P. Leite, J. Mylopoulos, From goals to aspects: Discovering aspects from requirements goal models, in *Proceedings of the 12th IEEE International Requirements Engineering*, Kyoto, Japan, 2004, pp. 38–47

Chapter 2
Reasoning About Dynamic Aspectual Requirements

Yijun Yu, Xin Peng, and Julio Cesar Sampaio do Prado Leite

Abstract Aspect-oriented requirements modelling separates the early crosscutting concerns as quality requirements such that one can reason about such requirements without cluttering with another. In this chapter, we propose a step further to reason about the dynamic goal models while the separated aspectual requirements are also dynamic. The key to this step is a list of change propagation rules for the goal models such that it is possible to reuse as much previous reasoning results as possible. To demonstrate, we use the Crisis Management System case study to indicate the application of these rules.

2.1 Introduction

Given a highly dynamic environment it is desirable that a software system be able to manage changes *continuously,* without suspension of the execution, whilst maintaining its essential requirements. In order to decide what is needed to change for satisfying the requirements, however, a system shall be aware of its current situation and the context in which it is situated. In support of requirements-driven self-managing systems, requirements reasoning needs to be made as dynamic as possible to take into account the new knowledge learnt during runtime.

We explore the issues of requirements-driven self-managing systems using a representation scheme, the goal-oriented non-functional requirements (NFR) framework [1, 2], that clearly differentiates functional and quality requirements.

Y. Yu (✉)
Centre for Research in Computing, The Open University, Buckinghamshire, UK
e-mail: y.yu@open.ac.uk

X. Peng
School of Computer Science, Fudan University, Shanghai, China

J.C.S. do Prado Leite
Departamento de Informática, PUC-Rio, Rio de Janeiro, Brazil

A. Moreira et al. (eds.), *Aspect-Oriented Requirements Engineering*,
DOI 10.1007/978-3-642-38640-4_2,

The NFR framework separates functions, which are modelled as hard goals (i.e. with crisp/binary satisfaction criteria), from quality requirements, which are modelled as soft goals (i.e. with non-crisp/non-binary satisfaction criteria, and using the term *satisficed* to acknowledge the distinction).

In relation to these classifications, functions of an implementation are composed by AND–OR rules to satisfy those high-level hard goals; and they are weaved through MAKE-BREAK-HELP-HURT contribution rules to satisfy those high-level soft goals. Goals are labelled by both their type (the function or the quality) and their topics (the domains) to which the type is being applied.

Our earlier work [3] introduced the notion of aspectual requirements to modularise the functions for the operationalisation of quality requirements (i.e. *advices* tasks) and to separate them from those functional requirements (i.e. *join-points* tasks) crosscut by the subject domains (i.e. *point-cuts* topics). The weaving algorithms for introducing the advising tasks into the join-points aim to maintain the equivalence of answers to the same deductive question, with or without the aspects: "Given a set of subgoals, are the high-level hard goals satisfied and high-level soft goals satisficed well enough?"

Given a model consisting of static rules and an a priori set of hard/soft goals, one could perform goal-based reasoning algorithms to get the answer. However, as we have just motivated earlier, these rules may no longer be static in real situations: changes to the hard/soft goals and their operationalised tasks, or even the rules, themselves, may change given that the context of a system is highly changeable, and the knowledge of the system requirements (awareness) is also allowed to be changed at runtime.

In this chapter, we aim to provide a theoretical answer to the following research question: "Is it possible to reason about the equivalence between the crosscutting requirements problem and the separated aspectual requirements problem while taking into account the changes to the requirements model as well as to the situations in the context?" The main contributions of this chapter are as follows:

1. Deal with change in the context of aspect-oriented requirements models, i.e. aspectual requirements models.
2. Propose a list of fundamental rules that characterises the equivalence of requirement aspect weaving in dynamic goal models.
3. Demonstrate the application of these rules in the common case study, the Crisis Management System [4].

The remainder of the chapter is organised as follows. Section 2.2 gives more background of goal-based reasoning and goal aspects using an illustrative example. Section 2.3 presents the list of equivalence rules that guarantees the dynamic aspectual requirements do not introduce problems to the dynamic goal reasoning. Section 2.4 presents an example application of the dynamic aspectual requirements. Section 2.5 summarises the limitations in this work, which points to a few future research directions. Section 2.6 concludes and points out a few interesting direction we hope to explore in future.

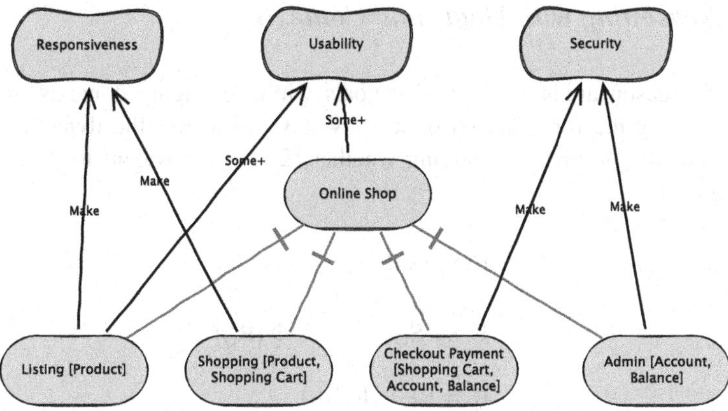

Fig. 2.1 The top-level hard and soft goals of an online shop

2.2 Background

In this section, we use the requirements model of an online shop as the running example to illustrate the problem and the existing solutions.

2.2.1 A Running Example

Figure 2.1 shows a simple goal model with the top-level hard goal "Online shop" decomposed by function into four sub-goals, "Listing [product]", "Shopping [Product, ShoppingCart]", "Checkout Payment [ShoppingCart, Account, Balance]" *and* "Admin [Account, Balance]". The canonical convention we adopted for these goals or subgoals is "type [topics]", named after the type of the primary function of these hard goals, along with the subject domains listed as the topics enclosed by square brackets, separated by commas. Meanwhile, they are contributing to three top-level soft goals indicated by the curly nodes, including "Responsiveness", "Usability" and "Security". As quality requirements, these soft goals do not have an absolute satisfaction, but they do have criteria to judge whether they are sufficiently implemented. Specifically, the "Listing" and "Shopping" hard goals *must* achieve the "responsiveness" because they are frequent operations; the "Checkout payment" and "Admin" hard goals *must* have "Security", because they both may access the customers' accounts and may update their balances; the hard goals "Listing" and "Shopping" may *help* "Usability" through memorising the potential customers' transactions as a shopping cart.

2.2.2 Reasoning with Goals and Contexts

In order to reason about the dynamic goals within changing contexts, we first transform, using the formulae introduced by Zave et al. [5], the dynamic goals' problem into the problem of judging whether (2.1) is equivalent to (2.2) in the following form:

$$E, S \Big| = R \tag{2.1}$$

$$\begin{aligned} &E, S_F, S_Q \Big| = R_F \wedge \Phi\left(R_Q\right) \\ &R = R_F \wedge \Phi\left(R_Q\right) \\ &S = S_F, S_Q \\ &E, S_F \Big| = R_F \end{aligned} \tag{2.2}$$

Here *E* stands for the environment, *R* stands for the requirements and *S* stands for the system specifications. Zave et al. [5] define the formula (2.1) as the requirements problem, whilst a refinement according to [1] can be formulated into (2.2) whereby S is separated into the functional tasks S_F, and the advising tasks S_Q, and R consists of the conjunction of both functional requirements R_F and the quality requirements R_Q and the evaluation of its fully/partially satisficed or not by $\Phi(R_Q)$.[1] Note that the composition of S_F and S_Q, denoted by the "," separator, can be achieved by aspect weaving [7].

With an extension to the temporal dimension *t*, now we would like to establish the equivalence of (2.1t) and (2.2t):

$$E(t), S(t) \Big| = R(t) \tag{2.1t}$$

$$\begin{aligned} &E(t), S_F(t), S_Q(t) \Big| = R_F(t) \wedge \Phi(t) \left(R_Q(t)\right) \\ &R(t) = R_F(t) \wedge \Phi\left(R_Q(t)\right) \\ &S(t) = S_F(t), S_Q(t) \\ &E(t), S_F(t) \Big| = R_F(t) \end{aligned} \tag{2.2t}$$

[1] An extension to Zave et al. has been proposed in Jureta et al. [6] to include the requirements other than the functional/quality, such as attitude, which are treated as part of the context here.

In other words, when at any given time *t*, the basic requirements problem shall hold. One may interpret the continuous satisfaction of requirements as a desirable self-management quality requirement at the process (meta-) level. With the help of satisfying additional monitoring [8], diagnosis [9] and feedback loop control [10] requirements derived from this process requirement, the systems may guarantee the satisfaction of the core functional requirements [11].

When the formula is focused on the runtime requirements of the software system product, the reasoning of the goal model is rather straightforward. Suppose that the top-level requirements are $R = R_F^{\text{Online shop}}$ ^ FS(R_Q^{Security}) ^ PS($R_Q^{\text{Usability}}$) ^ FS ($R_Q^{\text{Responsiveness}}$). Here FS and PS stand for "fully satisficed" and "partially satisficed," respectively, indicating the degree of the perceived quality criteria relating to the soft goals in parenthesis.

Then it is possible to specify $S_F = S_F^{Listing}, S_F^{Shopping}, S_F^{Checkout\ Payment}, S_F^{Admin}$ that given the context domains $E = E^{Product}, E^{Shopping\ Cart}, E^{Account}, E^{Balance}$ shall satisfy $R = R_F^{Online\ Shop}$ ^ $FS(R_Q^{Responsiveness})$ ^ $PS(R_Q^{Usability})$ ^ $FS(R_Q^{Security})$. In other words, the S_Q is required to be specified for each function as $S_Q^{Listing}, S_Q^{Shopping}$, $S_Q^{Checkout\ Payment}, S_Q^{Admin}$. Here we use "," to connect these domains, instead of "^" because the composition of them usually involves structural and behaviour semantics beyond simple logic conjunction. Nonetheless, the requirements problem $E, S| = R$ in (2.1) or $E, S_F, S_Q| = R_F$ ^ $\Phi(R_Q)$ in (2.2) can thus be refined into conjunctive sub-problems in the same form, with *E*, *S* and *R* substituted by the counterparts of the sub-problems. For examples, each sub-goal can be regarded as a sub-requirement for one of the sub-problems:

$$E^{Product}, S^{Listing}\Big| = R_F{}^{Listing} \wedge FS\left(R_Q{}^{Responsiveness}\right) \wedge PS\left(R_Q{}^{Usability}\right)$$

$$E^{Product}, E^{ShoppingCart}, S^{Shopping}\Big| = R_F{}^{Shopping} \wedge FS\left(R_Q{}^{Responsiveness}\right) \wedge PS\left(R_Q{}^{Usability}\right)$$

$$E^{ShoppingCart}, E^{Account}, E^{Balance}, S^{Payment}\Big| = R_F{}^{Payment} \wedge FS\left(R_Q{}^{Security}\right)$$

$$E^{Account}, E^{Balance}, S^{Admin}\Big| = R_F{}^{Admin} \wedge FS\left(R_Q{}^{Security}\right)$$

Note that here although the functional R_F and quality requirements R_Q are separated, their operationalisations are still to be refined into functional tasks S_F and advice tasks S_Q. In the next subsection, we explain how we represent the functional tasks as functions and advice tasks as aspects.

Now a simple version of the goal reasoning is to establish that $R_F^{Listing}$ ^ $R_F^{Shopping}$ ^ $R_F^{Payment}$ ^ R_F^{Admin} ^ $FS(R_Q^{Responsiveness})$ ^ $PS(R_Q^{Usability})$ ^ $FS(R_Q^{Security}) =$ *R*. From the known satisfaction result of the requirements on the left-hand side (i.e. $R_F^{Listing}, R_F^{Shopping}, R_F^{Payment}, R_F^{Admin}, FS(R_Q^{Responsiveness}), PS(R_Q^{Usability})$, $FS(R_Q^{Security})$) to the satisfaction of the requirements on the right-hand side (i.e. *R*), the reasoning is called *bottom-up* label propagation [12], whilst the opposite, reasoning from the known high-level goals in order to find the minimal plan or conjunction of sub-goals, is called *top-down* satisfiability (SAT) solution [13]. In either case, only goals are participating in the computation. Recently, Ali et al. [14] expand the semantics of goal reasoning to those of the context (set of topics) , such that it is also possible to reason about the contextual relationships in logic rules. The formula we presented, although looks simple, reflects more expressive reasoning rules because both the context and the goals can participate in the computation. By turning the missing goals or the missing context into wildcards, the same rule can be used to model all the rules [12–14]. More complete rules for requirements problems can be found in the canonical form [15] that also includes the *justification*.

$$\frac{E(t),\, S(t) \Big| = R_F(t) \;\wedge\; \Phi\left(R_Q(t)\right)}{E(t),\, S(t) \Big| = R(t)} \langle\langle justification \rangle\rangle \tag{2.3}$$

However, to reason about the justifications, a high-order logic or reification is required. For simplicity, in this chapter we only consider reasoning in the first-order predicate logic where the time t is treated as a special term in the predicates.

2.2.3 Reasoning with Aspectual Requirements

According to the systematic process in Yu et al. [3] using the conceptual construct of the V-graph model (see Fig. 2.2), the (hard) goals and soft goals are respectively operationalised into tasks. After the process, the tasks that operationalise the soft goals are separated from those tasks that operationalise the hard goals, as the advice tasks for the aspectual requirements. Moreover, the high-level contributions from the hard goals to the soft goals must be maintained by the low-level tasks when they are weaved together. Once they are separated, it is possible to specify the functional tasks S_F as functions and the advice tasks S_Q as aspects.

For example, the three soft goals are operationalised to three aspectual requirements. They weave their advising tasks (operationalisations) as modifications to the basic functions to guarantee the expected contribution relationship at a higher level. To illustrate that, we expand the high-level goal model Fig. 2.1 with one more level as a more concrete goal model in Fig. 2.3.

The "Listing [Product]" goal can be refined by either of the two alternatives: "Listing [Product, Persistence=Databases]" or "Listing [Product, Persistence=LDAP]", depending on the different mechanisms for persistence. Specifically, these two tasks can be separated into three tasks: one common functional task which does not specify the exact persistence mechanism "Listing [Product, Persistence=?]" and two alternative advice tasks "Database" and "LDAP". According to the documentation of the case study (i.e. http://oscommerce.com), the designer prefers to implement the product lists using LDAP service because

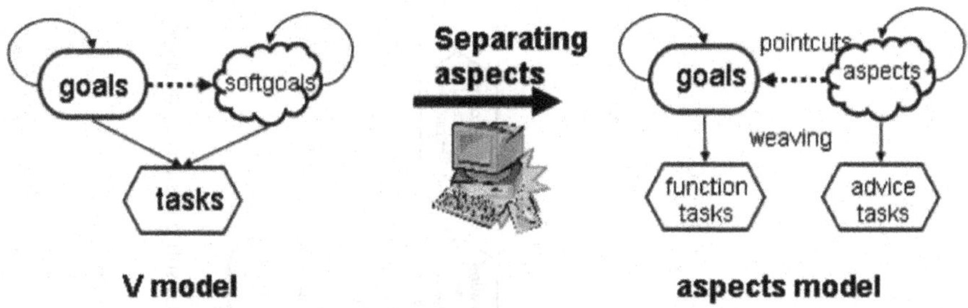

Fig. 2.2 The V-shaped graphs show conceptually how a tasks [1, Fig. 15]

it is more efficient in online shopping scenarios as customers frequently browse and select the products. Although a database solution is more scalable, it is not as responsive as the LDAP-based solutions. Therefore if the goal reasoning (top-down) is applied and $FS(R_Q{}^{Responsiveness})$ is required (on the right-hand side), one would find "$S^{\text{Listing [Product, Persistence = LDAP]}} = S_F{}^{\text{Listing[Product, Persistence = ?]}}, S_Q{}^{\text{Persistence [LDAP]}}$" in the plan because the contribution link from "Listing[Persistence=LDAP]" to "Responsiveness" is MAKE, whilst the contribution link from "Listing[Persistence=Database]" to "Responsiveness" is only HELP.

Similarly, the same trade-off needs to be made for the other hard goal "$S_F{}^{\text{Shopping [Produce, ShoppingCart, Persistence = ?]}}$". Although the connections from both the "Database" and "LDAP" tasks to the parent goals are "OR decomposition", once the trade-off decision is made in the reasoning, they can be simplified into "AND decomposition" because no matter which OR sub-goal of "Listing" or "Shopping" is chosen, they all need the "LDAP"-based implementations for the full satisficing of the Responsiveness soft goal.

In addition, "$S_F{}^{\text{Listing [Product, Persistence = ?]}}$" is refined into a task making use of the "$S_F{}^{\text{Listing [Product, Persistence = ?, Display = ?]}}$" and "$S_Q{}^{\text{Display [StyleBox]}}$", which presents user with the consistent look and feel in the whole website. In fact, this *Style Box* design should be applied to every page to be displayed, including both the listing and shopping pages. Therefore it is one of the candidate aspects.

Likewise, for the "Security" soft goal and all the sub-goals that require to *make* it satisfied (i.e. "Payment" and "Admin"), a common advice task "$S_Q{}^{\text{Autentication [Login, User, Credentials]}}$" is to be composed with the functional tasks "$S_F{}^{\text{Checkout Payment [Shopping Cart, Account, Balance, Authentication = ?]}}$" and "$S_F{}^{\text{Admin[Account, Balance, Authentication = ?]}}$". This makes the "Authentication [Login, User, Credentials]" another requirement aspect.

The third requirement aspect "Display [StyleBox]" has to do with "Usability". Although it is required to be partially satisfied by the "Listing" and "Shopping" sub-goals, having the *Style Box* is common to both and therefore crosscut every place in the program wherever the information is to be displayed as a web page.

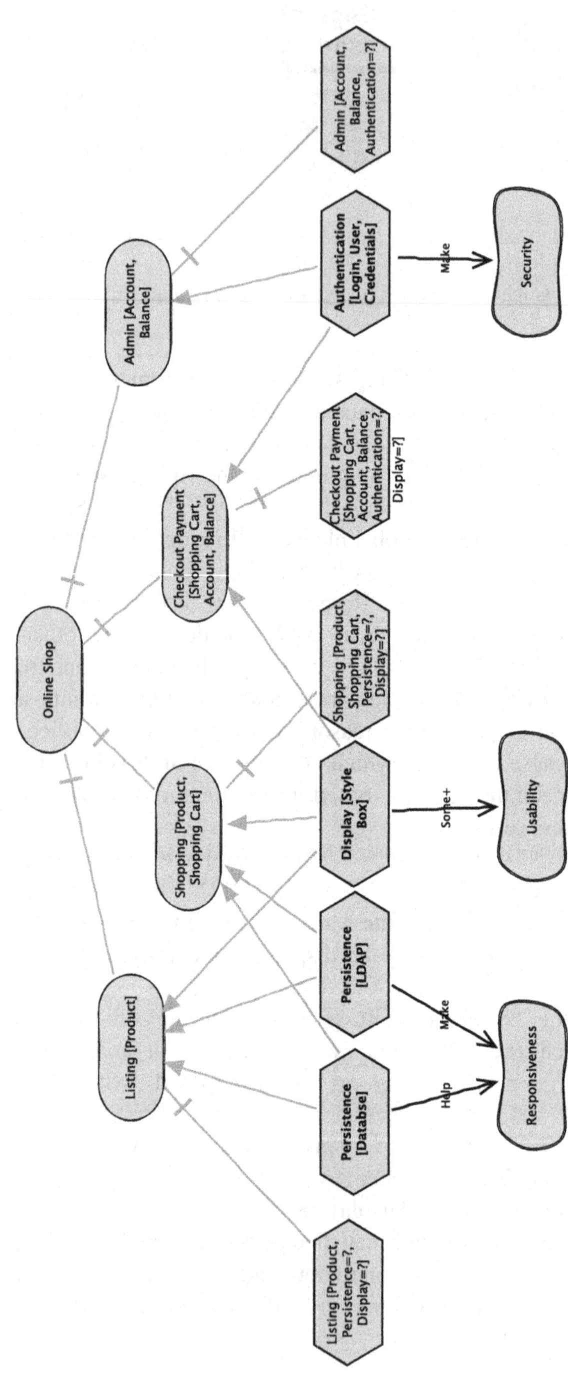

Fig. 2.3 The refined tasks of an online shop (cf. Fig. 2.1). Candidate aspectual requirements and their contribution to the hard and soft goals are highlighted

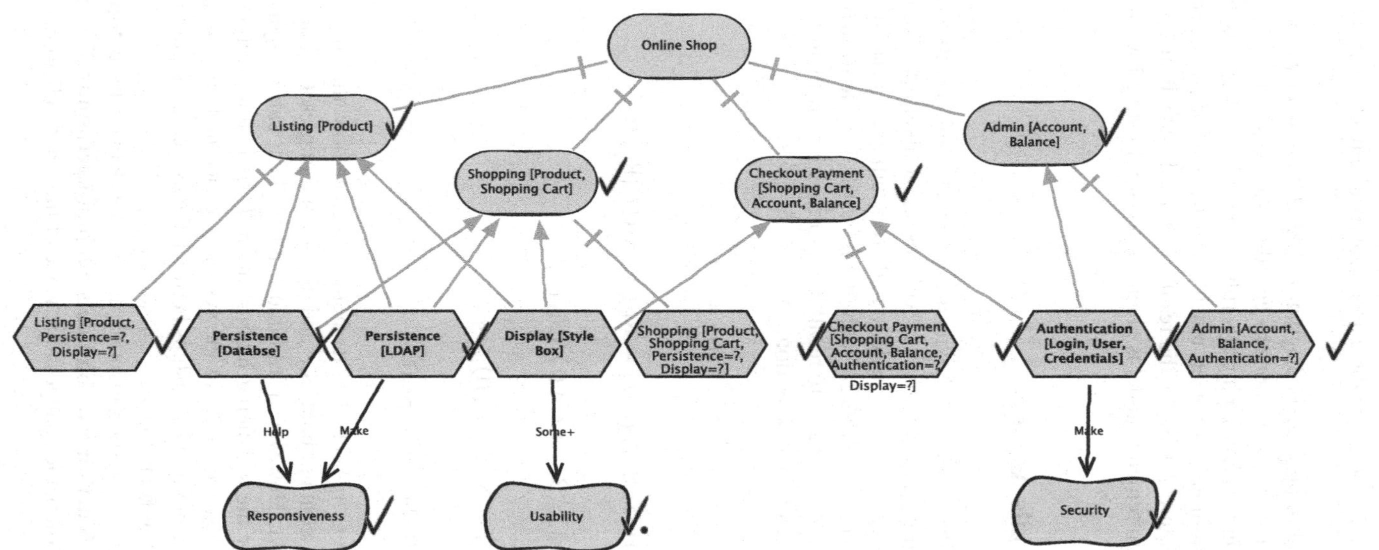

Fig. 2.4 Some reasoning results (cf. Fig. 2.3). In the NFR framework [2], the FS (satisfied/fully satisficed), PS (partially satisficed), CF(conflict), PD (partially denied), FD (denied/fully denied), and UN (unknown) labels are conventionally shown using the following *check marks*, respectively: ✓ ✓. ➘ ✗. ✗ ?

In Yu et al. [3] there are three other aspectual requirements; however, for the sake of discussions and illustration, these three aspectual requirements in the chapter are adequate.

Given the aspectual requirements diagram in Fig. 2.3, how do we perform the reasoning on then? In fact, it is to be done by encoding the rules (2.1) and (2.2) in the same way as any existing goal reasoning algorithm. The only difference is that, when presented to the requirements engineer, much fewer number of contribution links will be needed [3]. Figure 2.4 shows the results of how the labels are propagated once the aspectual requirements model is given, either top-down or bottom-up.

2.3 Dynamic Goals Aspects

In this section we define the notion of dynamic aspectual requirements and present a list of rules that can govern the changes with respect to them. As shown in the introduction section, our aim is to be able to find crosscutting concerns in dynamic requirement problems (2.1t) and (2.2t) such that it is still feasible to reason about the equivalence of (2.1t) and (2.2t). To recall these rules, we copy them here so that it is possible to revisit them in this section:

$$\mathrm{E}(\mathrm{t}), \mathrm{S}(\mathrm{t}) \Big| = \mathrm{R}(\mathrm{t}) \tag{2.1t}$$

$$\mathrm{E}(\mathrm{t}), \mathrm{S_F}(\mathrm{t}), \mathrm{S_Q}(\mathrm{t}) \Big| = \mathrm{R_F}(\mathrm{t}) \wedge \Phi(t)\ \big(\mathrm{R_Q}(\mathrm{t})\big)$$

$$\mathrm{R}(\mathrm{t}) = \mathrm{R_F}(\mathrm{t}) \wedge \Phi(t)\ \big(\mathrm{R_Q}(\mathrm{t})\big)$$

$$\mathrm{S}(\mathrm{t}) = \mathrm{S_F}(\mathrm{t}), \mathrm{S_Q}(\mathrm{t}) \tag{2.2t}$$

$$\mathrm{E}(\mathrm{t}), \mathrm{S_F}(\mathrm{t}) \Big| = \mathrm{R_F}(\mathrm{t})$$

After the discussion in Sect. 2.2, it should be clear now that the aspectual requirements indeed contain both S_Q and R_Q in the representation after the composition of S_F, S_Q. However, at runtime *t*, all of them can be dynamic (i.e. changeable). Even for the satisficing interpretation Φ *(t)* is not always constant, for example, when the survivability of the system is concerned [16]. To assist the maintenance of the reasoning relationships between the aspectual requirements, we need to establish a list of basic rules.

Since the weaving of a requirement aspect can be defined by **a tuple <soft goal Φ (R_Q), advice function S_Q, point-cuts S_F, join-operation ","** >, the basic reasoning rules concerning the changes to any one of them are as below:

- SG1—**soft goal change** Φ *(t)* (R_Q *(t)*): If a quality requirement R_Q changes its expected satisficing level Φ *(t)* due to the change of the satisficing criteria, then there is no need to change the tuple except that one must re-evaluate every rule involving $R_Q(t)$ either bottom-up, by label propagation or top-down, using a SAT solver reasoning. An example of such changes can be illustrated, for example, by modifying the "Usability" expectation from PS to FS. In that case, unless an operationalisation through the MAKE contribution link is found, it is not possible to satisfy the requirements model. In this case, one needs to consider the existing advising function inadequate or there could be an obstacle to fulfil the new soft goal. Introducing new advising function, such as "Common Look and Feel", "Multi Touch interface" may solve or at least alleviate this problem.
- SG2—**soft goal change** $S_Q(t) \rightarrow R_Q$ *(t)*: If the label of a contribution link from S_Q to R_Q changes, e.g. from HELP to MAKE or vice versa, then there is no need to change all tuples except that one must re-evaluate every rule involving $S_Q \rightarrow R_Q$ *(t)*. For example, if one modifies the label of the "Authentication" → "Security" contribution link from MAKE to HELP, to reflect the new situation that Denial of Service attack may hinder the system to serve all customers at all times. In this case, additional security measure needs to be introduced to mitigate the risk [17]. To do this at runtime means that the requirement aspect or its implementation needs to be extensible at runtime.
- AF1 (**advice function S_Q(t) changes):** This type of changes could happen when $E(t), S_F(t), S_Q(t)| = R(t)$ no longer holds even when R_Q is the same. For example, whether or not the contribution link between "Authentication" and "Security" is a MAKE or HELP relation depends on how strong the Login function is implemented. If it was encrypted using an algorithm that is no longer safe, for example, then the relationship $S_Q \rightarrow R_Q$ needs to be revisited.
- PC1 (**point-cuts $S_F(t)$, S_Q *(t)* changes):** It is perhaps the most frequent changes with respect to the aspectual requirements because the interface between S_F and S_Q affects the scope of the requirement aspect as well. Just as in AOP [18] whereby the signature of a method call used in the point-cut expression is changed would significantly change the scope of the aspect, it is also the case in the aspectual requirements. According to the definition of the point-cut of aspectual requirements, any changes to the contribution links between S_Q and R_Q, or S and R_Q, would lead to redefinition of the point-cuts. For example, modifying the topics of "Shopping" goal to include "Account" or "Balance", it would require the "Authentication" aspect to be weaved because they are sensitive to the mechanisms of protections. However, if there was no contribution link between "Shopping" and "Security", the high-level requirements model will be inconsistent with the lower one. A resolution is either recommending the removal of the "Account/Balance" access in the "Shopping" goal, or making it explicit that the same level of "Security" for "Admin" is required for the "Shopping" as well.
- JO1 (**join-operation "," semantics change**): Although AND decomposition is often the case for weaving aspectual requirements (as shown in all the three examples), sometimes other form of operation is allowed too. For example,

especially when even the $PS(R_Q^{usability})$ is not required, then one could even remove the application of the “StyleBox” aspect at the runtime. Therefore it is more appropriate to model the weaving operation as optional or OR decompositions in such cases. Otherwise, contextual conditions need to be added to the interface to enrich its semantics, e.g. by insisting on monitoring the context variable for the need of usability. In certain cases, even existing AND decomposition weaving operations can be sacrificed to guarantee the survivability of the system [16]. Therefore it is important to manage the join-operation dynamically.

2.4 Common Case Study Discussion

A common case study in the crisis management domain [4] is used in the book. Specifically, we use the car crash crisis management system (CCCMS) in our case study based on given requirements. In this case study, we show how goal aspects can be identified and represented and how the rules identified in Sect. 2.3 do apply for the dynamic goal aspects.

2.4.1 Goal Model

Figure 2.5 shows the top-level goal model of CCCMS. The top-level hard goal “Resolve Car Crash Crisis” is decomposed by function into four sub-goals, “Capture Witness Report [Witness, Crisis]”, “Create Mission [Mission]”, “Allocate Resource [resource]” and “Execute Mission [Mission]”. Besides these functional requirements, CCCMS is expected to meet quality requirements like “Facilitate Future Analysis”, “Security”, “Reliability” and “Mobility”, which are represented by soft goals. Specifically, all the sub-goals of “Resolve Car Crash Crisis” should help “Facilitate Future Analysis”, since historical analysis involves records about the whole crisis resolution process; the “Capture Witness Report”, “Allocate Resource” and “Execute Mission” must ensure “security”, because they are relevant to interactions with external uses and systems; “Allocate Resource” and “Execute Mission” must achieve “Reliability” and “Mobility” to ensure reliable communication with mobile rescue resources (e.g. firemen, doctors, policemen); all the sub-goals of “Resolve Car Crash Crisis” must ensure “Real Time”.

2.4.2 Goal Aspect Analysis

After goal refinement and operationalisation, we can get the refined goal model in Fig. 2.6. In the model, soft goals are separately operationalised into tasks,

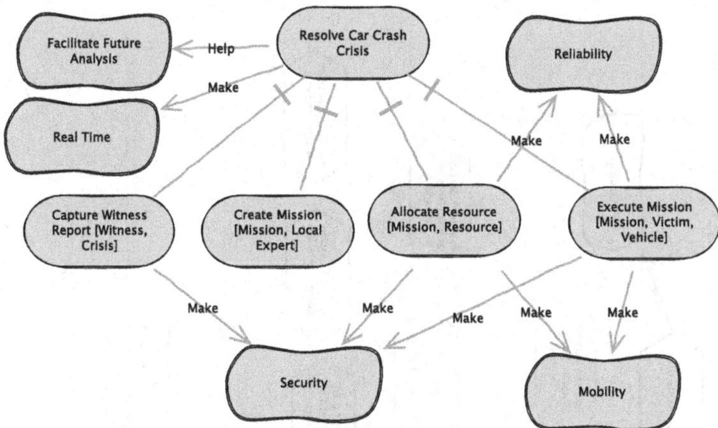

Fig. 2.5 The top-level hard and soft goals of CCCMS

which are weaved into relevant hard goals as advices. For example, as the operationlisations of "Facilitate Future Analysis", both the "Logging [Text]" and "Logging [Multimedia]" are weaved into the four sub-goals of the root goal as alternative implementation. They have different contributions to "Facilitate Future Analysis" and other soft goals. The "Logging [Multimedia]" means to record the crisis resolution process by audios and videos; thus it can achieve "Facilitate Future Analysis" but hurts "Real Time" at the same time.

By contrast, "Logging [Text]" records relevant events in text and thus can help "Facilitate Future Analysis" and has no obvious influence on "Real Time".

Based on the refined CCCMS goal model, we can identify candidate goal aspects as listed in Table 2.1. Besides "Facilitate Future Analysis", "Security", "Reliability" and "Mobility" are also identified as candidate goal aspects. All of them are operationalised into a set of tasks and linked with relevant hard goals by some point-cuts. The soft goal "Real Time" is not identified as a goal aspect, and although it actually constrains the implementation of basic functions, there are no obvious operationalisations for it at this level of abstraction in our modelling exercise.

2.4.3 Dynamic Goal Aspects

Given the goal aspects, we can determine the satisfaction levels of high-level goals in a *bottom-up* way or plan a minimum task set for specific top-level requirements by goal reasoning. For example, given the top-level requirements $R = R_F{}^{\text{Resolve Car Crash Crisis}} \wedge FS\left(R_Q{}^{\text{Facilitate Future Analysis}}\right) \wedge PS\left(R_Q{}^{\text{Real Time}}\right) \wedge FS\left(R_Q{}^{\text{Reliability}}\right) \wedge FS\left(R_Q{}^{\text{Security}}\right) \wedge FS\left(R_Q{}^{\text{Mobility}}\right)$, one would find "Logging [Multimedia]" in the plan (see Fig. 2.7), since it achieves "Facilitate Future Analysis" and hurts "Real Time".

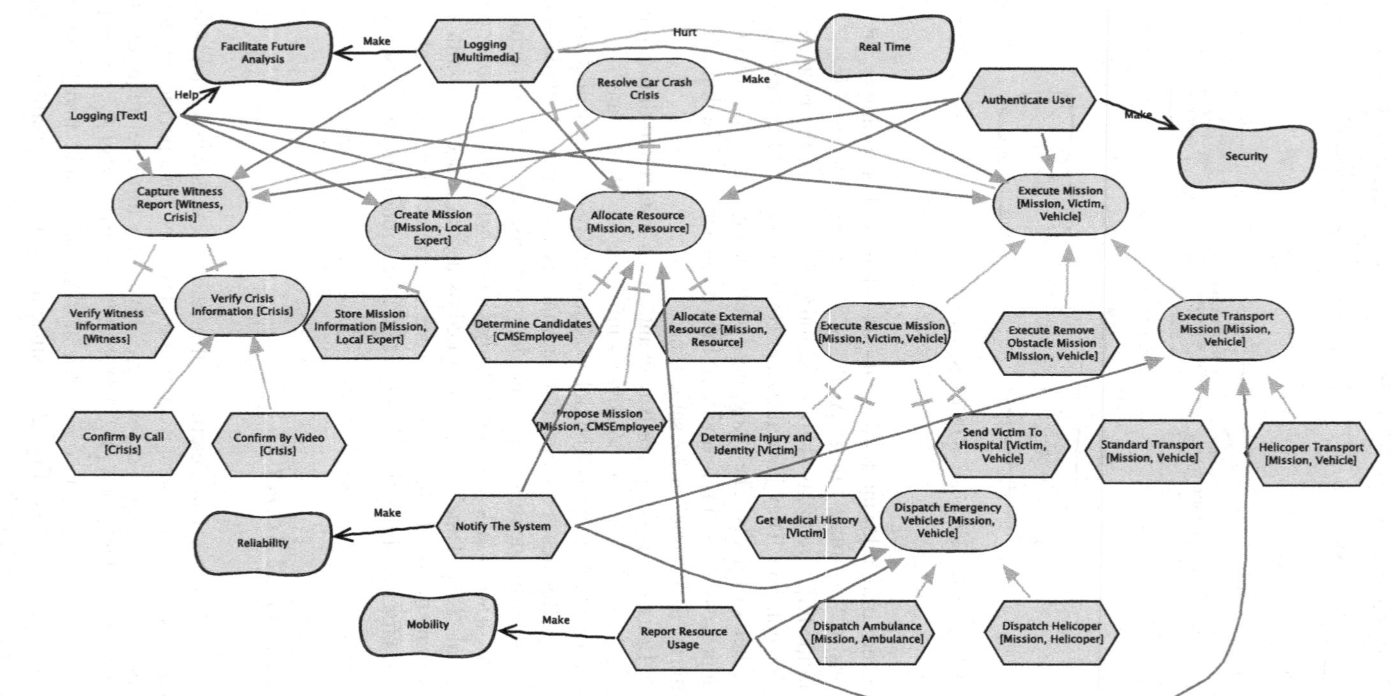

Fig. 2.6 Refined CCCMS goal model with candidate goal aspects

Table 2.1 Part of the identified goal aspects from CCCMS

Aspect (R_Q)	Advice Function (S_Q)	Point-cuts (S_F)
Facilitate Future Analysis	Logging	Capture Witness Report, Create Mission, Allocate Resource, Execute Mission
Security	Authenticate User	Capture Witness Report, Allocate Resource, Execute Mission
Reliability	Notify The System	Allocate Resource, Dispatch Emergency Vehicles, Execute Transport Mission
Mobility	Report Resource Usage	Allocate Resource, Dispatch Emergency Vehicles, Execute Transport Mission

Considering the changing environment and the runtime adaptation of CCCMS, the reasoning about goal aspects may change at runtime. Figure 2.7 shows an example of software goal change in CCCMS (Rule SG1), which involves a dynamic tradeoff between "Facilitate Future Analysis" and "Real Time" at runtime. In this scenario, the initial requirements include $\mathrm{FS}(R_Q{}^{\text{Facilitate Future Analysis}}) \wedge \mathrm{PS}(R_Q{}^{\text{Real Time}})$. Corresponding plan for this requirement includes "Logging [Multimedia]" for recording crisis processing logs. With the rapidly increasing user requests, real-time processing of requests becomes a more urgent requirement. And due to the conflict between "Facilitate Future Analysis" and "Real Time", the expected requirements change to $\mathrm{PS}(R_Q{}^{\text{Facilitate Future Analysis}}) \wedge \mathrm{FS}(R_Q{}^{\text{Real Time}})$. Accordingly, "Logging [Multimedia]" is replaced by "Logging [Text]" to achieve better satisfaction for "Real Time" with lowered satisfaction level of "Facilitate Future Analysis".

Another example of dynamic goal aspects in CCCMS is shown in Fig. 2.8, which illustrates the case of point-cuts change (Rule PC1). Initially, the hard goal "Create Mission" involves local expert in the creation of mission plans. At that time, it is irrelevant to the goal aspect "Security" and its advising task "Authenticate User", since it only involves local interactions within the crisis management centre. In some cases, remote experts are involved to evaluate the situation and define necessary missions, for example, when local experts are not available. Thus, "Create Mission" becomes a basic function that is relevant to security assurance, since it involves interactions with remote users. As a result, the point-cuts (i.e. the scope) of the goal aspect "Security" change to include "Create Mission" as shown in Fig. 2.8.

2.5 Limitations and Discussions

The proposed change propagation rules do cover the general types of changes in our modelling framework; however, there are several limitations known. As one can see from the CCCMS case study, all the change propagation rules are applicable. As they stand currently, however, the coverage of all possible changes

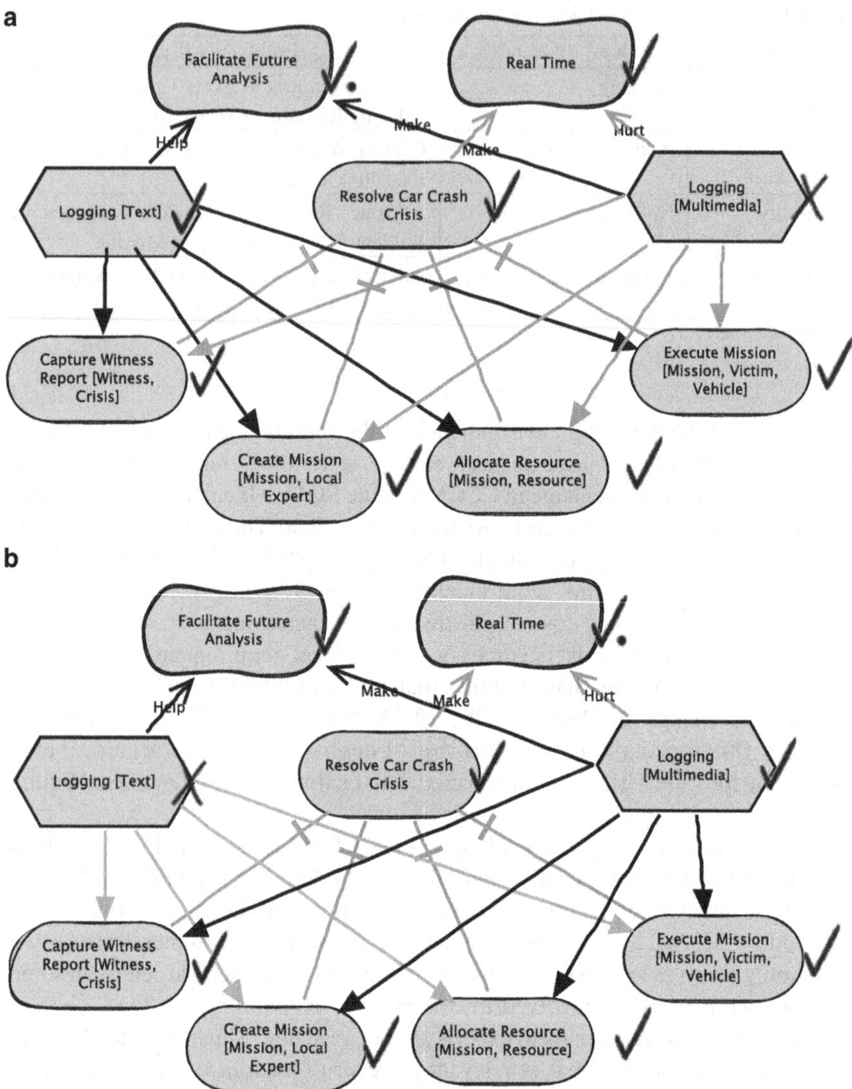

Fig. 2.7 Example of software goal change in CCCMS (Rule SG1) (**a**) before change (**b**) after change

to the crosscutting requirements is not complete. For instance, adding a quality soft goal would require additional aspectual requirements to be inserted into the model. However, without explicit analysis of such a new aspectual requirement, the crosscuts to existing functional requirements are likely missing when the topic names do not match. Therefore, a similarity-based computation is required to help requirements analysts to find more recalls.

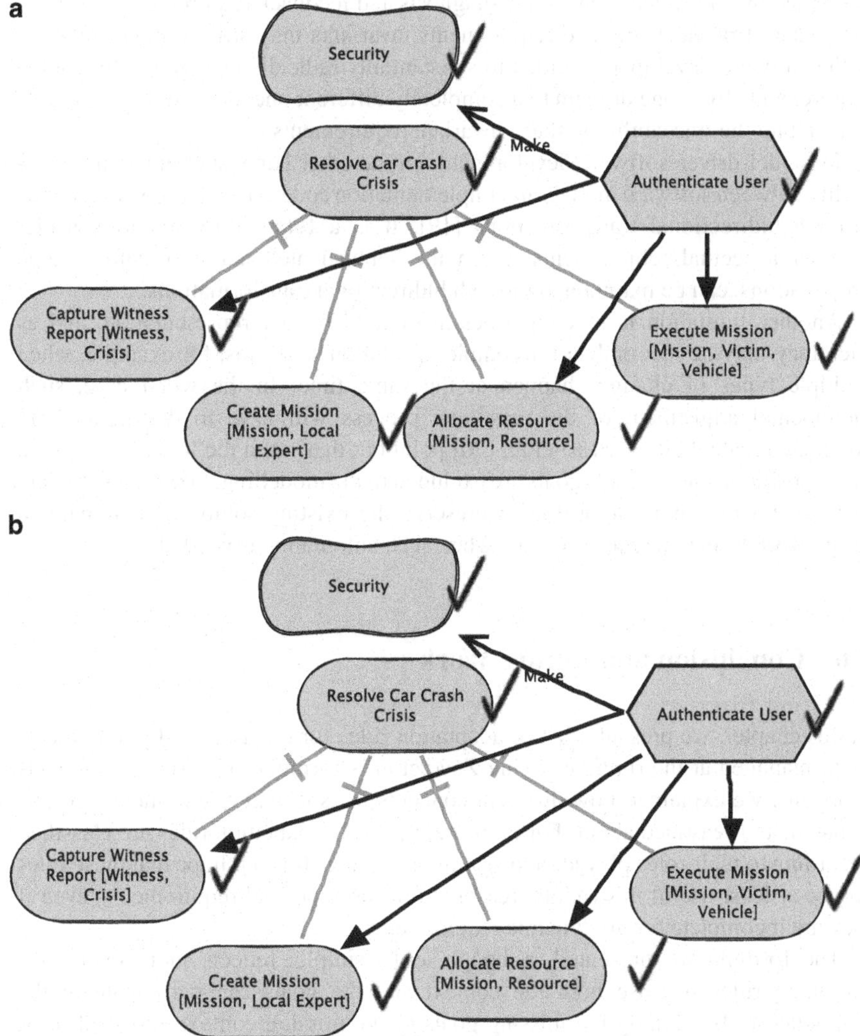

Fig. 2.8 Example of point-cuts change in CCCMS (Rule PC1) (**a**) before change (**b**) after change

It is worth to note that, currently, there is no knowledge about how invariant is the structure of the high-level goal structures. A possibility is that they tend to change more often for the application software for customer market, such as mobile apps than for those software systems of a mature domain, such as compilers and relational database management systems.

As we stated earlier, the continuous satisfaction of the "invariant" core requirements can be regarded as a quality requirement for the software evolution process. Our assumption is that such process-oriented quality requirements are to be addressed by additional monitoring, diagnosis and feedback requirements. Even so, the scope of product-oriented requirements invariants may still be rather relative. If the software developers decided to substantially/radically change the functional requirements from one domain to a completely different one, one would not be able to maintain the traceability to these invariant requirements.

In model-driven software development, on the other hand, such invariant traceability between software models and implementation code can be largely maintained through bidirectional transformations [19]. It is a future direction to consider whether aspectual requirements, given the sophisticated many-to-many change propagations, can be maintained through bidirectional transformations.

Another limitation is that our rules are bound by our representation, and as such they may be incomplete for complex evolution scenarios, for example, when multiple types of changes happen at the same time. In the worst case, such incremental adjustment of the reasoning process will have to degenerate into complete recalculations. Ernst et al. [20] point out that when the logic is as simple as propositional and the soft goals are excluded in the modelling, there is an efficient incremental reasoning algorithm to preserve the existing solutions. It remains a future work to include the soft goals when such automation is needed.

2.6 Conclusion and Future Work

In this chapter, we present a list of adaptation rules for the aspectual requirements to be managed at the runtime. Using Zave et al.'s formula for basic requirements problems, we explained how different concepts in aspectual requirements are formulated, and reasoned about. Furthermore, the basic adaptation rules are classified according to their roles played in the runtime changes. It is our hope that these rules can be at least useful in dynamic reasoning of the aspectual requirements, even if they are incomplete for all dynamic requirements.

The formula we presented, although looks simple, reflects more expressive reasoning rules because both the context and the goals can participate in the computation. By turning the missing goals or the missing context into wildcards, the same rule can be used to model all the rules [12–14].

The work has some limitations to be overcome in future. For example, we do not handle early aspects of other forms, such as natural language documents [21], or trust assumptions about the threat descriptions [22]. Also it is clear that having some form of tool support would greatly enhance the applicability of the methodology to larger and more interesting case studies. Currently we have implemented a simple form of aspect-monitoring framework based on our existing tool support of OpenOME [23] and OpenArgue [24]. Although they are able to perform the required reasoning tasks, it is still worthy to explore how well the work of incremental reasoning [20, 25] could be incorporated in the near future.

References

1. L. Chung, J.C.S. do Prado Leite, On non-functional requirements in software engineering, in *Conceptual Modeling: Foundations and Applications*, ed. by A.T. Borgida, V.K. Chaudhri, P. Giorgini, E.S. Yu (Springer, Berlin, 2009), pp. 363–379
2. J. Mylopoulos, L. Chung, B. Nixon, Representing and using nonfunctional requirements: a process-oriented approach. IEEE Trans. Softw. Eng. **18**(6), 483–497 (1992)
3. Y. Yu, J.C.S. do Prado Leite, J. Mylopoulos, From goals to aspects: discovering aspects from requirements goal models, in *Presented at the RE*, 2004, pp. 38–47
4. J. Kienzle, N. Guelfi, S. Mustafiz, Crisis management systems: a case study for aspect-oriented modeling, in *Transactions on Aspect-Oriented Software Development*, ed. by S. Katz, M. Mezini (Springer, Berlin, 2010), pp. 1–22
5. P. Zave, M. Jackson, Four dark corners of requirements engineering. ACM Trans. Softw. Eng. Methodol. **6**(1), 1–30 (1997)
6. I.J. Jureta, J. Mylopoulos, S. Faulkner, A core ontology for requirements. Appl. Ontol. **4**(3), 169–244 (2009)
7. N. Niu, Y. Yu, B. González-Baixauli, N.A. Ernst, J.C.S. do Prado Leite, J. Mylopoulos, Aspects across software life cycle: a goal-driven approach. Trans. Aspect Oriented Softw. Dev. **6**, 83–110 (2009)
8. M. Salifu, Y. Yu, B. Nuseibeh, Specifying monitoring and switching problems in context, in *15th IEEE International Requirements Engineering Conference*, 2007, pp. 211–220
9. Y. Wang, S.A. McIlraith, Y. Yu, J. Mylopoulos, Monitoring and diagnosing software requirements. Autom. Softw. Eng. **16**(1), 3–35 (2009)
10. X. Peng, B. Chen, Y. Yu, W. Zhao, Self-tuning of software systems through dynamic quality tradeoff and value-based feedback control loop. J. Syst. Softw. **85**(12), 2707–2719 (2012)
11. M. Salifu, Y. Yu, A.K. Bandara, B. Nuseibeh, Analysing monitoring and switching problems for adaptive systems. J. Syst. Softw. **85**(12), 2829–2839 (2012)
12. P. Giorgini, J. Mylopoulos, E. Nicchiarelli, R. Sebastiani, Reasoning with goal models, in *Conceptual Modeling—ER 2002*, ed. by S. Spaccapietra, S.T. March, Y. Kambayashi (Springer, Berlin, 2003), pp. 167–181
13. R. Sebastiani, P. Giorgini, J. Mylopoulos, Simple and minimum-cost satisfiability for goal models, in *Advanced Information Systems Engineering*, ed. by A. Persson, J. Stirna (Springer, Berlin, 2004), pp. 20–35
14. R. Ali, F. Dalpiaz, P. Giorgini, Reasoning with contextual requirements: detecting inconsistency and conflicts. Inf. Softw. Technol. **55**(1), 35–57 (2013)
15. X. Peng, Y. Yu, W. Zhao, Analyzing evolution of variability in a software product line: from contexts and requirements to features. Inf. Softw. Technol. **53**(7), 707–721 (2011)
16. B. Chen, X. Peng, Y. Yu, W. Zhao, Are your sites down? Requirements-driven self-tuning for the survivability of Web systems, in *Requirements Engineering Conference (RE), 2011 19th IEEE International*, 2011, pp. 219–228
17. V.N.L. Franqueira, T.T. Tun, Y.Yu, R.Wieringa, B. Nuseibeh, Risk and argument: a risk-based argumentation method for practical security, in *RE*, 2011, pp. 239–248
18. G. Kiczales, Aspect-oriented programming. ACM Comput. Surv. **28**(4es), 154 (1996)
19. Y. Yu, Y. Lin, Z. Hu, S. Hidaka, H. Kato, L. Montrieux, Maintaining invariant traceability through bidirectional transformations, in *ICSE*, 2012, pp. 540–550
20. N.A. Ernst, A. Borgida, I. Jureta, Finding incremental solutions for evolving requirements, in *Proceedings of the 2011 IEEE 19th International Requirements Engineering Conference*, Washington, DC, 2011, pp. 15–24
21. A. Rashid, A. Moreira, J. Araújo, Modularisation and composition of aspectual requirements, in *Proceedings of the 2nd International Conference on Aspect-Oriented Software Development*, New York, NY, 2003, pp. 11–20

22. C.B. Haley, R.C. Laney, B. Nuseibeh, Deriving security requirements from crosscutting threat descriptions, in *Proceedings of the 3rd International Conference on Aspect-Oriented Software Development*, New York, NY, 2004, pp. 112–121
23. J. Horkoff, Y. Yu, E.S.K. Yu, OpenOME: an open-source goal and agent-oriented model drawing and analysis tool, in *Presented at the iStar*, 2011, pp. 154–156
24. Y. Yu, T.T. Tun, A. Tedeschi, V.N.L. Franqueira, B. Nuseibeh, OpenArgue: supporting argumentation to evolve secure software systems, in *19th IEEE International Requirements Engineering Conference*, 2011
25. N.A. Ernst, J. Mylopoulos, Y. Yu, T. Nguyen, Supporting requirements model evolution throughout the system life-cycle, in *16th IEEE International Requirements Engineering, 2008. RE '08*, 2008, pp. 321–322

Part II
Concern Modelling and Composition

Chapter 3
Aspect-Oriented Compositions for Dynamic Behavior Models

João Araújo and Jon Whittle

Abstract The crosscutting problem can be observed at scenario modeling level where one model may present several tangled concerns, compromising requirements and system evolution. To avoid this problem, we can deal with aspectual scenarios by modularizing and thus separating them from other scenarios. Also, it is desirable to analyze how the crosscutting scenarios interact with other scenarios at early stages of software development; otherwise these interactions will only become clear during later stages when problems are much more expensive to solve. But to achieve that scenario modularization is not enough, we need efficient model composition mechanisms to allow the system to be analyzed and validated in its entirety. We introduce the Modeling Aspects Using a Transformation Approach (MATA), an expressive technique based on graph transformations, where aspectual scenarios, here represented as sequence diagram and state machines, will be modeled and composed efficiently. An example, based on a common case study, illustrates the usage of MATA's modularization and composition mechanisms.

3.1 Introduction

In general, crosscutting concerns, or aspects, make system evolution and maintenance costly because there is no clear separation of software artifacts. In this chapter, we consider aspects at the requirements analysis level. In particular, we concentrate on behavior modeling, e.g., scenario-based requirements modeling and state machine modeling.

J. Araújo (✉)
Departamento de Informática, Universidade Nova de Lisboa, Caparica, Portugal
e-mail: joao.araujo@fct.unl.pt

J. Whittle
Computing Department, Lancaster University, Lancashire, UK

A. Moreira et al. (eds.), *Aspect-Oriented Requirements Engineering*,
DOI 10.1007/978-3-642-38640-4_3, © Springer-Verlag Berlin Heidelberg 2013

A scenario is an example trace of desired or existing system behavior. Scenarios are a natural and intuitive way of specifying system and user interactions and are frequently used in requirements engineering [1] because they are easily understood by all stakeholders. A comprehensive set of scenarios can be difficult to specify, though, as there are several scenarios of different types to consider, such as exception and failure cases or scenarios that are called by several other ones. Many of these are aspectual in the sense that they crosscut other scenarios.

A crosscutting scenario is a scenario that crosscuts other scenarios [2], i.e., a scenario whose behavior constrains or modifies the behavior of non-aspectual scenarios it affects. But even they do not crosscut it is important to treat them as aspects in order to keep them separate for evolution purposes. A large system may be described by hundreds of scenarios that capture nominal or "happy day" scenarios, exceptional, alternative scenarios, etc. As with any large software artifact, there are many natural crosscutting scenarios.

The best way to deal with crosscutting scenarios is to separate them from other scenarios and model them independently. This modularization avoids tangled representations in the scenario models and facilitates scenario and consequently requirements evolution. On the other hand, if we neglect to model and analyze how the crosscutting scenarios interact with other scenarios earlier, there is a risk that these interactions will only become clear during later stages of software development when problems are much more costly to remedy. Thus, it is necessary at the requirements analysis stage to both model and compose scenarios in a way that will allow the entire set of scenarios to be validated. Aspects composition with core scenarios target an overall understanding of the system, offering, at the same time, the possibility to clearly understand the impact of an aspect scenario on a set of other base scenarios. Composition is a key technique because it allows the system to be inspected, analyzed, or tested in its entirety.

In behavior modeling, it is common among use case-based methods to first develop scenarios, given, for example, as UML sequence diagrams, as a way to describe use cases, and then later to use these scenarios as a guide in developing individual object behavioral descriptions, given as UML state machines. Aspects can be described at either the sequence diagram level or the state machine level.

In our approach, behavior will be modeled using UML diagrams, in particular, sequence diagrams and state machines. Sequence diagrams are a good way of modeling early requirements because they show interactions between system components and are very natural and intuitive to model. Although interactions give a global view of the requirements, to simulate the requirements, a local view of each system component is necessary. Therefore, a global scenario-based view can be converted into a local state machine-based view. This is a step necessary to move towards implementation. Aspects can also be separately represented at this stage. State machines can be used to model the local, internal behavior of system components and can be modeled taking into account the separation of aspectual and non-aspectual behavior and its composition also for validation purposes.

Since aspects can be identified at any stage of the software life cycle, composition can also take place at any of those stages. The effort involved in composition, however, may be different depending on when it takes place. This will be also discussed in this chapter.

We introduce an approach where aspectual scenarios, both at sequence diagram and state machine levels, will be modeled using MATA (Modeling Aspects Using a Transformation Approach) [3], a technique for modeling and composition of patterns based on graph transformations. In general, aspect orientation is a software reuse paradigm and perfectly suits the specification of patterns' models, as it provides efficient mechanisms to reuse and compose pattern's models to a specific application.

This chapter is organized as follows. Section 3.2 presents background on MATA. Section 3.3 introduces the approach. Section 3.4 discusses and illustrates the composition at scenario level (sequence diagrams). Section 3.5 does the same at state machine level. Section 3.6 discusses the trade-offs between the two model compositions. Section 3.7 compares with other related approaches. Section 3.8 draws some conclusions.

3.2 Background

Modeling Aspects Using a Transformation Approach (MATA) [3] is an aspect-oriented modeling language and tool that considers aspect composition as a special case of model transformation. MATA allows modelers to maintain aspect models separately, detect structural interactions between aspects automatically, and compose a chosen set of aspects automatically with a set of base models.

MATA provides a unified approach to aspect model composition. Any modeling language with a well-defined metamodel can be handled in the same way. Currently, UML class, sequence and state diagrams are supported, but extensions to other modeling languages would be straightforward and would provide the same capabilities in detecting interactions and automating composition.

In MATA, the joinpoint model is defined by a diagram pattern which allows for very expressive joinpoints and any base model element (or combination of elements) can be a pointcut. For example, a joinpoint may define a sequence of messages, i.e., MATA provides full support for sequence pointcuts at the aspect modeling level. This is in contrast to most previous approaches to aspect-oriented modeling that only allow joinpoints to be single model elements, such as a single message. Also, MATA supports more expressive composition types. For example, an aspect sequence diagram can be composed with a base sequence diagram, using parallel, alternative, or loop fragments as part of the composition rule. Most other approaches have often been limited to the before, after, around advice of AspectJ.

MATA is supported by a tool built on top of IBM's Rational Software Modeler. It has been applied in a range of application areas, including security modeling and software product lines.

3.2.1 MATA Description

Here we focus on MATA to model aspectual behavior by using and adapting sequence and state machine diagrams. To specify aspectual behavior, three stereotypes were created to define composition rules:

- <<create>>, applied to any model element, which states that the element will be created in the base scenario
- <<delete>>, applied to any model element, which states that the element will be deleted of the base scenario
- <<context>>, used with container elements that are created; which states that the element will not be affected by the other two stereotypes, rather it must exist in base scenario to be combined with it through pattern matching. It avoids creating an element inside a created element, forcing it to match an element in the base

The composition mechanism of MATA is based on graph transformations. MATA represents graph rules in UML's concrete syntax, with some extensions to allow more expressive pointcut and variable expressions. A graph transformation is a graph rule r: L → R from a left-hand side (LHS) graph L to a right-hand side (RHS) graph R. In MATA the composition of a base model, Mb, with an aspect model, Ma, which crosscuts the base, is specified by a graph rule, r: LHS →RHS:

- A pattern is defined on the left-hand side (LHS), capturing the set of points in Mb where new model elements should be added.
- The right-hand side (RHS) defines those new elements and specifies how they should be added to Mb.

Figure 3.1 shows two examples of MATA rules defined in the context of sequence diagrams. R1 specifies that the aspectual behavior consists of an interaction between two objects that must be instantiated to two objects in the base. The rule says that the fragment par (that specifies parallelism) and messages r and s in one of the sections of the fragment are created, i.e., they define the aspectual behavior that must be inserted in the base. However, since p is defined as <<context >>, it must be matched against a message with the same name in the base. The resulting composed model when applying R1 is shown on the top right-hand corner of the figure. Note that since q and b are not part of the rule they come after the par fragment. Rule R2 is similar; the main difference is the use of the "any" operator. This allows that, in the example, any sequence of messages between p and b can happen in the base (in this case, only the q message).

Variables in MATA are prefixed by a vertical bar "|", meaning that "|X" will match any model element (e.g., object names, object types, messages) with the same type of X. After specifying both kinds of scenarios, base and aspectual, a pattern matching is made between them. This means that the MATA tool tries to establish a connection between elements of each scenario, always respecting the composition rules defined in the aspectual scenario. The resulting composed scenario describes

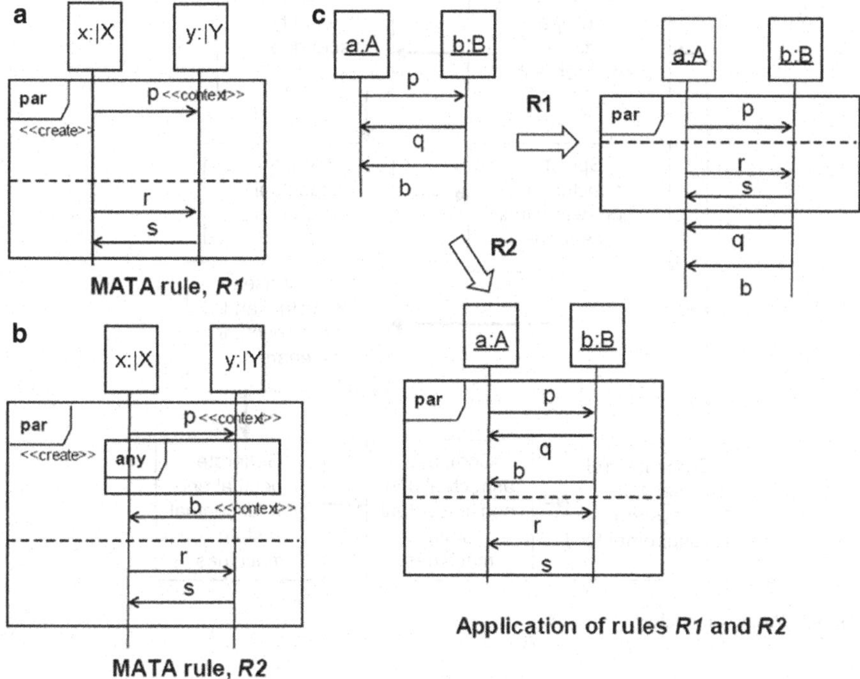

Fig. 3.1 Examples of MATA rules

the behavior of both scenarios, according to the rules defined. MATA allows more composition combinations than other existing aspect-oriented modeling tools and it also enables the identification of some aspect interactions.

Users may select a subset of the aspects and the tool generates the composed model for all of these aspects and the base. The user may also define an ordering of aspect composition in case one aspect needs to be composed before another. If an ordering is not specified, the tool selects an order non-deterministically.

Since MATA uses graph transformations as the underlying theory, it relies on an existing graph rule execution tool to apply graph rules. The graph rule execution tool used is AGG [4]. MATA converts a UML base model, captured as an instance of the UML2 metamodel, into an instance of a type graph, where the type graph represents a simplified form of the UML2 metamodel. MATA composition rules are converted into AGG graph rules and are executed on the base graph automatically. The results are converted back into a UML2 compliant model.

Critical pair analysis is always applied before composition and the results are presented to the user. Critical pair analysis is done by AGG and the results are converted into the IBM's Rational Software Modeler (RSM) so that detected dependencies and conflicts can be understood by the user. Critical pair analysis is not discussed any further as this not the focus of this chapter.

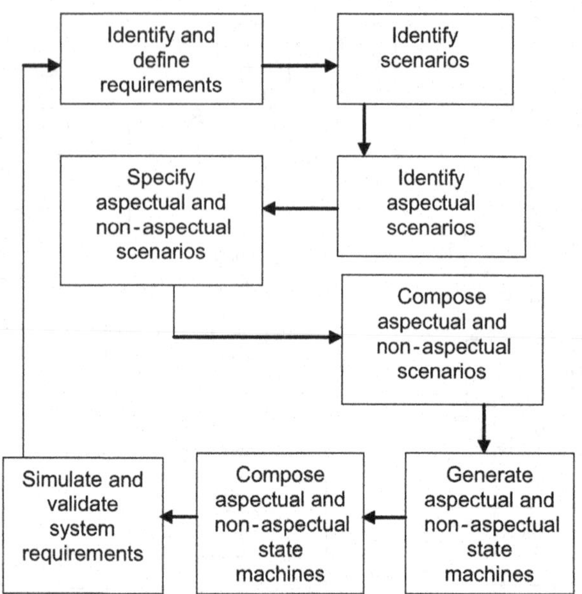

Fig. 3.2 Process model

MATA currently generates AspectWerkz [5] code from UML class diagrams and UML state diagrams. It takes a base model and a set of aspect models (selected by the user) and generates Java code for the base model and an AspectWerkz aspect for each of the aspect models. The details of the code generator are outside the scope of this chapter.

3.3 Behavioral Modeling with MATA

Here we describe the general process for modeling and composing with MATA, adapted from our previous works that used only pattern specifications [2,6]. We define a high-level process for developing and composing aspectual and non-aspectual behavior—see Fig. 3.2. Functional requirements, represented here as use cases, are refined to a set of scenarios. Aspectual scenarios, i.e., scenarios that crosscut other scenarios, are represented as aspectual sequence diagrams and non-aspectual ones as sequence diagrams. Aspectual and non-aspectual scenarios are composed through MATA graph transformations mechanisms.

Each aspectual or non-aspectual scenario is translated into a set of aspectual or non-aspectual state machines (one for each entity involved in the interaction). This can be done using the Whittle and Schumann state machine synthesis algorithm [7].

The result of the synthesis algorithm is a set of state machines—each object will have an aspectual and a non-aspectual state machine. The next stage of the process

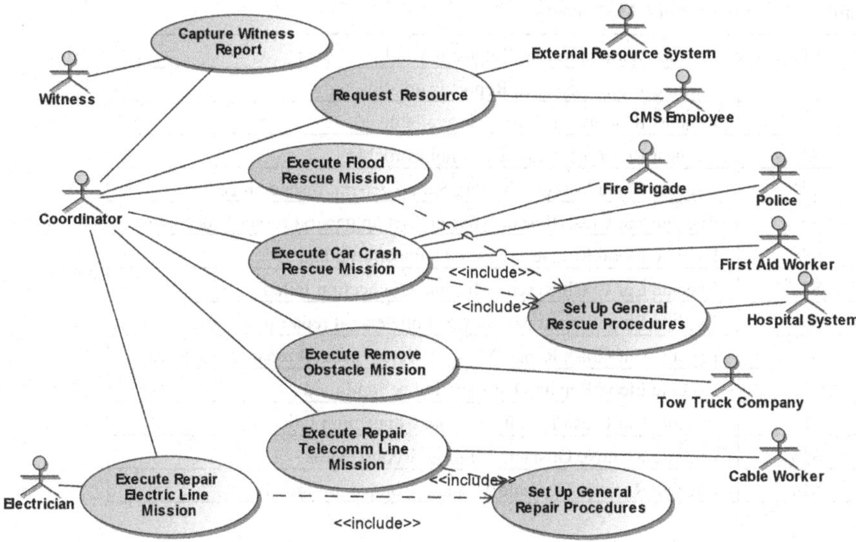

Fig. 3.3 Use case diagram for the Crisis Management System

composes the aspectual and non-aspectual state machine for each object. The result is an executable set of state machines that completely describe the requirements and in which aspectual and non-aspectual behavior has been woven. Validation of these state machines can now take place using a simulation harness. During simulation, it is likely that new scenarios will be discovered or inconsistencies and ambiguities will be found in the way that the aspects interact with the non-aspects.

In this chapter, the case study is also based on the Crisis Management System [8]. Here, we will assume that the system will give support to only car crash crisis and flood crisis.

3.4 Composition at Scenario Modeling Level

3.4.1 Identify Use Cases, Aspectual and Non-aspectual Scenarios

Figure 3.3 shows the use cases and actors that we will use to illustrate the approach. Basically, the coordinator is responsible for receiving a witness report of a car or flood crisis. Then s/he requests the necessary resources (either external or internal) to allow executing the necessary missions (e.g., rescue, repair, and remove obstacle missions).

Table 3.1 Partial set of CMS scenarios

S1	Capture Witness Report, Report is valid
S2	Capture Witness Report, Report is invalid
S3	Request Resource, Resource is available
S4	Request Resource, Resource is not available
S5	Execute Flood Rescue Mission, Set up general rescue procedures
S6	Execute Car Crash Rescue Mission, Set up general rescue procedures
S7	Execute Flood Rescue Mission, Connection failed
S8	Execute Car Crash Rescue Mission, Connection failed
S9	Execute Flood Repair Mission, Set up general repair procedures
S10	Execute Car Crash Repair Mission, Set up general repair procedures
S11	Execute Flood Repair Mission, Connection failed
S12	Execute Car Crash Repair Mission, Connection failed
S13	Execute Remove Obstacle Mission, Report status
S14	Execute Remove Obstacle Mission, Connection failed

Table 3.2 Aspectual Scenarios

A1	Set up general rescue procedures
A2	Set up general repair procedures
A3	Connection Failed

From the use case model we can identify in advance some crosscutting scenarios: it is the case of a use case being included by several other use cases. For example, setting up general procedures for a rescuing (or repairing) mission crosscuts specific rescuing (or repairing) missions scenarios.

More crosscutting scenarios are found after identifying a set of scenarios for each use case. Table 3.1 shows a non-exhaustive list of scenarios. Note that some exceptions can be also crosscutting such as "Connection failed."

This leads to the aspectual scenarios given in Table 3.2. For example, A1 is an aspectual scenario as it is repeated in the scenarios S5 and S6.

3.4.2 *Describe Aspectual and Non-aspectual Scenarios*

Figure 3.4 shows the MATA sequence diagram for interaction aspect A1. Firstly the victim's data are recorded (if available) and the respective medical records are requested. Also, depending on the status of the victim some action will be taken, but that depends on the type of the crisis involved. Finally, after the victim's status is updated, ambulance service is requested if needed. Note that the diagram contains one role name (|GeneralRescueProcedure) that must be instantiated to compose the aspect with the non-aspectual scenarios.

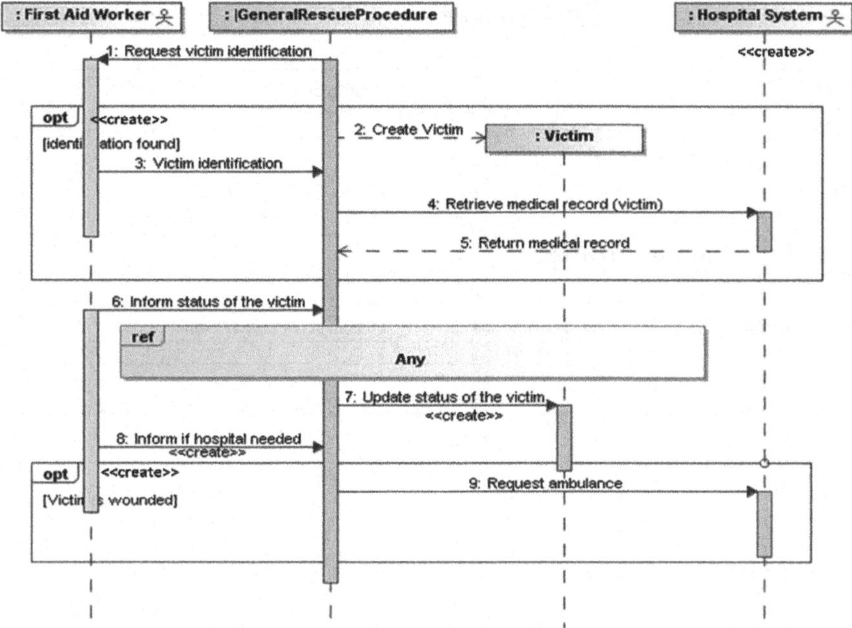

Fig. 3.4 The aspectual scenario "Set up general rescue procedures"

The non-aspectual (or base) scenario "Execute Car Crash Rescue Mission" is depicted in Fig. 3.5. Police service is requested at the same as the identification of the victim is requested. After the status of the victim is informed, if s/he is locked in the car the fire brigade team is requested.

3.4.3 Compose Aspectual and Non-aspectual Scenarios

The composed scenario is shown in Fig. 3.6. First we instantiate the roles: |GeneralRescueProcedure to CarCrashRescueProcedure. Then we compose, based on the graph transformations mechanisms of MATA.

3.5 Composition at State Machine Level

The separation of concerns should be maintained at the state machine level by deriving separately state machines from the aspectual objects (that shows only behavior relevant for the aspectual scenario it is involved in), i.e., aspectual state machines, and non-aspectual state machines from the non-aspectual objects (that shows the behavior relevant of the base scenario where it participates in).

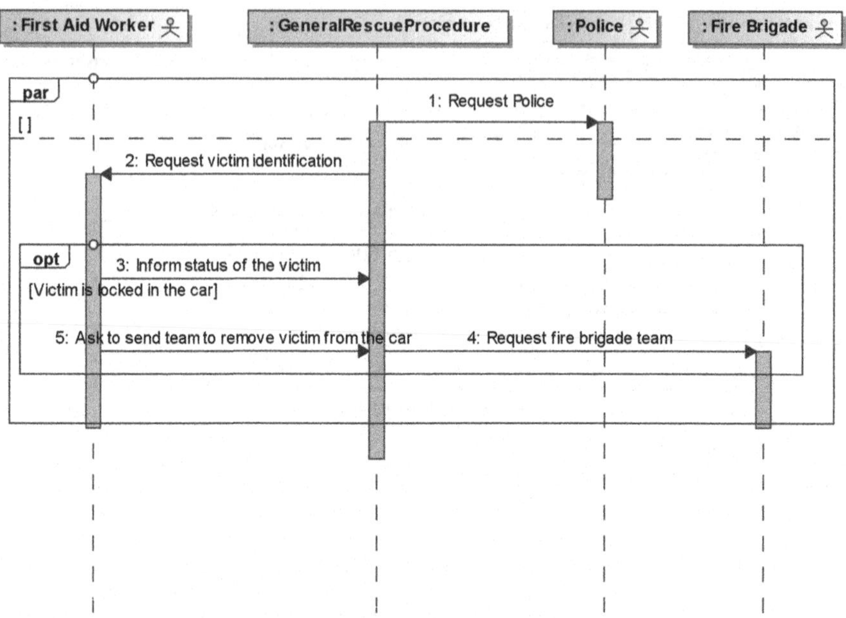

Fig. 3.5 Scenario for the Execute car crash rescue mission

In the example, the aspectual state machine for the |GeneralRescueProcedure object is shown in Fig. 3.7. It starts with the victim's identification request and, if available, victim's record is created. Then his medical record is requested. When the status of the victim is received, it is checked if s/he needs to go to the hospital. In this case an ambulance is needed. Note that we have a "Victim identification request," "Victim's status is received," "and Fire brigade requested" states—they serve as pointcuts, to allow composition with the base state machine.

In our example the non-aspectual state machine for the CarCrashRescueProcedure object is shown in Fig. 3.8. Police request occurs concurrently with victim's identification. After victim's status is received, fire brigade is requested in case s/he is locked in the car.

The composed scenario is shown in Fig. 3.9. Basically it complements the state machine in Fig. 3.8 with states and transitions created by the aspectual state machine in Fig. 3.7.

3.6 Discussion on the Two Composition Types

Developers wish to compose their aspect-oriented models with the core models in order to gain an overall understanding of the system. However, composition comes at a price; for budget and time constraint reasons it is not feasible to

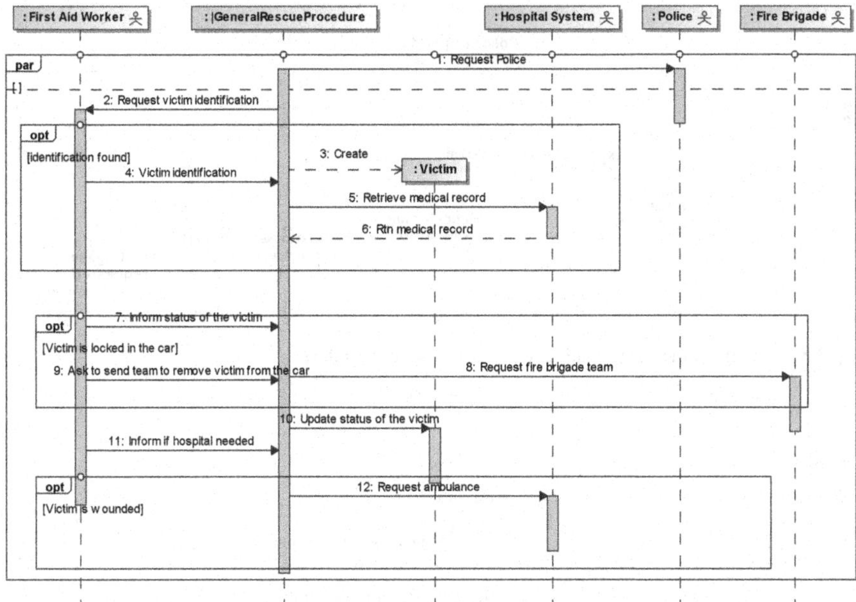

Fig. 3.6 Composed scenario

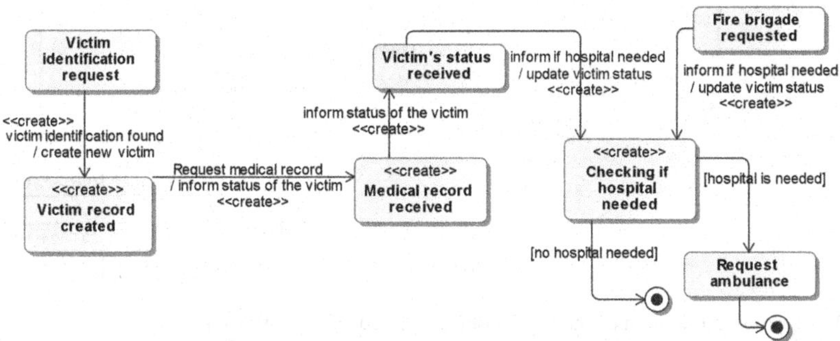

Fig. 3.7 Aspectual state machine for the object |GeneralRescueProcedure

compose at both interaction and state machine levels, even if the compositions are done automatically: there is also time and resources needed to analyze the compositions. The following questions naturally arise: what is the best time to perform composition? Is it more cost-effective to specify the composition as early as possible or as late as possible?

When developing aspects during analysis and design, there are three possibilities: compose aspects during scenario development and then convert to state machines; convert aspectual and non-aspectual scenarios first to aspectual and non-aspectual

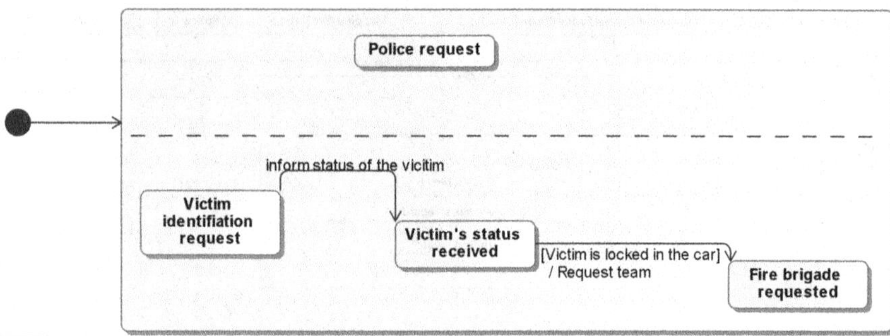

Fig. 3.8 State machine for the object CarCrashRescueProcedure

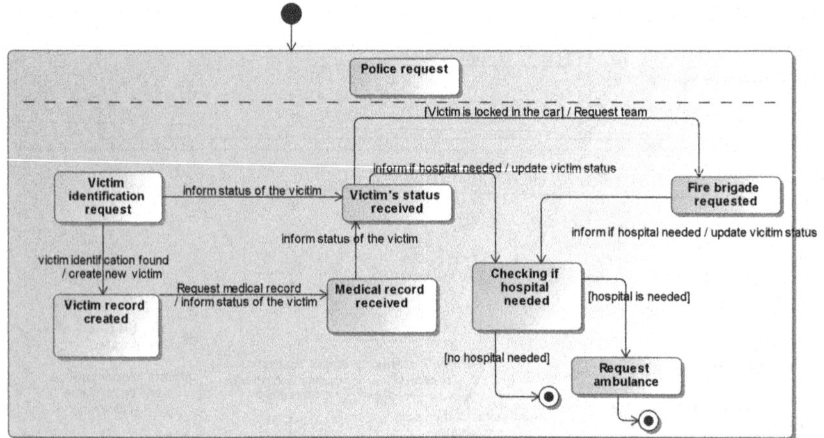

Diagram name	CarcrashSM
Author	joao
Creation date	23-09-2011 16:10
Modification date	17-04-2013 17:10

Fig. 3.9 Composed State machine for the object CarCrashRescueProcedure

state machines followed by composition; and compose scenarios and compose state machines.

With composition at the scenario level, the state machines need never be seen by the requirements engineer. Composition is specified purely in terms of scenario relationships and the executable state machines that are generated can be hidden. This has advantages for requirements engineers not trained in state-based techniques.

On the other hand, composition at the scenario level tends to be rather coarse grained. The user must provide composition operators that describe how to interleave messages from different scenarios. By composing instead at the state machine level, there is additional flexibility in describing the nature of the composition as composition can be defined in terms of states that are not specified in the scenarios.

At first glance, the effort of analyzing composition of aspectual scenarios is a function of the number of scenarios because each scenario is potentially crosscut. At the state machine level, each object has a state machine; therefore, the composition effort is a function of the number of objects. Typically, there are a large number of scenarios that could be crosscut by aspect scenarios. In contrast, there will typically be much fewer state machines because there are fewer participant objects than there are scenarios. This initial observation is naïve, as this may not be always the case as you may have a limited number of scenarios but a considerable number of objects—so it depends on the domain application. As a result, the preferred composition method depends on the particular application—the number of compositions might increase more in some cases than others.

There are, of course, other trade-offs between the two approaches. One important point is that scenario composition can lead to earlier detection of errors/inconsistencies/ambiguities. However, not all errors and conflicts can be identified at one level of abstraction. While some of them may appear at the scenario level, others may appear at the state machine level. Therefore, the synergy obtained from both approaches is higher than if only one is used. Certainly, this depends on budget constraints, the type of users, time constraints, and, last but not least, the available tools.

In summary, we observe that both strategies are useful. Some stakeholders may prefer to work with one diagram type as opposed to another. Composing at the scenario level, for example, has advantages for requirements engineers since sequence diagrams are generally easier to understand than state machines. Conversely, software designers might prefer a state machine-oriented view and would therefore prefer composition at the state machine level. In many cases, however, there is a real choice to be made between the approaches. A software engineer might develop some behavior models and aspectual behavior models and then ask him/herself whether s/he should compose earlier (i.e., during scenario modeling) or compose later (i.e., during state machine modeling). Note that we do not advocate either of these solutions, but expect that each one will be appropriate in different contexts.

3.7 Related Approaches

Generic aspects can be seen as a kind of design pattern. Hence, work on instantiating design patterns and applying aspect models is closely related. Indeed, there has been some work on automatically instantiating generic descriptions of design patterns [9] and using such techniques in aspect-oriented modeling [6].

Georg et al. [10] propose an aspect-oriented design approach that defines an aspect through role models to be woven into UML diagrams. The approach is similar to ours in that aspects are treated as patterns. In particular, interaction aspects may be modeled as interaction role models. However, the approach does neither allow concrete modeling elements in the role models, a flexibility provided by MATA, nor compose via graph transformations. Also, the approach relies on nonautomatic instantiations, a limitation subsumed by MATA.

Clarke and Walker [11] use UML templates to define aspects. The approach also is concerned more with how to specify the aspects rather than weaving aspects into non-aspectual models. It composes static structural properties of aspects with non-aspectual class models, but do not compose interaction properties of aspects with interaction models.

Song et al.'s work [12] also composes aspect sequence diagrams, but it has a very limited set of composition operators and does not provide tool support. However, it does address how to verify the result of the composition by annotating models with OCL expressions which could then be checked against the composed models. The work appears to be in its early stages, however.

Reddy et al. [13] compose aspect sequence diagrams by using special tags that allow an aspect to be broken into pieces and then inserted at different points in the base, e.g., at the beginning, in the middle, or at the end of the base messages. Nevertheless, the MATA approach is more general and subsumes these operators. Earlier work by the authors of this chapter also considered composition of sequence diagrams using a limited set of composition operators [2]. This work has also been subsumed by MATA.

Klein and Kienzle [14] describe a case study of composing aspect sequence diagrams. In this approach, one sequence diagram describes the pointcut and one sequence diagram describes the advice. The paper presents a case study using the semantic composition of scenarios described in [15]. The latter is important work that goes beyond syntactic mechanisms for defining pointcuts but instead relies on the semantics of the modeling language for matching an aspect. This reduces, to some extent, the fragile pointcut problem for aspect sequence diagrams but does incur a performance overhead. Such techniques could potentially be incorporated into MATA.

Katara and Katz [16] provide an approach for aspect-oriented modeling of sequence and state diagrams based on superimposition. This is quite similar to MATA in that aspects are defined as increments over other models (either the base or other aspects). However, the approach does not support a fully fledged pattern language for defining pointcuts, which limits the quantification possible. Although Katara and Katz do give consideration to identifying dependencies between aspects, these dependencies must be found manually and documented on a so-called concern diagram. MATA can be thought of as providing automated support for developing and/or validating such a concern diagram.

The WEAVR tool [17] considers actions in state machines as joinpoints and uses "around" advices to weave in aspect state machines. WEAVR is the first commercially available aspect modeling tool but focuses only on state machines.

In addition, it is tailored towards SDL state machines and concentrates on executable modeling so is more suited to detailed design rather than earlier analysis and design phases.

Related work that is closest to ours is joinpoint designation diagrams (JPDDs) [18]. JPDDs are similar to defining patterns using graph rules. Something similar to sequence pointcuts can be defined but the advices are limited to before/after/around. Furthermore, the advantage of using graph rules is the existence of formal analysis techniques. In addition, JPDDs focus on defining joinpoints and are not so much concerned with composition. MATA provides a full composition tool in which very expressive composition relationships can be specified. This is not possible with JPDDs.

More generally, model composition has been addressed outside of the AOSD community. In particular, Nejati et al. [19] investigates how to merge state machines using composition relationships and category theory. This is in many respects similar to our work but has a different goal in that it addresses how to reconcile models produced by different development teams.

3.8 Conclusions

This chapter discussed an approach for modeling and composing aspectual behavior, first at the scenario level and later at the state machine level using the MATA notation. MATA addresses aspect composition simply as model transformation. MATA tends towards the use of a generic model transformation language but tailors this to ensure familiarity of the language to modelers. In this sense, it is different than using a completely general transformation language, such as one based on QVT, but retains the power and flexibility of a generic transformation language. Dedicated aspect composition languages risk sacrificing expressiveness because a limited number of composition operators would be provided. MATA brings flexible composition without requiring any knowledge of programming or the need to understand the code in an existing composition framework.

The compositions at scenario and state machine levels were compared to evaluate the effort of aspect composition at different stages of an object-oriented analysis and design process. At scenario level, composition is specified purely in scenario terms. Once composition is done, the scenarios are converted to state machines. At design level, composition is done purely in terms of state machines. There are advantages and disadvantages to both composition moments. With composition at the scenario level, the benefits of composition can be seen by requirements engineers not familiar with state-based notations. On the other hand, composition at the interaction level tends to be rather coarse grained. The user must provide composition operators that describe how to interleave messages from different interactions. By composing at the state machine level, there is additional flexibility in describing the nature of the composition because composition can be defined in terms of states that are not specified in the interactions.

References

1. I. Alexander, N. Maiden (eds.), *Scenarios, Stories, Use Cases* (Wiley, New York, NY, 2004)
2. J. Whittle, J. Araújo, Scenario modeling with aspects, in *IEE Proceedings Software,* 2004
3. J. Whittle, P.K. Jayaraman, A.M. Elkhodary, A. Moreira, J. Araújo, MATA: a unified approach for composing UML aspect models based on graph transformation. Trans. Aspect Oriented Softw. Dev. **VI**, 191–237 (2009)
4. G. Taentzer, AGG: a graph transformation environment for modeling and validation of software, in *Conference on Applications of Graph Transformations with Industrial Relevance (AGTIVE)*, Charlottesville, VA, 2003, pp. 446–453
5. J. Boner, A. Vasseur, *Tutorial on AspectWerkz for Dynamic Aspect-Oriented Programming* (Aspect Oriented Software Development (AOSD), Lancaster, 2004)
6. J. Araújo, J. Whittle, D.-K. Kim, D.-K. Modeling and composing scenario-based requirements with aspects, in *International Conference on Requirements Engineering (RE)*, Kyoto, Japan, 2004, pp. 58–67
7. J. Whittle, J. Schumann, Generating statechart designs from scenarios, in *International Conference on Software Engineering (ICSE)*, Limerick, Ireland, 2000, pp. 314–323
8. J. Kienzle, N. Guelfi, S. Mustafiz, Crisis management systems: a case study for aspect-oriented modeling. Trans. Aspect Oriented Softw. Dev. **VII**, 1–22 (2010)
9. K. Kim, J. Whittle, Generating UML models from domain patterns, in *Software Engineering Research, Management and Applications*, 2005, pp. 166–173
10. G. Georg, I. Ray, R. France, Using aspects to design a secure system, in *8th IEEE International Conference on Engineering of Complex Computer Systems,* Greenbelt, MD, 2002
11. S. Clarke, R.J. Walker, Composition patterns: an approach to designing reusable aspects, in *International Conference on Software Engineering (ICSE)*, 2001
12. E. Song, R. Reddy, R. France, I. Ray, G. Georg, R. Alexander, Verifiable composition of access control and application features, in *ACM Symposium on Access Control Models and Technologies (SACMAT)*, Stockholm, Sweden, 2005, pp. 120–129
13. R. Reddy, A. Solberg, R. France, S. Ghosh, Composing sequence models using tags, in *Aspect Oriented Modeling Workshop at MODELS 2006*, 2006
14. J. Klein, J. Kienzle, Reusable aspect models, in *Aspect Oriented Modeling Workshop at MODELS*, 2007
15. J. Klein, L. Helouet, J. Jézéquel, *Semantic-Based Weaving of Scenarios* (Aspect-Oriented Software Development (AOSD), Vancouver, BC, 2006), pp. 27–38
16. M. Katara, S. Katz, *Architectural Views of Aspects* (Aspect-Oriented Software Development (AOSD), Boston, MA, 2003), pp. 1–10
17. T. Cottenier, A. van den Berg, T. Elrad, *Motorola WEAVR: Model Weaving in a Large Industrial Context* (Aspect-Oriented Software Development (AOSD), Vancouver, BC, 2007)
18. D. Stein, S. Hanenberg, R. Unland, *Expressing Different Conceptual Models of Join Point Selections in Aspect-Oriented Design* (Aspect-Oriented Software Development (AOSD), Bonn, 2006), pp. 15–26
19. S. Nejati, M. Sabetzadeh, M. Chechik, S. Easterbrook, P. Zave, Matching and merging of statecharts specifications, in *International Conference on Software Engineering (ICSE)*, 2007, pp. 54–64

Chapter 4
Semantics-Based Composition for Textual Requirements*

Ruzanna Chitchyan

This chapter is extensively based on the work initially published in [1].

Abstract Most current aspect composition mechanisms rely on syntactic references to the base modules or wildcard mechanisms quantifying over such syntactic references in pointcut expressions. This leads to the well-known problem of pointcut fragility. Semantics-based composition mechanisms aim to alleviate such fragility by focusing on the meaning and intention of the composition, hence avoiding strong syntactic dependencies to the base modules. In this chapter we present one such mechanism—requirements description language (RDL)—for textual requirements. The RDL enriches the natural language textual requirements with semantic information. Composition specifications are written based on these semantics rather than requirements syntax, hence providing improved means for expressing the intentionality of the composition, in turn facilitating semantics-based reasoning about aspect influences and trade-offs.

4.1 Introduction

The majority of current aspect-oriented (AO) composition mechanisms rely on syntactic references to enable the aspectual and base artifacts to be composed [1]. By syntactic references we mean use of specific naming conventions and structural references (e.g., to requirements ids, use case step numbers, etc.) or quantification over such elements using wildcards. When performing refactoring or maintenance activities this often leads to the well-documented *fragile pointcut*

*This chapter is extensively based on the work initially published in [1].

R. Chitchyan (✉)
Department of Computer Science, University of Leicester, Leicester LE1 7RH, UK
e-mail: rc256@le.ac.uk

A. Moreira et al. (eds.), *Aspect-Oriented Requirements Engineering*,
DOI 10.1007/978-3-642-38640-4_4, © Springer-Verlag Berlin Heidelberg 2013

problem[2, 3], whereby a structural change in the base modules may invalidate the aspect composition specifications. Further undesirable phenomena, such as *ripple effects* [3], can often occur. Additionally, when using syntactic references the compositions are always constrained by the syntax of the base artifacts [4], leading to loss in composition expressiveness. Thus:

- The requirements compositions have to be expressed in terms of the structure of the requirements rather than their semantics. As a result, the requirements engineer's (and stakeholder's) intentionality is lost in the mapping to a syntax-governed model. This complicates subsequent requirements analysis, for instance, by forcing the analyst to conduct trade-off analysis in terms of syntactic elements.
- The requirements engineer has to know ahead where the compositions will be applied and has to prepare these points by assigning ids or names to them or using specific naming conventions (in the rest of this paper such elements are referred to as *scaffolding*). If these points are not readily available in the requirements structure, the existing structure has to be changed before an unexpected composition can be defined.

Semantics-based composition mechanisms, e.g., [1, 5–7], aim to address these expressiveness and fragility problems of syntax-based mechanisms, and aim to support specification of compositions that:

- Require less scaffolding by relying on the meaning of the relationships to be captured by the composition rather than the structure of the base modules or specific naming conventions.
- Are more stable in the face of change, i.e., less fragile, and hence unaffected due to structural or syntactic changes in the base modules.
- Are able to directly capture the composition's intention, i.e., are more expressive, hence bridging the gap between the developer's intentions and the composition specification mechanism.

This chapter presents one such composition approach based on a Requirements Description Language (RDL). This work demonstrates how the richness of the natural language can be used in defining expressive semantics-based pointcuts in AORE compositions. This work uses the fact that the natural language itself has a clearly defined set of syntactic rules and semantic elements, precise enough to support definition of a flexible composition mechanism for requirements analysis. These compositions are not formalized. Though a more formal semantics would undoubtedly be more precise, the natural language semantics capture the stakeholders' needs as expressed in the elicited requirements and hence are more suited to aspect-oriented requirements analysis.

The following sections present the elements of the RDL (Sect. 4.2), show examples of its use for a Crisis Management Case study (Sect. 4.3), and briefly discuss the available results on the evaluation of this work and its automation support (Sect. 4.4).

4.2 Requirements Description Language

This work on RDL delivers a text-based requirements composition specification and analysis approach. This approach annotates the syntactic elements of the natural language and exploits the fact that each syntactic element has a designated semantic role—these semantic roles form the basis of expressive pointcut expressions in the RDL.

4.2.1 RDL Elements

The elements constituting the RDL are presented in the metamodel in Fig. 4.1.

The RDL is an XML-based language—the XML annotations help automate the analysis (as discussed in Sect. 4.4). We discuss the various RDL elements and its composition mechanism next.

The RDL is based on the symmetric view of AOSD [8–11]. It uses the concepts of concern and requirement.

A *Concern* represents both crosscutting and non-crosscutting elements. A Concern is a high-level unit for system partitioning, a container for localizing semantically related *requirements* (e.g., Crisis, Accuracy, etc.). Thus, the *Crisis* concern shown in Fig. 4.2 localizes the details related to crisis.

The initial set of concerns for each system can be selected from a concern repository [9], or identified via mining tools, e.g., [12, 13], domain analysis, stakeholder interviews, or ethnographic studies.

A concern can be simple (containing only requirements), or composite (containing other concerns as well as requirements), thus allowing hierarchical structuring of related requirements. Each concern is identified by its name and encapsulated within <Concern/> tags.

A *Requirement* is a description of a service the stakeholders expect of the system, the system behavior, and constraints and standards that it should meet [14]. One or more requirement elements are encapsulated within a concern; each requirement is identified by a unique identifier[1] (unique within its defining scope, which is the concern). Similar to concerns, requirements too can have sub-requirements.

The meaningful concern names and requirement ids are neither necessary nor utilized in the RDL compositions. They are used for ease of referencing in discussion and are a part of RE tradition.

Both *concern* and *requirement* can be multi-sentence elements. However, the smallest unit of meaningful interaction conveying a construct is a simple sentence, and in order to be able to reason about this "smallest meaningful construct" we

[1]A requirement may contain one or more sentences. We do not need to number each sentence separately. A sentence may have one or more clauses.

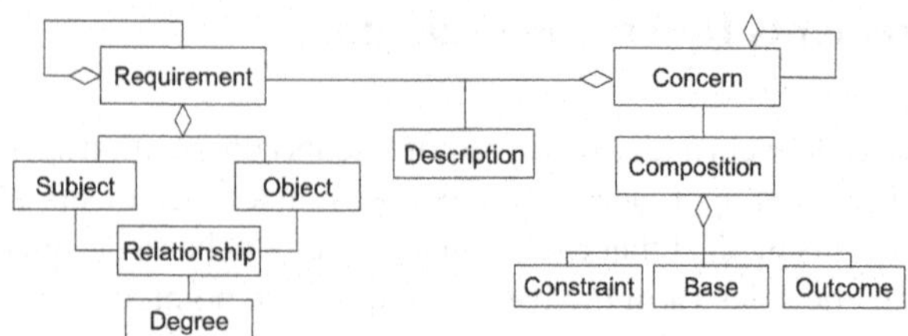

Fig. 4.1 RDL metamodel

need to define elements for its description. The main such elements in our RDL are *subject, object,* and *relationship.*

A *subject* is the entity that undertakes actions described within the sentence clause[2]. Subject in the RDL corresponds to the grammatical subject in the clause. Figure 4.2 demonstrates a subject—*system*—marked in a requirement or Accuracy concern (e.g., *data* is considered synonymous with *report*).

An *object* is the entity that is affected by the actions undertaken by the subject of the sentence, or in respect of which the actions are undertaken. Object in the RDL corresponds to the grammatical object in the clause. A clause could have several objects associated with (affected by) a single subject (e.g., Fig. 4.2 both *crisis report* and *witness* are objects.).

Relationship depicts the action performed (state expressed) by the subject on or with regard to its object(s). Relationships can be expressed by any of the verbs or verb phrases in natural language [e.g., *display* in requirement 2 of Fig. 4.2].

In order to support composition specifications involving a subject object or relationship denoted with different words representing the same semantics, a set of synonymous definitions must be provided. These synonyms could be provided either through a readily available standard electronic synonyms dictionary (e.g., WordNet [15]) or per project, augmenting a standard dictionary with a project-specific ontology.

The subject–relationship–object (S–R–O) structure carries the main semantic load of a sentence. Whereas subjects and objects denote the entities of significance in it, the relationship (i.e., verb) reflects the interaction between these entities. In our approach the relationship denotes the most central function, as it defines the functionality and/or properties that the subjects and objects provide. In order to be able to reason about the various types of relationships, we have used and adapted the linguistic studies of Dixon [16], Hale et al. [17], and Levin [18] that classify the verbs in accordance with their semantics (interested reader is referred to Chitchyan et al. [19–21] for more details). As a result of this (adapted) classification, we have a set of verb classes and subclasses (depicted in Fig. 4.3) that cover all English language verbs.[2] Each such class has a set of common semantic roles and

[2]Though this particular work focuses on English, the principle of verb classification is independent of language [16]. The same approach may be applied to other languages and a similar (though not identical) classification will result.

```
<Concern name="Accuracy">
  <Description"> Ensure accuracy of data. </Description>
 …
   <Requirement id="2"> The
    <Subject>system</Subject>
   <Degree type="modal" semantics="obligation" level="high">shall</Degree>
   <Relationship type="Move" semantics="Transfer_Posession">provide</Relationship>
    up-to-date
   <Object>information</Object>  to rescue
   <Object>resources</Object>
 …
</Concern>
```

Project Ontology
Data: weather data, witness data, terrain data, report, …

a

```
<Concern name="Crisis">
  <Requirement id="1">A
    <Subject>crisis management scenario</Subject> is usually
   <Relationship type="General_Action"
    semantics="Compare">triggered</Relationship> by a
    <Object>crisis report </Object>from a
    <Object>witness</Object> at the scene.
  </Requirement>
</Concern>
```

b

```
<Composition name="Accuracy Composition">
    <Constraint operator="apply">relationship="provide" and
    object="information"</Constraint>
    <Base operator="before">subject="data" or object="data" or
    relationship="report"</Base>
<Outcome operator="fulfil">
</Composition>
```

c

Fig. 4.2 Example of RDL elements

depicts their participation in a semantically related activity. For instance, all verbs of the Affect type involve three basic semantic roles—an Agent which moves or manipulates something (referred to as Manipulator role or Manip) so that it comes into contact with something or person that plays the Target role. Either the Manip or Target (or both) will be physically affected by this activity.

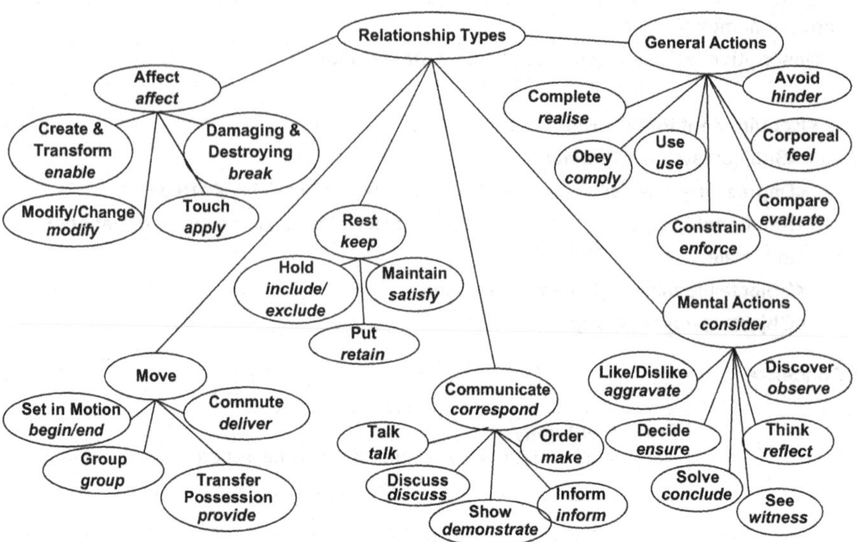

Fig. 4.3 Verb classes and composition operators (shown in *italics*)

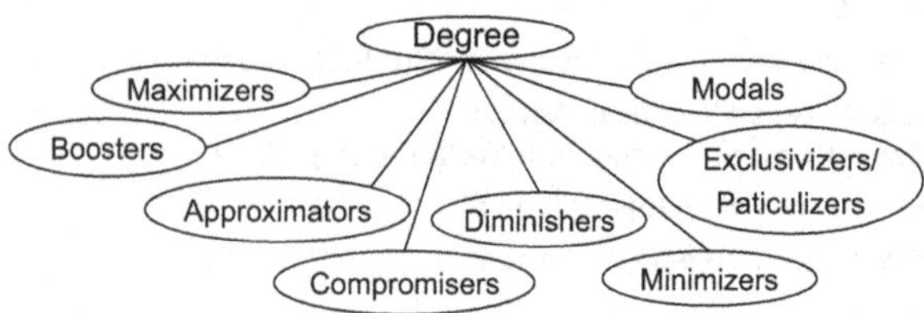

Fig. 4.4 Degree classes

In Fig. 4.3 the text in italics represents the composition operators (discussed in the next section) derived from these relationship semantics.

When specifying requirements stakeholders often qualify how important or significant a specific functionality or property is to them. In the RDL such qualifications are represented by the *Degree* element. Degree element depicts the strength of the relationship between the subject and object. An example for degree annotation is *<Degree type= "Modal" semantics= "Obligation" level= "high"> shall </Degree>* for the *shall* word in "The system *shall* provide … information…" requirement in Fig. 4.2.

The set of degree categories currently used in the RDL, i.e., the *type* attribute of Degree element in the RDL are presented in Fig. 4.4.

Each of these classes reflects a certain level of degree, for instance Maximizers (such as highly, completely, etc.) amplify some property to the top level, while Boosters (e.g., amply, considerably) amplify it but not to the maximum.

Of particular interest here is the group of Modals and related verbs: when a modal degree word (e.g., must, could, wish, etc.) qualifies a relationship, the relevance of that relationship (i.e., functionality or property) to the stakeholder is reflected ("shall provide"). The Modals have related levels, which can be high, medium, or low, depending on the semantics of a particular verb.

The RDL elements above are used for requirements description, irrespective of their modular structuring or contents. Composition is discussed next.

4.2.2 *Composition Elements and Their Use*

Composition is the assembling of the separately defined requirements modules with the aim of ensuring their desired interactions and revealing/addressing the undesired ones. A composition element in the RDL comprises three sub-elements: Constraint, Base, and Outcome. An example of composition is presented in Fig. 4.2.

A *Constraint* element specifies what checks and restrictions are to be placed on a set of requirements (provided by *Base* element) and what action must be taken in imposing these constraints. The required actions are specified by the constraint *operators* (see elements in italics in Fig. 4.3) which are derived from the relationship categories. Since each verb group has a dedicated meaning and a set of related roles, the corresponding operator denotes that these roles are expected to participate in a specific interaction. Thus, for instance, the *apply* operator used in Fig. 4.2 is derived from the *Touch* subgroup of the *Affect* group, and so has the semantics of *Agent* manipulating something (the *Manip* role) that comes into contact with a *Target* role, without disturbing it. These roles are normally filled in by the elements picked out by the Constraint and Base queries.

The query specified within the Constraint element is used to select concerns/requirements that will act as the constraint to be imposed [cf. query expression enclosed in the <Constraint/> tags in Fig. 4.2]. The query is semantics-based, i.e., it selects elements by their meaning, rather than structure or id or name. The benefits of such semantic queries are twofold. Firstly, we avoid syntactic matching in the composition specifications, thus avoiding unintended element matching. Instead compositions are specified based on the semantics of the requirements—for instance, the constraint query in Fig. 4.2 selects "the requirements in which information is provided" (more details are provided in Sect. 4.3.1). Secondly, it ensures that requirements compositions are semantically justified, rather than arbitrarily provided by a requirements analyst.

Base element provides a query for selecting the set of (points in) requirements that are affected by some constraints (provided by the *Constraint* element) and the temporal or conditional dependency between these requirements and the constraints. The query expression of the Base element, like that of the Constraint, is a semantic query. For instance, the base query in Fig. 4.2 selects "the requirement where data reports or is reported upon" (details are provided in Sect. 4.3.1).

The temporal and conditional dependencies are depicted by the base *operators*, which are founded on sequencing and conditional semantics in natural language

X before (after) Y	There is a temporal interval between requirements X and Y when X has completed but Y has not started yet.	XX YY
X meets (met by)Y	There is no temporal interval between requirement X ending and requirement Y starting (from perspective of X).	XXYY
X overlaps (overlapped by) Y	Requirement X has commenced before requirement Y; Y commences while X is in process; X completes while Y is in process (from perspective of X).	XXX YYY
X during (through) Y	Requirement Y has commenced before requirement X; X commences while Y is in process; X completes while Y is in process (from perspective of X).	XXX YYYYY
X starts (started by) Y	Requirement X has commences simultaneously with requirement Y; X completes while Y is in process (from perspective of X). This is a sub-type of during.	XXX YYYYY
X finishes (finished by) Y	Requirement Y has commenced before requirement X; X commences while Y is in progress; X and Y complete simultaneously (from perspective of X). This is a sub-type of during.	XXX YYYYY
X concurrent Y	Requirements X and Y are started and completed within the exact same temporal interval.	XXX YYY

Fig. 4.5 Selection of temporal operators for composition (based on Allen [22]). Here X and Y depict two requirements and their positioning towards each other reflects their temporal order

and reflect the ordering or conditional dependencies of requirements. Expressions such as "first… then," "once," "if," and alike are used to express such semantics. Our base operators fall into three categories:

- Sequential temporal operators: e.g., before, after, meets
- Concurrent temporal operators: overlap, during, starts, finishes and concurrent
- Conditional operators: if and if not

The temporal operators (Fig. 4.5) fully describe the relative temporal positioning of one item with respect to another [22], and all, besides concurrency, can be symmetrically inverted into another operator (e.g. *before* can be inverted to *after*, etc.). Since in the example in Fig. 4.2 we want to specify that the requirements where *"information is provided"* should be applied "some time before" the "data reports or reported upon," we use the *before* operator instead of the *"meets"* operator which is applicable when a no time lapse should be involved between base and constraint.

The *Outcome* element defines how imposition of constraints upon the base sets of requirements should be treated. For instance, the outcome element may specify a set of requirements that must be *satisfied* as post-conditions upon application of the Constraint or merely state that the Constraint has to be *fulfilled* [as is the case in Fig. 4.2].

We next discuss how the RDL facilitates expressive, semantics-based pointcut specifications.

4.3 Examples of Semantics-Based Compositions

Unlike other AORE approaches [23, 24] in which the smallest unit of reference for composition is normally a requirement, in RDL we use the elements that build the meaning of a requirement. Thus, we are able to select requirements by referencing their semantics without having to rely on any syntactic id.

Below we present some uses of the RDL.

4.3.1 Information Accuracy Composition

The composition for the Information Accuracy is shown in Fig. 4.2 with the concerns for Accuracy and Crisis shown in parts (a) and (b) of the figure. The Constraint query of this composition states that those *concern(s)* should be selected that contain one or more requirements that involve *provid*ing (relationship) *information* (object). This query will match the Accuracy concern in Fig. 4.2, as the relationship and objects of its requirements with id 2 correspond to the Constraint query criteria. Thus, the requirement 2 of the Accuracy concern will be selected without any reference to its name or to any of the ids of its requirements. If a synonym of the *provide* verb were used in the query instead, the respective requirements would still be matched. (If we wished to select the whole concern, we could have used *concern []* notation around the query, thus selecting the whole of the Accuracy concern.)

The Base query of this composition refers to requirements that involve *report*ing (relationship) or *data* (object or subject), which matches the requirement with id=1 in Fig. 4.2. Again, the point of interest for composition is defined without any syntactic reference. The Base operator is *before*, meaning that the constraint should be imposed immediately before the base.

Thus, the composition in Fig. 4.2 states that *immediately before* each requirement where the *data* is used in any way or something is *reported* is the requirement that "*provides information*" must be enabled. This intention of the composition is clear from the composition specification itself, without the need to look up anything from the participant concerns, thus providing a single point of reference for compositional reasoning.

This composition specification is also robust, unlike those in the syntactic counterparts. As long as *provision of information* is needed, the constraint of the composition will not change. Similarly, as long as the *data* is used in any way or anything is *reported*, the base also will be unaffected. This is true irrespective of any number of new requirements and concerns being added or removed from the specification.

The semantic queries used in the above example demonstrate that we can use the subject–relationship–object structure to find both the larger-grain entities, such as concerns, or requirements within which the given structure occurs, as well as a particular point, i.e., part of the sentence which contains this structure. In our automation of the RDL, if no "concern [ ]" expression is used, we refer to the S–R–O encapsulating requirement, though more fine-grained interpretations are also possible.

4.3.2 Assignment Operators in Composition

It should be noted that the semantic match for the queries defined by the S–R–O structure can be realized either per word *lemma* only, or per word *synonyms.*

A *lemma* is a reduction of the surface forms of the given word to its corresponding dictionary headword. For instance, *systems* will be reduced to *system*; *triggered* to *trigger*, etc. When matching "triggered" per lemma other surface forms of it (e.g., trigger) will also be matched, but no other synonym will.

On the other hand, when matching by synonym, both lemmas and synonyms of the given word are matched, so for instance, in case of "triggered," not only *trigger*, but also *initiate, activate, cause, prompt*, etc. will be matched.

Both of these matching techniques are significantly more expressive than the per string syntactic matching.

Normally the synonym-based matching is used in the RDL when the "=" operator is used. However, if required, a per lemma matching is also available via use of "= =" operator. This allows to define more narrow queries when needed, as well as to avoid confusion when a word is used in a specific sense but no project-specific lexicon is provided. For instance, with a standard synonym dictionary, if used with synonym assignment, *data* will match such words as *information*, *records*, *statistics*, etc. However, if we want only to match the word *data* itself, and if we have no project specific synonym dictionary or ontology of terms, the narrow per lemma assignment can be used.

4.3.3 Verb Classes in Composition

In addition to using the semantics of the S–R–O structure, other semantics of the RDL elements can also be used for querying. For instance, the semantics of the verb classes and subclasses (shown in Fig. 4.3) can be used to select requirements related to broad types of activities. One such example is shown in Fig. 4.6.

In this composition the constraint query is same as that in Fig. 4.2, but the *report* relationship in Base is described in terms of its semantic category: "Talk" (*semantics* attribute of the Relationship element in RDL used to capture the subclass of a generic verb class to which a given verb belongs (Fig. 4.3) [21][3]), thus the constraint will select the concern that contains requirements where the data is "talked" about

[3]The full schema for the RDL and meaning of each attribute is available from [21].

Fig. 4.6 Example of composition with verb class semantics

```
<Composition name="Communication Accuracy">
    <Constraint operator="apply">relationship="provide"
    and object="information"</Constraint>
    <Base operator= "before"> relationship.semantics = " Talk "and
object ="data" </Base>
</Composition>
```

Fig. 4.7 Example of degree element in composition

```
<Composition name="CompositionFirstRelease">
    <Constraint operator="include"> "Include requirements into
    1st release" </Constraint>
    <Base operator="if"> degree.semantics="Modal" and
    degree.level="high"</Base>
</Concern>
```

(e.g., report, discuss, argue, bicker, etc.). While some of these verbs are unlikely to be used with the given object, the others will depict a certain type of interaction reflected by the Talk subclass: i.e., the Speaker role (e.g., witness) talks about the optional Message role (e.g., data) with the Addressee role (e.g., police).

Such broader view queries are particularly useful when a requirements analyst wishes to establish an understanding of a particular interaction. Realistically it is not possible to write such queries for a syntax-based approach, as all individual verb statements in all concerns and requirements will have to be checked for the specific verbs and their corresponding extension points created/syntactic ids found and then listed in a pointcut/composition expression.

4.3.4 Degree Element in Composition

The Degree element and its attributes can also be used in queries. A query by relationship-related degree is shown in Fig. 4.7. In this example the constraint query does not select the constraint from the requirements, but provides it within the query statement.

The Base query selects requirements where the degree element of Modal type is used, as shown by the *degree.semantics= "Modal"* part of the query. The Modal type, due to the nature of the items included in this group, will always qualify verb phrases, i.e., relationships. This type of degree elements shows the level of the pertinence of the action/property defined by the verb phrase. The part of query stating *degree.level= "high"* uses the *level* attribute of the degree element which can be given high, medium, or low levels [21]. Thus, the base query will select the requirements where the relationship has a high level of pertinence, which may include requirements like "The credit card *must be validated* for payment," etc.

In addition, other types of the degree element (Fig. 4.4) indicate how the quality to which the degree relates should be treated. For instance, *degree.semantics= "Maximizer"* will select the set of requirements where a certain property must be maximized up to some given top level, while in case of use of Diminisher type the given level should be reduced, if possible.

4.4 Discussion

In this section we discuss two issues that are vital for the utility of the RDL approach: (1) Can it be automated? And (2) How does it compare to the syntax-based approaches?

The first issue is particularly relevant as the RDL utility will be void if it were to require a manual preprocessing of texts for tagset introduction and query processing.

Similarly, if the RDL were not to show any specific advantages over the existing syntax-based approaches, there would be no need for its use, even if the general idea for semantics-based composition was promising. Each of these issues is briefly discussed below.

4.4.1 Automation Support for RDL

Automation of RDL use is supported via two tools: the RDL annotations are automated through an extension of an existing natural language processing tool suite Wmatrix [25] while the composition definitions (based on the RDL tags) and visualization of the resulting interactions are supported by the MRAT Eclipse plug-in [26]. Both of these tools are briefly discussed below.

In order to support text annotation for the RDL described in this chapter, we have extended the functionality of **Wmatrix** tool in three areas by:

- Marking major *grammatical constituents of sentences* such as *subject, verb, and object.* This is achieved by building a set of patterns on top of the tags already assigned by the Wmatrix part of speech (POS) tagger. For example, a simple rule to link a verb to its object is as follows: N*o[.] (RR*/RG*/XXn3) VVN*v[.] This matches the sequence "Noun" (N*), followed by between 0 and 3 possibly negated "adverbs" (RR*/RG*/XX), followed by a past participle "verb" (VVN). In the case of a match, the noun is marked as the object of the verb.
- Explicit output of *lemmatization*, i.e., reducing similar words such as *systems* and *system* to the same base word (dictionary headword).
- *Classification* of verbs used in RDL is based on the work by Dixon [16]. In order to support this classification in Wmatrix we have defined a new tagset for verbs based on the RDL classification and have established a mapping from the Wmatrix verb categories onto this new tagset.

MRAT is implemented as an Eclipse plug-in and consists of an editor for revising RDL documents, and views for navigating and understanding requirement influences.

The editor is intended for revising RDL specification on the basis of inconsistencies, conflicts, and elaborations. MRAT offers automatic incremental building in terms of composition, outline-view integration, and editor features, such as syntax highlighting. Several views assist the editor by presenting RDL and synonym information, supporting development of pointcut expressions and navigating the composed document.

In addition to the editor and associated views, the tool has two more views for understanding composition information and influences: the Composition Definition View (CDV) and the Composition Time Flow View (CTFV).

The CDV provides composition-centric temporal visualizations. By explicitly showing the interactions of requirements in a multidimensional context, it is possible for the requirements engineer to identify and revise influences between requirements, as originally found by the discovery tool.

The CTFV supports conflict resolution and understanding by presenting requirements in a temporal visualization and providing contextual link derivation back to the composition source. This is the primary view for understanding how requirements are related as a result of mutual influence and for determining the source of a conflict. Conflicts and redefinitions (i.e., the case where the tool updates compositions to resolve some cases of temporal conflicts) are highlighted and the potential cause of the problem is displayed to the user.

4.4.2 Evaluation of RDL Compositions

The RDL composition mechanism has been compared [27] to a purely syntax-based composition approach [24] as well as a mixed one [28] which uses some elements of semantics and some syntax ones. For this evaluation, a case study was specified using the three approaches under evaluation, after which a set of change scenarios were applied to the initial requirements. The effect of the changes to compositions and modularity for all three approaches was quantified. While space limitations prevent us from going into detail of this comparative evaluation, the main results of it are summarized here:

- The RDL demonstrated the lowest number of concerns, compositions, and requirements affected when realizing all change scenarios. This is due to the fact that the RDL composition mechanism is fully decoupled from the structure of the requirements document: since this structure is not relied upon, any changes made to it do not propagate to the compositions.
- On average, the RDL used the smallest number of elements per composition to express the composition's intent; it also has the lowest standard deviation in the number of elements used per composition. The purely syntactic approach used both the highest average number of elements per composition, and had the highest standard deviation. This fact was explained by the higher level of abstraction of elements used in RDL compositions: no id or named requirement references were used. The syntax-based approach, on the other hand, needed

to either enumerate each element used in a composition via its "concern name-id" pair, or use wildcard-based quantification. The wildcard-based quantification, however, is often too broad, as well as fragile under change influence.
- RDL demonstrated a higher average **reachability** than those of the syntax-based alternatives, although RDL also demonstrated a higher standard deviation. This is explained by the scoping and lexicon definition characteristics of the composition reference mechanism. If a lexicon entry for an element is narrowly defined, the element will have relatively narrow reachability, bordering, in the worst case, with the named requirement like referencing mechanism of syntax based approaches, where only the joinpoints that exactly match the string of the given word are selected. However, such a narrow entry definition is rather unlikely. Normally a lexicon entry will be defined more broadly, and the broader its definition the wider the set of intended joinpoint that will be reached.

In summary, the initial evaluation of RDL demonstrates that this is a potentially promising approach for expressing interdependencies between concerns and requirements in a stable and intention preserving way.

4.5 Conclusion

In this chapter we have presented the RDL composition mechanism that abstracts away from the syntactic details in the AORE artifacts, hence helping the requirements engineer to focus on the meaning of the requirements-level compositions and interactions. The semantics exposed by the RDL and the semantics-based queries used in the composition specification facilitate reasoning about the stakeholders' intentions embedded within the natural language descriptions of requirements. Thus, the RDL and its supporting tools are a stepping stone towards more expressive pointcuts and intentional reasoning about concern dependencies and interactions at the requirements level.

References

1. R. Chitchyan, A. Rashid, P. Rayson, R. Waters. Semantics-based composition for aspect-oriented requirements engineering. in *AOSD '07* (ACM, New York, NY, 2007), pp. 36–48
2. A. Kellens, K. Mens, J. Brichau, K. Gybels, Managing the evolution of aspect-oriented software with model-based pointcuts, in *European Conference on Object-Oriented Programming (ECOOP)*. LNCS, vol. 4067 (Springer, 2006), pp. 501–525
3. P. Greenwood, T.T. Bartolomei, E. Figueiredo, M. Dósea, A.F. Garcia, N. Cacho, C. Sant'Anna, S. Soares, P. Borba, U. Kulesza, A. Rashid, On the impact of aspectual decompositions on design stability: an empirical study, in *ECOOP*, 2007, pp. 176–200
4. D. Stein, S. Hanenberg, R. Unland, Expressing different conceptual models of join point selections in aspect-oriented design, in *AOSD '06* (ACM, New York, NY), 2006, pp. 15–26
5. R. Knöll, M. Mezini, Pegasus: first steps toward a naturalistic programming language, in *OOPSLA, Onward Track* (ACM, 2006)

6. C.V. Lopes, P. Dourish, D.H. Lorenz, K.J. Lieberherr, Beyond AOP: towards naturalistic programming, in *International Conference on Object-Oriented Programming, Systems, Languages, and Applications (OOPSLA)* (ACM, 2003), pp. 198–207
7. K. Ostermann, M. Mezini, C. Bockisch, Expressive pointcuts for increased modularity, in *European Conference on Object-Oriented Programming (ECOOP)*. LNCS, vol. 3586 (Springer, 2005), pp. 214–240
8. A. Moreira, J. Araujo, A. Rashid, A concern-oriented requirements engineering model, in *Proceedings of the International Conference on Advanced Information Systems Engineering (CAiSE)*. LNCS, vol. 3520 (2005), pp 293–308
9. A. Moreira, J. Araujo, A. Rashid, Multi-dimensional separation of concerns in requirements engineering, in *International Conference on Requirements Engineering (RE)* (IEEE CS, 2005), pp. 285–296
10. S. Sutton, I. Rouvellou, Modeling of software concerns in Cosmos, in *International Conference on Aspect-Oriented Software Development (AOSD)*, 2002, pp. 127–133
11. P.L. Tarr, H. Ossher, W.H. Harrison, S.M. Sutton, N degrees of separation: multi-dimensional separation of concerns, in *ICSE* (ACM, 1999), pp. 107–119
12. E. Baniassad, S. Clarke, Theme: an approach for aspect-oriented analysis and design, in *International Conference on Software Engineering (ICSE)*, 2004, pp. 158–167
13. A. Sampaio, R. Chitchyan, A. Rashid, P. Rayson, EA-Miner: a tool for automating aspect-oriented requirements identification, in *International Conference on Automated Software Engineering (ASE)*, 2005, pp. 352–355
14. I. Sommerville, *Software Engineering*, 7th edn. (Addison-Wesley, Reading, MA, 2004)
15. WordNet (2006), http://wordnet.princeton.edu/
16. R.M.W. Dixon, *A Semantic Approach to English Grammar*, 2nd edn. (Oxford University Press, Oxford, 2005)
17. K.L. Hale, S.J. Keyser, *A View from the Middle* (MIT, Center for Cognitive Science, Cambridge, MA, 1987)
18. B. Levin, *English Verb Classes and Alternations: A Preliminary Investigation* (University of Chicago Press, Chicago, IL, 1993)
19. R. Chitchyan, S.S. Khan, A. Rashid, Modelling and tracing composition semantics in requirements, in *Early Aspects 2006: Traceability of Aspects in the Early Life Cycle Workshop (Held at AOSD'06)*, Bonn, Germany, 2006
20. R. Chitchyan, A. Rashid, Tracing requirements interdependency semantics, in *Early Aspects 2006: Traceability of Aspects in the Early Life Cycle Workshop Early Aspects WS (Held at AOSD'06)*, Bonn, Germany, 2006
21. R. Chitchyan, A. Sampaio, A. Rashid, P. Sawyer, S.S. Khan, Initial version of aspect-oriented requirements engineering model, in *Lancaster AOSD-Europe report (D36): AOSD-Europe-ULANC-17*, 2006
22. J.F. Allen, Maintaining knowledge about temporal intervals. Commun. ACM **26**(11), 832–843 (1983)
23. I. Jacobson, P.-W. Ng, *Aspect-Oriented Software Development with Use Cases* (Addison-Wesley, Reading, MA, 2005)
24. A. Rashid, A. Moreira, J. Araujo, Modularisation and composition of aspectual requirements, in *AOSD* (ACM, 2003), pp. 11–20
25. P. Rayson, Wmatrix (2006), http://www.comp.lancs.ac.uk/ucrel/wmatrix/
26. R.W. Waters, MRAT: a multidimensional requirements analysis tool, MSc. Dissertation, Lancaster University, Lancashire, 2006
27. R. Chitchyan, P. Greenwood, A. Sampaio, A. Rashid, A. Garcia, L. Fernandes da Silva. Semantic vs. syntactic compositions in aspect-oriented requirements engineering: an empirical study, in *Proceedings of the 8th International Conference on Aspect-Oriented Software Development (AOSD 2009)* (ACM, Charlottesville, VA), 2–6 Mar 2009, pp. 149–160
28. L. Silva, A guided strategy the modeling aspect-oriented requirements (in Portuguese), PhD, Rio de Janeiro, Catholic University of Rio de Janeiro (PUC-Rio), Brazil, 2006

Chapter 5
Composing Goal and Scenario Models with the Aspect-Oriented User Requirements Notation Based on Syntax and Semantics

Gunter Mussbacher, Daniel Amyot, and Jon Whittle

Abstract The Aspect-oriented User Requirements Notation (AoURN) combines goal-oriented, scenario-based, and aspect-oriented concepts into a framework for requirements engineering activities. AoURN's approach to composition takes the structure of AoURN's goal and scenario notations into account. Composition is hence tailored to these two notations to balance reusability of the aspect specification and the amount of duplication it requires. Furthermore, the composition mechanism of AoURN supports advanced interleaved composition rules in addition to the traditional before, after, and around composition rules. Interleaved composition allows two scenarios to be combined without losing sight of the overall behavior of each individual scenario. Finally, AoURN employs an enhanced composition mechanism based on semantic equivalences in each of its two sub-notations. The enhanced composition mechanism ensures that a certain class of refactoring operations may be performed on an AoURN model without interfering with the desired aspect composition. An example based on a common case study illustrates the usage of interleaved and semantics-based composition for AoURN's scenario model.

G. Mussbacher (✉)
Department of Electrical and Computer Engineering (ECE), McGill University, 3480 University Street, Montreal, QC, H3A 0E9, Canada
e-mail: gunter.mussbacher@mcgill.ca

D. Amyot
EECS, University of Ottawa, 800 King Edward, Ottawa, ON, Canada K1N 6N5
e-mail: damyot@eecs.uottawa.ca

J. Whittle
Department of Computing, InfoLab21, Lancaster University, Bailrigg, Lancaster LA1 4YW, UK
e-mail: whittle@comp.lancs.ac.uk

A. Moreira et al. (eds.), *Aspect-Oriented Requirements Engineering*,
DOI 10.1007/978-3-642-38640-4_5,

5.1 Introduction

The Aspect-oriented User Requirements Notation (AoURN) [1] extends the User Requirements Notation (URN) [2], standardized by the International Telecommunication Union, into a goal-oriented, scenario-based, and aspect-oriented framework. URN contains two sublanguages—the Goal-oriented Requirement Language (GRL) for goal modeling and Use Case Maps (UCM) for scenario modeling—to which AoURN adds aspect-oriented concepts, resulting in AoGRL and AoUCM.

URN is a requirements engineering language that supports the elicitation, analysis, specification, and validation of requirements. In addition, AoURN enables the specification of and reasoning about crosscutting concerns from the early requirements phase on. AoURN is a somewhat unusual modeling environment for aspect-oriented requirements engineering, because it combines two different notations. AoURN is hence most effectively applied in those requirements engineering activities for which goal or scenario models are deemed useful—ideally, AoURN is used to describe the high-level workflow of a concern *and* its impact on the overall system and stakeholder goals. The AoURN and URN notations are introduced as needed for the chapter in Sects. 5.2 and 5.3.

AoURN supports all basic composition rules found in many other scenario-based notations such as before, after, around, etc. AoURN also supports all basic composition rules found in many goal-oriented notations such as contributions, correlations, decomposition, and dependencies. This chapter hence does not focus on basic composition rules but explores the following three points in more detail: the implications of having two different notations in the AoURN framework, AoURN's support for interleaved composition, and AoURN's support for an enhanced composition mechanism based on language semantics.

1. Since AoURN consists of two rather different notations, it serves as an excellent example highlighting the need for tailored composition approaches that take the peculiarities of a notation into account (to be covered in Sect. 5.3) to reduce unnecessary modeling effort and improve the reusability of an aspect.
2. While basic composition rules (briefly overviewed for AoURN in Sect. 5.4) allow for the specification of a large class of aspects, more advanced composition rules may help by providing a clearer picture of the individual behavior of an aspect as well as the composed behavior. Interleaved composition is one such advanced composition rule. Interleaved composition avoids fragmentation of an aspect model and hence makes it easier to understand the aspect model, as will be discussed in Sect. 5.5 with the help of an example from a common case study, i.e., a crisis management system.
3. A well-known problem in the aspect-oriented community is the fragile pointcut problem [3–5] of syntax-based composition. Rather small changes in a model may have a significant impact on the specification of an aspect. AoURN hence employs an enhanced composition mechanism based on semantic equivalences [6] in each of its two sub-notations to ensure worry-free application of a certain

class of refactoring operations on the system model as will be discussed and illustrated again in Sect. 5.5.

Following the above-mentioned sections, this chapter then explains in more detail in Sect. 5.6 how composition is actually achieved in AoURN for basic and interleaved composition rules as well as for the results of semantics-based matching. The chapter closes with an overview of related work in Sect. 5.7 and a conclusion and an agenda for future work in Sect. 5.8.

5.2 Overview of the User Requirements Notation

This section gives a brief overview of the User Requirements Notation (URN). URN is a general purpose modeling language for the communication of and reasoning about requirements. URN supports the elicitation and specification of requirements for a proposed or an evolving system as well as the analysis and validation of requirements. URN consists of two sub-notations: the Goal-oriented Requirement Language (GRL) for goal modeling and Use Case Maps (UCM) for scenario modeling. GRL is a visual modeling notation for business goals and non-functional requirements of many stakeholders, for alternatives that have to be considered, for decisions that were made, and for rationales that helped make these decisions. UCM is a visual scenario notation that focuses on the causal flow of behavior optionally superimposed on a structure of components. UCM models often describe in more detail the alternatives considered in GRL models.

A GRL *actor* (⊖, see Fig. 5.1a for a summary of GRL model elements) represents a stakeholder of a system. A goal model shows the high-level business goals of interest to a stakeholder and the alternatives considered for achieving these high-level elements. *Softgoals* (⬭) differentiate themselves from *goals* (⬭) in that there is no clear, objective measure of satisfaction for a softgoal whereas a goal is quantifiable. *Tasks* (⬡) represent solutions to goals or softgoals that are considered for a system. Various kinds of *links* connect the elements in a goal graph. AND, XOR, and IOR decomposition links allow an element to be decomposed into sub-elements (+—). Contribution links indicate desired impacts of one element on another element (→), either expressed qualitatively (+ or –) or quantitatively as an integer value between −100 and 100. Correlation links (┈┈→) are like contribution links but rather indicate side effects than desired impacts. Finally, dependency links model relationships between actors, i.e., one actor depending on another actor for something (–▶–).

A UCM *map* contains any number of paths and components (see Fig. 5.1b for a summary of UCM model elements). *Paths* express causal sequences and may contain several types of path nodes. Paths start at *start points* (●) and end at *end points* (▮). *Responsibilities* (×) describe required actions or steps to fulfill a scenario. *OR-forks* (—<) (possibly including guarding conditions) and *OR-joins* (>—) are used to show alternatives, while *AND-forks* (—|=) and *AND-joins* (=|—) depict concurrency.

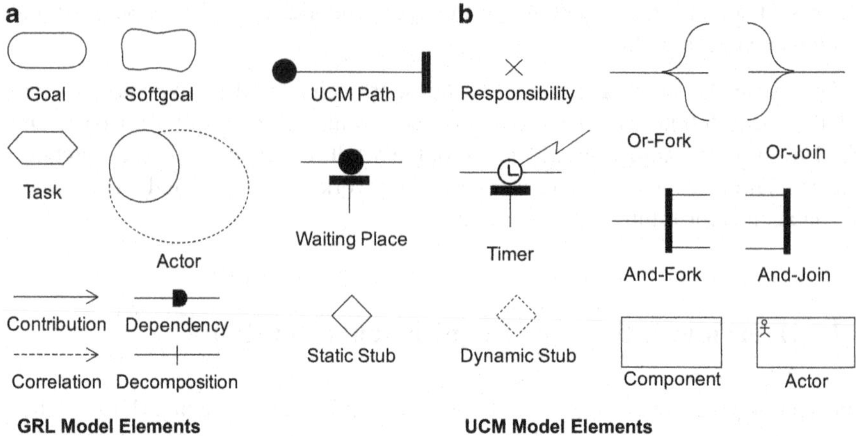

Fig. 5.1 Overview of URN notation

Loops can be modeled implicitly with OR-joins and OR-forks. Note that the UCM notation does not impose any nesting constraints. *Waiting places* (●) and *timers* (◷) denote locations on the path where the scenario stops until a condition is satisfied or another scenario arrives. A timer may also have a timeout path which is indicated by a zigzag line. Stubs (e.g., ◇ or ◇) allow hierarchical structuring of maps with various constraints imposed on the sub-maps depending on the stub type. Finally, *components* are used to specify the structural aspects of a system (e.g., □ for system component and 웃 for *actor*).

AoURN builds on URN by allowing patterns and composition rules to be specified for a crosscutting concern in addition to the aspectual properties of the crosscutting concern. This is explained in the following section.

5.3 Specification of Patterns and Composition Rules in AoURN

AoURN applies different composition approaches to its two sublanguages. Figure 5.2 gives an overview of the specification of aspects in AoURN. On the top left side, the specification of a logging aspect is shown for AoUCM and AoGRL (Fig. 5.2a, b, d). On the top right side, the impact of the logging aspect on an AoURN model is depicted (Fig. 5.2c, e). At the bottom, an alternative specification for the logging aspect is illustrated (Fig. 5.2f, g, h).

For AoUCM, the pattern (Fig. 5.2b) is clearly separated from the description of aspectual properties and the composition rule (Fig. 5.2a). Each is specified on its own *map* and the relationship between these two maps is formalized by *bindings* (illustrated in Fig. 5.2 by dashed arrows), which specify how the *in-/out-paths* of

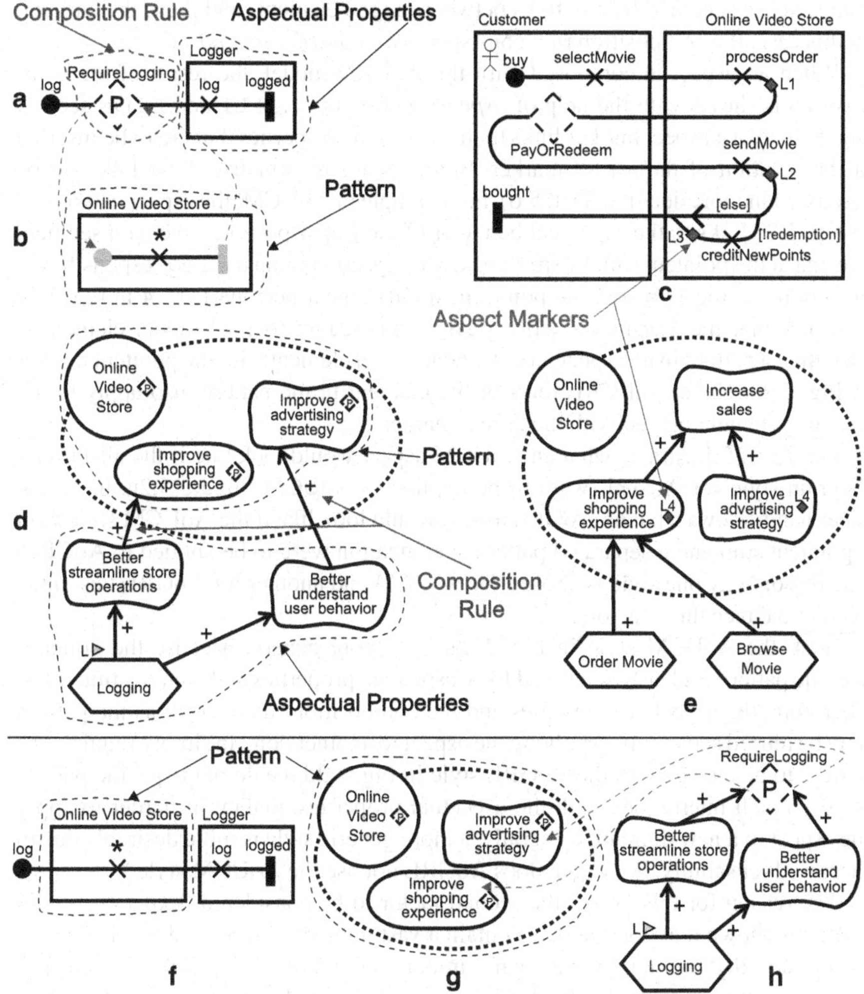

Fig. 5.2 Specification of patterns and composition rules in AoURN

a *stub* on a parent map are connected to the *start points* (●)/*end points* (▮) of a plug-in map, respectively. In Fig. 5.2, the pattern states that all *responsibilities* (×, e.g., `processOrder`) in the *component* `Online Video Store` (□) are to be matched. The composition rule is defined by the causal relationship between the *pointcut stub* (◈, e.g., `RequireLogging`) and the aspectual properties. In this case, the `log` responsibility of the `Logger` component is shown after the pointcut stub, hence describing an "after" composition rule.

For AoGRL, the pattern, aspectual properties, and the composition rule are all shown on the same goal graph (Fig. 5.2d). The goal model elements that belong to the pattern are identified by a tag, i.e., the pointcut marker (◈). The composition rule is hence specified by any links between tagged elements and those that are not. In this case, the composition rule consists of two *contribution links* (→).

When an aspect is composed with the AoURN model, the result of the composition is shown with the help of *aspect markers* (◆, e.g., `L1` and `L4`) as seen in Fig. 5.2c, e. An aspect marker links to the aspectual properties that are to be inserted at the location of the aspect marker. Bindings again formalize these links (to be discussed in more detail in Sect. 5.6). For example in AoUCM, the aspect marker `L1` in Fig. 5.2c links to the aspectual behavior of the Log aspect, i.e., the path segment starting at the pointcut stub `RequireLogging`, containing the `log` responsibility, and ending at the `logged` end point. In AoGRL, the aspect marker `L4` in Fig. 5.2e indicates that the `Improve shopping experience` goal model element is matching a pattern in an aspect, i.e., the goal model element with the pointcut marker in Fig. 5.2d. Hence, all GRL links of the element in the pattern also apply to the matched element tagged with the aspect marker.

Figure 5.2f illustrates what an AoUCM aspect would look like if the all-in-one-diagram style for AoGRL were to be applied to AoUCM. Figure 5.2g, h, on the other hand, shows what an AoGRL aspect would look like if the AoUCM style with a pointcut stub and a separated pattern specification were to be applied to AoGRL. The reason why one style is chosen for AoUCM and another for AoGRL lies in the need to balance three factors.

First, the AoUCM style in Fig. 5.2a, b is more generic because the domain-specific pattern is clearly separated from aspectual properties and composition rules. Therefore, the aspectual properties and the composition rule as well as the pattern may be reused separately. Applying the aspect to another domain simply requires the pattern to be changed. In the AoGRL style in Fig. 5.2d the domain-specific pattern is very much intertwined with the aspectual properties, making it harder to apply the aspect to a new domain. Generally, a more generic style is more desirable due to increased reusability. Why then does AoGRL not use the AoUCM style?

The reason for this lies in the second factor to be considered. Experience with GRL has shown that goal models contain a vast number of links and it is hence not uncommon that an element has many in-coming and out-going links. In scenario models, on the other hand, model elements are connected more sparingly. The same applies to the composition rules in goal models. Typically, a large number of links would have to be created going into or coming out of the GRL pointcut stub in Fig. 5.2h. For each such link, a binding needs to be specified essentially doubling the modeling effort compared to the all-in-one-diagram style. For AoUCM, this additional effort is negligible, because there are usually very few bindings that need to be specified. Finally and third, the concept of a stub already exists in UCM but not in GRL, making it more natural to use a pointcut stub in AoUCM compared to AoGRL. Therefore, AoGRL uses a different style than AoUCM.

The next section discusses the basic composition rules that may be specified for crosscutting concerns in AoUCM and AoGRL models and summarizes syntax-based matching.

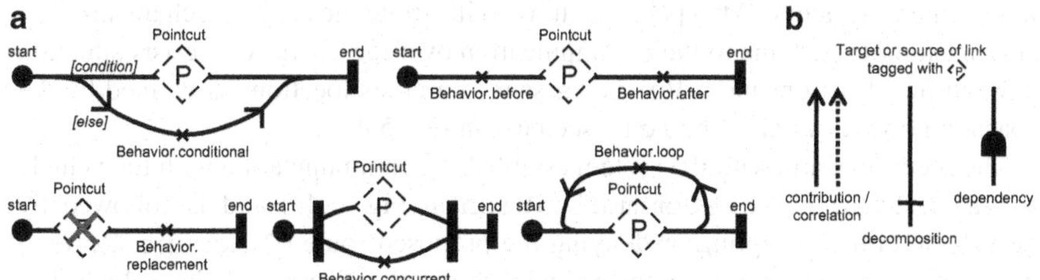

Fig. 5.3 Basic composition rules for AoUCM and AoGRL

5.4 Overview of Basic Composition Rules and Syntax-Based Matching in AoURN

Basic Composition Rules. AoURN's composition mechanism is exhaustive in that it makes use of the AoURN notation itself to describe composition rules instead of being constrained by a different composition notation. Figure 5.3a gives an overview of the more basic composition rules supported by AoUCM, but any combination of these composition rules and anything else that can be described with AoUCM may also be a composition rule. The same applies to AoGRL and its basic composition rules are shown in Fig. 5.3b.

Syntax-Based Matching. The pattern specified by an AoURN aspect is matched against the AoURN model. A successful match establishes a one-to-one mapping of each model element in the pattern with a model element in the AoURN model. This is generally a syntax-based approach that takes into account the following criteria. The type of the element in the pattern must match the type of the matched element. The elements' names must match. The elements' conditions must match. The causal relationship or type of GRL link of any two adjacent elements in the pattern must be the same as the one of the corresponding matched elements. The elements' UCM component or GRL actor must match. For AoUCM, the elements' location in their components must match (either first, last, or any location in the component). Finally, the metadata of the element in the pattern must be a subset of the metadata of the matched element. For a more detailed description of basic syntax-based matching, the reader is referred to [1].

The next section discusses more advanced matching and composition techniques of AoURN.

5.5 Interleaved Composition and Enhanced Matching Based on Semantics in AoURN

Two advanced composition mechanism supported by AoURN are interleaved composition and the ability to match a pattern against an AoURN model based on semantics and not just syntax. This section uses an example from the Crisis

Management System (CMS) [7] case study to illustrate these two mechanisms. The chosen example pertains to the communication over the course of a crisis situation between the System and a Vehicle sent to a crisis location, as defined by the Communicate with Vehicle scenario in Fig. 5.4.

The scenario starts with the system establishing communication with the vehicle (× establishVehicleCommunication in Fig. 5.4a) and is followed by the vehicle either accepting or denying the proposed route (◇ Accept Route) and finally the monitoring of the vehicle until the objective of the vehicle has been completed (◇ Monitor Vehicle). The *static stubs* (◇ Accept Route and Monitor Vehicle) in Fig. 5.4a are containers for *plug-in maps* shown in Fig. 5.4b, c. The continuation from an *in-path* of a stub to a *start point* on the plug-in map and from an *end point* on a plug-in map to an *out-path* of a stub is formally defined by a *plug-in binding* (illustrated with short, red, dashed arrows). The plug-in map of Accept Route states that the system keeps proposing a route to the vehicle until the vehicle accepts that route or the system runs out of possible routes. The plug-in map of Monitor Vehicle describes the various stages of the vehicle from being dispatched (× vehicleDispatched in Fig. 5.4c) to having arrived (× vehicleArrived) and having its objective completed (× vehicleCompletedObjective). After the vehicle has been dispatched, a *timer* (◷ ETAtimer) is set which guards against not receiving a location update from the vehicle by the estimated time of arrival (ETA). When a location update is received or the timer expires, the system assesses the situation and reacts to a vehicle breakdown by dispatching a new vehicle or to a route problem by updating the ETA. Once the vehicle has arrived, the scenario remains at a *waiting place* (●) until receiving confirmation from the vehicle that its objective has been completed.

The Communication Failure aspect is described in Fig. 5.5. In Fig. 5.5a, the aspect defines a failure start point (Ⓕ CommunicationNotAvailable) triggered when a communication failure occurs in the *target*, i.e., on the Communicate with Vehicle map or any of its sub-maps. If such a failure occurs, the system continues in manual mode and in parallel (modeled with an *AND-fork* ⊣⊏) waits for the communication to be available again. When that happens, the manual process is stopped, the vehicle status for each vehicle is established, and the scenario continues at the appropriate step in the scenario for each vehicle. Note that the *replication factor* for the Establish Vehicle Status *dynamic stub* (◇) ensures that as many instances of its plug-in map are executed as there are vehicles. Furthermore note that the appropriate step in the scenario is defined by connecting an out-path of the dynamic stub with an in-path of the pointcut stub. On the plug-in map of the dynamic stub, the system figures out what the vehicle status is and then exits the stub along one of its five out-paths, i.e., each out-path represents a vehicle status. Each in-path of the pointcut stub then connects to one stage in the scenario as described by the note in Fig. 5.5 (and formally defined again by plug-in bindings).

For example, if the system determines that the vehicle has been dispatched but has not yet reached its destination, then the communication failure scenario exits the dynamic stub along the third out-path and enters the pointcut stub along the third

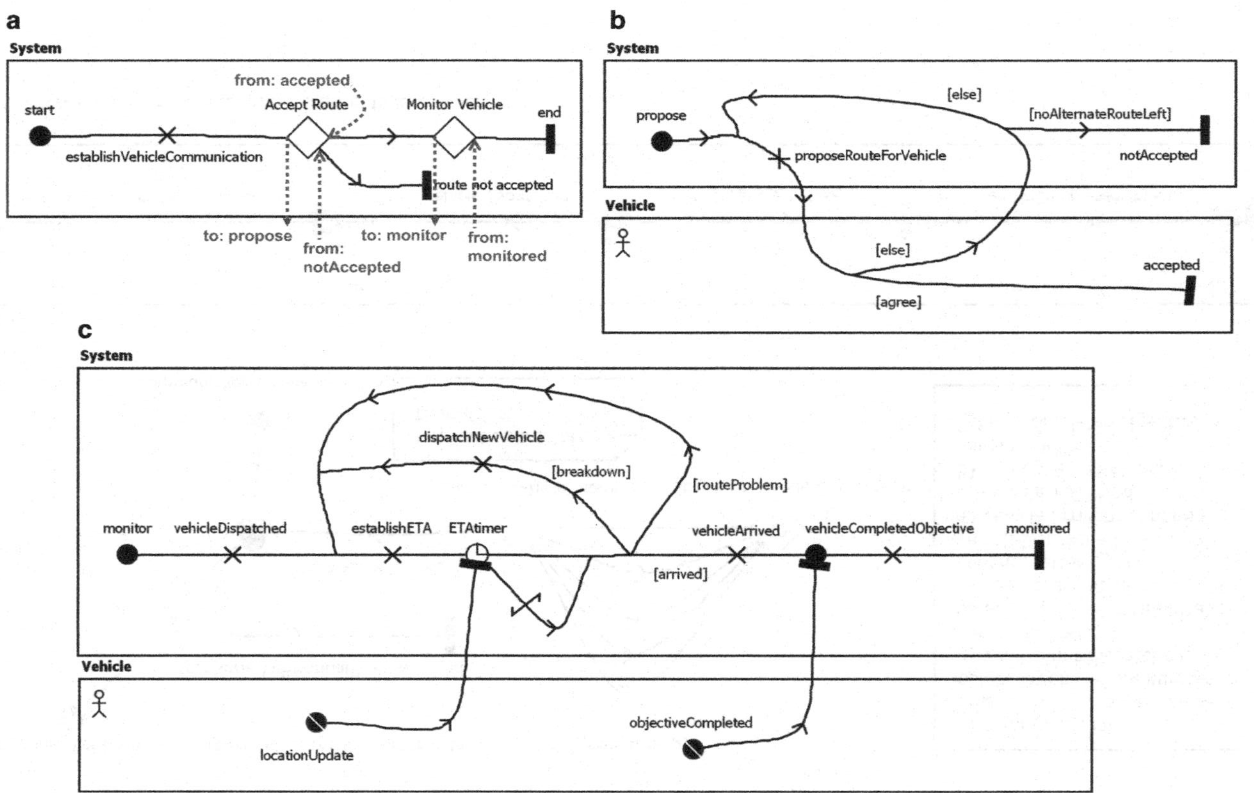

Fig. 5.4 AoURN scenario model: communicate with vehicle

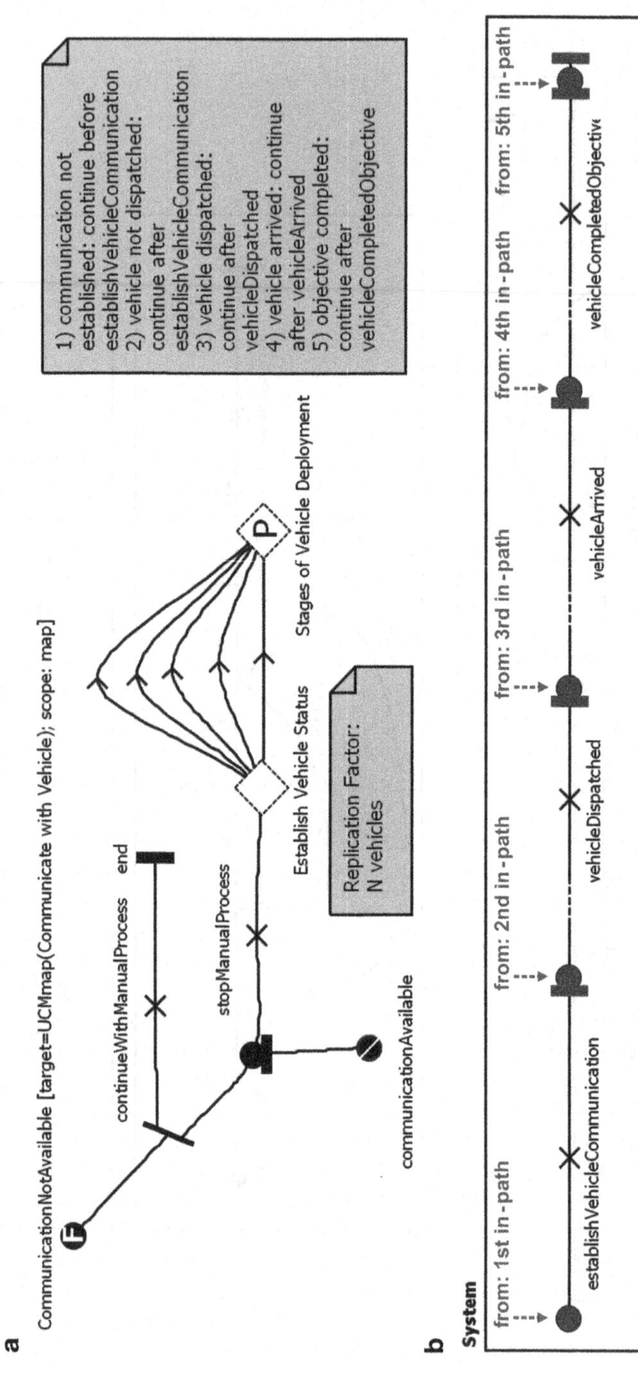

Fig. 5.5 AoURN scenario model: communication failure aspect

in-path which is connected to the start point after `vehicleDispatched` in the pattern (Fig. 5.5b). This has the effect that, when the `Communication Failure` aspect is composed with the scenario in Fig. 5.4, the communication failure scenario continues with the base scenario just after `vehicleDispatched` (Fig. 5.4c).

The pattern described in Fig. 5.5b is a series of responsibilities (from `establishVehicleCommunication` to `vehicleCompleted Objective`), which is reflected in the name of the pointcut stub `Stages of Vehicle Deployment`.

The *anything pointcut elements* (. . .) ensure that any number of model elements may occur between the responsibilities in Fig. 5.5b. The gray pairs of connected end points and start points are not taken into account by the matching mechanism but exist to enable interleaved composition. Depending on the bindings between the pointcut stub and the map with the pattern, aspectual behavior is added either before the whole pattern (an in-path of the pointcut stub is connected to the first start point), after the whole pattern (an out-path of the pointcut stub is connected to the last start/end point), or somewhere in between in an interleaved fashion (an in/out-path is connected to one of the three start/end points in the middle). Hence, an end point–start point pair provides a hook to interleave aspectual behavior with the matched scenario.

The example in Fig. 5.5 makes also use of a matching mechanism that takes *semantics* into account. A syntax-only approach yields no matches for the example, because such an approach cannot match against more than one map at a time. This is because a syntax-only approach does not understand that two responsibilities in a row are equivalent to one responsibility followed by a stub with a plug-in map with the second responsibility. An enhanced matching approach based on semantics, however, defines such a situation as a semantic equivalence and hence matches the same pattern to both models.

Without interleaved and semantics-based composition, the `Communication Failure` aspect would have to be split up into five individual aspects, each handling one of the five situations covered by the aspect in Fig. 5.5, i.e., each in-path of the pointcut stub has to be dealt with individually. This leads to a fragmentation of the overall behavior of the aspect as well as duplication, since the waiting place and the status check needs to be repeated in all five aspects.

Figure 5.6 shows various types of semantic equivalences that exist in AoURN models. The first and most straightforward equivalence type relates to whitespace (Fig. 5.6a) in the model such as direction arrows (>), empty points (O), connected end and start points (◗), but also OR-joins (⋝). These elements are simply ignored by the enhanced matching algorithm.

The second type of equivalence involves hierarchical structuring with a static stub, a dynamic stub, a synchronizing stub, an aspect marker but also GRL decomposition chains (Fig. 5.6b). Flattened models that are equivalent to all three types of stubs are defined in the URN standard [2] and are repeated in Fig. 5.6b. In contrast to a dynamic stub, a *synchronizing stub* requires all of its plug-in maps to finish before traversal may continue past the stub. The synchronizing stub is not

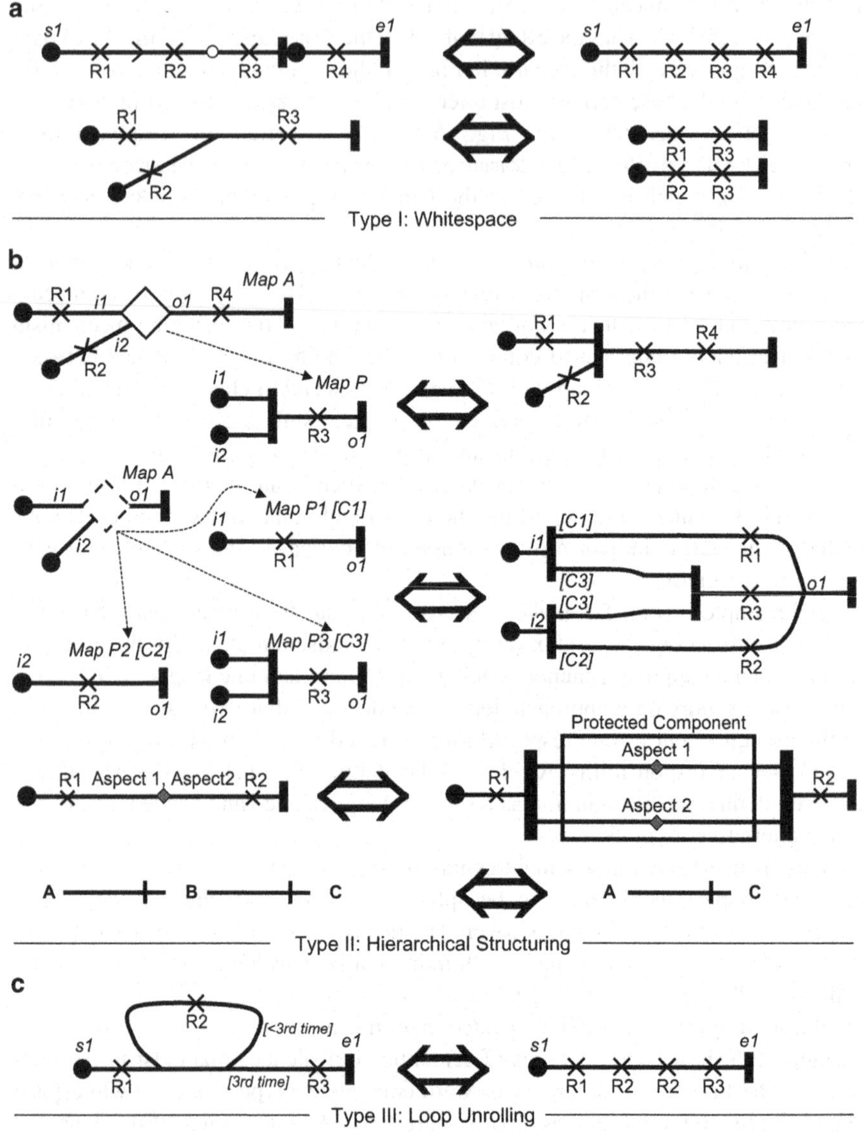

Fig. 5.6 Types of semantic equivalences

shown as it is the same as a dynamic stub, except that the OR-join `o1` is an AND-join (⊣⊢) instead. An aspect marker usually has the same structure as a static stub and is hence treated as such by the matching algorithm. An aspect marker may be a dynamic stub and contain more than one aspect map, if two aspects are applied to the same location in the AoUCM model and no ordering has been defined for these two aspects. In this case, it is undetermined which one of the two aspects executes first but they may not execute at the same time. This semantic constraint is expressed by the parallel branches inside a *protected* component in Fig. 5.6b.

The AoGRL example in Fig. 5.6b shows a chain of decompositions. It should be possible to match a longer chain (the one on the left) in the AoGRL model against a shorter chain (the one on the right) in the pattern. While an AoGRL decomposition chain is neither a true equivalence nor a true refactoring operation, because a shorter chain in the base model must not be matched against a longer chain in the pattern, it is nevertheless discussed here as it relates to hierarchical structuring. Matching of decomposition chains implicitly allows a series of decompositions and intentional elements in the AoGRL model to be matched against a single decomposition in the pattern.

Figure 5.6c covers loop unrolling, the third and last type of semantic equivalences in AoUCM models. Loop unrolling has been discussed in detail in [8]. While the findings of [8] could be incorporated into the AoUCM matching and composition approach, we focus on hierarchical structuring because (1) to the best of our knowledge this has not yet been addressed in literature, (2) it introduces additional challenges, particularly regarding how to layout the composed model, and (3) it is a much more common refactoring operation in AoUCM models than loop unrolling, based on our decade of experience in creating and maintaining UCM and AoUCM models.

In summary, the CMS example shows that interleaved composition and semantics-based matching nicely complement each other, making it possible to describe advanced composition rules very concisely. Furthermore, interleaved composition allows for a single pattern to be specified in a way that may span a large part of a system, thus avoiding fragmentation and duplication of the aspect specification. Finally, the `Communicate with Vehicle` scenario may be reorganized hierarchically by introducing new or removing existing stubs and plug-in maps without having to change the pattern of the `Communication Failure` aspect, thus ensuring that the aspect is still applied as desired. The following refactoring operations may be performed on AoURN models without interfering with an aspect specification:

1. Extracting a plug-in map and inlining a plug-in map (the reverse of the former).
2. Inserting/removing of a decomposition level in AoGRL models.
3. Adding/deleting of a direction arrow, an empty point, a pair of connected end and start points, and an OR-join.

These types of operations are applicable to most modeling notations as (1) most notations provide some form of hierarchical structuring that can benefit from extracting/inlining as well as many notations have (2) transitive modeling operations or (3) purely syntactical elements that do not change the meaning of the model but are visual aids for the modeler.

With a semantics-based matching mechanism in place that takes flattened AoUCM models into account, a first intuition is to use only the flattened model as the basis for the semantics-based matching algorithm, thereby reducing each

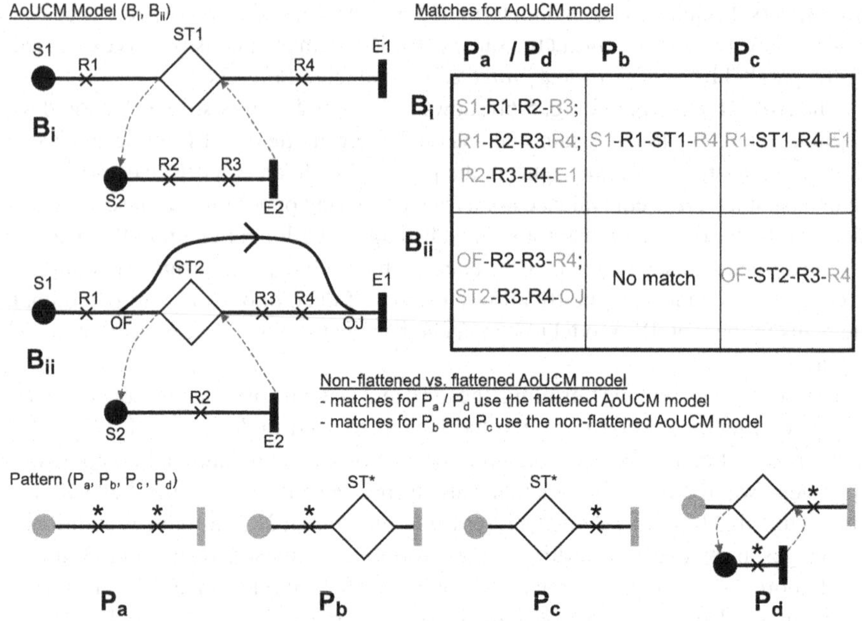

Fig. 5.7 Semantics-based matching of stubs

AoUCM model to its normalized form. Since the normalized form does not contain any stubs, a pattern with a stub cannot be matched. However, there is no good reason to exclude stubs from patterns, because a requirements engineer may want to match stubs explicitly. Therefore, the semantics-based matching algorithm expects a stub in the AoURN model, if a stub without a plug-in map is specified in the pattern. If a stub is not specified or the stub in the pattern contains a plug-in map, then the flattened model is used for the match. Therefore, a pattern that includes a stub with a plug-in map is flattened before matching it against the AoUCM model. Figure 5.7 gives examples of pattern matches against non-flattened and flattened AoUCM models.

Given the above definition, the patterns $\texttt{P}_{\texttt{a}}$ and $\texttt{P}_{\texttt{d}}$ are matched against the flattened AoUCM models, while $\texttt{P}_{\texttt{b}}$ and $\texttt{P}_{\texttt{c}}$ are matched against the non-flattened AoUCM. For example, the flattened model of $\texttt{B}_{\texttt{i}}$ is a single map consisting of a start point `S1`, the four responsibilities `R1`, `R2`, `R3`, and `R4` in a row, and an end point `E1`. This model is hence matched three times by $\texttt{P}_{\texttt{a}}$ and $\texttt{P}_{\texttt{d}}$ (**S1**–`R1`–`R2`–**R3**; **R1**–`R2`–`R3`–**R4**; **R2**–`R3`–`R4`–**E1**). $\texttt{P}_{\texttt{c}}$, on the other hand, matches against the non-flattened model $\texttt{B}_{\texttt{ii}}$, resulting in one match (**OF**-`ST2`-`R3`-**R4**). Note that the first and last mappings of each match are with the gray start and end points of the pattern.

The next section covers further details of the AoURN composition mechanism.

5.6 Composition in AoURN

Composition of aspects with an AoURN model involves the insertion of aspect markers into the AoURN model. While this is the case for AoGRL and AoUCM models, the mechanisms employed to achieve the insertion are quite different. The mechanisms, however, are in line with the way aspects are specified in the two sub-notations. In AoGRL, aspects are specified by adding tags to the model—in AoURN terminology these are called *metadata*. Hence, composition for AoGRL is also based on inserting metadata in the model. AoUCM, on the other hand, makes use of the stub concept and views aspect markers as types of stubs. Note that AoURN allows the composition of aspects to be ordered to resolve aspect interactions with the help of the *concern interaction graph* [1], but this is outside the scope of this chapter.

The remainder of this section first explains composition for basic AoGRL and AoUCM composition rules in Sect. 5.6.1. This is followed by more advanced composition rules involving interleaving in Sect. 5.6.2 and composition of the results of enhanced matching based on semantics in Sect. 5.6.3.

5.6.1 Basic Composition

For AoUCM, aspect markers, i.e., stubs, are added to the locations in the AoUCM model where an aspect needs to insert behavior. Plug-in bindings between the aspect marker and the aspectual properties specify clearly what behavior needs to be inserted. For example in Fig. 5.8a, the in-path of the aspect marker `L2` is connected to the out-path of the pointcut stub `RequireLogging` and the end point `logged` is connected to the out-path of `L2`. For AoGRL, on the other hand, metadata specifies (1) that an aspect marker has been added to an intentional element and (2) the connection between the AoGRL model element and the pattern. For example in Fig. 5.8b, `Improve shopping experience` has two metadata items attached to it after composition. The first (`aspect marker L4`) identifies that an aspect marker needs to be visualized for the element, while the second specifies the corresponding element in the pattern, i.e., the element with ID 78 (`to ref 78 match #1`). Since one element may be affected by many aspects, a unique identification number of the match is also captured in the second metadata item.

Aspect markers in AoUCM act like traditional UCM stubs except for one difference. In UCM, a scenario may return from a plug-in map only to the same stub from which it arrived at the plug-in map in the first place. This is not necessarily the case for aspect markers. Hence, aspect markers are grouped and a scenario may continue from a plug-in map to any aspect marker in the aspect marker group. An example for the need of aspect marker groups is the loop composition in Fig. 5.9. The scenario may enter the plug-in map through the *second* aspect marker `L1`

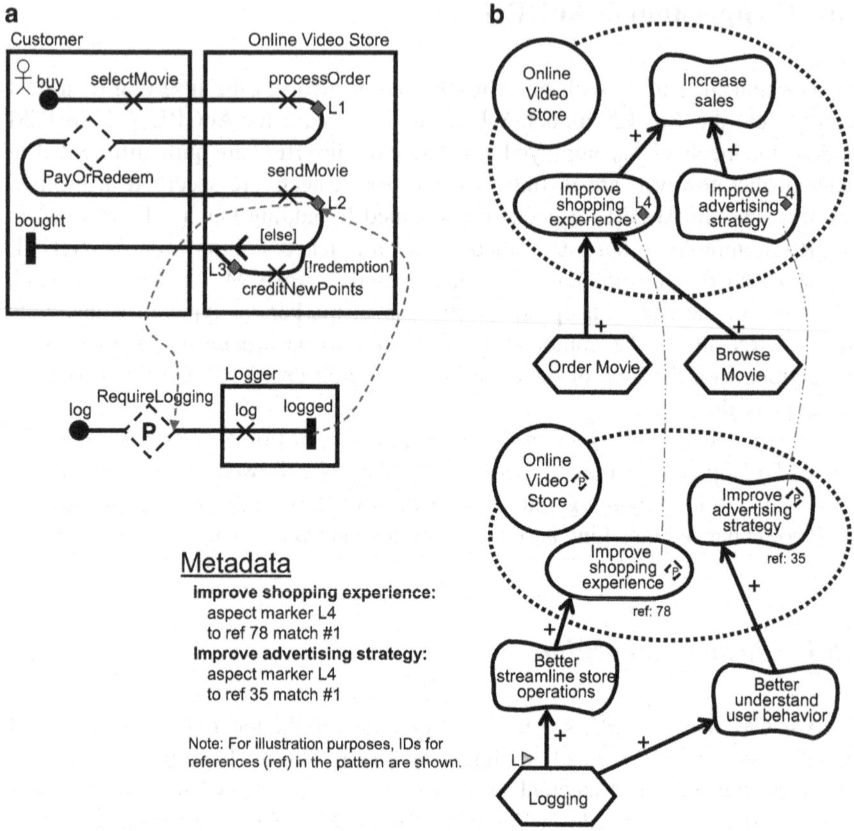

Fig. 5.8 Basic composition

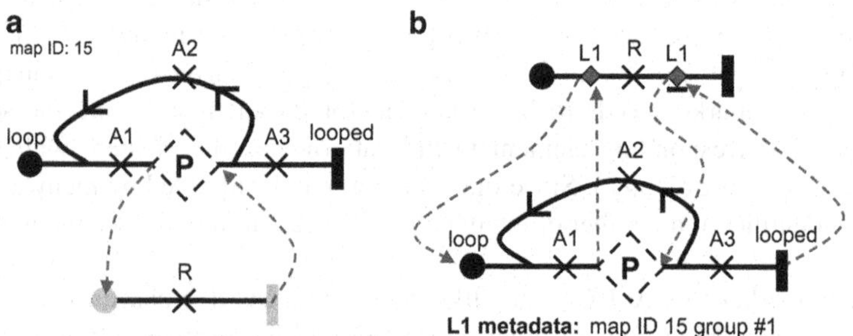

Fig. 5.9 Aspect marker groups

and exit the plug-in map through the *first* aspect marker `L1`, if the branch with responsibility `A2` is taken. The metadata defining the aspect marker group for the two aspect markers is `map ID 15 group #1`, assuming that the ID of the plug-in map is 15. A unique identification number of the match is again captured in the metadata item.

5.6.2 Advanced Composition: Interleaving

As an example for advanced composition, the results of applying the `Communication Failure` aspect in the CMS example from Sect. 5.5 are shown in Fig. 5.10. The composition mechanism adds five *tunnel exit aspect markers* (◗◆ in Fig. 5.10a, b) to the locations in the AoURN model identified by the pattern, i.e., one for each in-path of the pointcut stub (Fig. 5.10c).

AoURN provides visual clues for aspect markers that do not have two plug-in bindings—one from the aspect marker to the map of the aspect and another one back. Tunnel exit aspect markers only have a plug-in binding *from* the map of the aspect. *Tunnel entrance aspect markers* (◆◗) also exist and only have a plug-in binding *to* the map of the aspect. In the case of the CMS example, tunnel exit aspect markers are sufficient because the `Communication Failure` scenario unfolds as follows in the composed system. When a communication failure occurs, the Communication Failure aspect starts at its failure start point. The system switches to manual operation until communication is available again. When that happens, the system determines the status of each vehicle which leads the scenario to the pointcut stub along one of its in-paths. Each in-path is now connected to one of the tunnel exit aspect markers (Fig. 5.10c), because the composition mechanism inserted the aspect markers into the model and established their plug-in bindings. Depending on the status of the vehicle, the scenario takes one of the five plug-in bindings and continues by exiting one of the five aspect markers (`Ca` to `Ce`).

Interleaved composition also allows for more than one pointcut stub to be used in the specification of an aspect. Consider the example in Fig. 5.11. The `Pay Informant` aspect defines that before a meeting is scheduled a price needs to be negotiated, after the meeting is scheduled an initial sum is paid, and finally after the meeting the rest is paid.

The intention of interleaved composition is to combine two scenarios while maintaining the partial ordering of each scenario. This is the case in Fig. 5.11. However, the aspect could easily be specified such that the first pointcut stub links to `meet informant` while the second one links to `schedule meeting`, thus swapping the original partial ordering. In other words, the ordering of the pointcut stubs does not reflect the ordering of the corresponding path segments in the pattern. In the example in Fig. 5.11, this is not desirable, because it does not make sense to pay the rest before paying an initial sum. In general, the AoUCM composition mechanism for interleaving delivers desired results when the partial ordering of both scenarios is respected. The AoUCM specification style for aspects,

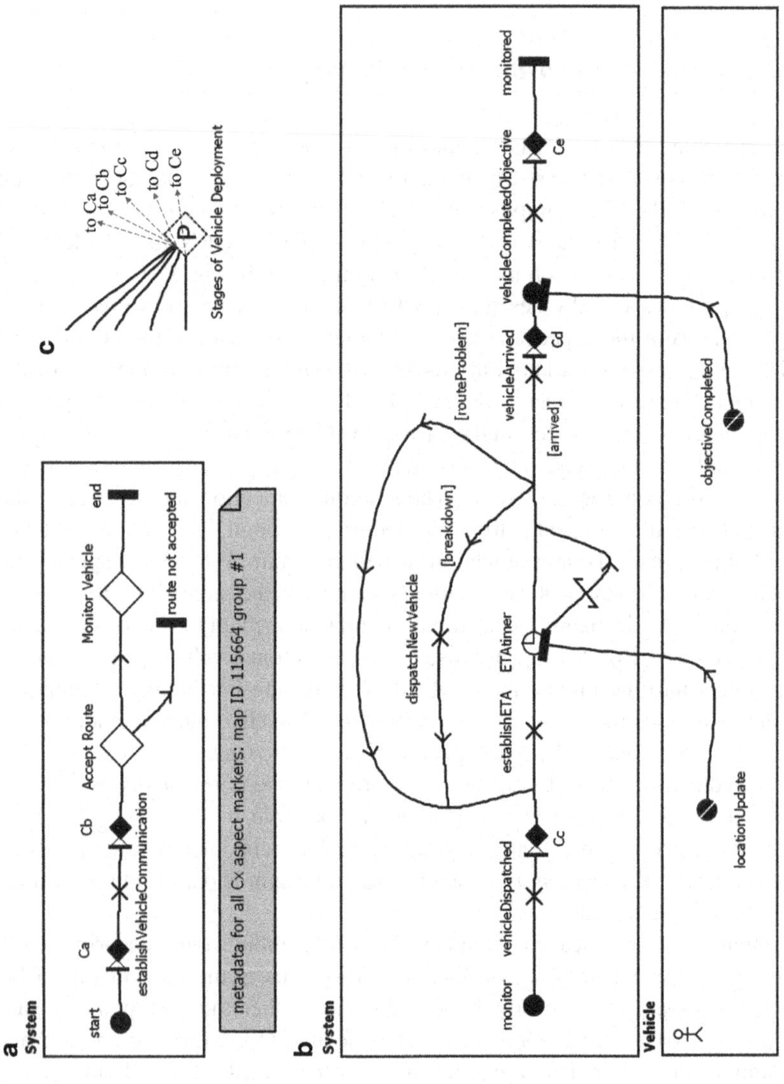

Fig. 5.10 Composition of communication failure aspect

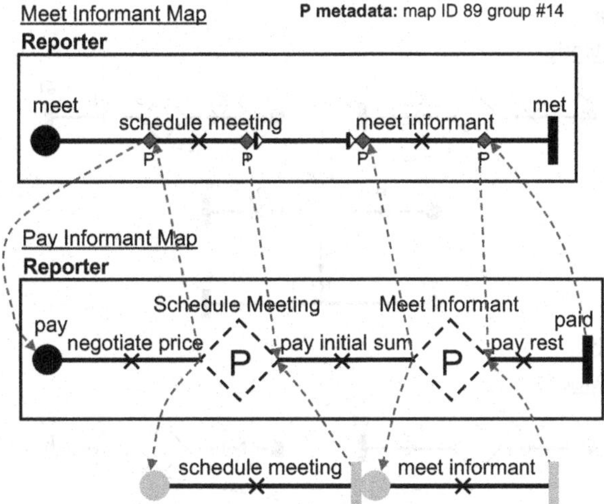

Fig. 5.11 Multiple pointcut stubs in interleaved composition

however, does not prevent the modeler from specifying aspects that violate this constraint, but comes with a disclaimer that the composition of such aspects needs to be thoroughly checked. The CMS example from Sect. 5.5 actually violates the constraint. The ordering of the pattern is quite clearly not reflected in the ordering of the pointcut stubs, since one pointcut stub links to all four path segments in the pattern. Nevertheless, the resulting composition is as desired due to the specific behavior of the aspect. In summary, while the AoURN approach to interleaved composition guarantees proper interleaving of two scenarios when adhering to the aforementioned constraint, the AoURN specification style also gives power to the requirements engineer to go beyond the intention of interleaved composition and allow even more advanced composition rules to be defined.

5.6.3 Advanced Composition: Semantics-Based Matching

Composition of models that use the enhanced matching mechanism based on semantics also has to consider special cases as shown in Fig. 5.12. The root problem with semantics-based matching is that a pattern may now be matched against a portion of the model that spans several maps, i.e., several hierarchical levels. The first special case involves shared plug-in maps while the second involves lost hierarchies.

In Fig. 5.12a, the pattern is matched by the hierarchy of maps that includes responsibility `R1` but not by the hierarchy of maps that includes responsibility `XYZ`. What happens when a scenario coming from the map with `XYZ` arrives at aspect marker `1b`? Should the scenario continue with the aspectual behavior (`A2`) or should this behavior be skipped? Furthermore, consider the situation where another aspect removes the aspect marker `1a` altogether. Should the aspect marker `1b` still be available? AoURN stipulates a pragmatic solution that is consistent with regular

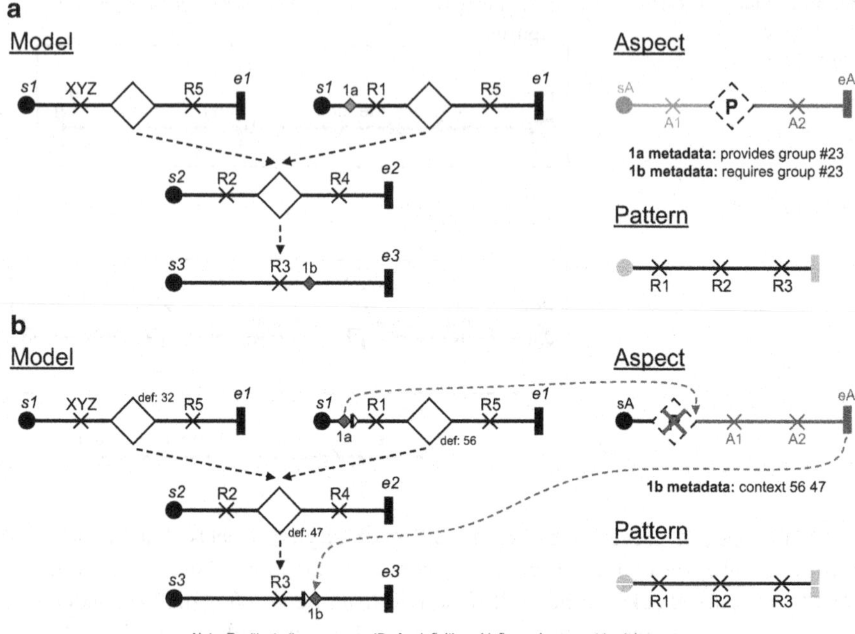

Fig. 5.12 Composition with shared plug-in maps and lost hierarchies

matches that do not span multiple maps. Thus, the aspect marker `1b` should be available only if the scenario arrives from the map with aspect marker `1a`.

To achieve this, metadata is added to the aspect markers. All aspect markers connected to a start point of the aspect (e.g., `1a`) are tagged with the metadata *provides group N*, with N being a unique number for this group of aspect markers. All remaining aspect markers for the aspect (e.g., `1b`) are tagged with the metadata *requires group N*. An aspect marker with the "requires" tag is only considered if an aspect marker with the "provides" tag was visited earlier in the scenario. Note that the special case of shared plug-in maps also applies to patterns whose match includes an OR-join that is not explicitly matched.

The second problematic case occurs when a *replacement pointcut stub* (❖) is used instead of a regular pointcut stub (Fig. 5.12b). A replacement pointcut stub indicates that the matched model elements are to be removed from the composed model. For example in Fig. 5.12b, when the aspect marker `1a` is reached, the scenario continues with `A1` and `A2` in the aspect, skipping over `R1`, `R2`, and `R3` (hence, removing them from the composed model), and then continues at aspect marker `1b`, because the end point `eA` is connected to the aspect marker `1b` and the aspect markers `1a` and `1b` belong to the same aspect marker group. Now, the problem is that the scenario continues with the bottom-level map but important contextual information has been lost. When the end point `e3` is reached, the scenario should continue with the mid-level map because `R4` used to be after `R3` in the original model. Yet, the scenario is not aware of the mid-level map at this point, because it never reached the stub after R1. Therefore, the matching algorithm collects information about lost hierarchies and attaches that information to the aspect marker 1b. For example, the metadata context 56 47 contains the list of IDs of the stubs that defines the lost hierarchy. With this context information, the scenario can adjust the stack of visited maps—adding the second-level map to it—and the scenario can continue with R4 as required.

For more details on the composition algorithms, the reader is referred to [1] and a proof-of-concept implementation in the jUCMNav tool [9].

5.7 Related Work

While many aspect-oriented modeling (AOM) techniques exist for requirements engineering such as use cases [10, 11], viewpoints [12], problem frames [13], and UML models [14, 15], none to the best of our knowledge addresses semantic equivalences in their matching and composition mechanisms with the exception of the following work in semantic-based aspect weaving. Chitchyan et al. [16] use natural language processing to take into account English semantics when composing textual requirements documents. A natural language-based approach could be combined with AoURN's matching approach as names of model elements must be matched. For aspect-oriented modeling, Klein et al. [8] weave UML sequence diagrams by matching semantically equivalent but syntactically different sequences. Klein et al. give a thorough explanation on how to deal with loops but do not address the problems related to hierarchical structuring and replacements discussed in Sect. 5.6.3. Furthermore, this work does not address complex layout issues that may have to be resolved when the woven end result is presented to the modeler.

Cottenier et al. [17, 18] match state machines at different levels of abstraction by performing a static control flow analysis to find matching patterns. Patterns are expressed with state machines at the behavioral specification level and then matched against more complex implementation state machines while taking the semantics of the behavioral specification into account. This orthogonal control flow-based approach could also be combined with AoURN's matching algorithm for the matching of UCM models. In the context of aspect-oriented programming, Bergmans [19] discusses the use of semantic annotations for composition filters. In the context of aspect interactions, Mussbacher et al. [20] use goal graphs to model and detect semantic-based interactions in aspect-oriented scenarios.

A recent taxonomy of syntactic and semantic matching mechanisms for AOM notations [21] identifies various pattern matching techniques in the AOM context and highlights the potential influence of approximation-based techniques from the database research community on more sophisticated matching mechanisms.

Interleaved composition is supported by graph transformation-based approaches such as MATA [15]. However, interleaving is restricted to one hierarchical level. AoURN, on the other hand, allows interleaved composition to be specified across the whole model.

5.8 Conclusion and Future Work

This chapter presents an overview of AoURN's composition mechanism. AoURN is an aspect-oriented requirements engineering language based on goal and scenario modeling that extends the international standard URN. The focus of the chapter is not the basic composition mechanism and syntax-based matching of AoURN, but rather two advanced composition rules that deal with interleaving and enhanced matching based on semantics. With AoURN's interleaved composition, two scenarios can be combined without losing sight of the overall behavior of the original scenarios. Moreover, interleaved composition helps reduce fragmentation and duplication in AoURN aspect specifications. Semantics-based matching, on the other hand, allows for a class of refactoring operations to be performed on an AoURN model without a risk of breaking the matches of an aspect's pattern. Interleaved composition and semantics-based matching empower the requirements engineer to specify advanced composition rules that span the whole AoURN model across several hierarchical levels.

The two sub-notations of AoURN also provide an opportunity to discuss and motivate the need for tailored composition mechanisms that take a notation's peculiarities into account to reduce unnecessary modeling effort and improve the reusability of an aspect.

AoURN has been applied to several case studies [1], most notably to the Crisis Management System (CMS) community challenge problem [22, 23]. AoURN covers sufficiently concerns at the requirements phase regardless of whether they are crosscutting or not as long as they can be described with goals and scenarios, but does not handle other forms of requirements such as constraints and data structures well. A combined application of AoURN, OCL, and domain concept modeling could improve the matching and composition capabilities of AoURN.

For future work, AoURN's composition mechanism could be improved by taking natural language semantics into account when matching an aspect's pattern against the model. Also, approximation-based techniques [21] could be employed to further improve the performance of AoURN's composition mechanism.

References

1. G. Mussbacher, Aspect-oriented user requirements notation, Ph.D. thesis, School of Information Technology and Engineering, University of Ottawa, Canada, 2010
2. ITU-T (2012). *User Requirements Notation (URN) – Language definition, ITU-T Recommendation Z.151 (10/12),* Geneva, Switzerland. http://www.itu.int/rec/T-REC-Z.151/en. Accessed 22 Oct 2012
3. M. Braem, K. Gybels, A. Kellens, W. Vanderperren, Inducing evolution-robust pointcuts, in *Second International ERCIM Workshop on Software Evolution (EVOL 2006)*, Lille, France, 2006

4. A. Kellens, K. Gybels, J. Brichau, K. Mens, A model-driven pointcut language for more robust pointcuts, in *Workshop on Software Engineering Properties of Languages for Aspect Technology (SPLAT! 2006)*, Bonn, Germany, 2006
5. C. Koppen, M. Stoerzer, Pcdiff: attacking the fragile pointcut problem, in *First European Interactive Workshop on Aspects in Software (EIWAS'04)*, Berlin, Germany, 2004
6. G. Mussbacher, D. Amyot, J. Whittle, Refactoring-safe modeling of aspect-oriented scenarios, in *Model Driven Engineering Languages and Systems*, ed. by A. Schürr, B. Selic. LNCS, vol. 5795 (Springer, 2009), pp. 286–300. doi:10.1007/978-3-642-04425-0_21
7. J. Kienzle, N. Guelfi, S. Mustafiz, Crisis management systems: a case study for aspect-oriented modeling, in *Transactions on Aspect-Oriented Software Development VII* (Springer, Berlin/Heidelberg, 2010), pp. 1–22. doi:10.1007/978-3-642-16086-8_1
8. J. Klein, L. Hélouët, J.M. Jézéquel, Semantic-based weaving of scenarios, in *Conference on Aspect-Oriented Software Development (AOSD'06)*, Bonn, Germany, 2006, pp. 27–38. doi:10.1145/1119655.1119662
9. jUCMNav website (2012), http://jucmnav.softwareengineering.ca/jucmnav. Accessed 22 Oct 2012
10. J. Araújo, A. Moreira, An aspectual use case driven approach, in *VIII Jornadas de Ingeniería de Software y Bases de Datos (JISBD 2003)*, Alicante, Spain, 2003, pp. 463–468
11. I. Jacobson, P.-W. Ng, *Aspect-Oriented Software Development with Use Cases* (Addison-Wesley, New York, NY, 2005)
12. A. Rashid, A. Moreira, J. Araújo, Modularisation and composition of aspectual requirements, in *2nd International Conference on Aspect Oriented Software Development (AOSD)*, Boston, MA, 2003, pp. 11–20. doi:10.1145/643603.643605
13. M. Lencastre, J. Araújo, A. Moreira, J. Castro, Towards aspectual problem frames: an example. Expert Syst. J. **25**(1), 74–86 (2008). doi:10.1111/j.1468-0394.2008.00453.x
14. S. Clarke, E. Baniassad, *Aspect-Oriented Analysis and Design: The Theme Approach* (Addison Wesley, New York, NY, 2005)
15. J. Whittle, P. Jayaraman, A. Elkhodary, A. Moreira, J. Araújo, MATA: a unified approach for composing UML aspect models based on graph transformation, in *Transactions on Aspect-Oriented Software Development VI* (Springer, Berlin/Heidelberg, 2009), pp. 191–237. doi:10.1007/978-3-642-03764-1_6
16. R. Chitchyan, A. Rashid, P. Rayson, R. Waters, Semantics-based composition for aspect-oriented requirements engineering, in *Aspect-Oriented Software Development (AOSD'07)*, Vancouver, BC, 2007, pp. 36–48. doi:10.1145/1218563.1218569
17. T. Cottenier, A. van den Berg, T. Elrad, Joinpoint inference from behavioral specification to implementation, in *ECOOP 2007*, ed. by E. Ernst. LNCS, vol. 4609 (Springer, 2007), pp. 476–500. doi:10.1007/978-3-540-73589-2_23
18. J. Zhang, T. Cottenier, A. van den Berg, J. Gray, Aspect composition in the Motorola aspect-oriented modeling weaver. J. Object Technol. **6**(7), 89–108 (2007). doi:10.5381/jot.2007.6.7.a4
19. L.M.J. Bergmans, Towards detection of semantic conflicts between crosscutting concerns, in *Workshop on Analysis of Aspect-Oriented Software(AAOS) at ECOOP 2003*, Darmstadt, Germany, 2003
20. G. Mussbacher, J. Whittle, D. Amyot, Modeling and detecting semantic-based interactions in aspect-oriented scenarios. Requirements Eng. J. **15**(2), 197–214 (2010). doi:10.1007/s00766-010-0098-4
21. G. Mussbacher, D. Barone, D. Amyot, Towards a taxonomy of syntactic and semantic matching mechanisms for aspect-oriented modeling, in *6th Workshop on System Analysis and Modelling (SAM 2010)*, Oslo, Norway, 2010, pp. 241–256. doi:10.1007/978-3-642-21652-7_15
22. G. Mussbacher, D. Amyot, J. Araújo, A. Moreira, Requirements modeling with the aspect-oriented user requirements notation (AoURN): a case study, in *Transactions on Aspect-Oriented Software Development VII* (Springer, Berlin/Heidelberg, 2010), pp. 23–68. doi:10.1007/978-3-642-16086-8_2
23. G. Mussbacher, bCMS case study: AoURN, in *ReMoDD*, 2011, http://www.cs.colostate.edu/remodd/v1/content/bcms-case-study-aourn. Accessed 22 Oct 2012

Chapter 6
Aspect-Oriented Goal Modeling and Composition with AOV-Graph

Lyrene Fernandes da Silva and Julio Cesar Sampaio do Prado Leite

Abstract As software complexity increases, so does the difficulty of manipulating its models. More complex models make it more difficult to define the impact of changes, to modify the models, or to reuse model parts in other projects. Part of the problem is that concerns are strongly interconnected. Traditional modularization minimizes this coupling. However, mostly, it considers only one dimension in software artifacts (for instance classes or functions). Therefore, the concerns in other dimensions are scattered and tangled, i.e., crosscutting. This chapter reports on the application of goals and aspect-oriented concepts in requirements modeling. Firstly, AOV-graph and its mechanisms to separation, composition, and visualization of crosscutting concerns are presented and after that, we discuss AOV-graph in the context of the Crisis Management case study.

6.1 Introduction

Requirements management is a challenge: requirements are the anchor for software construction, requirements evolve, and are intertwined [1]. The challenge is even greater if we consider the crosscutting nature of requirements whereby they influence or constrain each other [2]. An instance of the crosscutting nature of requirements is the feature interaction problem in telecommunications systems [3].

This chapter presents an approach for modeling requirements using concepts based on goal-oriented requirements engineering [4] where the relationships among requirements are explicitly modeled and analyzed in order to bring out their

L.F. da Silva (✉)
Universidade Federal do Rio Grande do Norte, Natal, Brazil
e-mail: lyrene@dimap.ufrn.br

J.C.S. do Prado Leite
Pontifícia Universidade Católica do Rio de Janeiro, Rio de Janeiro, Brazil
e-mail: julio@inf.puc-rio.br

A. Moreira et al. (eds.), *Aspect-Oriented Requirements Engineering*,
DOI 10.1007/978-3-642-38640-4_6,

crosscutting nature. To handle this crosscutting nature and overcome the complexity arising due to explicit representation of interactions, we present a language (called AOV-graph) and a process consisting of three activities: separation, composition, and visualization.

The particular strength of this approach is the usage of intentional modeling, that is, a modeling language that allows for the representation of goals, a higher abstraction than the usual function/task one. AOV-graph represents functional and nonfunctional requirements, exposes the interactions among requirements, and offers a new type of relationship to modularize these interactions. Its mechanism of composition is based on a semi-semantic strategy and it makes possible to select many joinpoints by using regular expressions, while its visualization mechanism can generate different and useful views for analyses of a model.

In order to make the context of crosscutting requirements more explicit, Sect. 6.2, exemplifies the web of relations when requirements are seen through the lens of crosscutting relationships. Section 6.3 presents AOV-graph: an aspect- and goal-oriented requirements language, its origin, grammar, and mechanisms for composition and visualization. Section 6.4 illustrates AOV-graph with the Crisis Management case study. Finally, in Sect. 6.5 we discuss the limitations of the current work and issues that we believe should be further investigated.

6.2 Motivation for AOV-Graph

Using a part of the Crisis Management System [5], we exemplify, with three different notations, the tangled and scattered nature of the crosscutting concerns. The notations used are (1) a use case, (2) a list of nonfunctional requirements, and (3) a goal model.

Figure 6.1 portrays the example, with these three notations, where we can observe some scattered and tangled functions and constraints, for instance:

1. In the use-case *Capture Witness Report* (Fig. 6.1a), the success scenario is tangled with availability, persistence, real-time, multiaccess, and adaptability nonfunctional requirements
2. The nonfunctional requirements (NFR) in the NFR list (Fig. 6.1b), are scattered in many use cases of the CRM, for instance, *Authenticate user*, *Assign internal resource*, *Request external resource*, *Execute super observer mission*, and others

However, these interactions (annotated in Fig. 6.1a, b) are not explicitly represented in the original CMS specification [5].

On the other hand, Fig. 6.1c presents a goal model (V-Graph) representing some requirements and relationships between concerns of CMS, which focus on the same requirements of Fig. 6.1a, b. In this model, gray tasks highlight *Capture Witness Report* requirements and their interaction with other concerns. This type of model makes the interactions between concerns more explicit compared to the previous models. However, as the number of interactions increases, although this model

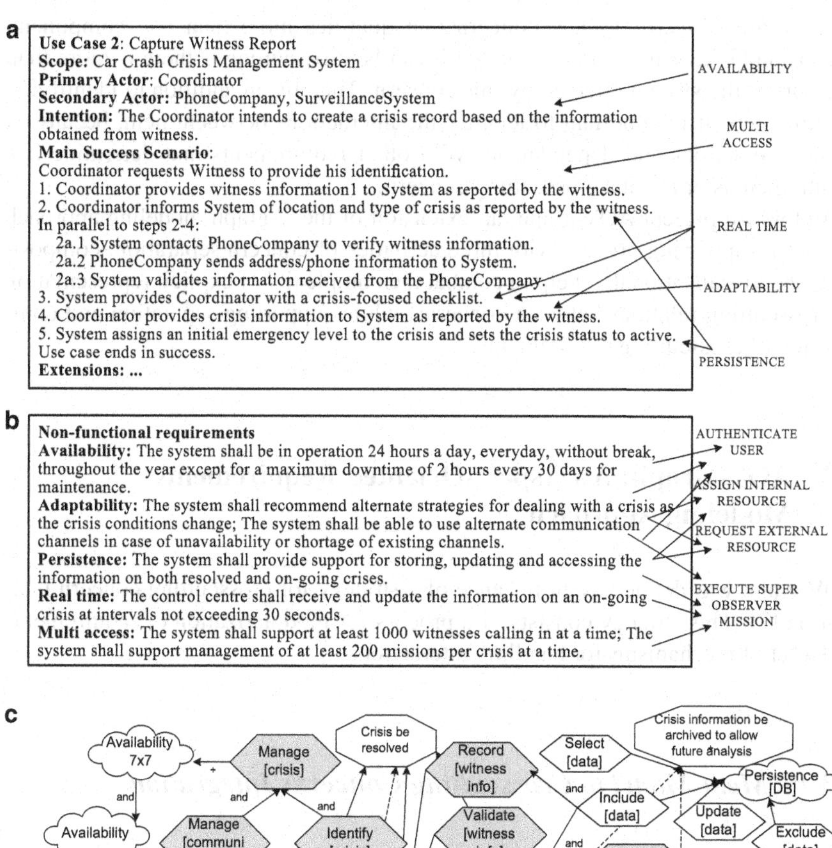

a

Use Case 2: Capture Witness Report
Scope: Car Crash Crisis Management System
Primary Actor: Coordinator
Secondary Actor: PhoneCompany, SurveillanceSystem
Intention: The Coordinator intends to create a crisis record based on the information obtained from witness.
Main Success Scenario:
Coordinator requests Witness to provide his identification.
1. Coordinator provides witness information1 to System as reported by the witness.
2. Coordinator informs System of location and type of crisis as reported by the witness.
In parallel to steps 2-4:
  2a.1 System contacts PhoneCompany to verify witness information.
  2a.2 PhoneCompany sends address/phone information to System.
  2a.3 System validates information received from the PhoneCompany.
3. System provides Coordinator with a crisis-focused checklist.
4. Coordinator provides crisis information to System as reported by the witness.
5. System assigns an initial emergency level to the crisis and sets the crisis status to active.
Use case ends in success.
Extensions: ...

b

Non-functional requirements
Availability: The system shall be in operation 24 hours a day, everyday, without break, throughout the year except for a maximum downtime of 2 hours every 30 days for maintenance.
Adaptability: The system shall recommend alternate strategies for dealing with a crisis as the crisis conditions change; The system shall be able to use alternate communication channels in case of unavailability or shortage of existing channels.
Persistence: The system shall provide support for storing, updating and accessing the information on both resolved and on-going crises.
Real time: The control centre shall receive and update the information on an on-going crisis at intervals not exceeding 30 seconds.
Multi access: The system shall support at least 1000 witnesses calling in at a time; The system shall support management of at least 200 missions per crisis at a time.

c

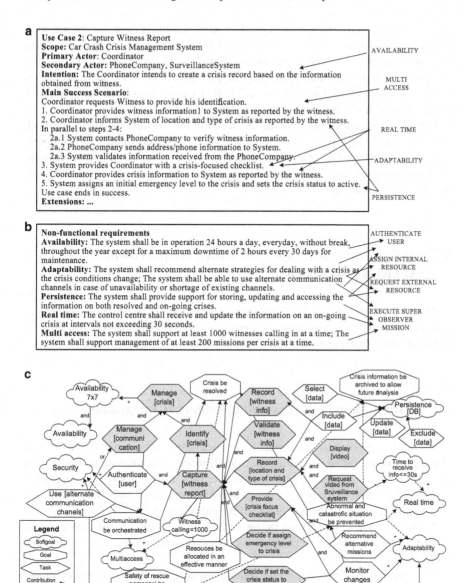

Fig. 6.1 Examples of crosscutting concerns into (**a**) a use case; (**b**) a nonfunctional requirements list; and (**c**) V-graph model

simply explicitly depicts the normally hidden interactions, this type of model may seem to be very complex.

We define a *concern* as any property or attribute that qualifies a system component. These components can be data, constraints, or functions. We define *crosscutting concerns* as any concern that qualifies more than one component. For example, security is a concern and it can be crosscutting if there is more than one part of the system affected by this concern. Thereby, in addition to identifying requirements, it is important to identify the interactions between them, because it is the interactions and dependencies with other requirements that determine if a requirement is or is not a crosscutting concern.

Below we present AOV-graph, an extension of the V-graph modeling approach [6] and a supporting process with three activities of concern separation, composition, and visualization that help to combat the complexity of explicit representation of crosscutting relations between concerns, while supporting separation and composition of crosscutting requirements.

6.3 AOV-Graph: An Aspect-Oriented Requirements Modeling Approach

AOV-graph was defined as an instance of a strategy for crosscutting concern integration [7]. This strategy consists of a process for modularization of requirements and a set of mechanisms for handling interactions.

6.3.1 Meta-Model to Crosscutting Concerns Integration

In this work, the process meta-model for crosscutting concerns integration consists of three activities, called Separation, Composition and Visualization (in light gray in Fig. 6.2). These activities are essential because they allow, respectively, separation and modularization of the system, composition of modules to build the system, and visualization of parts of the model and of the entire model.

Modularization is performed by an explicit description of how concerns are related each other. This description uses concepts inherited from aspect-oriented frameworks.

For Separation, AOV-graph and guidelines are provided in order to model requirements considering their crosscutting nature, i.e., to make explicit which requirements are scattered and how are they tangled. This information is recorded using a new notation for the *crosscutting* relationship type. By modeling the crosscutting concerns explicitly, we are able to observe them, and therefore, to analyze how the requirements interact.

Composition is an automatic process that combines the requirements modeled separately. This combination is made by interpreting crosscutting relationships and applying composition rules. Composition rules define how the information in crosscutting relationships is to be transformed, i.e., it indicates their semantics,

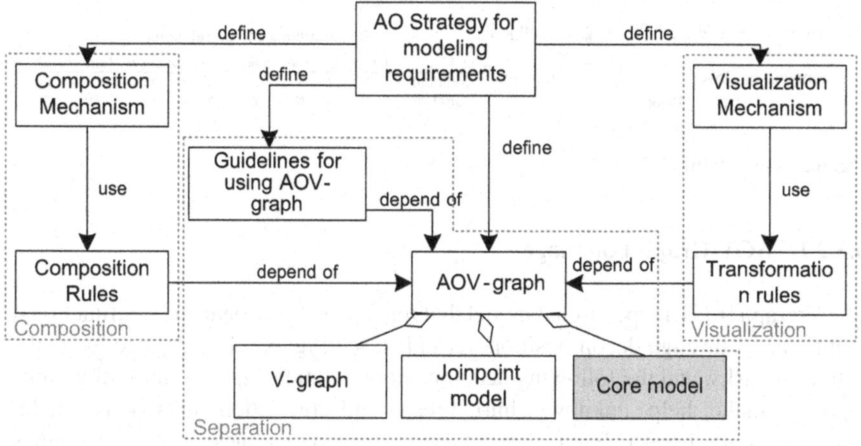

Fig. 6.2 Components used on integration of crosscutting concerns from [8, 9]

making their propagation possible. This process is similar to the "Weaver" of aspect-oriented programming languages [10], whose objective is to mix components and aspects.

Composition generates an integrated model. This model and the information about which views can be extracted from it are the inputs for the visualization activity. The visualization activity provides partial and complete views on the integrated model, making it possible to understand the system concerns individually or in conjunction.

In summary, this strategy provides a new way of thinking about, modeling and visualizing requirements. For this purpose, see Fig. 6.2, the composition and visualization mechanisms use composition and transformation rules, and they depend on the constructs of AOV-graph. Thereby, the separation, composition, and visualization are centered in AOV-graph, which consists of a Requirement Language, V-graph; a Core Model that represents crosscutting relationships; and a Joinpoint Model that defines how V-graph and the Core Model are related.

6.3.2 *Separation of Crosscutting Concerns*

As we discussed above, separation of crosscutting concerns is centered in the AOV-graph language. AOV-graph is an extension of V-graph, as it adds a crosscutting relationship to the notion of V-graph. The AOV-graph grammar and some guidelines for modeling are presented below.

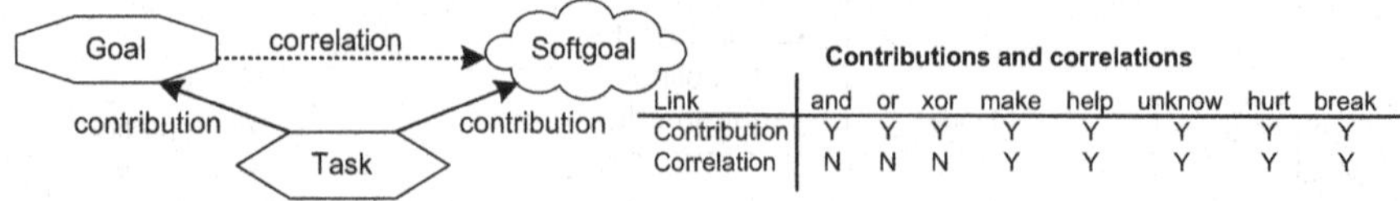

Link	and	or	xor	make	help	unknow	hurt	break
Contribution	Y	Y	Y	Y	Y	Y	Y	Y
Correlation	N	N	N	Y	Y	Y	Y	Y

Fig. 6.3 V-graph [6]

6.3.2.1 AOV-Graph Language

The V-graph [6] is a type of goal model that represents functional and nonfunctional requirements through decomposition trees [11], see Fig. 6.3. It is defined by goals, softgoals, tasks, and the following decomposition relationships—contribution links (and, or, make, help, unknown, hurt, break) and correlation links (make, help, unknown, hurt, break). Each element has a type and topics. The type defines a generic functional or nonfunctional requirement, for example, Security and Management. The topic defines the context of that element, for example, user and communication.

Softgoals, goals, and tasks represent requirements on three abstraction levels. This is important because in the same model we can represent reasons and operations, the context and how each element contributes to achieve the system goals. Furthermore, there are useful results in goal modeling, as one can immediately use previous work on: how to analyze obstacles to the satisfaction of a goal [12]; how to qualitatively analyze the relationships in goal models [4]; how to analyze variability [13]; how to analyze conflicts among goals through a propagation mechanism of labels [14]; how to identify aspects in goal models [6]; and how to provide goal reuse [15].

AOV-graph grammar and its joinpont and core models are explained as follows. Figure 6.4 shows the AOV-graph grammar in BNF notation.

Goal_model: Each *goal_model* consists of *name, identifier*, and a set of *components* and *relationships* (line 2 in Fig. 6.4). The *components* can be *softgoals, goals*, and *tasks* and each one of them consists of *name*, *type*, *topic*, *decomposition_label*, and a set of *components* and *relationships* (lines 4–6 in Fig. 6.4). This *decomposition_label* represents contribution relationships between the contributing component and its parent, and can assume labels *and, or, make, help, unknown, hurt, and break* (line 12 in Fig. 6.4). *Relationships* are defined by *correlationRel*, representing correlation relationships and *crosscuttingRel*, representing crosscutting relationships (lines 10 and 17 in Fig. 6.4). Each *correlationRel* is defined by a *correlation_label*, *source*, and *target*. Contributions and correlations are one-to-one relationships.

Joinpoint: In AOV-graph, *joinpoints* are elements of types *softgoal*, *goal*, and *task* (line 16 in Fig. 6.4). Instances of these types can be referred as *pointcuts* and they can be identified by composition mechanism: directly by their names or identifiers; or indirectly by regular expressions defining name, type, or topic.

```
1   <aspect_oriented_model> := <goal_model>
2   <goal_model> := goal_model (<name>; <id>){<component> <relationship>} | <goal_model>
<goal_model>
3   <component> := <softgoal> | <goal> | <task> | <softgoal_ref> | <goal_ref> | <task_ref> |
<new_element_type> | < component > < component >
4   <softgoal>:=softgoal(<name>;<softgoal_id>;<decomposition_label>;(<type>); (<top-ic>))
{<component><relationship>}
5   <goal> := goal (<name>; <goal_id>; <decomposition_label> ; (<type>) ; (<topic>))
{<component><relationship>}
6   <task> := task (<name>; <task_id>; <decomposition_label> ; (<type>) (<topic>))
{<component><relationship>}
7   <topic> := <name> | <topic>; <topic>
8   <type> := <name> | <type>; <type>
9   <relationship> := <correlationRel> | <crosscuttingRel> |  <relationship> <relation-ship>
10  <correlationRel> := correlation <correlation_label> {source=<component>
target=<component >}
11  <correlation_label> := break | hurt | unknown | help | make
12  <decomposition_label>:=and | or | xor | break | hurt | unknown | help | make
13  <goal_ref> := goal_ref = <goal_id> <decomposition_label>
14  <softgoal_ref> :=  softgoal_ref = <softgoal_id> <decomposition_label>
15  <task_ref> :=  task_ref = <task_id> <decomposition_label>
16  <joinpoint> := <softgoal_ref> | <goal_ref> | <task_ref>
17  <crosscuttingRel> := crosscutting {source=<joinpoint>
<pointcut><advice><intertype_declaration>}
18  <pointcut> := pointcut (<name>; <pointcut_id>) : <pointcut_expression> | <pointcut> <pointcut>
19  <pointcut_expression> := <operand> |  not <operand> | <pointcut_expression> and
<pointcut_expression> | <pointcut_expression> or <pointcut_expression>
20  <operand> := <primitive> (<joinpoint>) | <primitive> (<regular_expression>)
21  <primitive> := include | substitute
22  <regular_expression> := <value>; "<joinpoint>"; <atribute_type>; <path>
23  <atribute_type> := id | name | type | topic
24  <advice> := advice <advice_type>: <a_it_expression> {<advice_body>} |  <advice> <advice>
25  <advice_type> := after | before | around
26  <a_it_expression> := <pointcut_id> | not <pointcut_id> | <a_it_expression> and <a_it_expression> |
<a_it_expression> or <a_it_expression>
27  <intertype_declaration> := intertype <intertype_type>: <a_it_expression>
{<intertype_declaration_body>} |  <intertype_declaration> <intertype_declaration>
28  <intertype_type> := attribute | element
29  <advice_body> := <joinpoint> | <advice_body>; <advice_body>
30  <intertype_declaration_body> := new_element_type {<new_element_type>} |
<joinpoint> | <intertype_declaration_body> ; <intertype_declaration_body>
31  <new_element_type> := <name>=<value> | <new_element_type>; <new_element_type>
32  <text> := <letter> | <digit>
33  <name> := <text>
34  <value>:=<text>
35  <path> :=<text>
36  <task_id> := <text>
37  <softgoal_id> := <text>
38  <goal_id> := <text>
39  <pointcut_id> := <text>
```

Fig. 6.4 AOV-graph Grammar

Instances of goal, softgoal, and task are also used in the description of *advice* and *intertype declarations bodies*. Furthermore, since these types have a *decomposition_label* attribute (lines 13–15 in Fig. 6.4), it is possible to define in *advice* and in *intertype declarations* which will be the labels of the new relationships created by the composition mechanism.

CrosscuttingRel: Although the concept of a crosscutting relationship is based on aspects of AspectJ [16], aspects are first-order components to represent crosscutting concerns while crosscutting relationships (*crosscuttingRel*) are not first-order elements and only represent how crosscutting concerns are related. We choose to define a type of relationship in opposition to a first-order abstraction because:

- Crosscutting relationships are less intrusive than aspects because they are not another abstraction to model requirements; therefore, the techniques and guidelines used by V-graph can remain unchanged.
- With crosscutting relationships, the identification and description of information about how a concern is crosscutting can be postponed until interactions between requirements are known and then they can be substituted by a crosscutting relationship, without having to change the structure and organization of requirements. This characterizes a late binding approach, as opposed to an early binding approach.
- Since each concern is represented in the same way (by first-order elements of AOV-graph), it is easier to reuse concerns that in some projects are crosscutting, whereas in others they are not. We consider that one concern can be crosscutting or not, depending on its context and kind of modeling language.
- With crosscutting relationships, information about "what" is crosscutting, represented by elements of AOV-graph, is separated from information about "how" it is crosscutting, represented by crosscutting relationship.

Each *crosscuttingRel* is described by *pointcuts*, *advice*, and *intertype declarations* (line 17 in Fig. 6.4). These elements are associated to the types defined in the *joinpoints*. Next, we describe the semantics of these elements in AOV-graph.

- *Pointcuts—Pointcuts* can refer to any element whose types are defined in the *joinpoint* model (i.e., softgoal, goal, and task). In pointcuts, operator *OR* states that if the operands refer to the children of the same parent then only one operand will be changed, while operator *AND* states that every operand will be equally affected, and operator *NOT* excludes operands reported in the pointcut.
- *Advice—Advice* defines which elements of the source model are scattered and tangled at the *pointcuts*. This information is used by the composition mechanism in order to *include* or *exclude* relationships in an AOV-graph model. In the AOV-graph, advice can be one of the three types: *before*, *after*, or *around*. Since V-graph models do not model sequence of actions, but rather follow a top-down or left-right order, we use these types of advice to define (1) before—elements are inserted *before* pointcuts as a decomposition of their parent; (2) around—elements are inserted as a decomposition of the affected pointcuts; and (3) after—elements are inserted *after* pointcuts as a decomposition of its parent. Although the *before* and *after* types generate elements in the same point in the tree structure, they can be used to analyze how the requirements are coupled.
- *Intertype declarations*—Intertype declarations are used in order to change the structure of elements in the goal model, i.e., new *goals*, *softgoals*, *tasks*, and *attributes* can be created and scattered for many *jointpoints* in accordance with

```
crosscutting (source = Persistence){
  pointcut (p1): include (Record.*)
  advice (around): p1 {task_ref=(Include [data]; and;T3.1;)}
  intertype declaration (element): p1 { task = (Verify if [data] exists already; T3.5; and) }}
```

Fig. 6.5 Example of crosscutting relationship

some criteria. For example, it would be possible to create an attribute actor to indicate which stakeholders are interested in which requirements.

Figure 6.5 illustrates an example of crosscutting relationship, which defines one pointcut using regular expression (line 2), one around advice (line 3), and one intertype declaration element (line 4). The pointcut refers to *every* (denoted by *) goal, softgoal, and task starting with *"Record"* string, and in each one of these elements two tasks will be added: *Include [data]* and *Verify if [data] exists already*. These two tasks are operationalizations of Persistence (defined in first line of Fig. 6.5); they have a generic context (specified by the word in brackets) in order to be applied to any type of data (*data*).

6.3.2.2 Guidelines for Concerns Modularization

With AOV-graph, concerns are modeled as a graph of goals, softgoals and tasks. As a result of interactions among these concerns, the engineer can decide to create crosscutting relationships. Although each graph or sub graph can be considered as a concern, it is recommended that the separation should be done by modeling each concern as a distinct goal_model rather than by a sub-tree, mainly when a concern presents:

1. High complexity—it involves many variables and it is difficult to analyze all its parts at the same time; or
2. It can potentially be used (reused) in other domains; or
3. It is apparently independent of the others—it should have high cohesion and low coupling[1]

Likewise, in AOV-graph, it is recommended to use crosscutting relationships when a concern:

1. Is repeated many times in the model, or it contributes to satisfaction of many other concerns, representing the scattering problem; or
2. Contributes for satisfaction of concerns in distinct tree (separated goal models), representing the tangling problem.

[1]The usual heuristics of software design can be applied in this context: we observe if the concept has wholeness, that is, its contents are enough to explain it and nothing more, thus it is cohesive; and we also observe that information exchanged with other entities (integration) is performed without exposing the concept itself, so that interfaces to other entities are not intrusive to the concept.

Advice and intertype declaration group tasks, goals, and softgoals that affect one or several pointcuts. Therefore, the more elements are grouped in an advice or intertype declaration, the better it is to use crosscutting relationships. That is, when crosscutting relationships are used, the quantity of relationships that has to be individually defined decreases. Consequently, the visual representations of the model are better than it would be without crosscutting relationships, and it is also easier to manipulate such models.

6.3.3 Composition of Crosscutting Concerns

By using crosscutting relationships, we decrease the number of individually defined relationships (contributions) between goals, softgoals, and tasks because each crosscutting relationship "modularizes" several interactions which otherwise will be repeated in order to associate the same concern (source) to many elements (target). Therefore, pointcuts group points that are affected in the same way, while advice and intertype declarations group behaviors or structures that are repeated in several points. For instance, Fig. 6.5 presents a crosscutting relationship, in which the source is Persistence and the target are all tasks starting with "Record" string, which may be represented by a one-to-many relationship before composition. However, this relationship defines, by using pointcuts, advice, and intertype declarations, a many-to-many relation, since, for example, there is a contribution between each one of tasks in advice and each pointcut.

Composition rules determine how the composition mechanism transforms an input model into an integrated model; they take into account the semantics of the constructs of crosscutting relationships and the syntax of the AOV-graph.

Table 6.1 presents the composition rules created for AOV-graph. There are two actions specified in crosscutting relationships by the primitives *include* and *substitute*. The combination of *operators*, *primitives*, *advice types*, and *intertype declaration types* determines which transformations are to be made at each pointcut.

Figure 6.6 presents a composition example (a) describes an input goal model, (b) defines a crosscutting relationship, and (c) describes the result of the composition process. In Fig. 6.6c, task-refs in bold are the elements added by composition and described by advice and intertype declarations in Fig. 6.6b.

6.3.4 Visualization of Crosscutting Concerns

During the requirements definition, as well as the design process, i.e., during the elaboration of solutions, the developer needs to be able to obtain different views on the base model in order to analyze the solutions created from different viewpoints and perspectives.

Therefore, a visualization mechanism is fundamental in facilitating requirements modeling. An automatic mechanism for generation of views can accelerate the

Table 6.1 Composition rules

Operator	Semantic
AND	Affect all operands
OR	Affect only one of operands if it has the same parent
NOT	Exclude an operand of set of points to be affected

Primitive	Type of Intertype declarations or advice	Semantic
Include	*Advice* before	Include the elements defined in the advice body BEFORE the pointcut as children of its parent element
	Advice after	Include the elements defined in the advice body AFTER the pointcut, as children of its parent element
	Advice around	Include the elements defined in advice body as children of the pointcut
	Intertype declaration element/attribute	Include the elements defined in *intertype* body into the source element and into the pointcut
Substitute	Advice Before/around/after	Substitute the *pointcut for* elements defined in advice body
	Intertype declaration element/attribute	Include the elements defined in *intertype* body into the source element and into the pointcut

a

```
goal_model (Safety; GM5) {
  sofgoal Safety (and; S5;) {
    task Monitor [emissions of crisis] (and; T5.1;) {}
    task Determinate [safe operating distances and perimeter
(and; T5.2;){}
    task Monitor [weather] (and; T5.3){}
    task Monitor [criminal activity] (and; T5.4;){}
    task Monitor [terrain conditions] (and; T5.5;){}
}}...
```

b

```
crosscutting (source=Mobility){
   poitcut (p2): include (Determinate safe operating distances
and perimeter) and include (Monitor [weather]) and
include(Monitor [criminal activity]) and include (Monitor
[terrain conditions])
    advice (around): p2 {
      task_ref = (Provide [location sensitive info];and;T4.2;)
      task_ref=(Access [maps, terrain and weather conditions
and routes];and;T4.4;)
}}
```

c

```
goal_model (Safety; GM5) {
 sofgoal Safety (and; S5;) {
  task Monitor [emissions of crisis] (and; T5.1;) {
    task_ref = (Provide [location sensitive info];and;T4.2;)
    task_ref=(Access [maps, terrain and weather conditions and routes];and;T4.4;)}
  task Determinate [safe operating distances and perimeter (and; T5.2;){
    task_ref = (Provide [location sensitive info];and;T4.2;)
    task_ref=(Access [maps, terrain and weather conditions and routes];and;T4.4;)}
  task Monitor [weather] (and; T5.3){
    task_ref = (Provide [location sensitive info];and;T4.2;)
    task_ref=(Access [maps, terrain and weather conditions and routes];and;T4.4;)}
  task Monitor [criminal activity] (and; T5.4;){
    task_ref = (Provide [location sensitive info];and;T4.2;)
    task_ref=(Access [maps, terrain and weather conditions and routes];and;T4.4;)}
  task Monitor [terrain conditions] (and; T5.5;){
    task_ref = (Provide [location sensitive info];and;T4.2;)
    task_ref=(Access [maps, terrain and weather conditions and routes];and;T4.4;)}
}}...
```

Fig. 6.6 Example of composition

modeling process. Since views deal with scoping, they are instrumental in dealing with complex models. Therefore, the developer can analyze the correctness and completeness of one concern or a set of concerns at a time.

We have defined a set of views for the AOV-graph. Such views are classified as (1) service and (2) model views.

Service views represent parts of the system that complement each other, for instance, security view, functional requirements view, persistence view, and so on. They are partial views, focusing on one or a subset of concerns at a time.

Model view is a representation where we can explicitly model functional and nonfunctional requirements using softgoals, goals, and tasks. This is its dominant decomposition manner, an intention-oriented decomposition. Moreover, hierarchy and topics of the AOV-graph provide new perspectives of the system, based on, for example, situations and data. Furthermore, relationships between goals, softgoals, and tasks provide a perspective of interaction or traceability and so on. Using this implicit knowledge, rules to transform the information from an AOV-graph into different models have been defined, such as architectural specifications [17], scenarios, features models [18], class diagrams, and entity-relationship models [8, 9].

View as services or as models are not disjointed categories, i.e., we also can generate views as models for one limited set of services.

6.4 AOV-Graph in Action

Here, we illustrate AOV-graph[2] by using Crisis Management case study [5]. Although CMS document defines artifacts as, requirements, features models, and architecture, we use only requirements and use cases to create an AOV-graph model of CMS. These sections define 6 functional requirements, 11 nonfunctional requirements, and 10 use cases. Interpreting and modeling the CMS requirements as a goal-oriented model resulted in a graph whose complexity is a direct result of modeling the requirements interaction in an explicit way, you can see the complete graph in [21], and Fig. 6.9 in Appendix gives a general idea of how complex these interactions can become. Next, some views of this graph are discussed.

6.4.1 Crisis Management System AOV-Graph

We applied the heuristics defined in Sect. 6.3.2.2 to the given information sources (functional requirements, nonfunctional requirements, and use cases). The full model (attached in Appendix) is centered on the goal of "Crisis be resolved." We used the available CMS materials to modularize related goals and softgoal and used the task concept to provide the fine detail. However, the point that this exercise aims to stress is the fact that we have explicitly mapped the relationships among requirements, that is, their interaction.

[2] AOV-graph has been also applied to other case studies [18–20].

Figure 6.7a shows a high-level abstraction view of the correlation between CMS goals (such as Crisis be resolved, Communication be orchestrated, Safety of rescue personnel be provided, Crisis information be archived to allow future analysis) and some of its nonfunctional requirements (Reliability, Safety, Security, Mobility, Multi access, Availability, Adaptability, Accuracy, Real time, Persistence, Logging). By definition, each correlation indicates that there is some task contributing to both, the correlated goal and softgoal.

CMS functional requirements and each nonfunctional requirement were modeled as separated goal models, for instance, in Fig. 6.6a, is presented the goal model about Safety; the graphical representation of this goal model can be seen in Fig. 6.9 in Appendix, where each cluster (represented by rectangle) portrays a distinct model. We then modeled their interactions, using contributions, correlations, and crosscutting relationships. Crosscutting relationships were defined when goals, softgoals, and tasks affected different points in the same model or in distinct models, indicating scattered and tangled information (for instance in Fig. 6.7d the task Receive [final mission report] contributes to Execute [rescue mission] and three other tasks, indicating that it is scattered).

Figure 6.7b presents a small example of CMS tasks, which involves manage crisis and missions. A description of a crosscutting relationship from Fig. 6.7b is shown in Fig. 6.7c stating that in order to execute any type of mission, it is necessary to perform some tasks of monitoring. The composed AOV-graph model for this relationship is showed in Fig. 6.7d, providing contributions from each subtask of Monitor (mission) to all kind of missions to be executed.

This case study contains five other crosscutting relationships: from Mobility to Safety, from Logging to Monitor (crisis), from Safety to Monitor (crisis), from Manage (crisis) to some softgoals, and from Adaptability to Manage (crisis), presented in Fig. 6.8. These crosscutting relationships are not explained here for space reasons.

6.4.2 *Observations from the Crisis Management Case Study*

Crisis Management AOV-graph model is comprised of 27 softgoals, 6 goals, and 79 tasks, see Table 6.2. These elements were modularized in 12 goal models, which refer to Crisis Management, Reliability, Safety, Security, Mobility, Multiaccess, Availability, Adaptability, Accuracy, Real time, Persistence, and Logging.

After composition, 48 contributions were generated; this represents an increase of 44.44 % on the total of contributions. The reasons for that are believed to be:

1. Scattering of some elements, since they are operationalizations of other elements. For instance, in order to execute any type of mission, tasks associated with the beginning and the end of mission are necessary.
2. Tangling of some concerns, since in order to attain one of them other concerns are involved. For instance, in order to *Monitor [mission]*, the tasks named *Monitor [weather]*, *Monitor [terrain]*, and *Monitor [criminal activity]* need to be achieved.

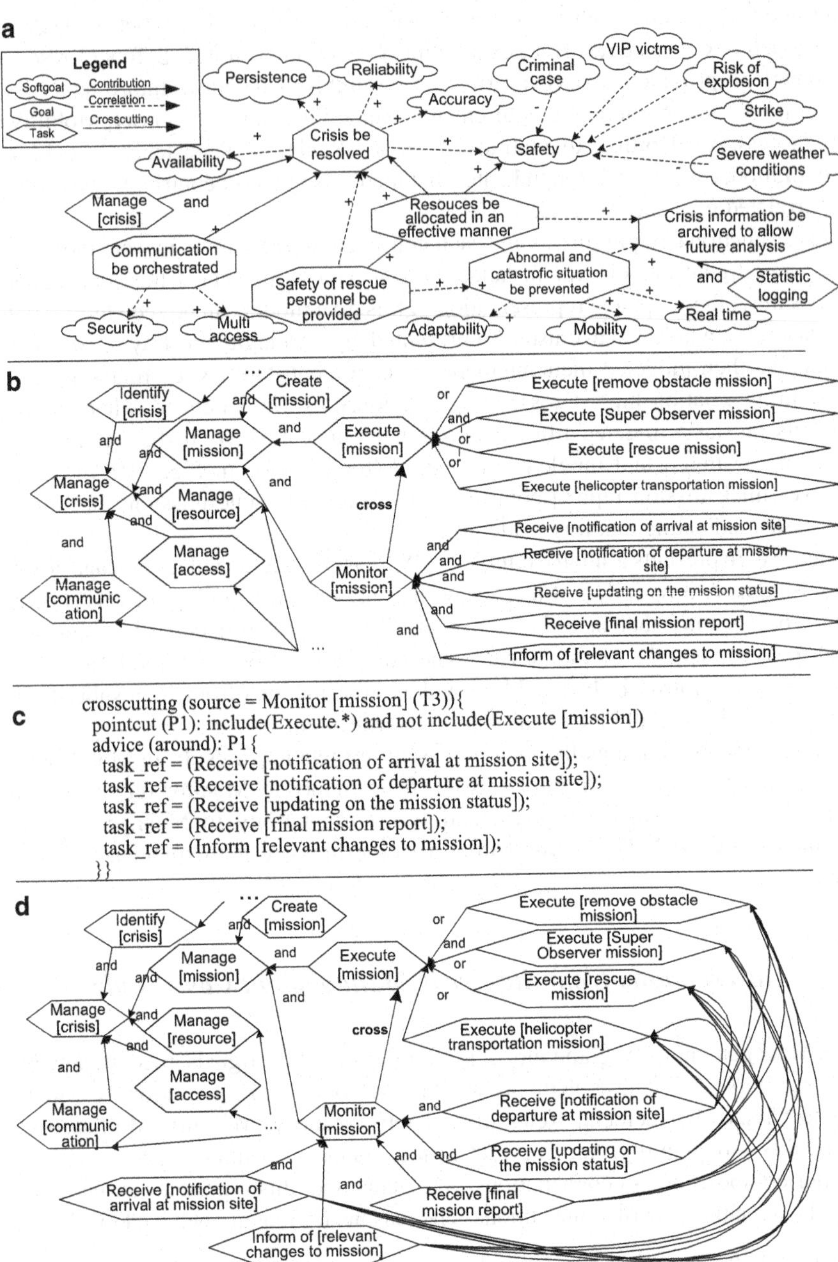

Fig. 6.7 CMS views: (**a**) correlations between CMS goals and softgoals; (**b**) some of CMS tasks and a crosscutting relationship; (**c**) description of the crosscutting relationship showed in (**b**); and (**d**) AOV-graph of (**b**) after composition

```
crosscutting (source=Mobility){
 pointcut (p2): include (Determinate safe operating distances and perimeter) and
include (Monitor [weather]) and include(Monitor [criminal activity]) and include (Monitor
[terrain conditions])
advice (around): p2 {
      task_ref = Provide [location sensitive info];
      task_ref=Access [maps, terrain and weather conditions and routes];}}

crosscutting (source=Logging){
 pointcut (p3): include (Receive [notification.*) and include(Receive [final mission report])
 advice (around): p3 { task_ref = Record info for logging; }}

crosscutting (source=Safety){
 pointcut (p4): include (Monitor [mission])
 advice (around): p4 {
      task_ref = Monitor [weather];
      task_ref = Monitor [criminal activity];
      task_ref = Monitor [terrain conditions];
      task_ref = Determinate safe operating distances and perimeter;}}

crosscutting (source=Manage [crisis]){
 pointcut (p5): include (Reliability [communication]) and include (Real time) and
include (Multi access) and include (Accuracy) an include (Use [alternate communication
channels])
 advice (around): p5 {
      task_ref = Manage [communication];}}

crosscutting (source=Adaptability){
 pointcut (p6): include (Inform of [relevant changes to mission])
 pointcut (p7): include(Provide [crisis focus checklist])
 advice (around): p6 and p7{
      task_ref = Manage [changes];
      task_ref = Recommend [alternate missions];}
 advice (around): p6 { task_ref = Recommend [alternate resources];}}
```

Fig. 6.8 CMS' crosscutting relationships

Table 6.2 Statistics about crisis management case study

Elements	Quantity before composition	Quantity after composition
Goals	6	6
Sofgoals	27	27
Tasks	79	79
Crosscutting relationships	6	6
Correlations	20	20
Contributions	108	156

If we consider only one view with the twelve 12 models together (showed in Fig. 6.10 in Appendix), this tangling and scattering makes it difficult to visualize, model, and analyze them. Furthermore, if no automatic visualization mechanism is used, the work for writing and maintaining these models is enormous.

This case study helps to illustrate how we use AOV-graph to separate, compound, and visualize concerns, helping us to analyze the system requirements. However, due to the nature of this case study, some features of AOV-graph have not been explored. These are negative contributions and correlations, primitive substitute, before and after advice types, and attribute intertype declaration.

6.5 Final Remarks

This chapter presented AOV-graph, a strategy to deal with the scattering and tangling problems in goal models. This strategy is based on the idea that the crosscutting nature of concerns comes from interaction between them. A given concern can be crosscutting in some context and non-crosscutting in other contexts. Therefore, this strategy contributes to requirements engineering by:

1. Defining a crosscutting relationship which modularizes interactions, helping to deal with system complexity
2. Providing composition and visualization mechanisms, which help to analyze and model the requirements

Although this approach helps to address the modularization of concerns there are some limitations and challenges:

1. Sophisticated tools are necessary to provide separation, composition, and visualization. Reqsys [18] is a tool to analyze if an AOV-graph specification is syntactically correct, however, it does not include graphical edition of AOV-graph models, interaction with the generated views, neither are all of the parameters of composition defined.
2. AOV-graph only provides partial semantic composition. As showed by related research [22], semantic composition provides a better modularization than syntactic composition. Furthermore, we believe that other composition operators should be investigated, for instance, mechanisms to describe the sequence of compositions and primitives such as "merge" and "overlap."
3. There is a need to trace crosscutting concerns in requirements from and to other activities of development process.
4. Also experimentation using AOV-graph and traditional approaches, in parallel, with well-defined metrics is important to better evaluate this and other approaches. Some initiatives in this context have been conducted [19, 22] but each approach is yet only used by its authors.

A.1 Appendix

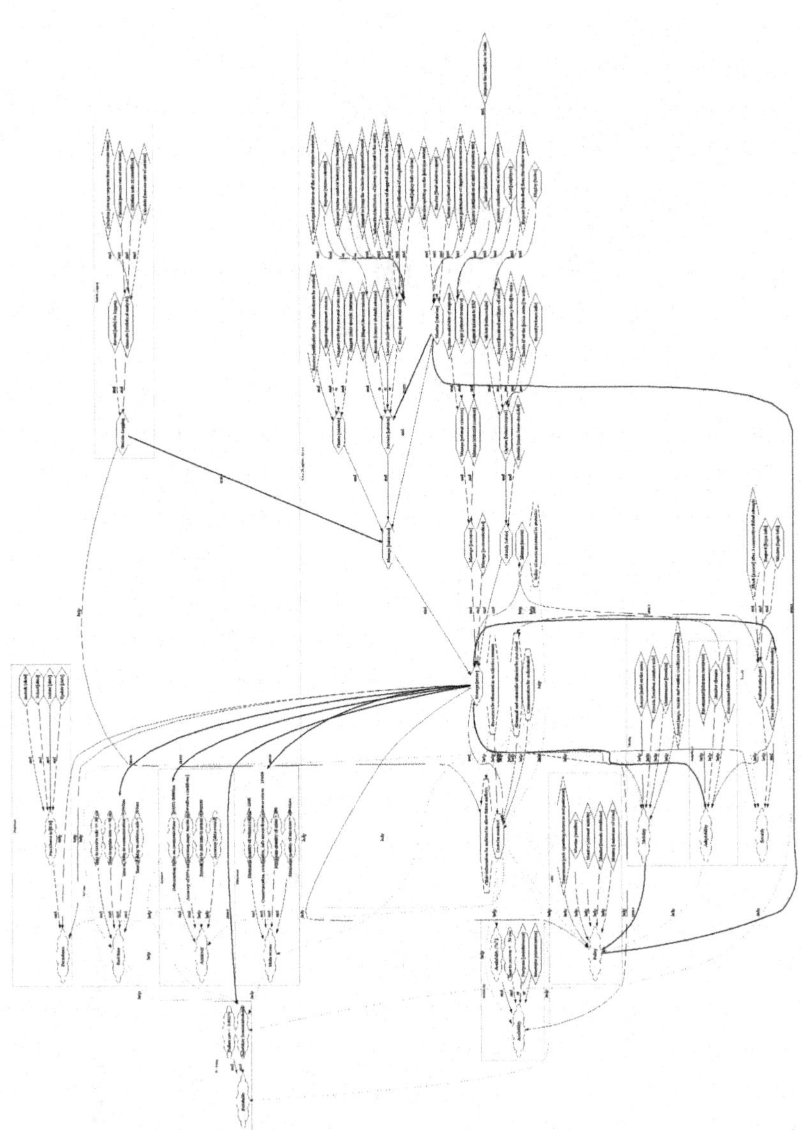

Fig. 6.9 AOV-graph before composition [21]

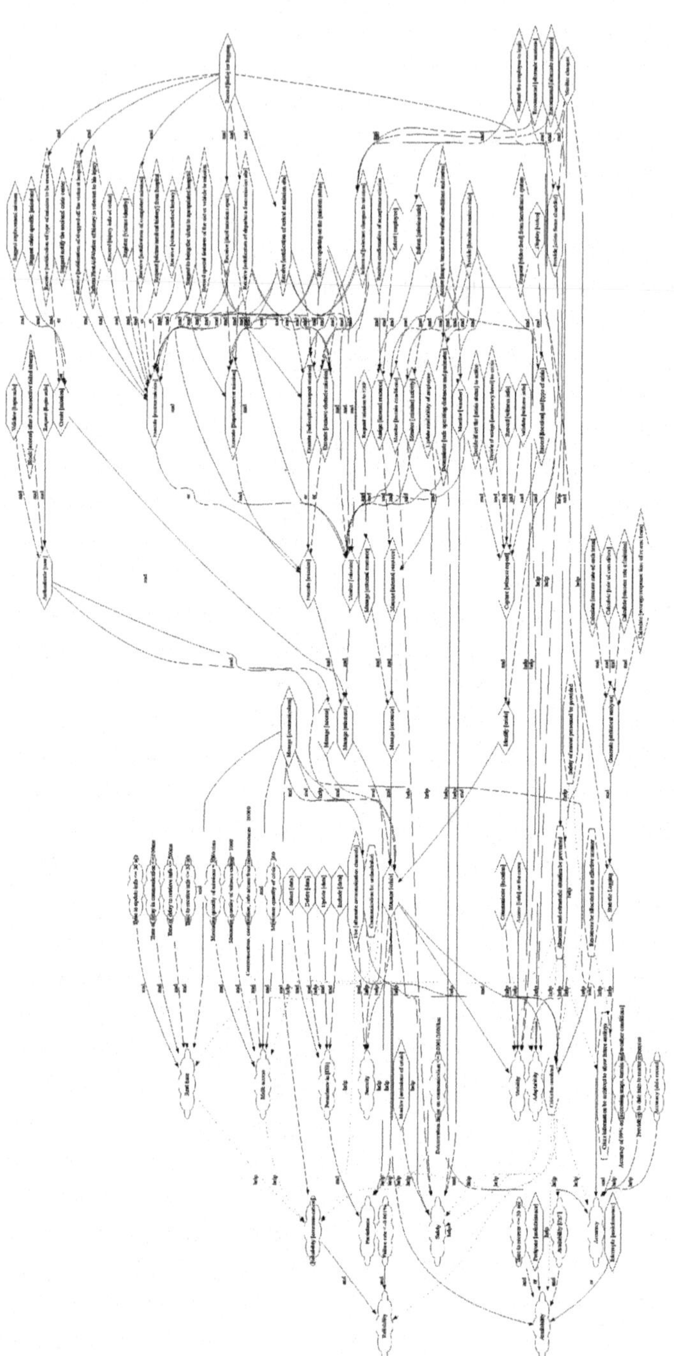

Fig. 6.10 AOV-graph after composition [21]

References

1. W.N. Robinson, S.D. Pawlowski, V. Volkov, Requirements interaction management. ACM Comput. Surv. **35**(2), 132–190 (2003)
2. B. Tekinerdoğan, A. Moreira, J. Araújo, P. Clements, Early aspects: aspect-oriented requirements engineering and architecture design, in *Proceedings of the Early Aspects Workshop at AOSD*, ed. by B. Tekinerdoğan, A. Moreira, J. Araújo, P. Clements, 2004, pp. 3–14
3. M. Jackson, P. Zave, Distributed feature composition: a virtual architecture fortelecommunications services. IEEE Trans. Softw. Eng. **24**(10), 831–847 (1998)
4. L. Chung et al., *Non-functional Requirements in Software Engineering* (Kluwer Academic, Boston, MA, 2000)
5. J. Kienzle, N. Guelfi, S. Mustafiz, Crisis management systems a case study for aspect-oriented modeling. Resource document. TAOSD Special Issue (2009), http://www.cs.mcgill.ca/~joerg/taosd/TAOSD/TAOSD_files/AOM_Case_Study.pdf. Accessed 26 Aug 2011
6. Y. Yu, J. Leite, J. Mylopoulos, From goals to aspects: discovering aspects from requirements goal models, in *Proceedings of the 12th IEEE International Symposium on Requirements Engineering*, ed. by N. Maiden, 2004, pp. 38–47
7. L.F. Silva, J.C.S.P. Leite, An aspect-oriented approach to model requirements, in *Proceedings of the Requirements Engineering Doctoral Consortium, 13th IEEE International Requirements Engineering Conference*, ed. by N. Day, Paris, France, 2005
8. L.F. Silva, An aspect-oriented strategy for requirements modeling (in Portuguese), Theses, Pontificia Universidade Católica do Rio de Janeiro, 2006, http://www.2.dbd.puc-rio.br/pergamum/biblioteca/php/mostrateses.php?open=1&arqtese=0210666_06_Indice.html. Accessed 26 Aug 2011
9. L.F. Silva, J.C.S.P. Leite, Generating requirements views: a transformation-driven approach, in *Electronic Communications of the East: 3rd Workshop on Software Evolution Through Transformations*, ed. by R. Heckel, J. Favre, T. Mens. ISSN 1863–212, vol. 3, 1–14, 2006, http://www.journal.ub.tu-berlin.de/eceasst/issue/view/3. Accessed 26 Aug 2011
10. G. Kiczales, E. Hilsdale, J. Hugunin, M. Kersten, J. Palm, W. Griswold, An overview of Aspectj, in *Proceedings of the European Conference On Object-Oriented Programming*, ed. by J.L. Knudsen, 2001, pp. 327–254
11. J. Mylopoulos, L. Chung, B. Nixon, Representing and using nonfunctional requirements: a process-oriented approach. IEEE Trans. Softw. Eng. **18**(6), 483–497 (1992)
12. A. Lamsweerde, E. Letier, Handling obstacles in goal-oriented requirements engineering. IEEE Trans. Softw. Eng. **26**(10), 978–1005 (2000)
13. B. Gonzalez, M. Laguna, J.C.S.P. Leite, J. Mylopoulos, Visual variability analysis with goal models, in *Proceedings of the 12th IEEE International Symposium on Requirements Engineering*, ed. by N. Maiden, 2004, pp. 198–207
14. P. Giorgini et al., Reasoning with goal models, in *Proceedings of the 21st International Conference on Conceptual Modelling*, ed. by S. Spaccapietra, S.T. March, Y. Kambayashi, 2002, pp. 167–181
15. J.C.S.P. Leite, Y. Yu, L. Liu, E.S.K. Yu, J. Mylopoulos, Quality-based software reuse, in *Proceedings of the Conference on Advanced Information Systems Engineering*, ed. by O. Pastor, J. Falcão e Cunha. LNCS, vol. 3520 (Springer, 2005), pp. 535–550
16. Aspectj (2011), Aspectj Project, http://www.eclipse.org/aspectj/. Accessed 26 Aug 2011
17. L.F. Silva, T.V. Batista, A. Garcia, A.L. Medeiros, L. Minora, On the symbiosis of aspect-oriented requirements and architectural descriptions, in *Proceedings of the 10th International Conference on Early Aspects: Current Challenges and Future Directions*, ed. by EDITORES, 2007, pp. 75–93
18. L. Santos, L.F. Silva, T. Batista, On the integration of the feature model and Pl-Aovgraph, in *Proceedings of the 2011 International Workshop on Early Aspects*, ed. by EDITORES, 2011, pp. 31–36

19. P. Greenwood et al., On the contributions of an end-to-end AOSD Testbed, in *Proceedings of the Workshop in Aspect-Oriented Requirements Engineering and Architecture Design at ICSE*, ed. by EDITORES, 2007, p. 8
20. E. Figueiredo et al., Detecting architecture instabilities with concern traces: an exploratory study, in *Proceedings of the WICSA/ECSA*, ed. by EDITORES, 2009, pp. 261–264
21. L.F. Silva, CMS AOVgraph, http://https://sites.google.com/site/lyrene/. Accessed 24 Apr 2013
22. R. Chitchyan, P. Greenwood, A. Sampaio, A. Rashid, A. Garcia, L. Silva, Semantic vs. syntactic compositions in aspect-oriented requirements engineering: an empirical study, in *Proceedings of the 8th ACM International Conference on Aspect-Oriented Software Development*, ed. by A. Garcia, N. Niu, A. Moreira, J. Araujo, 2009, pp. 149–160

Chapter 7
Aspect Composition in Problem Frames

Maria Lencastre, João Araújo, Ana Moreira, and Jaelson Castro

Abstract Problem frames (PFs) is a problem domain-oriented approach, focusing on understanding the problem, instead of its design solutions. PFs support the identification of problem domains, provide mechanisms to analyse and structure problems and promote reusability by dealing with different types of known problems. The motivation for this work is the early evidence that Jackson's problem frames include many scattered and tangled model elements that correspond to crosscutting requirements. This chapter offers specific guidelines to define and compose crosscutting concerns in PFs. The proposed approach uses a specification template for aspectual requirements and abstract problem diagrams. The advantage lays on providing support for modularization of requirements and domain knowledge.

7.1 Introduction

Problem frames (PFs) is a problem domain-oriented approach, aiming at focusing users' attention on the problem at hand instead of premature design solutions. PFs provide a way to analyse and structure problems, rather than modelling requirements by using more subjective concepts, such as goals and dependencies [1]. They support the identification of problem domains and their types, supplying rational principles for problem analysis. Indeed, PFs provide specific guidance on how to deal with different types of known problems, therefore promoting reusability [1].

M. Lencastre (✉)
Escola Politécnica de Pernambuco, Universidade Estadual de Pernambuco, Recife, Brazil
e-mail: maria@dsc.upe.br

J. Araújo • A. Moreira
Departamento de Informática, Universidade Nova de Lisboa, Caparica, Portugal
e-mail: joao.araujo@fct.unl.pt; amm@fct.unl.pt

J. Castro
Centro de Informática, Universidade Federal de Pernambuco, Recife, Brazil

A. Moreira et al. (eds.), *Aspect-Oriented Requirements Engineering*,
DOI 10.1007/978-3-642-38640-4_7,

PFs emphasize that the best way to solve a complex problem is to decompose it—not only does a good decomposition help to solve a problem but also to understand it better. Each decomposed subproblem has its own concern and projections of the world and of the system, taken from the original problem. Subproblems can include parallel structures and also be composite problem frames; two or more subproblems can be concurrent, and this can be considered a composition concern.

Despite considering modularity, the Problem Frames approach does not include a specific way to deal with scattered problems, as Aspect-Oriented Requirements Engineering (AORE) does. The concept of an aspect as "a concern that cuts across the base modules derived from the dominant separation of concerns criterion, plus automated support to weave the separately described aspects back into the base modules" [2] is not present in PFs. PFs simply propose their definition as problem diagrams.

Crosscutting concerns usually affect large portions of requirements models, compromising their modularity and consequently their evolution. Models built using PFs approach are no exception. There are requirements that appear in many (sub) problems diagrams, so they are scattered among several diagrams. Some of them match well-known problems and, in this case, the correlation of these requirements to the appropriate existing, and known, problem frame is a natural consequence of Jackson's proposal.

In this chapter we show how to deal with PF's corresponding problems' information in the aspect-oriented context and how to compose the aspects with the model elements they crosscut in order to allow their future recomposition. We illustrate the approach using a subset of the Crisis Management System (CMS) [3], the Car Crash Crisis Management System (CCMS).

The remainder of this chapter is organized as follows. Section 7.2 presents an overview of PFs. Section 7.3 introduces an aspect-oriented approach for PFs and Sect. 7.4 applies that approach to the CCMS, showing a proof-of-concept example. Section 7.5 presents some related work and Sect. 7.6 draws some conclusions.

7.2 Problem Frames Overview

Problem Frames are a software engineering approach appropriate for describing problem domains, defining requirements and decomposing a problem into subproblems [1]. Problem frames clearly separate the description of the problem from its solution. Both problem and solution descriptions are based on domains, which are composed of phenomena, and their interactions. A domain can be thought of as a collection of related phenomena (such as entities, events and states), which represent part of a physical domain in the world where the effects, that is the phenomena, are observable. A machine domain is a domain that must be designed and built, in the form of software, to solve a problem. *Problem frames* are problem patterns that aim at facilitating problem identification and solution (each problem pattern presents the associated frame, characteristics, difficulties and solution methods). The steps for building a PFs specification are (1) draw the problem's context diagram; (2) describe problems and subproblems diagrams and (3) decompose subproblems until each subproblem is simple enough to be seen as an instance of a recognized problem frame.

Next we will illustrate all the three PFs' diagrams, using the CCMS, which handles car crash management. Afterwards we discuss the approach and present some extensions (related to problem composition).

7.2.1 *Problem Frames Diagrams*

The PFs approach includes three main diagrams for requirements elicitation and for denoting the intermediate results in requirements specification development: the *Context diagram* structures and delimits the problem; the *Problem diagram* defines the requirements that need to be satisfied for the problem at hand; the *Frame diagram* (also called *Problem frame* diagram) describes familiar subproblem classes, previously documented in PFs notation, that an application to be developed could rely on.

7.2.1.1 Context Diagram

The aim of the context diagram is to structure and delimit the problem as separated domains, together with the machine to be built—the system—denoted by a rectangle with a double vertical line. This diagram also shows how these domains interact with one another through the interface of shared phenomena.

Figure 7.1 illustrates an example for the CCMS, where the main domain representing the system is the *CarCrash* domain and the other ones are *Witness*, *Coordinator*, *SuperObserver*, *SurveillanceSystem*, *PhoneCompany*, *ExternalResourceSystem*, *Worker* (e.g. paramedics, police), *Victim*, and the *CrisisScenario*. The interactions between these domains are represented by the text between brackets linking the domains, i.e., the respective phenomena. The interactions are built based on the descriptions adapted from the original requirements document [3]. An example of an interaction is discussed next.

"A crisis occurs, representing a real scenario; a *Witness* contacts the *Coordinator*, which captures his/hers report, and confirms through the system (CCMS) the *Witness*' given data, a service supplied by the *PhoneCompany* services. If necessary, the *Coordinator* asks the CCMS a video about the local of the crisis, available through a request to the *SurveillanceSystem*". The interface phenomena are *ScenarioInfo*, *WitnessReport*, *WitnessInfo*, *Address*, *Phone*, *RequestVideo* and *Video*.

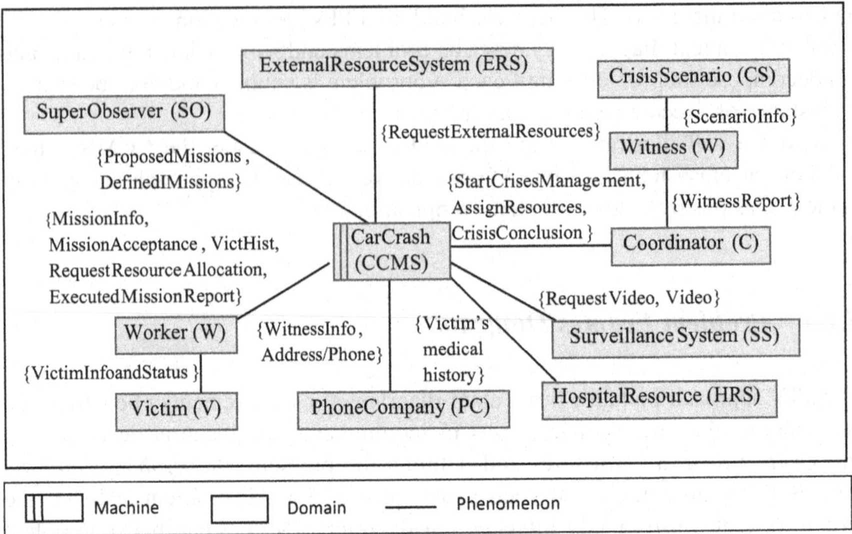

Fig. 7.1 Context diagram for car crash management system

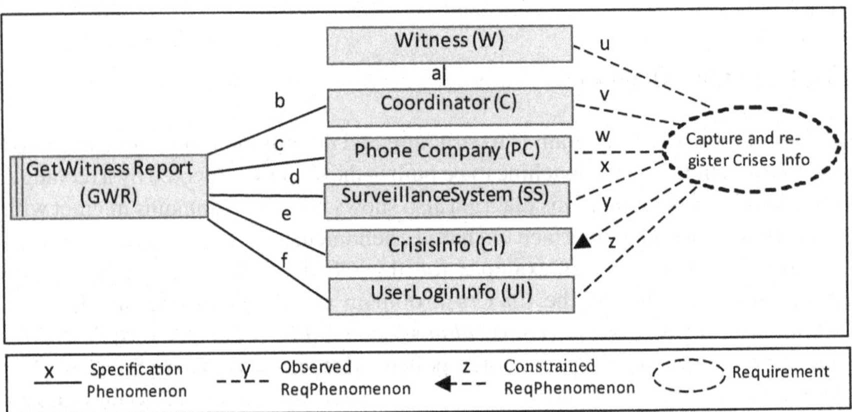

Fig. 7.2 Problem diagram for *GetWitnessReport*

7.2.1.2 Problem Diagram

Problem requirements provide a starting point for the problem analysis; they represent the machine, the requirements to be achieved and the interaction between the involved domains that are part of the problem on focus. Problem diagrams are developed for all the functionalities offered by CCMS. An example of a problem diagram is shown in Fig. 7.2, for the *GetWitnessReport* problem.

The *GetWitnessReport* problem can be detailed as: "a subsystem is needed to help the *Coordinator* to create a crisis record based on the information obtained

Table 7.1 Interaction phenomena for the problem *GetWitnessReport*

a	W! {WitnessInfo, CrisisInfo}
b	GWR!{CrisisCheckList} C! {GiveCrisisInfo (CrisisDetails, WitnessedTime), WitnessInfo (fname, lname, phone, address)} C! {AssignInitialEmergencyLevel, ActivateCrisisSatus}
c	GWR!{CheckWitnessInfo} PC!{WitnessInfoResult (phone,address)}
d	GWR! {RequestVideo (local, time)}, SS!{SendVideo}
e	GWR! StoreCrisisInfo
U	{Crisis witness report and info}
V	{Crisis activation, Witness info validated}
w	{SuppliesWitnessInfo}
X	{SuppliesCrisisVideo}
Y	{CrisisInfo stored}
z	{InformationChecked}

from a Witness". The dotted ellipse in the problem diagram of Fig. 7.2 represents the problem's requirement that defines what must be supported by the machine; the rectangles are the problem domains that interact with the machine *GetWitnessReport*. The interface phenomena, on the left-hand side, are expressed at the specification level (those with letters from "a" to "f"), and on the right hand side at requirements level (from "u" to "z"). Table 7.1 presents the corresponding interface phenomena also called shared phenomena, which represent the interaction between the involved domains, identifying the domain that makes the control.

The interface phenomena GWR! {CrisisCheckList}, detailed in letter "b", means that the subsystem GWR is controlling the CrisisCheckList and sending it to the *Coordinator*. Observe that the interface phenomena on the right-hand side are at the requirements level; if the requirements constrain a domain, a dotted line with an arrow is used; otherwise it is only a reference. Note, for example, that the constraint in *CrisisInfo* has only the stored information about confirmed crisis.

The Problem Diagram has a main concern, which is to get the witness report (capture and register info). However, a problem diagram also contemplates the idea of *particular concerns*, that is, *concerns* that are common to some or to almost all problems; but, these are secondary, not the main concerns of those problems. Such concerns arise from the nature of particular requirements or interfaces or problem domains. An example of a *particular concern* is the *AuthenticateUser* problem, which is common to several problems. Particular concerns are represented in specific problem diagrams, and the common domain represents the way both problems interact. This interaction among subproblems results in the composition of concerns that can be represented by a specific problem diagram addressing composition concerns.

The *AuthenticateUser* (*AU*) problem is presented in Fig. 7.3 and Table 7.2. The intention is to authenticate the *CMSEmployee* to allow its access to the system. The AU subsystem first requests *CMSE* for a login id and password. The *CMSE* enters his login id and password and the *AU* subsystem validates the login information

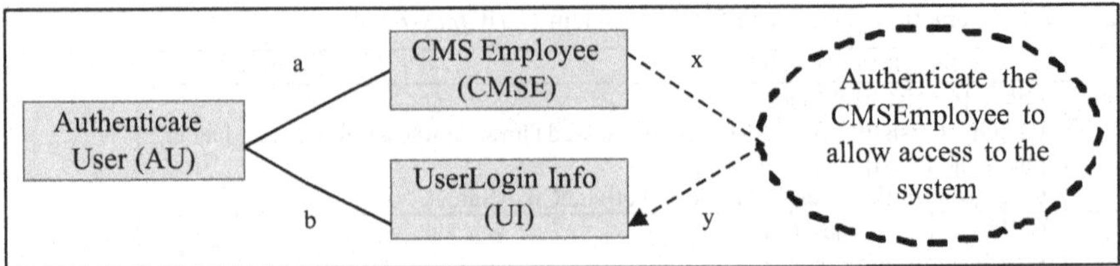

Fig. 7.3 *AuthenticateUser* problem diagram

Table 7.2 Interface phenomena of *AuthenticateUser* problem diagram

x: {RequestAccess, CancelAccess} {GetAccesstoSystem , notGetAccesstoSystem}
a: {AU!PromptsforLogin, CMSE!EntersLoginandPssw}
{AU!Allowsaccess, notAllowaccess}
{CMS!CancelAuthenticationProcess}
b: {AU!ValidateInfo}
y: {InformationChecked}

with the *UserLoginInfo* previous registered. Observe that the *CMSE* can cancel the authenticate process access if s/he so wishes.

7.2.1.3 Problem Frame Diagram

The Problem Frame diagram represents a well-known, recurrent class of application problems. In our example, we introduce the *Request Management* problemframe, a class of problems where "a person requests the system, that is the machine, a service that is provided by an outside system (e.g. a public system), to which the main system is connected; the results are returned as resources". Figure 7.4 details this problem frame. The diagram includes types of domains and phenomena. For example the B, in the *Person* box, states that the domain is Biddable (meaning that it has unpredictable behaviour), the C in *ServiceProvider* states that this domain is Causal (meaning that its properties can be formally described and are expected to hold) and the X in *Resource* informs that the domain is lexical (i.e. symbolic). The shared phenomena are also presented in an abstract form.

Table 7.3 presents the corresponding interface phenomena. While "x" represents phenomena at requirements level, defining that a person requests a service and that specific information (the "requiredInformation") will be needed, "a" represents a phenomenon at the specification level, explicitly defining which domain is responsible by the interaction and what is the object of the interaction. For example, in the case of P! {RequestService} we can observe that it is followed by "[causal]" which indicates that it is a command that is sent by the Person, but P!{RequestInfo [symbolic]} shows that an information is being sent by the person, as "[symbolic]"

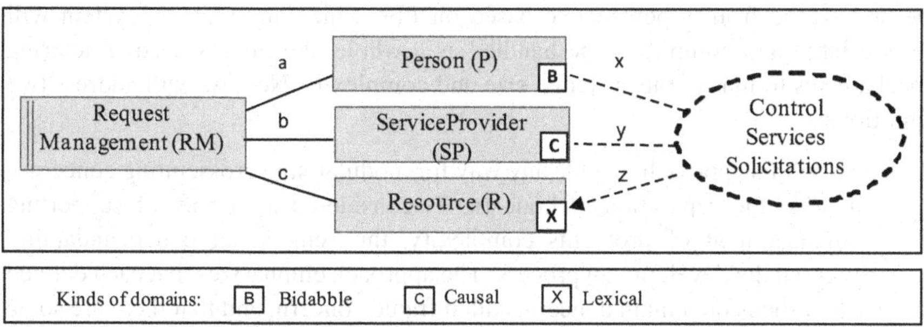

Fig. 7.4 Request management problem frame

Table 7.3 Interaction phenomena for the RequestManagement problem frame

x	{RequestsService, requiredInformation}
a	P!{RequestService [causal]} RM!{RequestSpecificInfo [causal]} P!{RequiredInfo [simbolyc]}
y	{Requested for Service and Services Provider}
b	RM!{RequestService [causal]} SP!{ConfirmService [symbol], ResourceInfo [symbol]}
z	{RegisteredResourceInfo [symbol]}
c	RM! {DatastoredforResource }
Obs: marks for kinds of phenomena: [symbol] for data and [causal] for commands	

represents phenomenon that is a representation of physical data. The logic for the appropriate sequence of the phenomena interaction will only be present in the argumentation of the main frame concern.

An example of a problem in CCMS that matches this problem frame is: when the Coordinator requests a video to the CCMS related to what occurs at the location of the crisis, at the respective time, this service is only available through a specific request to the Surveillance System—an outside system.

In the PFs approach, concerns are also "aspects of a problem demanding the developer's attention" [1]. In the next subsection we will make some considerations about PFs, considering also the motivation and concepts from Aspect-Oriented Requirement Engineering (AORE).

7.2.2 *Analysing How the PFs Approach Addresses Crosscutting Concerns and Composition*

In [4] the author says that aspect technology may offer some utility in understanding and implementing problem composition and specification; in turn, the goals of aspect technology can be clarified through the analysis of how problems may be understood from a perspective based on PFs. Since any realistic system will be too large and complex to be handled as a whole, developers need structuring mechanisms to master the systems' size and complexity. Next we will address two questions:

1. Does the PFs approach include any way for modularising crosscutting concerns?

   In PFs, the separation of concerns is considered as a way of supporting the management of problems complexity, thus enhancing understandability throughout the development process. The approach emphasizes that each defined problem focus on a main concern, called frame concern, and that there are some other secondary concerns (also part of the problem), which are generally present in several other problems—what Jackson calls particular concerns. This attempt of removing the scattering parts of the problems to specific problem diagram could result in the same problem analysed in [2], caused by the introduction of implicit tangling between the newly separated problem diagrams (concerns) and the other concerns (the main problem diagram).

   Conclusion: Jackson's proposal could also be problematic: the analyst cannot tell, without an exhaustive search, which problems the scattered properties (problems) affect. In the CCMS example, the *AuthenticateUser* problem can be seen as the one which has scattered properties in the system. As pointed out in [2], the aspect-oriented solution makes the impact explicit by modularizing aspects into two parts: one that describes the requirements of the aspect concern itself and another that describes the breadth of its impact.
2. Is the PFs' composition enough to represent composition rules?

   The original PFs approach [1] does not propose explicit ways to compose problems. It mentions only that the composition could be made through the interaction of different problems through common domains, and interaction among subproblems gives rise to composition concerns, such as precedence and parallelism. Other works on PFs address the question of how to combine the solutions structures of the simple subproblems to obtain a solution structure for a complex problem. In [5] the idea of an architectural frame, called an AFrame (a combination of known architectural styles, such as pipe-lines, with problem frames), is introduced as an elaboration of the problem frame diagram to accommodate an early architectural decision. So, the decomposition is guided by the chosen architecture and many composition requirements become trivial. In [6] the task of composing conflicting requirements is addressed using the Composition Frame, which includes the specification of a composition controller (like an architectural connector) to solve requirement which are in conflict. In [7] the authors present a pattern-based software development process using problem frames and corresponding architectural patterns. In [8], the authors present a lightweight approach to dealing with behavioural inconsistencies at run-time. Requirement Composition operators are introduced that specify a run-time prioritization to be used on occurrence of a feature interaction.

   Conclusion: PFs composition alternatives help composition process, however there is no way of defining a specific point—an aspect—for gathering what is scattered. Consequently, there is no way of representing composition rules for the logic that is gathered in an aspect.

We will show that PFs can be improved by the aspect-oriented concepts to encapsulate scattered data (domains, phenomena and requirements) hence achieving better modularisation. Next subsection builds on this by extending PFs to specify aspects. Due to the difficulty of managing PFs diagrams (the involved syntax and semantic) and aiming at a future automation, a BNF [9] specification is proposed for the PFs diagrams and extensions for aspects incorporation.

7.3 Modelling and Composing PF Using Aspects

This section starts by discussing two crosscutting concepts in the problem frames approach, i.e. aspectual requirements and aspectual problem frames.

Aspectual requirements are proposed to encapsulate in a single form the scattered requirements that appear in many (sub)problems' diagrams; this therefore represents an extension of PFs approach. An example of an aspectual requirement is the *AuthenticateUser* problem, which is scattered in several problems, such as *GetWitnessReport* and *AssingInternalResources*.

Aspectual problem frames correspond to the matching of a known problem frame by more than one problem. What is innovative is that this allows addressing the aspectual requirements in a standardized way, through the problem frame. An example of this is the *RequestManagement* problem frame, which is used in several parts of our example, as in *WitnessInformationValidation*, *VideoRequest* and *VictimInfoRequest*. This occurs because all these examples match the *RequestManagement* problem frame, so we can use the pattern proposed by *RequestManagement* for all of them, instead of defining a specific aspectual requirement for each one.

This section also explores how to represent and compose aspects in PFs using aspect composition rules. Although different works on PFs focus on how to combine the solution structures of simple subproblems to obtain a solution structure for a more complex problem, once again they do not deal with crosscutting concerns. Next we will detail the whole proposed process.

7.3.1 *Process for Modelling and Composing Aspects*

Figure 7.5 depicts an approach for modelling and composing problem frames using aspects. This approach is based on our previous work [10] and consists of three major steps: build the problem frames specification, identify aspectual elements, modularise and specify aspects. Each one of these steps is explained next.

1. **Build the problem frames specification**. This activity includes the following three steps: drawing the context diagram to determine where the problem is

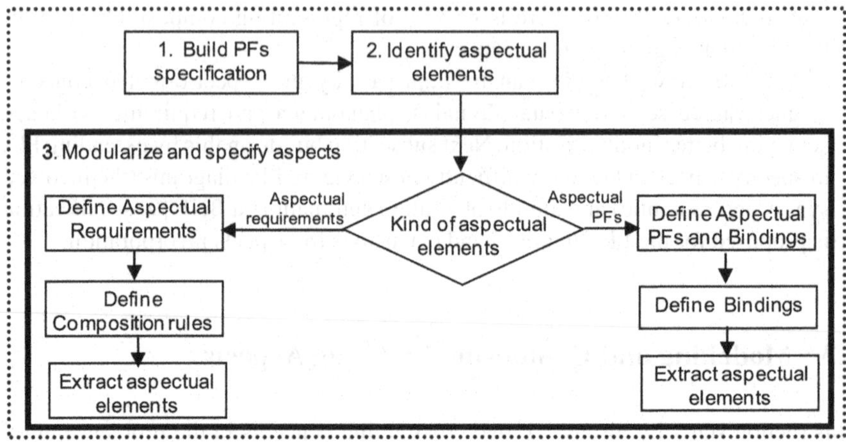

Fig. 7.5 Process for modelling and composing problem frames using aspects

```
Create aspectReq
 <aspectual requirement name> for
 <crossproblem name> which appears in
 <problem name>, <problem name>, {<problem name>};
```

Fig. 7.6 Specification of an aspectual requirement

located, as well as the parts of the world it considers; defining the problem requirements, providing a starting point for the problem analysis; representing each requirement using a problem diagram. Observe that each problem must be decomposed into simpler and smaller (sub)problems, and problem analysis continues until each problem is simple enough to be seen as an instance of a recognized class of problems, that is, a problem frame.

2. **Identify aspectual elements**. Aspectual elements may be aspectual requirements or aspectual problem frames. Here the match between problems and a problem frames must be listed.
3. **Modularise and specify aspects**. Each aspectual element, identified in step 2, is specified, and composition rules are defined for it.

   Thus, for each identified **aspectual requirement**:

- Modularise and specify it using the specification template presented in Fig. 7.6. To achieve this, create a new name for this specification (of an aspectual requirement), defines the name of the *crossproblem* (i.e. scattered problem) and enumerate the names of the base problems crosscut by this crossproblem.
- Define composition rules to capture how the crosscut problems are recomposed (aspect weaving), to represent again the original problems. Figure 7.7 illustrates this definition.

```
Compose problem <problem name> with <aspectual requirement name>
Add domain <domain name>
Connect <domain name> to machine <machine domain>
Add specPhen <phenomenon name> between
 machine and domain <domain name>, {, <phenomenon name> between
 machine and <domain name>}
Add reqPhenObserved  <phenomenon name> domain <domain name>, {,
 <phenomenon name> between requirement and domain <domain name>};
Add reqPhenConstrained  <phenomenon name> domain <domain name>,
 {, <phenomenon name> domain <domain name>};
```

Fig. 7.7 Specification of composition rules for an aspectual requirement

```
Create aspectualProblemFrame <aspectual Problem Frame name>
related to <problemFrame name>
which appears in problems <problem name>, <problem name>
 {,<problem name>};
```

Fig. 7.8 Specification of an aspectual problem frame

```
Bind machine <problem frame machine name> to <problem machine name>
Bind domain <problem frame domain name> to <problem domain name>
 {, domain <problem frame domain name> to <problem domain name>}
Bind requirement <problem frame requirement name> to <problem re
 quirement name>
Bind specPhen <problem frame phenomenon name> to <problem phenomenon
 name> between machine and <domain name>
 {,<problem frame phenomenon name> to <problem phenomenon name>
 between machine and domain <domain name>}
Bind reqPhenObserved <problem frame phenomenon name> to <problem
 phenomenon name> domain <domain name> {,<problem frame phenomenon
 name> to <phenomenon name> domain <domain name>}
Bind reqPhenConstrained <problem frame phenomenon name> to <problem
 phenomenon name> domain <domain name>{,<problem frame phenomenon
 name> to <problem phenomenon name> domain <domain name>}
```

Fig. 7.9 Specification of composition for aspectual problem frame

- Extract the corresponding aspectual elements from subproblems, where the aspectual requirements are found, since they will be represented through the composition rules associated with this aspectual requirement.

Similarly, for each identified **aspectual problem frame**:

- Define it giving the list of problems that this specific problem frame crosscuts (use the specifications template presented in Fig. 7.8).
- Define the composition rule, by instantiating it to each concrete solution (use the specification template presented in Fig. 7.9).
- Extract the corresponding aspectual elements from subproblems, where the aspectual problem frame was found.

Next we will concentrate on the third step of the process, which modularises and specifies aspects.

7.3.2 Aspectual Requirements Specification

The specification of an aspectual requirement is shown in the template presented in Fig. 7.6. The specification includes the definition of:

- The aspectual requirement name, which must be unique, and represents the aspect that is being defined.
- The crossproblem name, that is, the one which appears scattered along several other problems; the name of the problem where the cross problem appears. Note that there must be at least two problems crosscut by the cross problem.

In order to complete the process of the aspectual requirements definition, composition rules are specified to register how to re-establish connections between domains and phenomena which will be removed from the original problems (crosscut by an aspectual requirement). The composition rule specification template is presented in Fig. 7.7. Three operators are available: *compose*, *connect* and *add*. The *compose* operator is used to re-establish the link between an existing problem and an aspectual requirement which crosscuts it. The rule includes the addition of involved domains, present in the aspectual requirement; the *connect* operator to define the link between the existing machine that attends the requirement which is been analysed and the *add* operator for the addition of phenomena at both requirement and specification levels.

7.3.3 Aspectual Problem Frames Specification

For the representation of an aspectual PF we rely on the specification template illustrated in Fig. 7.8. It includes arguments such as the name given for the *aspectualProblemFrame* name, the *problemFrame* name which appears in several other problems and the names of problems where the PF appears.

The definition of composition rules, for the aspectual problem frame, is also needed. As shown in Fig. 7.9, this composition consists of a set of instantiation steps, where abstract elements are replaced with concrete elements through the *Bind* command (that simply makes the correlation of problem frame elements and the matched problems).

7.4 Proof-of-Concept Example

We now illustrate the process depicted in Fig. 7.5, detailing each step building for a proof-of-concept using the CCMS.

7.4.1 Build Problem Frames Specification

This step consists of four other substeps: draw the context diagram (Sect. 7.2.1.1); define requirements; describe problems and subproblems, representing each requirement using a problem diagram; and identify matching subproblems and problem frames. The context diagram was presented in Fig. 7.1. The remaining substeps are discussed next.

7.4.1.1 Define Requirements

Requirements will be the starting point for the problem analysis; they will define subproblems that must be solved through the construction of a subsystem. The main concerns of the CCMS application represent the key requirements: get witness report; start a crisis management; define missions adequate to solve a crisis; request services; assign resources (internal and external); execute missions; conclude a crisis management; user authentication; etc.

7.4.1.2 Describe Problem and Subproblems

In order to illustrate this step we will focus on the *GetWitnessReport* problem, presented in Sect. 7.2.1.2. Recall that the purpose is to build a system that helps the Coordinator creating a crisis record based on the information obtained from a witness. The *GetWitnessReport* problem can be defined using the specification in Fig. 7.10, which requires information from the respective problem diagram (Fig. 7.2 and Table 7.1). This specification format helps us maintaining a specification pattern similar to the aspects specification, which will be presented next. Afterwards, information that can be represented as an aspect will be removed from this specification (see Fig. 7.11).

GetWitnessReport can be further decomposed into the following subproblems:

1. *WitnessInformationValidation*: *Coordinator* inserts witness information in the System (location and type of crisis and witness information) and this checks the validation of the witness information.
2. *Video Request*: if the crisis location is covered by camera surveillance, a video is requested to the *Surveillance System.* Then the coordinator confirms, or not, the situation that the witness describes.

```
Create Problem with
Machine GetWitnessReport GWR
Requirement {Capture and Register Crises Info}
Add domain {Witness W, Coordinator C, PhoneCompany P, Surveillance
 System SS, CrisisInfo CI, UserLoginInfo UI}
Add specPhen {WitnessInfo, CrisisInfo}between domain W and domain C,
 {CrisisCheckList} between domain GWR and domain C
 {RequestAccess, CancelAccess, GiveCrisisInfo (CrisisDetails, Witnes
 sedTime), WitnessInfo (fname, lname, phone, address)} between
 domain C and domain GWR,
 {AssignInitialEmergencyLevel, ActivateCrisisSatus} between domain C
 and domain GWR,
 {CheckWitnessInfo} between domain GWR and domain PC,
 {WitnessInfoResult (phone,address)} between domain PC and
 domain PC,
 {RequestVideo(local,time)} between domain GWR and domain SS,
 {SendVideo} between domain SS and domain CWR,
 {StoreCrisisInfo} between domain GWR and domain CI,
Add reqPhenObserved {Crisis witness report and info} domain W,
 {Crisis activation, Witness info validated, GetAcesstoSystem, not
 GetAccesstoSystem} domain C
 SuppliesWitnessInfo domain PC, SuppliesCrisisVideo} domain SS
 {Information Validated} domain AU
Add reqPhenConstrained {CrisisInfo stored} domain CI;
```

Fig. 7.10 Specification for GetWitnessReport problem

```
Create aspectreq AuthUser_aspect for AuthenticateUser
which appears in {GetWitnessReport,AssignInternalResource};
```

Fig. 7.11 Specification of AuthUser aspectual requirement

3. *GetCrisesInformation*: system provides crisis-focused checklists (type of crisis, local) and the *Coordinator* provides crisis information.
4. *Crisis Activation*: the system assigns an initial emergency level to the crisis and sets the crisis status to active.
5. *AuthenticateUser*: the system shall authenticate users on the basis of the access policies when they first access any components or information (this functionality was not present in the original example; we included it here to help illustrating the process).

7.4.1.3 Identify Matching Problem Frames

The problem frames that match the existing subproblems are defined in Table 7.4. The *RequestManagement* problem frame (from Fig. 7.3 and Table 7.2) can be used to request a video from Surveillance System (an external system)—Video

Table 7.4 Subproblems and problem frames that match them

Subproblem	Problem Frames
WitnessInformationValidation	*RequestManagement*
VideoRequest	*RequestManagement*
GetCrisesInformation	*SimpleWorkpieces*
CrisisActivation	*SimpleWorkpieces*

Table 7.5 Aspectual requirements and aspectual problem frames

Aspectual element	Subproblem	Kind of aspect
RequestManagement	*WitnessInformationValidation* *VideoRequest, CarCrashRescue,* *RequestVictimInfotoHospital,* *PhoneRequestManagementSystem*	Aspectual PF
SimpleWorkpiece	*GetCrisis Info*	Aspectual PF
AuthenticateUser	*GetWitnessReport* *AssingInternalResources*	Aspectual Requirement

Request subproblem; and the same occurs with *WitnessInformationValidation* the subproblem, which requests witness data from the Phone Company. On the other hand, *GetCrisisInformation* and *Crisis Activation* can be represented as a *Simple Workpieces* problem frame presented in [1], where system's users send commands to an edition tool, which in turn updates or queries a specific stored data.

7.4.2 *Identify Aspectual Elements*

Table 7.5 classifies different sub(problems), considering if they are aspectual requirements or aspectual problem frames. Several (sub)problems were analysed from the whole CCMS, and three aspectual elements were selected to help to illustrate the process: *RequestManagement, SimpleWorkpiece* and *AuthenticateUser*.

7.4.2.1 Modularise and Specify Aspects

In PFs, the identification of crosscutting aspectual requirements can be done through the observation of the associations between the subproblems' concerns that crosscut each other. The aspects specification can be defined using the specification language proposed in [10]. This step is divided into two other steps, one for aspectual requirements and another for aspectual problem frames. Both cases are detailed next.

Table 7.6 Aspectual requirements elements

Subproblem	Aspectual requirement
GetWitnessReport	*AuthenticateUser*
AssignInternalResources	*AuthenticateUser*

```
Compose problem GetWitnessReport with AuthUser_aspect
Add domain UserLoginInfo UI
Connect UI to machine GetWitnessReport GWR
Add specPhen {PromptsforLogin, GetAccesstoSystem (result}
 between domain GWR and domain CMSEmployee,
 {EntersLoginandPssw, CancelAuthenticationProcess} between
 domain CMSEmployee and domain GWR,
 {ValidateInfo} between domain GWR and domain UI
Add reqPhenObserved {GetAccesstoSystem, notGetAccesstoSystem}
domain CMSEmployee
Add reqPhenConstrained InformationChecked domain UI};
```

Fig. 7.12 Specification of composition rules for aspectual requirement

```
Remove domain {UserLoginInfo (UI)}from problem GetWitnessReport
Remove specPhen
 {RequestAccess, CancelAcces} between domain C and domain GWR,
Remove reqPhenObserved
 {Information Validated} domain UI
```

Fig. 7.13 Elements extraction from *GetWitnessReport* using AutheUser _ aspect

7.4.2.2 Aspectual Requirements

In our example we specify the aspectual requirement *AuthenticateUser* which is present in *GetWitnessReport* and *Assign Internal Resources* (see Table 7.6).

The *AuthenticateUser* problem is represented in Fig. 7.3 and Table 7.2. Then, we can modularise and specify the aspectual requirement using the proposed specification template (presented in Fig. 7.11).

After, we can define composition rules to capture how an aspect affects the model elements it crosscuts, using the specification template presented in Fig. 7.12. The goal is to show how to recompose the *AuthenticateUser* with *GetWitnessReport* problem.

Moreover, we can extract the corresponding aspectual elements from subproblems where they were found. This corresponds to checking for related model elements, that is, the domains and phenomena that are part of it (see Fig. 7.13). In our example we use the *GetWitnessReport* and extract elements related to *AuthenticateUser* problem (from Fig. 7.3).

Figure 7.14 presents the *GetWitnessReport* diagram after removing the elements identified in Fig. 7.13, which are related to *AuthenticateUser*.

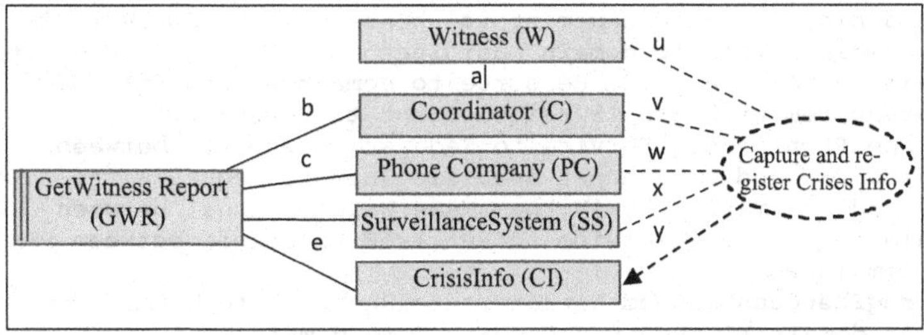

Fig. 7.14 *GetWitnessReport* after Elements extraction from *AuthenticateUser*

Table 7.7 Aspectual problem frames (the match of subproblems and problem frames)

Subproblem	Aspectual problem frames
WitnessInformation Validation	*RequestManagement*
VideoRequest	*RequestManagement*
CarCrashRescue	*RequestManagement*
Request VictimInfotoHospital	*RequestManagement*
PhoneRequestManagementSystem	*RequestManagement*

```
Create aspectualProblemFrame RequestManagement_aspProblFrame
related to RequestManagement
which appears in problems
  {ValidateWitnessInformation,  RequestVideo, CarCrashRescue,
  Request VictimInfotoHospital, PhoneRequestManagementSystem};
```

Fig. 7.15 Specification of an aspectual problem frame

7.4.2.3 Aspectual Problem Frames

We illustrate this step using *RequestManagement* aspectual problem frame, previous classified in Table 7.6. It corresponds to the problem frame presented in Fig. 7.3 and Table 7.2. It is described as "a worker (coordinator, or any worker) requests services through the system to a Service Provider, generally some specific information is required and must be supplied by the worker. At the end the service is provided, and the associated information is stored in the system database". Observe that *RequestManagement* problem frame matches several problems in CCMS (see Table 7.7), so it is considered an aspectual problem frame, specified in Fig. 7.15, considering the specification detailed in Fig. 7.8.

Figure 7.16 presents the binding of *PhoneRequestManagementSystem* to *RequestManagement* problem frame, whose specification was first detailed in Fig. 7.9. The result can be seen in Fig. 7.17 and Table 7.8, which presents the resulting problem diagram.

```
Bind machine RequestManagement to PhoneRequestManagement PRM
Bind domain Person to domain Coordinator C, ServiceProvider to
  domain PhoneCompany PC, Resource to domain WitnessInfo WI
Bind requirement ControlServiceRequest to VerifyWitnessInfo
Bind specPhen RequestService to RequestWitnessInfo between
  domains PRM and C, Request_Specific_Info to RequestWitnessInfo,
  RequiredInformation to {WitnessName,WitnessPhone} between C and
  domain PRM, RequestService to RetriveWitnessInfo between PRM
  and domain PC
Bind reqPhenConstrained DataStoredforResource to WitnessInfo-
  Stored domain WI, RegisterResourceInfo domain WI
Bind reqPhenObserved {Requests Service, required information} to
  {Requested for Service, PersonInformsatPhoneCompany}
```

Fig. 7.16 Specification of composition for aspectual problem frame

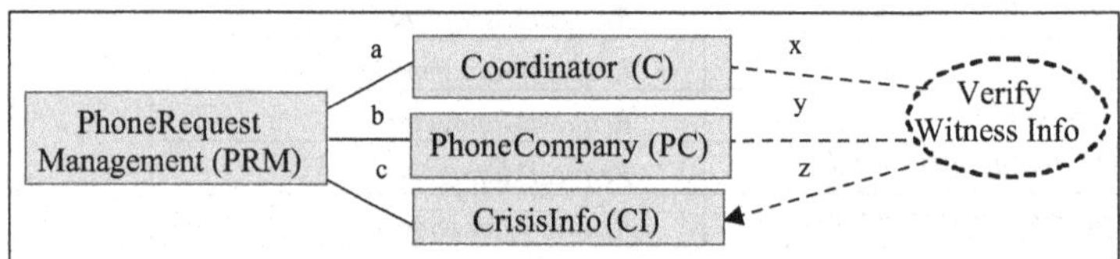

Fig. 7.17 Problem diagram PhoneRequestManagement based on RequestManagement aspectual PF

Table 7.8 Interaction phenomena for PhoneRequestManagement

A	PRM! {RequestWitnessInfo} C!{WitnessName, WitnessPhone}
B	PRP! {RetriveWitnessInfo} PC!{PhoneAdreess Record}
C	PRM!{StoreCirisisInfo}
X	Informs witness information
Y	PersonInfoatPhoneCompany
Z	WitnessInfoStored at the Crisis Management Database

After the composition was specified, the aspectual elements can be extracted from the original problems where they were found. We can observe that the elements could also be extracted from Fig. 7.10, where the *GetWitnessReport* was specified together with *PhoneRequestManagement*. This is done in a similar way as it was done in Fig. 7.13 Specification of Elements extraction from *GetWitnessReport* problem using *AuthUser_aspect*.

7.5 Related Work

In [11] it is described how to derive security requirements from crosscutting threat descriptions using the PFs approach. A threat description is a descriptive phrase of the form "*performing action X on asset Y could cause harm Z*"; the purpose is specific, it aims at illustrating how representing threats as crosscutting concerns aids in determining the effect of security requirements on the functional requirements.

Despite of existing efforts to facilitate the problem decomposition task and the combination of basic problem frame, there is in fact low knowledge and consensus about how effectively the PFs approach must analyse software complex problems and how to explore the decomposition in an aspectual sense. Our work contributes to narrow the gap between the concepts proposed for aspects [2].

Another form of composition was proposed in [12] where problem frames are composed together with MATA [13] sequence diagrams, to represent the composition scenarios for the PFs aspectual scenarios. The integration of MATA concepts with PF makes it possible to achieve a higher level of sophistication, giving support to more expressiveness in terms of aspects description, composition, and involved domains.

Regarding other AORE techniques, described in this book, we can make some comparison with the proposed approach.

The Requirements Description Language (RDL) uses textual specifications written in natural language for expressing the dependencies and interactions between requirements groups (e.g., use cases). RDL uses annotations, where these annotations are added to the syntactic elements of the natural language. They take advantage of the fact that each syntactic element has a selected semantic role. Our approach could be integrated with this approach where the requirements specifications in RDL would guide the construction of problem diagrams.

MATA is an expressive aspect modelling approach which represents aspects through patterns; it is also a composition language for structural and behavioural models. MATA supports a richer set of model composition operators in comparison with previous approaches to aspect-oriented modelling. Our work on PFs could benefit from the integration with MATA as presented in [12], by refining problem diagrams into scenarios, where the behaviour associated with an aspectual problem diagram could be specified using an aspectual scenario.

7.6 Conclusions

A central advantage of PFs is that problems can be broken into subproblems until a known problem class, previously documented and characterized by a problem frame, is identified. As proposed by Jackson [1], each problem frame is of a familiar and documented class, the concerns it raises can become, over time, fully documented and well known to the competent developers. These concerns may be associated with particular types of problem domain, of requirement or of relationship between the machine and the problem domains.

Considering the early evidence that Jackson's problem frames include many model elements that can be seen as aspects, this chapter outlines some specific guidelines to define and compose crosscutting concerns in PFs based on [10]. The proposed approach uses a specification template for aspectual requirements and abstract problem diagrams. The advantage lays on providing support for modularisation of requirements and domain knowledge. This approach [12] and the one proposed discussed here are complementary and their use can be chosen by the analyst, if s/he founds that it is possible and appropriate to define the elements that are crosscut by an aspect through a behaviour pattern or if it is better to enumerate the specific joinpoints.

The advantage of [12] approach lays on the fact that the integration of the MATA concepts with PFs gives support to more elegant and modularised way of representation and reuse. Also it makes possible to achieve a higher level of sophistication, allowing representing aspect concepts as patterns and achieving composition by combining those patterns using a set of operators. It gives support to more expressiveness in terms of aspects description, composition and involved domains, as it details structural and behavioural scenarios.

It is important to analyse what has been improved in relation to the original PFs approach. Some points that we can evaluate are based on the following questions:

- Could we distinguish how further the original PFs approach was far from the aspect approach? Many considerations were done about existing structures; and it was considered that PFs approach does not represent the full concept of aspects that helps improving modularity.
- Do we include concepts that could encapsulate crosscutting concerns in a single module? Yes, this was the proposed extension, the aspects were defined and the elements were removed from the places where they were scattered—including not only requirements (such as the example of Authenticate User) but also the involved domains and phenomena.

Some other questions arise but remain still unanswered after this study:

- Does the proposed extension introduce more simple diagrams for building or to interpret? Probably not, as other concepts were included.
- Has the number of diagrams increased or the complexity of diagrams reduced? Probably yes for both, but we need to apply metrics to evaluate those issues.
- Are the composition rules better than the other PFs composition existing alternatives? We need to carry on an empirical study to compare the alternatives.
- Is it simple to use the proposed approach without an appropriate tool? No, the proposed approach is not simple to be specified and managed if there is no available tool due to the involved details and complexity. The problem increases with the problems scalability.

All these questions must be evaluated in future work. Here we present only a first step.

References

1. M. Jackson, *Problem Frames: Analysing and Structuring Software Development Problem* (Addison-Wesley, New York, NY, 2001)
2. E. Baniassad, P. Clements, J. Araújo, A. Moreira, A. Rashid, B. Tekinerdogan, Discovering early aspects. IEEE Softw. **23**, 61–70 (2006)
3. J. Kienzle, N. Guelfi, S. Mustafiz, Crisis management systems: a case study for aspect-oriented modeling, in *Transactions on Aspect-Oriented Software Development VII*, ed. by S. Katz, M. Mezini (Springer, Berlin Heidelberg, 2010), pp. 1–22
4. M. Jackson, Problems, subproblems and concerns, Position Paper, in *Early Aspects Workshop at AOSD*, 2004
5. L. Rapanotti, J. Hall, M. Jackson, B. Nuseibeh, Architecture-driven problem decomposition, in *Proceedings of the 12th IEEE International RE'04*, Kyoto, 2004
6. R. Laney, L. Barroca, M. Jackson, B. Nuseibeh, Composing requirements using problem frames, in *Proceedings of the RE'04*, 2004, pp. 122–131
7. C. Choppy, D. Hatebur, M. Heisel, Component composition through architectural patterns for problem frames, in *XIII Asia Pacific Software Engineering Conference*, 2006
8. R. Laney, T. Thein, M. Jackson, B. Nuseibeh, Composing features by managing inconsistent requirements, in *Ninth International Conference on Feature Interactions in Software and Communication Systems ICFI'07*, 2007, pp. 141–156
9. BNF (2007), http://www.cui.unige.ch/db-research/Enseignement/analyseinfo/AboutBNF.html. Accessed 25 Aug 2007
10. M. Lencastre, J. Araújo, A. Moreira, J. Castro, Towards aspectual problem frames: an example. Expert Syst. J. **25**(1), 74–86 (2008). doi:10.1111/j.1468-0394.2008.00453.x (Blackwell Publishing Ltd. Expert Systems)
11. C. Haley, R. Laney, B. Nuseibeh, Deriving security requirements from crosscutting threat descriptions, in *Third International Conference on AOSD'04* (ACM Press, Lancaster, 2004)
12. M. Lencastre, A. Moreira, J. Araújo, J. Castro, Aspects composition in problem frames, in *16th IEEE International Requirements Engineering Conference*, Barcelona, 2008. IEEE CS Press Conference Proceedings, available at IEEE CS Digital Library, 2008
13. J. Whittle, P. Jayaraman, MATA: a tool for aspect-oriented modeling based on graph transformation, in *Workshop on Aspect Oriented Modeling at MODELS'07*, 2007

Part III
Domain-Specific Use of AORE

Chapter 8
Mapping Aspects from Requirements to Architecture

Pablo Sánchez, Ana Moreira, João Araújo, and Lidia Fuentes

Abstract Different approaches provide support for aspect-oriented requirements engineering and for architectural design. Thanks to the first, requirements can be elicited, analysed, and specified in an aspect-oriented fashion. Similarly, software architecture can be designed taking into account the aspectual nature of certain concerns, improving component modularisation and, therefore, component reusability and architecture evolution and adaptability. Nevertheless, these two kinds of approaches emerged in isolation. As a consequence, it is yet not clear how to derive an aspect-oriented architecture from an aspect-oriented requirements specification. This chapter describes *Model-Driven Development for Early Aspects* (MDD4EA), an approach that aims at automating this process by using model transformations. The whole process is illustrated with a subset of the Car Crisis Management System case study.

P. Sánchez (✉)
Dpto. Matemáticas, Estadística y Computación, Facultad de Ciencias, Universidad de Cantabria, Santander, Cantabria, Spain
e-mail: p.sanchez@unican.es

A. Moreira • J. Araújo
Departamento de Informática, Universidade Nova de Lisboa, Caparica, Portugal
e-mail: amm@di.fct.unl.pt; joao.araujo@fct.unl.pt

L. Fuentes
Dpto. Lenguajes y Ciencias de la Computación, ETSI Informática, Universidad de Málaga, Málaga, Spain
e-mail: lff@lcc.uma.es

A. Moreira et al. (eds.), *Aspect-Oriented Requirements Engineering*,
DOI 10.1007/978-3-642-38640-4_8,

8.1 Introduction

In the last decade, several approaches have appeared for handling crosscutting concerns at the requirements [3, 7, 8, 24, 33] and architectural design levels [4, 6, 29–31]. While aspect-oriented requirements approaches offer support to elicit, analyse, and model requirements taking into account their crosscutting nature early in the software development life cycle, aspect-oriented architectural languages help to improve the modularisation of software architectures, encapsulating crosscutting concerns, such as *Authentication* or *Integrity*, in particular kinds of components, which communicate with the other components by means of special composition mechanisms.

Although all this work has contributed to the support for aspect orientation throughout the software development process, little attention has been paid on how to construct an aspect-oriented software architecture from an aspect-oriented requirements specification. That is, there is a need to understand how to link these approaches together.

This chapter contributes to fill this gap by providing a process to automatically derive aspect-oriented software architectures from aspect-oriented requirements models by means of model transformations. The method proposed, *Model-Driven Development for Early Aspects*, uses AORA [9], an aspect-oriented requirements engineering approach and CAM [30], and an aspect-oriented architectural component model, although its underlying ideas can be used with different approaches.

The hypothesis for our work is as follows: most crosscutting concerns, such as *Integrity* or *Authenticity*, are recurrent across many different systems. In most cases, a solution that satisfies these crosscutting concerns can be described in a generic form, independently from the system where they are demanded. For instance, we can describe how to check *Integrity* of a message by simply assuming that there are generic messages that might be corrupted and therefore something needs to be done to ensure *Integrity*. Thus, what we need to do to satisfy a crosscutting concern is to analyse the predefined solutions that are currently available, select the one that best fits the system needs, and then instantiate such a solution. This instantiation process often only requires the application of a set of well-defined steps. This process can be precisely specified by means of a model transformation that is executed by a computer.

The main benefit of using model transformations is to avoid repetitive, laborious, and error-prone manual tasks, hence reducing the development effort. Consequently, the quality of the end product increases due to the elimination of errors introduced by a manual instantiation of a pattern solution. We will illustrate how our MDD4EA works using a subset of the Car Crisis Management case study [20, 21].

Following this introduction, this chapter is structured as follows: Sect. 8.2 offers a brief background on AORA and CAM, the two specific aspect-oriented approaches used by MDD4EA, which is discussed in Sect. 8.3. Section 8.4 illustrates our approach with the CCMS case study. Section 8.5 comments on related work and Sect. 8.6 summarises the chapter and outlines future work.

8.2 Background

8.2.1 AORA

The Aspect-Oriented Requirements Analysis (AORA) approach defines three primary tasks: identify concerns, specify concerns, and compose concerns [9]. In AORA, a concern is a matter of interest to one or more stakeholders and which localises one or more related requirements.

The identification of concerns can be accomplished by using traditional requirements elicitation techniques, such as ethnographic studies, analysis of the initial requirements, transcripts of stakeholders' interviews, etc. Other good sources for concern identification are existing catalogues, such as the non-functional requirements catalogue offered by Chung [11].

The specification of concerns is achieved through the systematic description of a set of properties that characterise each concern. These properties are collected in a pattern-like template and form the basis for several types of analysis possible, including the identification of conflicts between aspectual requirements. These properties are name, description, associated stakeholders, classification (functional or non-functional), type (derived attribute which classifies the concern as crosscutting or non-crosscutting), list of responsibilities, list of stakeholders' importance, list of contributions (positive or negative) between this concern and the others in the system, and list of concerns required to help supporting the responsibilities listed. The required concerns element acts as a dependency reference to other concerns in the system and is used to identify crosscutting concerns (i.e. concerns that are required by more than one other concern). The stakeholders' importance property assigns priorities to concerns from the stakeholders' perspective, in a first attempt to help in the conflict resolution process.

The composition of concerns allows an incremental analysis of impact of possible concern configurations. Each composition specification is analysed by taking into account the required concerns in the concern template. A composition rule shows how a set of concerns can be composed together using predefined operators. At this stage, conflicting situations may be detected when concerns contributing negatively to each other and having the same importance need to be composed together in the same joinpoint (or match point in AORA's terminology). If conflicts are identified, AORA offers multi-criteria decision techniques to handle them (this is discussed in Chap. 13).

8.2.2 CAM

This section provides some background of the UML 2.0 Profile for CAM [30], the aspect-oriented architectural notation we have selected to model our architectural design. We have opted for this notation, instead of other options (e.g. AspectualACME [17], Fractal [28], or PRISMA [27]) because (1) it is a UML 2.0 Profile, so the models that conform to it can be used as inputs for model transformations, (2) mature tool support can be easily obtained with little effort, and (3) we have considerable previous experience in using it.

UML 2.0 Profile for CAM organises a software architectural model in two main views:

1. A *structural view*, which specifies its constituent components and interfaces, and how these components and interfaces are interconnected. This structural view is modelled using UML 2.0 component diagrams.
2. A *behavioural view*, which models the interactions between these components. This behavioural view is modelled using UML 2.0 sequence diagrams.

In the UML 2.0 Profile for CAM, components are represented as common UML 2.0 components. Provided and required interfaces are represented in the usual UML 2.0 notation. CAM components never interchange messages directly. Instead, they communicate through their ports. Messages sent to a port from outside a component are forwarded to the component internals, while messages sent to the port from the inside are forwarded to the connected external components. This approach enables the sender to declare required interfaces and to send messages to its own ports when communicating with the environment, rather than identifying an external target component directly. Components defined in this way are assembled by wiring them together by means of provided and required interfaces.

Aspects are considered a special kind of component in CAM. These special *aspect* components are composed with the other components differently from traditional components. In addition to traditional component composition, which is based on connecting required with provided interfaces, operations of aspect components can be *spontaneously* invoked as a consequence of the occurrence of a certain event in a running system. Aspects are depicted as UML 2.0 components stereotyped as *«aspect»*. As usual components, they can provide and require interfaces and they must communicate through ports.

How aspect components are *spontaneously* invoked when a certain event occurs in the system is specified in the behavioural view of the software architecture. In the behavioural view, a component operation, an advice in AspectJ terminology [19], must be implicitly invoked. This is indicated by stereotyping the messages with *«aspectual»* in a sequence diagram, from a component port to the aspect. This does not mean there is an explicit call from the component to the aspect, or that component is explicitly connected to the component. Rather, this means that between the time when a port receives a message and the message is dispatched inside or outside, a piece of crosscutting behaviour is executed without the knowledge of the affected component. The call to the crosscutting behaviour is performed implicitly by the aspect-oriented weaver as a result of the weaving process, i.e. the component is oblivious of this call. We would also like to point out that common components are not explicitly connected to aspectual components.

Figure 8.1 shows how and when aspects can be executed on a sending/receiving message between components according to the CAM Profile, and how an aspect

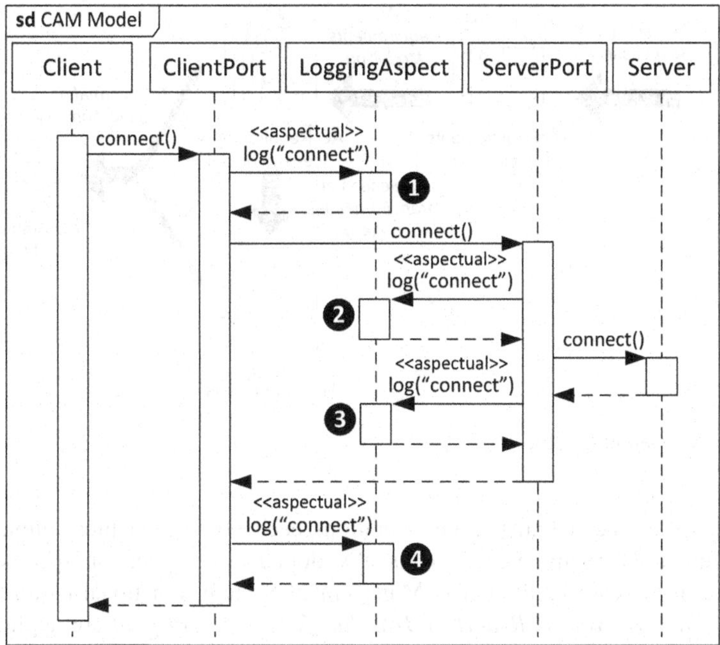

Fig. 8.1 Aspect execution in the CAM Profile

execution must be specified concerning the exact point of a sending/receiving message that it crosscuts. We have selected a simple example where a client connects to a server through an invocation to a *connect* method. In order to keep track of connections, a logging aspect is used. So, for instance, if we want to specify the *log* advice must be triggered after the Server receives the method call but before it executes it, we would place a call stereotyped *«aspectual»* between the point in which *ServerPort* receives the call from outside and the point in which *ServerPort* dispatches this call to the Server component internals (Fig. 8.1, label 2). Other interception points, like BEFORE_SEND, AFTER_RECEIVE, or AFTER_SEND, are indicated in Fig. 8.1 (labels 1, 3, and 4, respectively).

8.3 Model-Driven Development for Early Aspects

This section provides a general overview of MDD4EA (Model-Driven Development for Early Aspects). Our aim is to derive an aspect-oriented architecture from an aspect-oriented requirements specification, preserving, whenever possible, the information contained in the requirements specification.

Mapping requirements associated with functional concerns is not difficult. We need to identify the components that will carry out the computations and assign

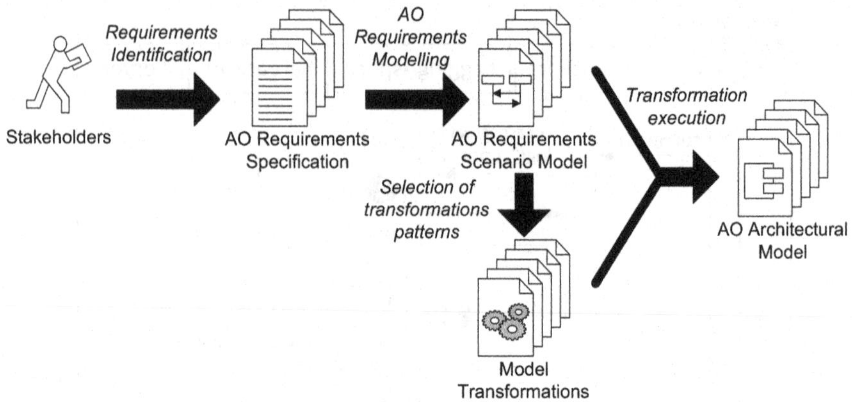

Fig. 8.2 Overview of the process

responsibilities, i.e. identify what operations each component must implement. These functional requirements are usually domain or application specific. For instance, in the case of the Crisis Management System, functional requirements such as *Capture Witness Report* or *Translate Victim To Hospital* are application-specific and they will rarely be reused by other systems, especially outside the Crisis Management domain.

On the other hand, the mapping of requirements associated with non-functional crosscutting concerns is often based on the systematic application of predefined solutions that are often reused across different applications and domains. For example, to map a concern such as *MessageIntegrity* to a part of an architectural model, there are well-identified solutions in the literature, such as adding checksums or other kind of redundant codes to messages to ensure integrity [18, 39]. Thus, we would need to introduce some logic to check checksums and ask for message resending when a message is identified as corrupted.

These kinds of solutions are often composed of a set of well-identified elements that need to be systematically incorporated into an architectural model to ensure *Message Integrity*. The instantiation of these solutions requires few or no creativity, as these solutions are often based on the systematic application of a set of steps and operations, which can, in most cases, be described algorithmically. So, this instantiation process can be encapsulated in a set of model transformations that are automatically executed by a computer.

In summary, the hypothesis for our approach is that the architectural demonstration of crosscutting concerns can be encapsulated in model transformations that accept, as input, requirements models and automatically generate an architectural design model. Nevertheless, some guidance might be required from the software architect during this process, as it is discussed later. MDD4EA general process is depicted in Fig. 8.2.

8.3.1 Step 1: Requirements Identification

The goal of the *Requirements Identification* step (Fig. 8.2) is to generate an aspect-oriented requirements specification using any of the existing aspect-oriented requirements engineering approaches (such as the ones shown in Chaps. 2, 3, or 14. As we mentioned before, MDD4EA is independent of the aspect-oriented requirements engineering approach selected.

In general, requirements can be described with different granularities. In this work, we use the classification proposed by Cockburn [14]. Following this classification, requirements can be described at different levels of granularity: *sky* (broad system goals), *kite* (more detailed goals containing several subgoals), *sea* (a single system interaction), or *mud* (low-level and highly detailed requirements).

The output of this step is a requirements specification describing in detail the system concerns, be them functional, such as *Capture Witness Report*, or non-functional, such as *Integrity*. Only one constraint is imposed on the output of the process: the system must be decomposed into a set of scenarios, each one containing only one non-crosscutting sea-level functional concern (a single interaction with the system) and any number of aspectual requirements that have an impact on the functional concern. The reason for this restriction is that these fine-grained scenarios are affected by fewer aspectual requirements, since they contain fewer elements than coarse-grained (kite or sky-level) ones. This means that the development of automatic model transformations and the trade-off analysis at the requirements and architecture levels will be easier.

More complex scenarios can be obtained through consecutive composition of fine-grained ones. For instance, sky and kite-level scenarios might be obtained by composing sea-level ones. This will be shown later with the help of the CCMS case study.

8.3.2 Step 2: Aspect-Oriented Requirements Modelling

To execute a model transformation we need to provide a model as input so that it can carry out the appropriate computations to produce the output model. So, the second step of our approach is to elaborate a requirements model using the requirements identified in the previous step.

We have opted for building UML models, due to the wide range of mature tools currently available in the market. If we were to develop our own requirements modelling notation, we would need to develop our own tool support, which would have been more costly, time-consuming, and error-prone. In addition, development teams are not tied to a specific tool developed by us, but thanks to the use of UML, they can use their favourite UML editors.

To model aspect-oriented requirements in UML, we have developed a UML Profile that permits expressing a requirements specification (the output of the previous step) as a UML 2.0 model. Using this Profile, aspect-oriented requirements are modelled as a set of scenarios, each one containing one non-crosscutting functional concern that may be affected by several aspectual concerns. So, the output of this second step is an aspect-oriented requirements scenario model in UML.

8.3.3 Step 3: Selection of Transformation Patterns

When mapping a certain concern, specially crosscutting concerns, several solutions may be initially available. For instance, when mapping *Response Time* to an architectural design, the following three alternatives might be potential solutions: (1) do nothing if there are enough hardware capabilities to ensure a good response time, (2) add a cache to the system, and (3) do a combination of the previous two strategies.

It is the responsibility of the software architect to analyse the different available alternatives and select the most appropriate one according to the system qualities required and the user needs. Each of these solutions has associated a certain pattern whose instantiation can be encapsulated into an executable model transformation. This means that the software architect must only configure the transformation process to select the model transformations that correspond to the patterns he wants to instantiate. Hence, the output of this step is a set of model transformations ready to be executed.

8.3.4 Step 4: Transformation Execution

The model transformations selected in the previous step are automatically executed, generating as output an aspect-oriented architectural model. This model is generated incrementally by automatically transforming each individual scenario created in Step 2.

To transform each scenario, each non-aspectual functional requirement is processed first, and then, an architectural solution that satisfies the aspectual requirement is injected into the generated architecture to ensure that all the information contained in the requirements model issued at the architectural level. The architectural model is expressed using the UML 2.0 Profile developed for CAM [30].

We would like to point out that aspectual requirements are not always transformed into an architectural artefact. According to [33, 35], aspectual requirements may be mapped to architectural decisions or architectural constraints that might not be possible to express in UML. Or else, an aspectual requirement may simply be postponed and not addressed at the architectural level. To properly handle this issue, an auxiliary traceability repository would help to record (a) the reason behind a specific architectural decision, (b) the architectural constraint and the elements it affects, and (c) the reason why a concern cannot be addressed immediately and, instead, is deferred to be handled later. Traceability is, however, beyond the scope of this chapter. The interested reader can refer to [2, 10, 35].

The goal of this work is to generate an aspect-oriented software architecture, which is expressed in the UML 2.0 Profile for CAM. However, a development process continues beyond the architectural design, although the following stages in the development process are not addressed in this book. Nevertheless, there are several paths that can be followed after generating this aspect-oriented software architecture. It is up to each development team to decide which path should be followed. We enumerate several of these options below:

1. The CAM aspect-oriented software architecture can serve as a basis for a manual detailed design or implementation of the software system. This detailed design or implementation can be done either using an aspect-oriented language or a non-aspect-oriented one. In the former case, aspects and pointcuts identified at the architectural level help to write pointcuts and aspects in our aspect-oriented language. In the latter case, the designer or developer would need to manually weave the aspectual components with the components they crosscut and the benefits achieved by the aspect-oriented decomposition will be lost. So this option is not recommended unless it is strictly required.
2. The CAM aspect-oriented architecture can be used to automatically generate (see [15]) a DAOP-ADL description, which is used to run an application on the DAOP platform [29, 30]. The DAOP platform is a distributed component and aspect-based platform, where aspects and components are dynamically composed at runtime using the information provided by the DAOP-ADL aspect-oriented architectural description language [30].
3. The CAM aspect-oriented architecture can be used to automatically generate, by means of model transformations, a UML design model for the application [32]. In this case, the model transformation is on charge of weaving the aspects with the components these aspects crosscut, producing a non-aspect-oriented UML model as output.
4. An aspect-oriented detailed design model can be automatically derived from the CAM aspect-oriented architectural model by means of model transformations [32]. In this case, the separation of concerns achieved at the architectural level is preserved at design time.
5. The CAM aspect-oriented architecture can also be used to automatically generate code for different languages [16], both aspect-oriented (AspectJ and JBoss AOP) and non-aspect-oriented ones (Java).

Next section illustrates the different steps in our approach by applying it to the CCMS case study.

8.4 From Aspectual Requirements to Architecture: The Case for CCMS

This section illustrates our approach, depicted in Fig. 8.3, by using the CCMS.

8.4.1 *Requirements Identification*

The first step of our approach identifies the requirements the system under development must fulfil. Any of the AORE techniques currently available can be used for this purpose. For this chapter, we have chosen the Aspect-Oriented Requirements Analysis (AORA) [8, 9] approach, since we have previous experience in handling it. AORA, like most of the AORE approaches, starts by identifying concerns, then specifies them, and later composes them to reason about aspect interactions and conflicts. This approach starts by identifying the kite-level concerns. Examples of these kite-level concerns are the following:

- Capture Witness Report: A car crash is reported by a witness. The witness can be involved in the car crash. A crisis employee, who plays the role of crisis coordinator, must gather information about the incident (such as location and victims' state) as reported by the witness.
- Confirm Crisis Scenario: When an employee of the crisis management agency arrives to the location of the car crash, the crisis scenario is confirmed. New elements, such as damages to the road infrastructure, might be added. Similarly, elements can be modified or removed from the crisis scenario, according to the employee criteria. The employee might, for instance, add photos of the car crash to allow insurance companies to determine responsibilities later.
- Identify Victim: One of the tasks of the crisis management employee is to identify the victims. This is key to locate his or her medical history, as needed, as well as to notify relatives as soon as possible.
- Message Integrity: Messages might be corrupted when transmitted. So, message integrity should be ensured.
- Message Authenticity: The system needs to communicate with several public services, such as firemen, ambulances, and hospital. Nevertheless, the sender of these messages should be authenticated to avoid anonymous malicious users that can send erroneous messages to the services. This would avoid, for instance, a terrorist organisation deviate ambulances to a distant place from the one where the attack is planned.
- Privacy: Due to legal issues and personal data protection, identity of the victims involved in the car crisis should be encrypted to preserve personal data privacy.
- Response Time: Certain communications have associated a maximum response time, in order to ensure the crisis is attended in an adequate and reasonable time frame.

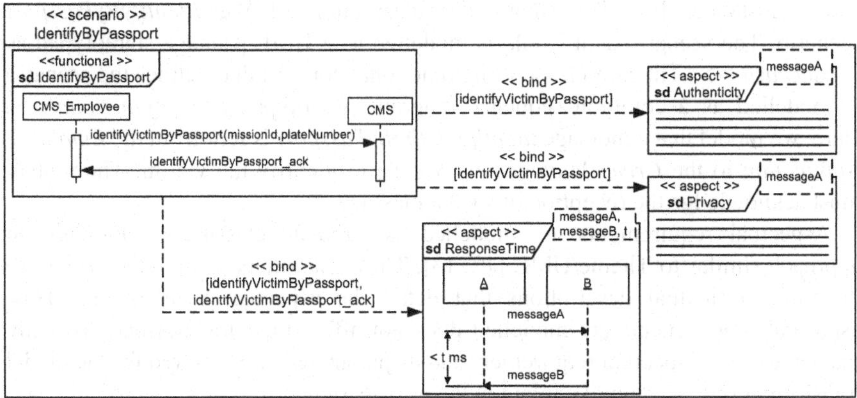

Fig. 8.3 IdentifybyPassport sea-level scenario

So, the next step is to refine these concerns to sea-level granularity. Kite-level scenarios would be refined to more fine-grained ones. For instance, the *Confirm Crisis* concern might be refined into the *AddCrisisElement*, *ModifyCrisisElement*, *RemoveCrisisElement*, or *AddPhoto* concerns. Similarly, the *Move to Hospital* concern is decomposed into *Find Hospital*, *Report Movement Init*, and *Confirm Victim Arriva l*concerns. The *Identify Victim* concern is refined into the *IdentifyByCarPlate*, *IdentifyByIdCard*, *IdentifyByPassport*, and *IdentifybyCreditCard*.

These sea-level concerns are affected by several crosscutting concerns. All sea-level scenarios are affected by the *Message Integrity, Message Authenticity*, and *Response Time* crosscutting concerns. Moreover, the identification scenarios, e.g. *IdentifyByCarPlate* and the *AddPhoto*, are affected by the *Privacy* crosscutting concern.

So, once we have identified the concerns the system under development must address, the next step is to create a requirements model that can be used as input to the model transformations. This is explained next.

8.4.2 Aspect-Oriented Requirements Modelling

Each sea-level scenario is modelled in UML 2.0 using the *Aspectual Scenario Modelling (ASM) UML Profile* we developed for this purpose. The ASM Profile allows the construction of requirements models based on scenarios.

Each sky-, kite-, and sea-level scenario is modelled as a package. For the case of sea-level scenarios, each package contains a single non-crosscutting functional concern that describes a single interaction with the system by means of a sequence diagram.

For instance, Fig. 8.2 shows the description of the *IdentifyByPassport* scenario. The scenario as a whole is modelled as a UML package stereotyped as <<*scenario*>>. The non-crosscutting functional concern that defines the scenario is modelled as a common sequence diagram stereotyped as <<*functional*>>. Here, we model that a message *identifyVictimByPassport* is sent from the *Employee Application* to the *Crisis Management System* to identify the victim. The system must acknowledge the reception of such a message.

Aspectual requirements are modelled as template classifiers, following an approach similar to Theme/UML [12, 13]. These classifiers can contain sequence diagrams or textual descriptions that detail the aspectual requirements. How aspectual requirements are modelled does not affect their transformations. Only the name of the aspectual requirement and its parameters are required for the model transformations, as we will explain in the next section.

These classifiers describe the aspectual requirements in a general and abstract way, referring only to template parameters instead of concrete elements coming from the functional concern it affects. For instance, in Fig. 8.2, *ResponseTime* is modelled as a sequence diagram using generic messages *messageA* and *messageB*. This allows this aspectual requirement to be reused in other scenarios. On the other hand, *Privacy* and *Authenticity* are described by means of textual descriptions.

Aspectual requirements are composed with non-crosscutting functional requirements by means of <<*bind*>>relationships, also inspired by Theme/UML [12, 13]. These relationships instantiate the aspectual requirements for particular non-crosscutting functional concerns, specifying how and where the aspectual requirements must crosscut the functional requirement as indicated by the actual parameters.

8.4.3 Selection of Model Transformations

Next we select the set of model transformation patterns that will be used to transform the requirements model created in the previous step into an architectural model. To clarify why we need to select between different alternatives, we will describe how the model transformation process works, i.e. what rules drive this transformation process.

8.4.3.1 Model Transformation Rules

This subsection explains how model transformations have been designed to automatically generate an aspect-oriented architectural model from an aspectual requirements model. The transformation process follows a bottom-up style, that is, from sea-level to kite-level scenarios. The transformation of the sea-level scenarios is defined through the rules described next.

1. Functional concerns (described by means of sequence diagrams) are transformed into architectural artefacts, according to the following steps:

   a. For each lifeline representing a different domain object in the sequence diagram, a component with a port is added to the architecture model. The name of the component is the name of the type of the lifeline.
   b. If a lifeline A receives a message in the requirements model, an interface IA is incorporated into the architectural model. In addition, a provided relationship is established between the component A (resulting from transforming the lifeline A following the rule 1.a) and the newly created interface IA. The operation invoked by the message is added to the interface IA, with their corresponding parameters.
   c. For each lifeline B that sends a message to a lifeline A, a required relationship from the corresponding component B (created previously by transformation of lifeline B fulfilling rule 1.a) and the newly created interface IA is added to the architectural model (according to rule 1.b).

   These steps create the structural view of the architectural model, describing the components that comprise the architecture and their connections.

2. Each interaction (i.e. the sequence diagram) describing a functional concern is transformed into an interaction in the architectural model (i.e. an architectural sequence diagram). This interaction contains the transformation of all the messages that do not appear as parameters in any of the bind relationships, i.e. that are not affected by any aspect. So, the sequence diagram generated will be incomplete until the non-functional crosscutting concerns are transformed. Messages affected by aspects are not included as they might be intercepted, reified, or modified by the aspects.
3. Aspectual requirements and the messages affected by them are transformed into architectural artefacts using pattern-based transformations, where a certain pattern encapsulates the design of a suitable solution for the aspectual requirement. This pattern is instantiated using the parameters of the bind relationship that composes the aspectual requirement with the functional requirement. Each pattern has its own model transformation. So, before executing this transformation process, we must select which one we want to instantiate. This transformation step only requires the name of the aspectual requirement, which determines the pattern to be injected and the actual values of the bind relationship, which provides the values for instantiating the pattern.

   Note that as mentioned in the previous section, the way in which an aspectual requirement is modelled does not affect the transformation process. Thus, the description of an aspectual requirement serves for documentation only. This last step completes the behavioural view created in the second step.

   The transformation of kite-level scenarios does not require any special effort, as their structure is simply copied into the architectural model. Constraints attached to kite-level scenarios about the composition of smaller scenarios are also copied as composite scenarios into the architectural model. Thus, as the composite scenarios are simply copied, they will be correct if the result of the transformation of their constituent parts is correct, that is, if the result of transforming the sea-level scenarios that constitutes the kite- and sky-level scenarios is correct.

The reader interested in the details of how these model transformations were specified using the QVT (*Query, View, Transformations*) language can refer to [36].

We will illustrate this process with an example from the case study in the remaining in this section.

8.4.3.2 Selection of a Pattern for Each Aspectual Requirement

As mentioned before, several patterns that satisfy a given aspectual requirement might exist. For example, in the case of *MessageIntegrity,* it can be supported by techniques such as Checksum (CRC), one-way hash algorithm (MD5, SHA1) and a digital signature [18, 39]. It is the software architect's responsibility to select the appropriate transformations or solutions that best satisfy the aspectual requirements, taking into consideration trade-offs between these requirements and stakeholders needs.

To specify which specific pattern will be used, each stereotype *«aspect»* of the ASM Profile has a tagged value called *architecturalSolution*. Once the software architect selects a specific solution for an aspectual requirement, s/he sets the name of this tagged value to the name of the selected model transformation. This ensures that when generating the software architecture, only the transformation corresponding to the pattern of the selected solution is instantiated.

Message Privacy

Privacy requires some kind of encryption. Multiple encryption algorithms have been created. Modern algorithms are based on ciphering messages using asymmetric key cryptosystems. In these systems, senders cipher messages using a public key, known by everybody. Once the message has been encrypted, it can be decrypted only using the corresponding private key, which is only known by the receiver. As mentioned previously, we are looking for a fast algorithm with an adequate security, low network overhead, and resource consumption. In this case, a simple RSA algorithm is enough to satisfy our goals.

Message Authenticity

Authenticity requires the verification of the identity of entities involved in a communication. There are several algorithms to achieve authenticity [18, 39]. All these algorithms are based on adding some code, called *MAC (Message Authentication Code)*, to the message being sent so that the receiver can verify the authenticity of the sender by carrying out some calculus with such a code as an input. Each algorithm provides different levels of reliability, performance, network overhead, and resource consumption. In our cases we need a fast algorithm—in a crisis, carrying out the right actions in time with a minimum network overhead is key. Due to the latency of the wireless networks we need to communicate with the crisis scenario and use low resource consumption, as the crisis employee at the crisis scenario will use a mobile device with limited hardware resources. In the light of these requirements, the RSA algorithm, the one used for encryption, seems a suitable choice.

Message Integrity

Integrity requires mechanisms to ensure that the message is not corrupted between the moment it leaves the sender and the moment it reaches the receiver. Traditional algorithms [18, 39], such as MD5, RSA, hash functions, and CRC, add extra data to the message before sending it. Then, they use mathematical mechanisms to allow the receiver to check if the message was corrupted. If corruption is detected, the sender is notified and the message is resent. As before, we are looking for a fast algorithm with an adequate reliability, low network overhead, and resource consumption. In this case, MD5 seems a suitable choice.

Response Time

There are several good solutions available to handle *ResponseTime*. For example, we could use a specialised data centre with replicated servers that ensure a bounded workload and therefore a bounded response time. This is not, however, an architectural decision and should, therefore, be postponed. Moreover, we might need to create a specific implementation, in a concrete software platform and with a concrete hardware support before analysing how much time each request needs to be processed. Using these data, we might simulate different workloads and calculate the response time for each request in different crisis scenarios, with a different number of users communicating with the system. In the light of these data, we might conclude that our system satisfies this requirement, or we might need to do further work. Nevertheless, few can be done at the architectural level. What we can do at the architectural level is described as follows. Each request needs to be processed within a certain period of time. We can attach time constraints to the architectural specification to guarantee that the component is implemented in such a way that the constraint will be taken into consideration. We select this solution, which is already encapsulated in a reusable model transformation.

It should be noted that the order in which aspects are applied to a requirement might be relevant. For this reason, a tagged value *executionOrder* is added to the stereotype *«aspect»* of the ASM Profile. This tagged value is an integer, whose value must be between -1 and the number of aspects involved in a scenario, minus 1.

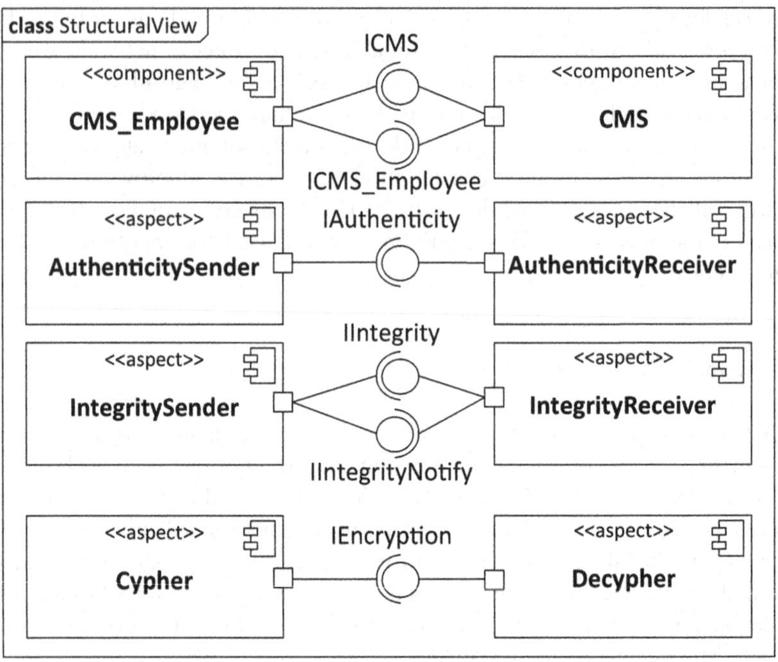

Fig. 8.4 Architectural model generated—structural view

A −1 value specifies the order is not relevant. A positive number indicates the place in the execution order for this aspect. An OCL constraint checks if two aspects in same scenario do not have the same value for *executionOrder*. In our case, *Integrity* must be the last aspect executed. The reason is that as *Privacy* and *Authentication* will change the contents of the message, the MD5 redundant code must be calculated for the final message that will be sent to the network. In the case of *Privacy* and *Authenticity*, the execution order seems initially not relevant. So, we assign maximum priority (0) to *Privacy* and execute *Authenticity* in second place.

The following section shows the results of executing the selected model transformations to the requirements models shown in Sect. 8.4.2.

8.4.4 Execution of the Model Transformation

This section shows and describes the architectural model obtained as a result of executing the model transformations selected in Sect. 8.4.3 using the scenario of Fig. 8.3 as an input.

The architectural model is expressed in the UML 2.0 Profile for CAM [30]. Figure 8.4 depicts the structural view of the generated architecture in terms of components, ports, and interfaces, which are connected to ports using provided and

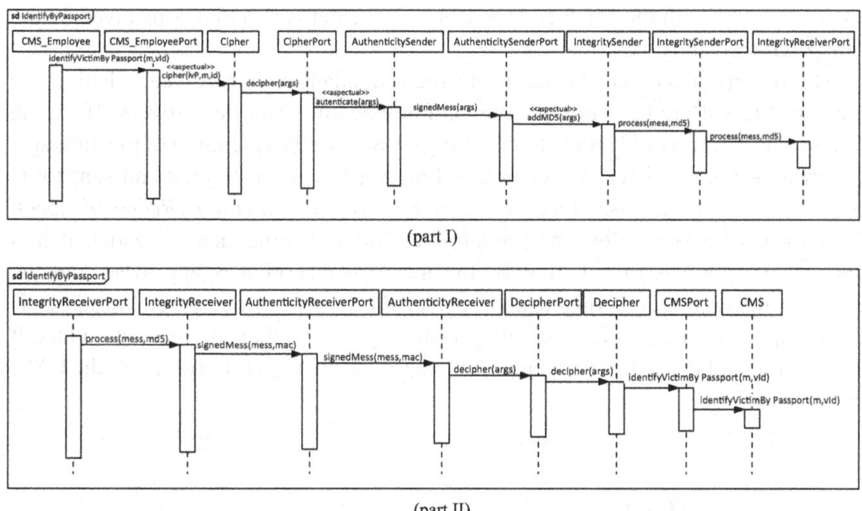

(part I)

(part II)

Fig. 8.5 Behavioural view for the IdentifyByPassport success scenario

required relationships. Figure 8.5 shows the behavioural view corresponding to the transformation of the *IdentifybyPassport* scenario.

As a result of processing the lifelines of the functional concern in Fig. 8.3, the *CMS_Employee* and the *CMS* components are created. As the *CMS_Employee* sends messages to the *CMS*, an interface *ICMS* is created by the model transformations. This interface is provided by the *CMS* and required by the *CMS_Employee*. The same reasons drive the creation and connection of the *ICMS_Employee* interface and all the remaining others.

As a consequence of transforming the aspectual requirements, components for ensuring *Authenticity*, *Integrity* and *Privacy* are added. These components are created by the pattern-based transformations that provide the selected solutions for these aspectual requirements.

How these components work together is illustrated in the behavioural view of Fig. 8.5 (parts I and II). This scenario has been shortened and split into two separate diagrams for convenience. It represents the success scenario—as integrity and authentication checks produce positive results. Firstly, the *CMS_Employee* component sends a message through its port to identify a victim by his or her passport number. This message is intercepted by a *Cipher* aspectual component, which must cipher the arguments of this message. After ciphering the message arguments, the *Cipher* message will send a *decipher* request to the *Decipher* component in the receiver side. This message is intercepted by the *AuthenticitySender* aspect, which signs the message and sends it to the *AuthenticitySender* component, also in the receiver side. This signed message is intercepted again by the *IntegritySender* aspect, which adds a MD5 code to this message. No additional aspect is executed, so the message with the MD5 code is sent over the network and it is received by the *IntegrityReceiver* aspect.

The *IntegrityReceiver* checks, using the redundant code received, whether the message has suffered corruption while communicating over the network. If so, the *IntegrityReceiver* would request to the *IntegritySender* the resending of the message. If corruption is not detected, the original message is reconstructed and sent to its original target. In our case, it was a *signedMess* for the *AuthenticityReceiver* aspect. This aspect checks whether the sender is a valid and authenticated sender. If it is not, an exception is raised. If it is, the message reception is approved, and the original message reconstructed and sent to the target. In our case, the target is the *Decipher aspect*, which uses its private key to decipher the message. Once it has been deciphered, it is delivered to the appropriate target, in our case, the CMS *component*.

8.5 Related Work

To the best of our knowledge this is one of the first approaches that address the problem of deriving aspect-oriented software architectures from aspect-oriented requirements model using model transformations. MDD4EA, our approach, was firstly presented in Sánchez et al. [34, 36]. This chapter has reviewed this work and it has illustrated the method with a new case study. Moreover, support for dealing with the problem of aspect precedence has been added. In this section, we comment on related work.

There are several works combining AOSD and MDD at different development phases [1, 5, 22, 37, 38]. However, the focus of all these works is not on automatically deriving aspect-oriented architecture designs from aspect-oriented requirements specifications.

Silaghi and Strohmeier [37] propose an approach that integrates component-based software engineering, model-driven development, and aspect-oriented programming. All these technologies are put together in a software development method for enterprise, middleware-mediated applications. This work focuses on architecture specification, detailed design models, and implementation, but not on how to go from requirements models to architecture models.

The proposal presented by Barbosa et al. [5] models PIM and PSM levels using Subject-Oriented Design and Composition Patterns in UML. The idea is to reduce scattering and tangling in class and interaction diagrams when they realise CIM use cases. The approach models each MDA level with a set of models (ViewCIM, ViewPIM, and ViewPSM) representing different aspects and viewpoints that stakeholders perceive of the software system. Therefore, the work supports the specification, modelling, and transformation of large complex systems from multiple views (CIM, PIM, and PSM views), but, once again, automatic transformations of requirements models to architecture models are not addressed.

Another approach, closer to ours, is the AOMDF (Aspect-Oriented Model-Driven Framework) proposal (Simmonds et al. [38]), which proposes an MDD/MDA generation process to transform aspect-oriented models in different phases of the software life cycle. AOMDF focuses on the detailed design development phase, not addressing requirements analysis models.

Deriving aspect-oriented architectural models from an aspect-oriented requirements specification has been addressed in [10, 35]. This work offers some guidelines and heuristics to support the required mappings. However, these mapping processes are manual, since they do not cope with new MDD techniques.

ATRIUM (Architecture Traces from RequIrements applying a Unified Methodology) [23] is a methodology for developing interactive systems, where functional and non-functional requirements are equally managed. It also introduces a process for the semi-automatic generation of software architectures. ATRIUM starts with the construction of a goal model, which considers functional and non-functional requirements. Operationalisations for these goals are created. An operationalisation provides a design decision and a design rationale, which contributes to traceability between requirements and design decisions. Next, one or more architectural styles are selected, and by using them, a scenario model is constructed. Finally, this scenario model is used to automatically generate a proto-architecture. Model transformation between scenario models and architectural models is implemented in QVT. The process is supported by a tool called MORPHEUS. This approach is very similar to ours. Indeed, the ATRIUM authors were highly inspired on our work. The only differences are (1) they rely on their own metamodel for requirements engineering, instead of a UML Profile as we do; (2) their tool support is oriented to the .NET platform.

Mussbacher et al. [26] presented a set of model transformation rules for mappings aspect-oriented requirements models to aspect-oriented design models. The requirements models are expressed using aspect-oriented use case maps, in the AoURN notation [25]) whereas the design models use RAM [21]. Although this approach focuses on automating the transformation process, they do not address the derivation of the architecture.

8.6 Conclusions

This chapter presented a (semi) automatic approach to generate aspect-oriented architectural designs from aspect-oriented requirements models. While the architectural models are expressed in the UML 2.0 Profile for CAM, the requirements models are expressed in the ASM UML 2.0 Profile. The transformation process ensures that the information contained in the requirements models is preserved at the architectural level. This helps to bridge the gap between aspect-oriented requirements and aspect-oriented architectures. This gap is even more noticeable in aspect orientation than in traditional development techniques since, in addition to the classical misalignment between requirements specification and architecture design, aspect-oriented requirements engineering and aspect-oriented architecture design approaches have emerged in isolation from each other. Therefore, an automatic process to map requirements-level aspects into architectural-level aspects has not existed for years. This mapping is the major contribution of this chapter.

The approach has been applied to several case studies in addition to the one discussed in this chapter. We refer the interested reader to Sánchez et al. [36]. As a result, pattern solutions for eight crosscutting concerns have been created and are available to be reused across different projects.

The only shortcoming we have found in our approach is related to the transformation of the functional concerns. In some cases, automatically generated architectures need to be slightly refactored to incorporate some creative solutions. This would be the case if we wanted to have several distributed *Crisis Management* sites that uses information from a central database. In this case, we would need a component for managing the connections between the *Crisis Management* sites and the central database. This component will not appear in the requirements models, so it would not be generated at the architecture level. The main issue here is that the discovery of this emerging component relies on a certain expertise and creativity of the software architect that was not captured by the automatic model transformation. In addition, with the current transformations, it is not possible to define several provided or required interfaces for a component.

Therefore, as future work, we will investigate further how to transform functional concerns into architectural models. Moreover, we will investigate the conflicts, dependencies, and interactions between scenarios, how to deal with requirements information which cannot be naturally mapped into an architecture and more powerful techniques for trade-off analysis.

Acknowledgements We thank Daniel Sardonil for his value technical pieces of advices about encryption, authenticity, and data integrity. This work has been partially supported by the projects TIN2008-01942 funded by Spanish Ministry of Science and Innovation and P09-TIC-05231 (FamiWare) funded by Andalusian Government and the EC STREP Project AMPLE IST-033710.

References

1. P. Amaya, C. Gonzalez, J. Murillo, Towards a subject-oriented model-driven framework, in *Proceedings of the 1st International Workshop on Aspect-Based and Model-Based Separation of Concerns in Software Systems, AB-MBSoC, 1st European Conference on MDA-Foundations and Applications, (ECMDA-FA).* Electronic Notes on Theoretical Computer Science, vol. 163(1) (Nuremberg, Germany, 2005), pp. 31–44
2. N. Anquetil, U. Kulesza, R. Mitschke, A. Moreira, J.-C. Royer, A. Rummler, A. Sousa, A model-driven traceability framework for software product lines. Softw. Syst. Model. **9**(4), 427–451 (2010)
3. E. Baniassad, S. Clarke, Theme: an approach for aspect-oriented analysis and design, in *Proceedings of the 26th International Conference on Software Engineering (ICSE)*, Edinburgh, Scotland, UK, 2004, pp. 158–167

4. O. Barais, E. Cariou, L. Duchien, N. Pessemier, L. Seinturier, TranSAT: a framework for the specification of software architecture evolution, in *Proceedings of the 1st International Workshop on Coordination and Adaptation Techniques (WCAT), 18th European Conference on Object-Oriented Programming (ECOOP)*, Oslo, Norway, 2004
5. P. Barbosa, C. González, J. Murillo, MDA and separation of aspects: an approach based on multiple views and subject oriented design, in *Proceedings of the 6th International Workshop on Aspect-Oriented Modelling (AOM), 4th International Conference on Aspect-Oriented Software Development (AOSD)*, Chicago, IL, 2005
6. T. Batista, C. Chavez, A. Garcia, U. Kulesza, C. Sant'Anna, C. Lucena, Aspectual connectors: supporting the seamless integration of aspects and ADLs, in *Proceedings of the 20th Brazilian Symposium on Software Engineering (SBES)*, Florianopolis, Brazil, 2006
7. I. Brito, A. Moreira, Integrating the NFR framework in a RE model, in *Proceedings of the 3rd International Workshop on Early-Aspects (EA), 3rd International Conference on Aspect-Oriented Software Development (AOSD)*, Lancaster, England, 2004
8. I. Brito, F. Vieira, A. Moreira, R. ribeiro, Handling conflicts in aspectual requirements compositions, in *Journal of Transactions on AOSD*, ed. by A. Rashid, M. Aksit. LNCS, vol. 4620 (2007) (Special issue on Early Aspects), pp. 144–166
9. I. Brito, Aspect-oriented requirements analysis, Ph.D. thesis, Departamento de Informática, Faculdade de Ciências e Tecnologia, Universidade Nova de Lisboa, 2008
10. R. Chitchyan, M. Pinto, A. Rashid, L. Fuentes, COMPASS: composition-centric mapping of aspectual requirements to architecture, in *Transactions on Aspect-Oriented Software Development IV*, ed. by A. Rashid, M. Aksit. LNCS, vol. 4640 (2007), pp. 3–53
11. L. Chung, B.A. Nixon, E. Yu, J. Mylipoulos, *Non-Functional Requirements in Software Engineering* (Springer, Berlin, 1999)
12. S. Clarke, Extending standard UML with model composition semantics. Sci. Comput. Program. **44**(1), 71–100 (2002)
13. S. Clarke, E. Baniassad, *Aspect-Oriented Analysis and Design: The Theme Approach* (Addison-Wesley, New York, NY, 2005)
14. A. Cockburn, *Writing Effective Use Cases* (Addison-Wesley, New York, NY, 2000)
15. L. Fuentes, M. Pinto, P. Sánchez, Generating CAM aspect-oriented architectures using model-driven development. Inf. Softw. Technol. **50**(12), 1248–1265 (2008)
16. N. Gámez, Code generation from architectural descriptions based on xADL extensions, Master Thesis, Dpto. Lenguajes y Ciencias de la Computación, Universidad de Málaga, Julio, 2007
17. A. Garcia, C. Chavez, T. Batista, C. Sant'Anna, U. Kulesza, A., Rashid, C.J. Pereira de Lucena, On the modular representation of architectural aspects, in *Proceedings of the 3rd European Workshop on Software Architecture (EWSA)*, ed. by V. Gruhn, F. Oquendo. LNCS, vol. 4344 (Nantes, France, 2006), pp. 82–97
18. J. Katz, Y. Lindell, *Introduction to Modern Cryptography: Principles and Protocols* (Chapman and Hall/CRC, Boca Raton, FL, 2007)
19. G. Kiczales, E. Hilsdale, J. Hugunin, M. Kersten, J. Palm, W.G. Griswold, An overview of AspectJ, in *Proceedings of the 15th European Conference on Object-Oriented Programming (ECOOP)*, ed. by Jørgen Lindskov Knudsen. LNCS, vol. 2072 (Budapest, Hungary, 2001), pp. 327–355
20. J. Kienzle, N. Guelfi, S. Mustafiz, Crisis management systems: a case study for aspect-oriented modeling. Trans. Aspect Oriented Softw. Dev. **7**, 1–22 (2010)
21. J. Kienzle, W. Al Abed, F. Fleurey, J.M. Jézéquel, J. Klein, Aspect-oriented design with reusable aspect models. Trans. Aspect Oriented Softw. Dev. **7**, 272–320 (2010)
22. V. Kulkarni, S. Reddy, Separation of concerns in model-driven development. IEEE Softw. **20**(5), 64–69 (2003)
23. F. Montero, E. Navarro, ATRIUM: software architecture driven by requirements, in *Proceedings of the 14th International Conference on Engineering of Complex Computer Systems*, Postdam, Germany, 2009, pp. 230–240
24. A. Moreira, A. Rashid, J. Araújo, Multi-dimensional separation of concerns in requirements engineering, in *Proceedings of the 13th International Conference on Requirements Engineering (RE)*, Paris, France, 2005, pp. 285–296

25. G. Mussbacher, D. Amyot, J. Araújo, A. Moreira, Requirements modeling with the aspect-oriented user requirements notation (AoURN): a case study. Trans. Aspect Oriented Softw. Dev. **7**, 23–68 (2010)
26. G. Mussbacher, J. Kienzle, D. Amyot, Transformation of aspect-oriented requirements specifications for reactive systems into aspect-oriented design specifications. MoDRE **2011**, 39–47 (2011)
27. J. Pérez, I. Ramos, J. Jaén, P. Letelier, E. Navarro, PRISMA: towards quality, aspect-oriented and dynamic software architectures, in *Proceedings of the 3rd International Conference on Quality Software (QSIC)*, Dallas, TX, 2003, pp. 59–66
28. N. Pessemier, L. Seinturier, T. Coupaye, L. Duchien, A model for developing component-based and aspect-oriented systems, in *Proceedings of the 5th International Symposium on Software Composition (SC)*, ed. by W. Löwe, M. Süholt. LNCS, vol. 4089 (Vienna, Austria, 2006), pp. 259–274
29. M. Pinto, L. Fuentes, J.M. Troya, DAOP-ADL: an architecture description language for dynamic component and aspect-based development, in *Proceedings of the 2nd International Conference on Generative Programming and Component Engineering (GPCE, 2003*), ed. by F. Pfenning, Y. Smaragdakis. LNCS, vol. 2830 (2003), pp. 118–137
30. M. Pinto, L. Fuentes, J.M. Troya, A dynamic component and aspect-oriented platform. Comput. J. **48**(4), 401–420 (2005)
31. M. Pinto, L. Fuentes, J.M. Troya, Specifying aspect-oriented architectures in AO-ADL. Inf. Softw. Technol. **53**(11), 1165–1182 (2011)
32. M. Pinto, L. Fuentes, L. Fernández, Deriving detailed design models from an aspect-oriented ADL using MDD. J. Syst. Softw. **85**(3), 525–545 (2012)
33. A. Rashid, A. Moreira, J. Araújo, Modularisation and composition of aspectual requirements, in *Proceedings of the 2nd International Conference on Aspect-Oriented Software Development (AOSD)*, Boston, MA, 2003, pp. 11–20
34. P. Sánchez, J. Magno, L. Fuentes, A. Moreira, J. Araújo, Towards MDD transformations from AO requirements into AO architecture, in *EWSA 2006*, pp. 159–174
35. P. Sánchez, L. Fuentes, A. Jackson, S. Clarke, Aspects at the right time, in *Transactions on Aspect-Oriented Software Development (TAOSD) IV*, ed. by A. Rashid, M. Aksit. LNCS, vol. 4640 (2007), pp. 54–113
36. P. Sánchez, A. Moreira, L. Fuentes, J. Araújo, J. Magno, Model-driven development for early aspects. Inf. Softw. Technol. **52**(3), 249–273 (2010)
37. R. Silaghi, A. Strohmeier, Integrating CBSE, SoC, MDA, and AOP in a software development method, in *Proceedings of the 7th Enterprise Distributed Object Computing Conference (EDOC)*, Brisbane, Australia, 2003, pp. 136–146
38. D. Simmonds, A. Solberg, R. Reddy, R. France, S. Ghosh, An aspect oriented model driven framework, in *Proceedings of the 9th Enterprise Distributed Object Computing Conference (EDOC)*, Enschede, The Netherlands, 2005, pp. 119–130
39. S. Vanstone, P. van Oorschot, A. Menezes, *Handbook of Applied Cryptography* (CRC, Boca Raton, FL, 1996)

Chapter 9
Maintaining Security Requirements of Software Systems Using Evolving Crosscutting Dependencies

Saad bin Saleem, Lionel Montrieux, Yijun Yu, Thein Than Tun, and Bashar Nuseibeh

Abstract Security requirements are concerned with protecting assets of a system from harm. Implemented as code aspects to weave protection mechanisms into the system, security requirements need to be validated when changes are made to the programs during system evolution. However, it was not clear for developers whether existing validation procedures such as test cases are sufficient for security and when the implemented aspects need to adapt. In this chapter, we propose an approach for detecting any change to the satisfaction of security requirements in three steps: (1) identify the asset variables in the systems that are only accessed by a join-point method, (2) trace these asset variables to identify both control and data dependencies between the non-aspect and aspect functions and (3) update the test cases according to implementation of these dependencies to strengthen the protection when a change happens. These steps are illustrated by a case study of a meeting scheduling system where security is a critical concern.

9.1 Introduction

Security requirements are about protecting assets of a system from the harms caused by malicious attackers [1]. As one of well-known crosscutting concerns, changes to security implementation can often lead to failures to satisfy other requirements in the system. Implementing security requirements as security aspects could help modularise the protection mechanisms that would otherwise clutter the non-security

S. bin Saleem (✉) • L. Montrieux • Y. Yu • T.T. Tun
Centre for Research in Computing, The Open University, Buckinghamshire, UK
e-mail: s.b.saleem@open.ac.uk

B. Nuseibeh
Centre for Research in Computing, The Open University, Buckinghamshire, UK

Lero – The Irish Software Engineering Research Centre, Limerick, Ireland

A. Moreira et al. (eds.), *Aspect-Oriented Requirements Engineering*,
DOI 10.1007/978-3-642-38640-4_9,

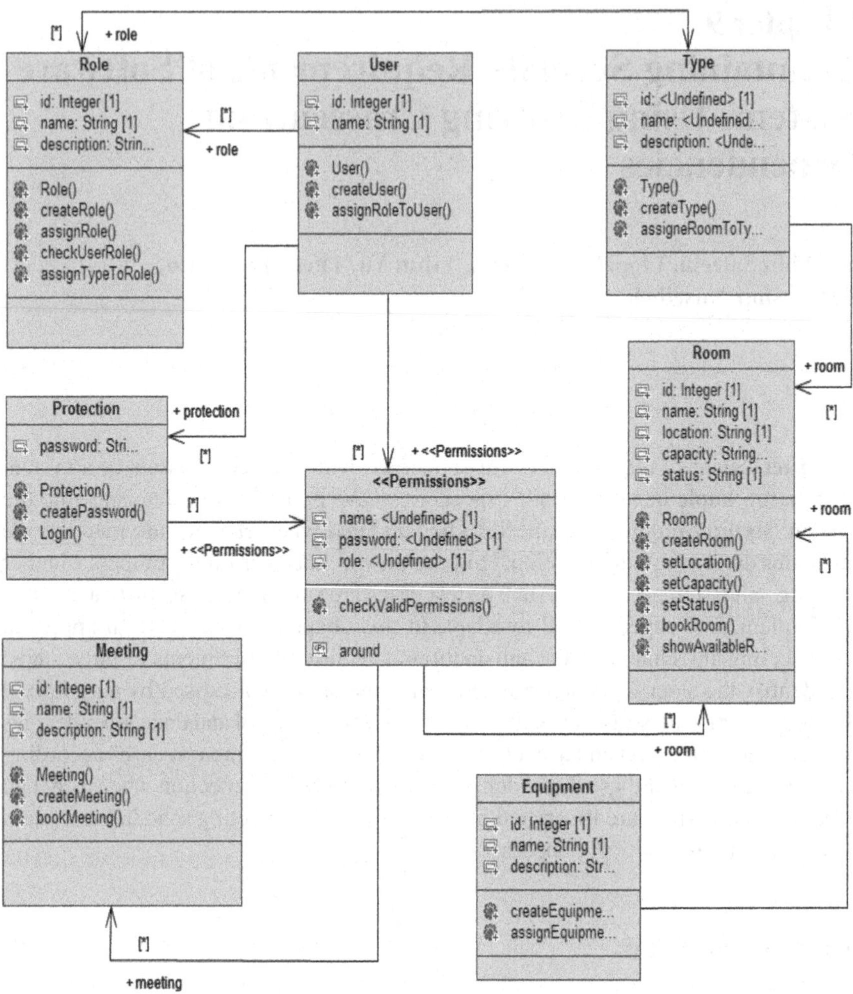

Fig. 9.1 The class model of a secure meeting scheduler system

functions of the system [1]. However, any part of the system including both aspect and non-aspect functions can change, making it difficult to maintain the satisfaction of security requirements. Here we use aspect functions to refer the advising functions inside the aspect and we use the join-point methods to refer to where the aspect is weaved.

An example is shown in Fig. 9.1: the class diagram of a secure meeting scheduler system. In this system, the `Permissions` aspect implements a security requirement. The purpose of this security requirement is to ensure that only the authorised users could be allowed to view/edit relevant information about the meeting rooms. The aspect crosscuts the join-point methods `bookMeeting` in the `Meeting` class and `showAvailableRoom` in the `Room` class. Through a test case, the satisfaction of this security requirement is checked that only an authorised user can book a meeting or list available room(s), and an unauthorised user cannot do so. When change happened to any function, usually one has to update the test case in order to check the satisfaction of the same security requirement. The difficulty here is that such an update could be ad hoc because most of the time the security requirements are stated at a higher level of abstraction and are tested implicitly by the test cases.

In this chapter, we propose an approach for detecting any change to the satisfaction of security requirements in three steps: (1) identify the asset variables in the systems that are only accessed by a join-point method; (2) trace these asset variables to identify both control and data dependencies between the non-aspect and the aspect functions; (3) update the test cases according to these dependencies to strengthen the protection when a change happens. An *asset variable* refers to a variable in the code that is being protected by the security aspect. For example, `Equipment.name and Room.name` are asset variables in the meeting scheduler system. The main contributions of this work are twofold:

1. We explicitly represent the security requirement as assets' protections in concrete test obligations or test cases.
2. We update such test obligations by making use of the change impact analysis on the assets variables and protection conditions.

The proposed steps will be illustrated by a small case study of a meeting scheduling system where security is an important concern. The remainder of the chapter is organised as follows. Section 9.2 discusses related work and background before explaining our approach in detail. Section 9.3 presents our dependency analysis framework that focuses on the satisfaction of security requirements before and after the code has changed. Section 9.4 details the application of this framework to a case study that exposes interesting research challenges. Finally, we conclude in Sect. 9.5 with an outlook for the future research directions.

9.2 Background

Before explaining our framework, we first discuss some related work in the area of aspect-oriented requirements (early aspects), evolving security requirements and dependency analysis.

9.2.1 Aspect-Oriented and Evolving Security Requirements

Rashid et al. [2] proposed the concept of "early aspects" as a form of crosscutting concerns in requirements. The notion of eliciting or identifying early aspectual requirements seeks to prevent the introduction of crosscutting concerns at a later design and implementation stage. There are many possible definitions of security requirements as discussed by Mellado et al. [3]. However, in this work we adopt the same definition of *security aspects* as in [1], where it is defined as the way to protect the assets of the system because of cross cutting relationship between the threat descriptions and functional requirements. Here threat descriptions are the set of concerns to define relationship between the threats and system objects. Similarly, we adopted the definition of *security requirements* as in [4], which is defined as the way to protect important assets of the system from the harm caused by the malicious attacker. As we consider the requirements and aspects in the problem world rather than in the solution world, therefore we adopted the Haley's definitions. However in this work our focus is on the change impact analysis with respect to implementation of the security aspects.

Security-related code tends to be scattered throughout many classes, and structurally separating security concerns, e.g. access control, was a challenge until the proposal of Aspect-Oriented Programing (AOP) paradigm. There are many approaches proposed to solve the problem of separating security concerns using Object-Oriented Programming (OOP) paradigm that includes modularising different concerns. However, the problem of when and where to call a security mechanism was not satisfactorily solved using the OOP paradigm. A security implementation often calls other modules inside the system. The internal encryption mechanism is an example of such a system, where key selection depends on the communication channel. Therefore, it is hard to update all the system calls in response of change requests when lines of code are in the thousands. The AOP is a solution to this problem that not only specifies the behaviour of a specific concern but also binds the relevant applications. Win et al. [5] conducted case studies on a Personal Information Management System (PIM) and FTP server to implement security requirements using aspect technology. They have confirmed that implementing security using AOP is useful to explicitly separate the security logic from the application logic. In this way, it is much easier for developer to take care of the applications part and security experts to check that whether a security policy is correctly implemented. Second, separating module (aspect) and binding (point-cut) help to cope with unanticipated changes. The aspect and point-cut are concepts used in the AspectJ, which is a Java extension of the AOP. A similar study has been conducted by the Viega et al. [6] to check the benefits of writing secure code using AOP extension of the C programming. They also reported that using AOP is very useful to design security into the application without mixing the security and application logic. Hence, the existing literature supports aspectual implementation of security is better than the non-aspectual implementation. Therefore, based on this fact we are using aspectual implementation of security in our study.

Haley et al. described functional requirements and threat descriptions as two types of concerns to derive security requirements using aspect-oriented techniques [1]. The functional requirements are set of concerns that help in understanding the different objects in the system to perform an operation. On the other hand, threat descriptions describe relationships between threats and objects. In case of the security requirement, the objects are assets that need to be protected. In this study, we are using the term asset variable to refer asset objects because assets are implemented as variables in the system code. Second, in this study we are doing change impact analysis at the code level rather than at the design level. Therefore, it makes more sense to call these asset implementations as asset variables. We named the locations of system where an object (asset) is implemented and a security mechanism is called to protect this asset as join-point functions. Similarly, we name the functions where assets and security mechanisms are not called as non-join-points. This convention of name is in line with the Haley's definition that join-points are locations where objects are shared among functional requirements and threat descriptions.

Many forms of early aspects models have been proposed, including goals [10] and problem frames [1], the targeted requirements are goal- or problem-oriented models. Yu et al. [7] identify aspectual requirements from soft goals; on the other hand Haley et al. [1] identify them using problem frames. It is worth noting that most early aspects frameworks treat security requirements as one of the non-functional requirements. However, Haley et al. [1] define the point-cuts of security aspects specifically based on the definition of security requirements [4], i.e. *protecting assets from harms of malicious attacks*. They also suggested that security requirements can be expressed as trust assumption made by the domain expert about security of the system. Recently, Franqueira et al. [8] have extended the security requirements argumentation process of Haley et al. [4] to strengthen the trust assumptions by conducting risks assessment.

The idea of tracing and validating security aspects using requirements-driven approach is not new by itself, as Niu et al. [9] have demonstrated the feasibility to support the whole aspect development life cycle using the goal-oriented approach. However, our work reported here is different in that we focus on change impact analysis of security aspects. Unlike the runtime-monitoring framework proposed by Salifu et al. [10], in this work we concentrate on the analysis at the development time. Nhlabatsi et al. [11] survey the literature on security requirements and software evolution, where the *management of evolving security requirements* is identified as an outstanding research issue.

9.2.2 Existing Security Dependency Analysis Frameworks

The term *dependency* refers to a relationship among different elements of a program or between two different programs relying on each other to perform a particular task. Such dependencies play an important role in program execution and are classified into data and control dependencies [12]. A data dependency exists when the output of a program becomes the input for another program. On the other hand, a control dependency is related to the ordering and conditions of the execution of the program. Ferrante et al. have introduced the Program Dependency Graph (PDG) to represent the relationship between different programs based on the data data and control dependencies [13]. Similarly, Pugh have proposed an approach to remove false data dependencies to prevent program transformation [14] and later improved the approach by using integer programming [15]. Both of the proposed approaches aim to improve the program understanding, for instance, when analysing changes to the programs. A *security requirement dependency* is defined as a relationship between the aspect and non-aspect functions to protect an asset variable of a program.

In the field of network security, Yau and Zhang [16] refer network security dependency as a relationship between two nodes in the network when a program or service intruded by an attacker in one node helps to attack the other node. Therefore, they consider that it is important to identify such security dependency relationships among all the nodes. Johansson [17] have introduced that security dependency exists between two nodes of a network when they depend each other for their security. He categorises them into acceptable and unacceptable dependencies: an acceptable dependency means that a less sensitive system of a network depends on the more sensitive system for its security and an unacceptable dependency is referred as a relationship when the more sensitive system depends on the less sensitive system for its security. For example, it is acceptable, if a workstation depends on a domain controller for its security. A domain controller depending on a workstation for its security is unacceptable. However, these works are not at the program level; therefore they are not directly applicable to the scope of security program aspects. However, all these works stressed the need to manage program dependencies, which is also true for security implementation to avoid the risk of attack on the entire system in case of attack on one vulnerable module. Therefore managing security dependencies at the program level is equally important to minimise the risk of system wide attacks.

To the best of our knowledge, there is still a need to perform dependency analysis of evolving security requirements that are implemented using security aspects.

9.3 A Dependency Analysis Framework for Security Aspects

An overview of our proposed framework is presented in Fig. 9.2, showing inputs, outputs and the three steps.

The inputs to the SDF include (1) a system that already has the security requirements implemented as a list of security aspects, (2) a set of test cases that check the satisfaction of security requirements and (3) a set of changes to the implementation of the system. The outputs from the SDF include both (1) a set of updated test cases and (2) a list of updated security aspects that may enhance the protections.

Specifically, the framework can be seen as three consecutive steps: initially (1) the concrete assets to be protected are identified from the differences between join-point and non-join-point functions. Without weaving the protection into the join-points, one may assume that certain assets are unprotected. Therefore their identification can be helped by existing join-point control flows; (2) from these identified asset variables, program slicing [18] can be performed to obtain

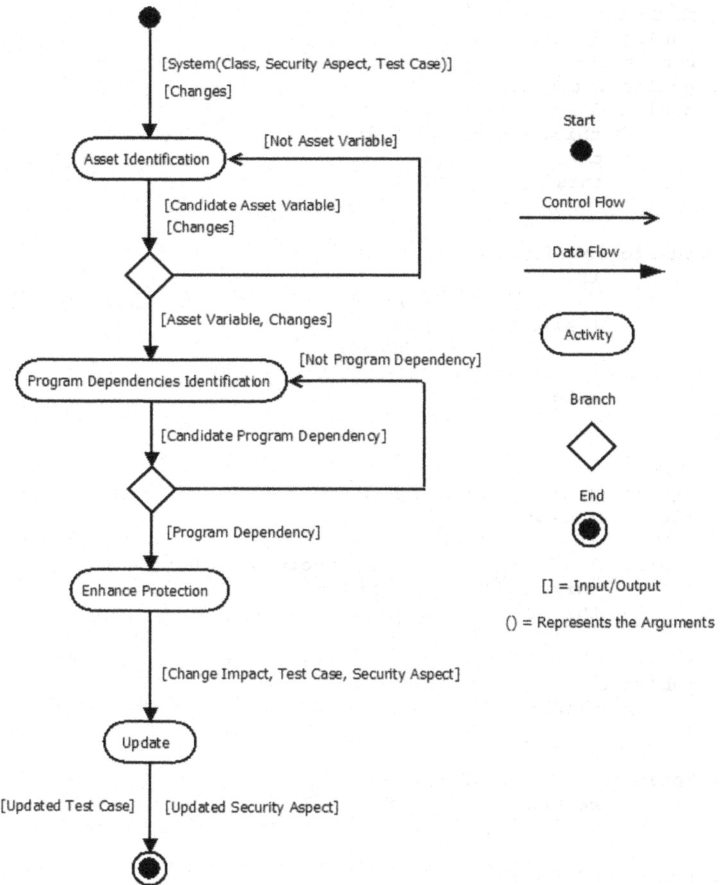

Fig. 9.2 An overview of our SD framework in three steps

the control and data dependencies that may leads to the unwanted exposure of these asset variables due to the changes to the functions; and finally (3) from these analysed dependencies, the test cases and security aspects are inspected to check whether the exposed asset values are covered by the new test obligations or by extending the scope of protection through an updated point-cut.

The detail of each step is demonstrated through a running example consisting of three classes (i.e. `Employee`, `User` and `Role`), one aspect (i.e. `CheckPermission`) and one test case (i.e. `SRTestCase`).

The implementation of all these classes is shown in Fig. 9.3. The class `Employee` has instance variables `age` and `salary` and a method `getSalary()` to get the value of the salary according to person's age. Similarly, the class `User` has two variables `userName` and `authorized` and two methods `access ()` and `hasPermissions ()`. The aspect `CheckPermission` is implemented

```
public class Employee {
        public String person;
        public int age;
        public int salary;
        public Employee(String person) {
                this.person= person;
                this.age = 0;
                this.salary =0;
        }

        public int getSalary() {
                if(age<60){
                        salary=100000 + 5000 * (age - 60);
                } else if(age>=60){
                        salary=100000;
                }
                return salary;
        }
}
public class User {
        public String userName;
        public boolean authorized;

        public User(String userName, boolean authorized) {
                this.userName = userName;
                this.authorized = authorized;
        }

        public int obtainSalary(Employee person) {
                return person.getSalary();
        }

        boolean hasPermissions() {
                return authorized;
        }
}
public aspect CheckPermission {
        pointcut p(): (call(public int Employee.getSalary())
        &&args());

        int around(): p() {
                if (((User)thisJoinPoint.getThis()).hasPermissions())
        {
                return proceed();
                } else {
                return -1;
                }
        }
}
```

Fig. 9.3 Listings of the running example: the `Employee` and `User` classes and the `CheckPermission` aspect

to run whenever a `getSalary()` function is called; the advice part of the aspect runs around the `getSalary()` function call and returns the control to calling methods when the user has the right permissions as indicated by the truth value

```
import static org.junit.Assert.*;
import org.junit.Test;
public class SRTestCase {

        @Test
        public void testSecurity() {
                User user = new User("Saad", false);
                assertEquals(-1, user.obtainSalary(new Em-
                ployee("Lionel")));
                user.authorized = true;
                assertTrue(-1 != user.obtainSalary(new Em-
                ployee("Lionel")));
        }
}
```

Fig. 9.4 The security implementation validated as a unit test

returned from the implemented `hasPermissions()` function. Otherwise, the advice code aborts the further execution of the program.

In this running example, the security requirement to be maintained is "*to protect the salary from the unauthorised users to view or to change*". The test case in Fig. 9.4 checks whether the security requirement is correctly implemented.

The first type of change considered here is (C1) which is due to introduction of a new requirement in the program. For example the system context is changed and now salary is calculated based on the new retirement `age` "65". This change should be reflected in the program by modifying `age` constant variable from "60" to "65". The second type of change (C2) is about updating existing implementation of the system. For example, the `setAge()` method in `Employee` class needs to be updated to reflect salary calculation according to the new age. The third type of change (C3) is about a scenario when a new security mechanism is introduced in the system. For example now the system security is checked using the direct access control (by user permission) to the indirect role-based access control (by user-role-permission). Given these inputs, one can analyse whether these changes could lead to the security requirement not being satisfied anymore.

The first step of our proposed approach is applied as follows. The join-point being protected by the advice in the `CheckPermission` aspect is `Employee.getSalary()` whereby `salary` is identified as an asset variable to be protected from viewing or changing by unauthorised users, e.g. when it is called by the `obtainSalary()` method.

After identifying the asset variable, in the second step we analyse both the data and control dependencies: `Employee.age` and `User.authorized` are found between the aspect (`User.obtainSalary`, `CheckPermisson.around`) and non-aspect functions (`Employee.getSalary`, `User.hasPermissions`), respectively. The guard condition for the `getSalary()` computes `User.authorized`, i.e. a control dependency; the computation of `salary` itself makes use of the variable `Employee.age`, thus a data dependency.

In the third step, we need to combine the program dependencies with the following proposed changes to tell whether there is a need to update the security aspect.

Fig. 9.5 C1: Change to the `Employee` class

```
public class Employee {

        public int getSalary() {
                if(age<65){
                salary=100000 + 5000 * (age - 65);
                } else if(age>=65){
                salary=100000;
                }
                return salary;
        }
}
```

9.3.1 Change Due to a New System Requirement (C1)

For the change of the retirement age (see the underlined parts in Fig. 9.5), a change to the computation of the asset `Employee.getSalary()` is detected because of the data dependencies. Although it has to do with *integrity*, however, this change will not be detected as a threat to the asset for malicious access (*authorisation*). Therefore there is no need to update the `CheckPermission` aspect or the corresponding `SRTestCase` test case.

9.3.2 Change Due to an Update of Existing Implementation (C2)

On the other hand, if a user has the permission to modify the `Employee.age`, as suggested by adding a method to update `Employee.age`, e.g. by using the `setAge()` method in Fig. 9.6.

In this case, although the `Employee` class is not changed, it is mandatory to protect the `Employee.age` by the same level of permissions. Therefore it is required to update the point-cut expression in the `CheckPermission` aspect as follows: **pointcut** `p():(`**call**`(`**public** `* Employee.getSalary()` || **public** `* Employee.setAge())&&` **args**`());`

9.3.3 Change Due to a New Security Mechanism (C3)

The third example change introduces role-based access control into the system by modifying the `User.hasPermission()` method, as shown in Fig. 9.7.

Here, the control dependency to `hasPermissions()` has changed because the system is now giving access based on the user's role. Although this change does not influence the interface between the `CheckPermission` aspect and

```
/* New function setAge is added to the Employee class*/
public class Employee {
        public void setAge(int ageArg){
                this.age=ageArg;

        }
}

public class User {
        public String userName;
        public boolean authorized;
        Role userrole;

        public User(String userName, Role userRole) {
                this.userName = userName;
                this.userrole=userRole;
        }

        public int obtainSalary(Employee person) {
                person.setAge(40);
                return person.getSalary();
        }


}
```

Fig. 9.6 C2: Change to the `User` class

```
public class Role {

        public String role;
        public boolean authorized;

                public Role(String role, boolean authorized) {
                        this.role=role;
                        this.authorized=authorized;
                }
                boolean hasPermissions(){
                        return this.authorized;
                }
}

public class User {
        boolean hasPermissions() {
                return userrole.hasPermissions();
        }
}
```

Fig. 9.7 C3: Change according to role-based access control mechanism

the join-points, it requires the test case `SRTestCase` to check the satisfaction of security requirement differently, as shown in Fig. 9.8.

In summary, we have shown that analysis of the data dependencies on the asset variables and the control dependencies on the protection condition results in the

```
public class SRTestCase {

        @Test
        public void testSecurity() {
                Role student = new Role("Student", false);
                User userRightRole = new User("Saad",student);
                assertEquals(-1, userRightRole.obtainSalary(new Em-
                ployee("Lionel")));
                Role professor = new Role("Professor", true);
                User userWrongRole = new User("Saad",professor);
                assertTrue(-1 != userWrongRole.obtainSalary(new Em-
                ployee("Lionel")));

        }

}
```

Fig. 9.8 C3: change to the test case is required

identification of changes in the security aspects or the security test cases. In the following section, we show an application of the methodology to a case study in order to discuss some general issues.

9.4 Application to the Meeting Scheduler System

Since the common case study does not provide source code, we could not use it for our proposed approach. To illustrate our approach, we have used the Meeting Scheduler system exemplar case study, extended with the security requirements. This case study is selected because of simplicity and sufficiency to represent the problem [19]. We handle the Meeting Scheduling problem for the members of the Computing department of the Open University based in the Jennie Lee Building (JLB). It involves the physical and social contexts of the members of the department. The roles of the people include faculty members, full-time PhD students, secretaries, course team members, tutors and research fellows, etc. For simplicity, in this study only these regular roles of stakeholders are considered to interact with the system; other roles such as visitors are not considered. Since laptops and USB keys are assets in the meeting rooms of the building, security measures have been taken to protect the open-plan areas and the meeting rooms. Great care has been taken to ensure that the measures do not hinder people performing their jobs. By looking at the meeting scheduler problem in JLB and interviewing the stakeholders inside the building, one can construct a secure meeting scheduling system.

Figure 9.1 shows a simplified class diagram of the secure Meeting Scheduler system design. The `Protection` class is part of the `Permissions` aspect in the design, which crosscuts the `showAvailableRoom` and `createRoom` join-point functions. Both functions share a common asset variable: the information of available meeting rooms inside the building (`Room.roomList`). In this example, the Permissions aspect verifies that the users have the right permissions before they access any information relevant to the meeting rooms. Any change to the advising function checkValidPermisions or to the join-points functions must be inspected against the implementation of the security requirement. The security requirement is to protect the information of available rooms from the access of unauthorised potentially malicious attackers. Otherwise, either the system would not function anymore or all the users would have permissions to access relevant information about meetings rooms.

Suppose the Permissions aspect is originally implemented by checking the username and password against a predefined list of access control (User.userList). A change (C”1) has happened such that not only the available meeting room but also valuable equipment such as projectors are considered as the assets (Equipment.equipmentList).

Another change (C”2) is to do with introducing Role-Based Access Control (RBAC) (User.roleList) to the users. To analyse whether the current implementation can still satisfy the security requirement or not, we applied the dependency analysis methodology as follows.

First we identified the asset variables Room.roomList and Equipment.equipmentList from the join-point functions showAvailableRoom, createRoom and createEquipment. In the second step, we identified data dependencies reading room information between Room.readRoom and Equipment.readEquipment. In this case, the equipment is inside a room; therefore we always need to read the room information to know the whereabouts of the equipment. Similarly, we identified the control dependency between User.userList and User.roleList because assignment of a role to a user depends on the condition that the user must be valid. In this way, system always checks the validity of the user before checking his/her role. These dependencies could be exploited by malicious attackers when change happened to the asset variables. In this case study, the Equipment.name, Room.name and Meeting.name are classified as asset variables.

After the proposed change C”1, createEquipment was added into the system, making it necessary to include it into the scope of protection as well. The original implementation of the Permissions aspect worked perfectly for both createEquipment and createRoom functions. However, when C”2 happened, it was found that the security requirement for the showAvailableRoom function was not fulfilled. The reason is that different users now have different roles and the Permissions aspect did not consider the roles of users while giving access to the system. It means the Permissions aspect still relies on the control dependency User.userList instead of User.roleList in case of change from *access list* to *RBAC* protection mechanism. This change to the protection mechanism is not reflected in the system; therefore the control dependency User.userList leads to the exposure of asset variables Room.roomList and Equipment.equipmentList. In an initial attempt, function call to check the roles of user was made inside the showAvailableRoom join-point function. However, the change was not effective because createEquipment and createRoom are not directly involved with RBAC.

After this change, however, the system did not show available rooms and still the system security requirement is not satisfied according to security requirement test case. Actually, still the change was made to only the join-point function `showAvailableRoom`. To respond to the change for satisfying the security requirement, the advising function of the `Permissions` aspect and the other join-points should be changed as well. Not only the join-point and advising function but also this change in security requirement should be tested by a new unit test case. Later to reflect the change, we removed the RBAC check from inside the `showAvailableRoom` function and updated the `Permissions` aspect with the RBAC check instead. In this way, the new check in permission aspect depends on the `User.roleList` variable instead of depending on `User.userList`. Similarly, the security requirement's test case is also updated by checking the permissions based on the role rather than based on the users.

9.5 Conclusion

In this chapter, we have illustrated the need for a systematic approach to handle changes made to security-critical programs, using a running example and our meeting scheduler case study. There are two main observations: (1) Change can happen to any part of the system, including both the aspect and non-aspect part of the implementation. When a change happens, the validation procedure (test cases) for the security requirements may need to be updated even if the security requirements have not changed; (2) both control and data dependencies can have impact on the validation of security requirements. Therefore, it is important to check whether the implementation of security aspects can catch the problematic changes, for instance, the point-cut expressions that need to be updated in order to include more changing functions into the scope.

In future, we aim to automate some part of the analysis so that it is possible to reduce the workload for the developers when the system is changed frequently. Also we aim to apply the framework to a substantially larger case study in the public domain so that our findings can be generalised and shown to be useful for security practitioners.

References

1. C.B. Haley, R.C. Laney, B. Nuseibeh, Deriving security requirements from crosscutting threat descriptions, in *Proceedings of the 3rd International Conference on Aspect-Oriented Software Development* (ACM, New York, NY, 2004), pp. 112–121
2. A. Rashid, P. Sawyer, A. Moreira, J. Araujo, Early aspects: a model for aspect-oriented requirements engineering, in *Proceedings of the IEEE Joint International Conference on Requirements Engineering, 2002*, 2002, pp. 199–202

3. D. Mellado, C. Blanco, L.E. Sánchez, E. Fernández-Medina, A systematic review of security requirements engineering. Comput. Stand. Interface **32**, 153–165 (2010)
4. C.B. Haley, R. Laney, J.D. Moffett, B. Nuseibeh, Security requirements engineering: a framework for representation and analysis, in *IEEE Transactions on Software Engineering*, vol. 34, 2008, pp. 133–153
5. B.D. Win, W. Joosen, F. Piessens, *Developing Secure Applications through Aspect-Oriented Programming*. Aspect-Oriented Software Development (Addison-Wesley, New York, NY, 2002), pp. 633–650
6. J. Viega, J.T. Bloch, P. Ch, Applying aspect-oriented programming to security. Cutter IT J. **14**, 31–39 (2001)
7. Y. Yu, J.C.S. do Prado Leite, J. Mylopoulos, From goals to aspects: discovering aspects from requirements goal models, in *Proceedings of the Requirements Engineering Conference, 12th IEEE International* (IEEE Computer Society, Washington, DC, 2004), pp. 38–47
8. V.N.L. Franqueira, T.T. Tun, Y. Yu, R. Wieringa, B. Nuseibeh, Risk and argument: a risk-based argumentation method for practical security, http://re11.fbk.eu/accepted
9. N. Niu, Y. Yu, B. González-Baixauli, N. Ernst, J.C.S. do Prado Leite, J. Mylopoulos, Aspects across software life cycle: a goal-driven approach, in *Transactions on Aspect-Oriented Software Development*, ed. by S. Katz, H. Ossher, R. France, J.-M. Jézéquel, vol. VI (Springer, Berlin, 2009), pp. 83–110
10. M. Salifu, Y. Yu, B. Nuseibeh, Specifying monitoring and switching problems in context, in *Requirements Engineering Conference, 2007. RE '07. 15th IEEE International*, 2007, pp. 211–220
11. A. Nhlabatsi, B. Nuseibeh, Y. Yu, Security requirements engineering for evolving software systems. Int. J. Secure Softw. Eng. **1**, 54–73 (2010)
12. N. Wilde, Understanding program dependencies, Carnegie Mellon University, Software Engineering Institute SEI-CM-26, 1990 (26 pages) (University of West Florida)
13. J. Ferrante, K.J. Ottenstein, J.D. Warren, The program dependence graph and its use in optimization. ACM Trans. Prog. Lang. Syst. **9**, 319–349 (1987)
14. W. Pugh, D. Wonnacott, Eliminating false data dependences using the Omega test. SIGPLAN Not. **27**, 140–151 (1992)
15. W. Pugh, D. Wonnacott, Going beyond integer programming with the Omega test to eliminate false data dependences. IEEE Trans. Parallel Distribut. Syst. **6**, 204–211 (1995)
16. S.S. Yau, X. Zhang, Computer network intrusion detection, assessment and prevention based on security dependency relation, in *23rd International Computer Software and Applications Conference* (IEEE Computer Society, Washington, DC, 1999), p. 86
17. Island Hopping: Mitigating Undesirable Dependencies – TechNet Magazine Blog – Site Home – TechNet Blogs, http://blogs.technet.com/b/tnmag/archive/2008/02/27/island-hopping-mitigating-undesirable-dependencies.aspx
18. M. Weiser, Program slicing, in *IEEE Transactions on Software Engineering*. SE-10, 1984, pp. 352–357
19. A. Van Lamsweerde, R. Darimont, P. Massonet, Goal-directed elaboration of requirements for a meeting scheduler: problems and lessons learnt, in *Proceedings of the Second IEEE International Symposium on Requirements Engineering* (IEEE Computer Society, Washington, DC, 1995), p. 194

Chapter 10
Using Aspects to Model Volatile Concerns

Ana Moreira, João Araújo, Jon Whittle, and Miguel Goulão

Abstract A rapidly changing market leads to software systems with highly volatile requirements. In many cases, new demands in software can often be met by extending the functionality of systems already in operation. By modularizing volatile requirements that can be altered at the client's initiative or according to market demands, we can build a stepping-stone for management of requirements change. The volatility must be managed in a way that reduces the time and costs associated with updating a system to meet the new requirements. In this chapter, we present an approach for handling volatile concerns during early life cycle software modeling. The key insight is that techniques for aspect-oriented software development can be applied to modularize volatility and to weave volatile concerns into the base software artifacts.

10.1 Introduction

A key barrier to the success of modern systems is the time required to deal with volatile requirements. As Firesmith [9] says: "The more volatile the requirements, the more important it becomes for the requirements process to support the quick and easy modification and addition of requirements." This chapter discusses a modeling method that copes with requirements change by explicitly externalizing volatile concerns and treating them as candidate aspects. In general, volatile concerns may or may not be crosscutting, but techniques for modeling aspects may be reused because both aspects and volatile concerns share the same basic needs—independency,

A. Moreira (✉) • J. Araújo • M. Goulão
Departamento de Informática, Universidade Nova de Lisboa, Caparica, Portugal
e-mail: amm@fct.unl.pt; joao.araujo@fct.unl.pt; mgoul@fct.unl.pt

J. Whittle
Computing Science Department, University of Lancaster, Lancashire, UK
e-mail: whittle@comp.lancs.ac.uk

A. Moreira et al. (eds.), *Aspect-Oriented Requirements Engineering*,
DOI 10.1007/978-3-642-38640-4_10,

modular representation, and composition with a base description. By representing volatile concerns using aspect-oriented techniques, volatility is modularized and requirements modifications can be rapidly composed into an existing system, leading to efficiency gains in handling requirements creep.

In our approach, both volatile and crosscutting concerns are modeled as aspects by using extended pattern specifications and are composed using specialized techniques for pattern specification composition. Pattern specifications (PSs) were proposed in [10] as a way of formalizing the reuse of models. The notation for pattern specifications is based on the Unified Modeling Language (UML). A pattern specification describes a pattern of structure or behavior defined over the roles which participants of the pattern play. It can be instantiated by assigning modeling elements to play these roles. Pattern specifications are a practical and flexible way to handle aspects at the modeling level. By identifying volatile concerns, they can be modeled as pattern specifications and then instantiated and composed with a base system in a number of different ways. Requirements change amounts to replacing a pattern specification and reapplying the composition strategy.

This chapter aims at demonstrating the value of early externalization of volatile business rules and constraints to support concern change using aspects. This is achieved by proposing an evolutionary model that includes the concepts of aspect orientation and its advantages [12].

Modeling volatile concerns as candidate aspects, independently of those concerns being crosscutting or not, is a way to support change, since volatile concerns may become crosscutting in the future. Also, since it improves modularization and consequently a better separation of concerns, it facilitates the introduction and removal of business rules because it is easier to add a new aspect to a running system than to add a new set of classes or methods.

The remainder of this chapter is structured as follows. Section 10.2 introduces some background work. Section 10.3 gives an overview of our method for modeling volatile concerns. Section 10.4 applies the method to a case study. Section 10.5 evaluates the presented method according to general and specific criteria. Section 10.6 discusses related work and Sect. 10.7 concludes the work and suggests directions for further research.

10.2 Background

Pattern Specifications (PSs) PSs [10] are a way of formalizing the reuse of models. The notation for PSs is based on the Unified Modeling Language (UML) [17, 18]. A pattern specification describes a pattern of structure or behavior defined over the roles which participants of the pattern play. Role names are preceded by a vertical bar ("|"). A PS can be instantiated by assigning concrete modeling elements to play these roles. A role is a specialization of a UML metaclass restricted by additional properties that any element fulfilling the role must possess. Hence, a role specifies a subset of the instances of the UML metaclass. A model conforms to a

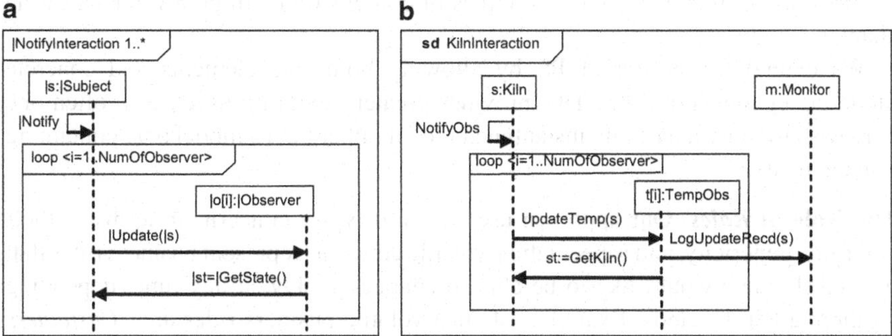

Fig. 10.1 An IPS (**a**) and a conforming sequence diagram (**b**)

PS if its model elements that play the roles of the PS satisfy the properties defined by the roles. Thus, a conforming diagram must instantiate each of the roles with UML model elements, multiplicity, and other constraints. Note that any number of additional model elements may be present in a conforming diagram as long as the role constraints are maintained.

PSs can be defined to show static structure or dynamic behavior. We will focus on dynamic behavior, applying use case pattern specifications (UCPS), activity pattern specifications (APS), and interaction pattern specifications (IPS). For example, an IPS defines a pattern of interactions between its participants, consisting of a number of lifeline roles and message roles which are specializations of the UML metaclasses Lifeline and Message, respectively. Each lifeline role is associated with a classifier role, a specialization of a UML classifier. (A similar reasoning applies to UCPS and APS.)

Figure 10.1 shows an example of an IPS (taken from [10]), where Fig. 10.1a formalizes the Observer pattern. A conforming sequence diagram is shown in Fig. 10.1b. Note that the partial ordering on the message roles must be satisfied. An instantiation rule can take the form: Replace |Subject with Kiln. Figure 10.1b conforms to 1a because the roles in 1a can be instantiated as follows:

```
|NotifyInteraction -> KilnInteraction; |s -> s; |Subject
-> Kiln; |Notify -> NotifyObs; |o -> t; |Observer ->
TempObs; |Update -> UpdateTemp; |st -> st; |GetState ->
GetKiln.
```

Note that PSs offer more than mere parameterization (for parameterization UML templates could be used instead). PSs consist of roles, which can be instantiated to zero, one, or any number of model elements, roles may have attached constraints and any model element playing the role must fulfill those constraints, and PSs have a well-defined notion of conformance which makes them suitable for composition. This composition is valid if and only if the result of the composition conforms to the pattern specification. Many examples of composition will be given later in the chapter.

We extend the notion of PS by allowing both role elements and concrete modeling elements in a PS. This provides greater flexibility in reuse as often one may wish to reuse a partially instantiated model rather than a model only containing role elements.

The Role of *Roles* Our approach uses roles to typify concerns in terms of their volatility, genericity, and aspectuality. Volatile concerns represent business rules that the stakeholders would like to be able to change quickly, at any time, depending on the market demands. Examples of such volatile business rules are *"Customers whose transactions amount to at least five million euros annually are awarded a position on the company executive board"* or *"Off-peak customers get a 5 % discount"*. In traditional software development approaches, the specification, and consequent implementation, of these volatile requirements is hardwired to core modules that cannot be changed without having to recompile the application. By externalizing these volatile concerns and specifying them as role elements (or, more generally, role models) we are offering a mechanism to instantiate each business rule differently whenever needed (genericity). For example, a volatile concern can be given as a use case role and later be instantiated to a concrete use case.

Roles are also used to represent crosscutting concerns. The advantage is that the resulting role model can be instantiated and composed differently depending on which model it crosscuts. In general, both volatile and crosscutting concerns can be modeled as a PS, and this can be done at multiple levels of abstraction—e.g., a crosscutting use case can be refined into an APS.

Crosscutting Models We define an aspect-oriented model to be a model that crosscuts other models *at the same level of abstraction*. This means, for example, that a requirements model is an aspect if it crosscuts other requirements models; a design model is an aspect if it crosscuts other design models. In particular, a use case is not necessarily an aspect. Although a use case always cuts across multiple implementation modules, it is only an aspect if it cuts across other use cases.

In this chapter, we restrict the definition of an aspect-oriented model further and say that a model is an aspect only if it crosscuts other models written from the same perspective. For example, a model showing global component interactions does not, according to our definition, crosscut a model showing internal component behavior. Although the models are defined at the same level of abstraction, they are written from different perspectives—a global and a local perspective. In terms of UML, this means that we are only interested in crosscuts defined over diagrams of the same type. We therefore do not consider, for example, sequence diagrams that crosscut state machines or use cases that crosscut class diagrams.

Composition Models Keeping separate the definition of the rules that indicate how base and aspect models are weaved together is as important as representing crosscutting models in a modular fashion. Separating aspects is good for improved modularization and evolution, and composition is necessary to facilitate reuse of both base and aspectual models, to understand the overall picture, and to reason about the necessary trade-offs between conflicting properties.

Composition is achieved through composition rules. These rules weave together compatible models by means of specific operators. Compatible models are those at the same level of abstraction and that were built from the same perspective. Composition operators function as the glue that keeps together aspectual and base models. They are similar to *advices* (*before, after*, and *around*) in AspectJ [12] except that here operators are specific to UML diagrams.

10.3 Modeling Volatility

One of the prime objectives of our approach is to develop a means to handle requirements that have a high probability of changing during their life cycle. These volatile requirements may be business rules that the stakeholders would like to be able to change quickly, at any time. Some of these volatile requirements may be part of coarse-grained concerns and therefore be difficult to identify during the early stages of the software development. Our goal is to modularize volatile requirements, handling them as first class entities. This facilitates requirements change, promoting software system evolution. In traditional software development approaches the specification, and consequent implementation, of these volatile requirements is hardwired to core modules that cannot be changed without having to recompile the application (or at least a part of it).

The key insight is that volatility can be handled in the same way as aspects, since both concepts share the same basic needs—independency, modular representation, and composition with a base description. By representing volatile requirements using aspect-oriented techniques, volatility is modularized and requirements modifications can be rapidly instantiated and composed into an existing system. Therefore, the process we propose focuses on requirements evolution, where classification, composition, and instantiation form the most important tasks to achieve the adequate flexibility needed for evolvable systems (see Fig. 10.2).

The process starts with the identification of the main problem domain concerns (step 1). Each concern is then classified (step 2) enduring or volatile and is described in terms of its main elements in a template as shown in Tables 10.1 and 10.2. Classification and description of concerns may lead to their refactoring (step 3). Concerns may be iteratively identified, classified, described, and refactored.

Concerns are represented (step 4) using UML diagrams or pattern specifications. Enduring concerns are modeled using UML diagrams. Volatile concerns, crosscutting concerns, and constraints are modeled as pattern specifications. The representation of these concerns as roles requires that the original concern definition is modified to become nonspecific, thus allowing several concrete instantiations (step 5).

Concern evolution (step 7) allows new concerns to be identified, classified, refactored, and represented, iteratively. At this stage, the outcome of the process is a

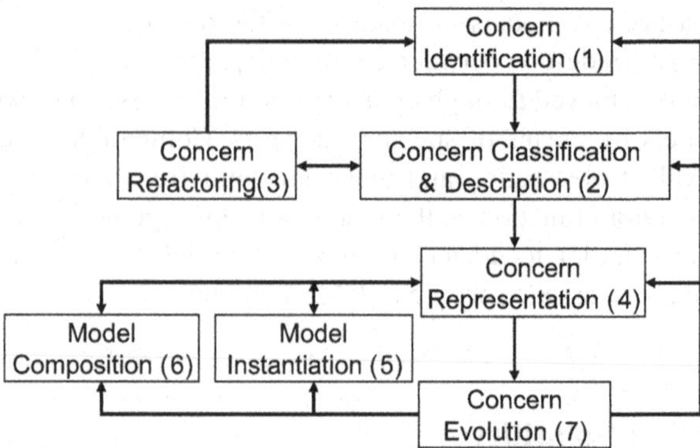

Fig. 10.2 Aspect-oriented evolutionary model for volatile concerns

Table 10.1 *Order Handling* description

Concern #	C1a
Name	Order Handling
Classification	Enduring
Stakeholders	Shuttle, Passenger
Interrelationships	C1b, C2
List of pre-conditions	
(1) There is a new order	
List of responsibilities	
(1) Broadcast order (2) Receive bids (3) Store bids	

Table 10.2 *Choose Bid* description

Concern #	C1b
Name	Choose Bid
Classification	Volatile
Stakeholders	Shuttle
Interrelationships	C1a
List of pre-conditions	
(1) There should be at least one order	
List of responsibilities	
(1) Get offers (2) Select winning bid (3) Store Choice (4) Make decision known	

specification where core concerns and concern roles are kept separate. Instantiation and/or composition (steps 5 and 6) can take place at the level of granularity of elementary concerns or models. While instantiation offers the opportunity to make concrete decisions regarding volatile concerns, which have been marked as role elements, composition serves to weave the instantiated concerns into a base model consisting of enduring services. During composition conflicts may be identified and solved by means of trade-off analysis, similarly to what is discussed in Chap. 14. Here we will ignore conflict analysis and focus on composition using a set of generic directives and a technique similar to the one in [10].

We now illustrate the process outlined in Fig. 10.2 using an automated transport system[1] in which transport contractors bid to fulfill passenger transport orders.

10.3.1 Concern Identification

The identification of concerns starts with the identification of the stakeholders and follows by inspecting existing documents that describe the problem, existing catalogues [4], models from previous business modeling [22], stakeholders' interviews transcripts, and results from searching techniques [20].

For example, in the automated transport system, passenger orders can be bid on by all transport contractors and the lowest bid wins. In the event of two lowest bids, the first arriving bid wins. Successful completion of an order results in a monetary reward for the shuttle involved. In case an order has not been completed in a given amount of time, a penalty is incurred. The following two concerns can be identified from this example: (C1) Passenger orders can be bid for by all transport contractors and the lowest bid wins. In the event of two lowest bids, the first arriving bid wins. (C2) Successful completion of an order results in a monetary reward for the shuttle involved. In case an order has not been completed in a given amount of time, a penalty is incurred.

10.3.2 Concern Classification and Description

Concerns are classified according to longevity, which can be enduring or volatile. Enduring concerns are "relatively stable requirements which derive from the core activity of the organization and which relate directly to the domain of the system" [21]. Volatile concerns "are likely to change during the system development or after the system has been put into operation" [21].

For example, concern C1 above might be classified as both enduring and volatile. While the first sentence refers to something stable as it is likely that shuttles will always have to bid for business in this system, the second implies a choice process which is likely to change depending on organization policies. This leads to a natural refactoring of this concern into two separate concerns—one to capture the enduring part and one to capture the volatile part (cf. Sect. 10.3.3 below).

---

[1]Shuttle system description found at http://scesm04.upb.de/case-study-1/ShuttleSystem-CaseStudy-V1.0.pdf.

Each concern is described in more detail using a template that collects its contextual and internal information. Tables 10.1 and 10.2 illustrate the templates for concern C1 (refactored into C1a and C1b). The row "Interrelationships" lists the concerns that a given concern relates to. (The reader can consult [4, 8] on several kinds of relationships.) A responsibility is an obligation to perform a task, or know certain information.

10.3.3 Concern Refactoring

Attempts to assign the enduring/volatility categorization lead to a refactoring of the requirements, thus increasing the granularity. For example, in the automated transport system example, the concern "(C1) Passenger orders can be bid for by all transport contractors and the lowest bid wins. In the event of two lowest bids, the first arriving bid wins." could instead be represented as two separate concerns—one for the bidding (C1a) and one for the decision on who wins in the event of two equal lowest bids (C1b). Identified volatile concerns may be redefined to represent a more generic concern. For example, C1b, if originally defined as *Choosing From Equal Bids*, can be generalized to *Choose Bid*. Such a generalization promotes evolution since you may want to change the bidding policies in the future.

The classification process helps to refactor the list of concerns into a list with consistent granularity level. This is because increased granularity is often needed to be able to specify the fact that part of a concern is enduring or volatile. As an example, for concern (C1) above, one would like to say that the first part of the concern (the bidding process) is enduring whereas the second part (dealing with two lowest bids) is volatile—one might, for example, later wish to use a different selection strategy in which bidders with strong performance histories win equal bids. Such a classification would lead naturally to splitting concern (C1) into two concerns (C1a) and (C1b). Applying a classification strategy consistently across a set of concerns leads to a consistent level of granularity in concern representation.

10.3.4 Concern Representation

Our approach represents concerns using UML use case and activity models. Elements in a model representing crosscutting or volatile concerns are marked as roles and the model becomes a pattern specification model. Thus, we may use Use Case Pattern Specification (UCPS) and Activity Pattern Specifications (APSs).

Build Use Case Models A UCPS is a modified use case model with use case roles, each one representing volatile constraints and services. It incorporates use case roles, where concerns are mapped into use cases, volatile constraints and services are mapped into use case roles, stakeholders are mapped into actors, and

Input: a list of stakeholders and classified concerns
Output: a UCPS
For each concern *C*:
  Create a new use case or use case role corresponding to *C*
    If *C* is enduring, describe *C* as a concrete use case
    If *C* is volatile, describe *C* as a use case role
    If *C* is crosscutting, describe *C* as a use case role
  If *C* has a relationship, *R*, to concern *C'* in its template description, create a relationship between the use cases or use case roles corresponding to *C* and *C'*
    If *C* is a constraint, attach the `<<constrain>>` stereotype to this relationship
  Map Stakeholders that interact with the new use cases into actors

Fig. 10.3 Guidelines to map concerns to a UCPS

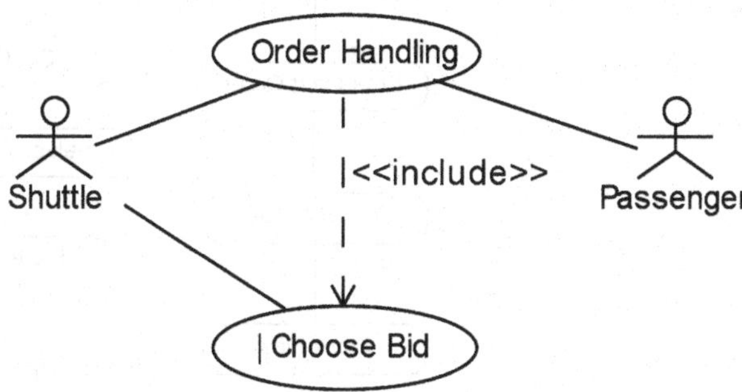

Fig. 10.4 Transport UCPS

interrelationships help in identifying relationships between use cases. Figure 10.3 summarizes the process of building a UCPS.

Most use case relationships are given in the usual manner (with `<<include>>` and `<<extend>>`). Those that are derived from constraints will, however, be related with other use cases by using the new relationship `<<constrain>>`, meaning that the origin use case restricts the behavior of the destination use case. (Origin and destination are indicated by the direction of the arrow representing the relationship.) Some of the use cases derived from constraint concerns are typically global properties, such as nonfunctional requirements. Figure 10.4 illustrates an example of a UCPS for the transport system, where C1a and C1b are represented by use cases. Note how C1b is given as a role use case, pointing out the clear distinction between enduring and volatile concerns—a reader of the model can immediately see where the volatility lies.

Identify Crosscutting Concerns Crosscutting concerns are those that are required by several other concerns. This information can be found in the concerns' templates, or by analyzing the relationships between use cases in the UCPS. For example, one use case that is included by several other use cases is crosscutting.

Fig. 10.5 Guidelines to map UCPS to activity diagrams or APSs

Input: a UCPS and the list of concern templates
Output: an APS for each use case role or crosscutting use case; an activity diagram for each use case

For each use case *U* corresponding to a concern *C*:
- If *U* is a use case, create a new activity diagram:
  - *U*'s activity diagram is a set of activities, one for each responsibility in *C*, connected by appropriate transitions
- If *U* is a use case role or crosscutting use case, create an APS:
  - *U*'s APS is a set of activities and activity roles that represent responsibilities in *C*, connected by appropriate role transitions

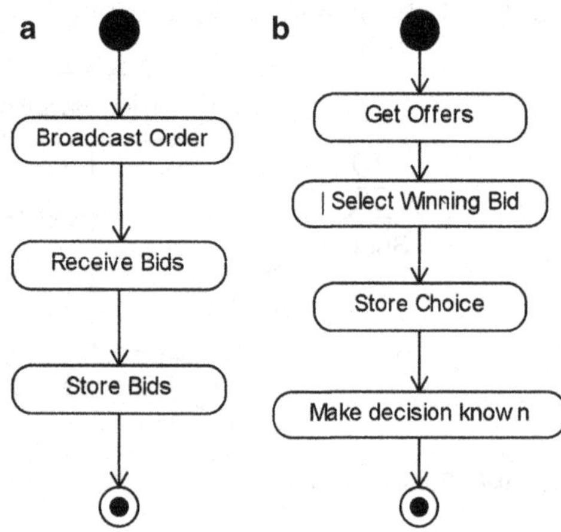

Fig. 10.6 *Order Handling* (**a**) and *Choose Bid* APS (**b**)

Build Activity Models Activities describe use cases and activity roles describe use case roles or crosscutting use cases. Figure 10.5 gives the process for creating an activity pattern specification from the UCPS. Each responsibility listed in the concern's template corresponds to an activity in an activity diagram or an activity role in an APS. The nature of the concern (crosscutting, enduring, or volatile) decides whether activities or activity roles are used. For example, C1b is volatile; therefore, one or more of its responsibilities will correspond to activity roles in the activity diagram. Activity roles are those that correspond to the responsibilities that are primarily responsible for making the concern volatile. In this case, responsibility 2 of C1b will correspond to a role activity (Fig. 10.6).

10.3.5 Model Instantiation

Model elements can be instantiated by a rule of the form:

```
<step #.> Replace |<modelElement A>
  with <modelElement B>
```

This means that *modelElement A* is eliminated and substituted by *modelElementB*, including its context. Instantiation is done for each particular configuration of the system. For example, consider our concern (C1b), represented in the UCPS as `|Choose Bid`. The instantiation rule is as follows:

```
1. Replace |Choose Bid
  with Choose From Bids (Equal Bids Choice Based On
   Arrival Time)
```

An instantiation for APS in Fig. 10.6 is as follows:

```
2. Replace |Select Winning Bid
   with Select Lowest Bid (Equal Bids Choice Based On
   Arrival Time)
```

Note that only volatile concern roles will need instantiation. The remaining roles elements might be used as "join points" for composition (Sect. 10.3.6).

10.3.6 Model Composition

For the purpose of this chapter we define two basic composition operators: **Insert** and **Replace**. The **Insert** operator can be used together with the two clauses **after** and **before**, meaning that a particular model element can be inserted after or before a certain point in the base model, respectively. The **Replace** operator, on the other hand, can be used together with the simple **with** clause, meaning that a model element replaces another (similar to an instantiation), together with a **choice** ([]) clause, meaning that more than one alternative is possible, together with a **par** (||) clause, meaning parallelism, etc. The clause **Compose** encapsulates a composition rule (c.f. Sect. 10.4.3 for concrete examples).

Composition and instantiation can be applied independently from each other in an incremental fashion, leading to consecutive refinements of abstract requirements models into more concrete analysis models, supported by a set of guidelines and heuristics. Composition is achieved by defining composition rules that explicitly specify how two or more models of the same type (e.g., activity diagrams and APSs) are weaved together. In a more traditional aspect-oriented view, only crosscutting concerns would be composed with base modules. Here, we use composition to weave aspectual or volatile models to base models. A composition rule consists of a set of instantiation steps, where PS elements are replaced with concrete elements or other PS elements:

```
Compose <PS A> with <PS B>
 <step #.> Replace |<A> with <B>
 <step #.> Insert <A> {after, before} <B>
 <step #.> Insert <A> {after, before} <B>
                   where <statement>
 <step #.> Delete <A>
```

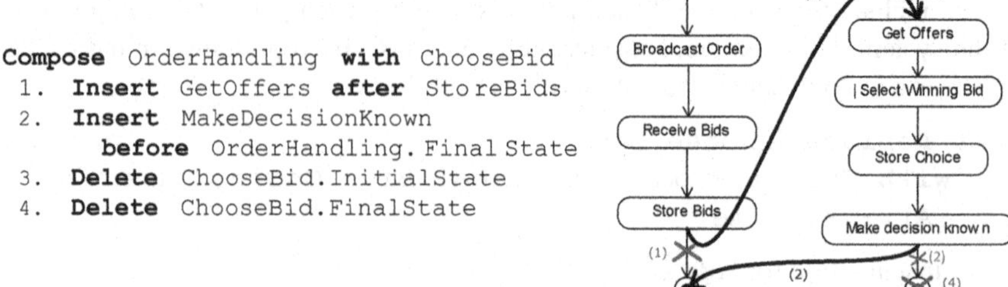

Fig. 10.7 Composition rule (*left*); OrderHandling & ChooseBid composed (*right*)

<step #.> **Delete** <B>

where "A" and "B" may be model elements (or models in the case of the **Insert** operator). A composition rule can, of course, be more complex than this, involving, for example, decision and parallel operators. The full description of a composition language is beyond the scope of this chapter, and we leave it for future work.

For our example, an obvious composition rule is to put together the activity diagram **OrderHandling** and the APS **ChooseBid** (Fig. 10.7 (left)). The resulting model is illustrated in Fig. 10.7 (right) where transitions (1) and (2) represent the effect of the two **Insert** operators. In this particular case, the choice of a particular method for choosing the winning bid would be performed after this composition. When the requirements change (i.e., volatile concerns change), composition can be used to update the model in an efficient and modular way.

By inserting `GetOffers` after `StoreBids` (1), we are actually replacing the flow that existed between `StoreBids` and the `FinalState` node of `OrderHandling`, thus leaving it dangling. The `InitialState` of `ChooseBid` also loses its flow to `GetOffers`. The flow from `MakeDecisionKnown` to `ChooseBid`'s `FinalState` is replaced in (2), so that `MakeDecisionKnown` now flows to `OrderHandling`'s `FinalState` (which ceases to be dangling). (3) and (4) delete the `InitialState` and `FinalState` of `ChooseBid`, which became dangling, so they are automatically removed from the composed model.

10.3.7 Concern Evolution

Evolution should cope with changes in concerns that are already part of the system and with new functionalities or constraints not yet part of the existing system. In the former, the system is prepared to handle the change, by either defining a new instantiation rule, or else by changing one or more composition rules. For example, a change in the process used to select the winning bid (C1b) is easily handled at all levels by choosing different rules (i.e., UCP and APS):

```
1. Replace |Choose Bid
   with Choose From Bids (Equal Bids Choice Based On
   History)
2. Replace |Select Winning Bid
  with Select Lowest Bid (Equal Bids Choice Based
  On History)
3. Replace |select Winning Bid
   with select Lowest Bid (Equal Bids Choice Based
   History)
```

In cases where we have to remove a concern, we need to remove all dependencies on this concern from all the composition rules. Coping with new requirements or constraints requires the reapplication of the method to identify the corresponding new concerns. These are integrated with the existing system by adding or changing existing composition rules.

10.4 Case Study

This section validates the approach described in the previous section by means of an example of the crisis management system, applied to car crashes: rescuing the victims of a car accident.

When a car crash is reported and confirmed, handling it typically involves two sorts of missions: a rescue mission, so that the people involved in the accident can receive appropriate medical care, and a repair mission, so that the accident location is cleared of any debris and traffic can flow through it normally again. The rescue mission typically involves a first aid professional transmitting injury information to an hospital, identifying the car crash victims, removing them from the crashed cars, administering first aid, and, if necessary, taking the accident victims to the hospital.

10.4.1 Concerns Identification

The crisis coordinator and the crisis management system employee are the most direct users of a crisis management system. There are other important stakeholders that also provide key information to the system, such as crisis victims, witnesses, and other stakeholders who help conducting some of the system's missions, such as first aid workers and professionals in charge of reinstating a normal situation by repairing properties damaged during the crisis. Other important stakeholders include the owners of the crisis management system, and civil protection organizations. In this chapter, we identify a non-exhaustive list of concerns for these systems—a

Table 10.3 List of concerns for the crisis management system

Concern #	Concern name	Concern description
F1	Witness report	Receive a crisis report from a witness
F2	Entity resource request	Request resources to handle crisis
F3	Authentication	The system must authenticate its users.
F4	Internal resources assignment	The system must support a sensible resources assignment.
F5	Mission execution	The system must support mission execution
NF1	Response time	The system must react in time in order to handle crisis situations fast enough so that victims can be rescued with efficiency and effectiveness.
NF2	Availability	The system must be available in order to be used
NF3	Legal issues	Legal issues might be raised to handle responsibilities in mission execution.

Table 10.4 Concerns classification

	Enduring	Volatile
Concerns	F1, F2, NF2	F3, F4, F5, NF1, NF3

more detailed analysis of such systems can be found in [13]. Some of the identified concerns reflect functional requirements, namely F1, F2, F3, F4, and F5, in Table 10.3. Others, namely, NF1, NF2, and NF3, reflect nonfunctional requirements that are typical of these systems. Table 10.3 presents a short description of each of these concerns.

10.4.2 From Classification to Refactoring

Concerns can be classified enduring or volatile. Table 10.4 identifies which concerns are considered as enduring and which are regarded as volatile.

The enduring concerns are those we expect to be stable in the future. A crisis management system is expected to handle crisis reports from victims (F1), as well as to supporting the request of external resources (F2) in a stable manner. The nonfunctional requirement *Availability* (NF2) is also considered enduring, as this sort of systems is expected to be virtually always available. Other concerns are more volatile. For instance, we need an authentication feature in the system (F3), but the exact way system user authentication is performed may evolve, over time. The same applies to internal resources assignment, which are constrained by factors external to this system, such as legal constraints, budget restrictions, or crisis management policy changes, among others. With respect to missions, this is a too generic concern, which we refactor into two more specialized concerns: rescue missions (F5a) and repair missions (F5b). The exact way rescue and repair missions are conducted is also bound to evolve, with the occurrence of new kinds of crises, the change in available means to deal with them, and so on. In this chapter, we consider two kinds of crises, car crashes and floods, each leading to different

Table 10.5 Refactored list of concerns

Concern #	Concern name	Description	Classification
F1	Witness report	Receive a crisis report from a witness	Enduring
F2	Entity resource request	Request resources to handle crisis	Enduring
F3	Authentication	The system must authenticate its users.	Volatile
F4	Internal resources assignment	The system must support a sensible resources assignment.	Volatile
F5a	Rescue victim	Victims may need to be rescued, receive special help and first aid and, if necessary, to be sent to the hospital for further treatment.	Volatile
F5a1	Rescue victim from car	A car crash rescue may involve removing the victim from the car and provide the victim with first aid.	Enduring
F5a2	Rescue victim from flood	A flood rescue involves providing the victim with first aid and, if necessary, transporting the victim to the hospital, or that is not necessary, transport the victim to a safe location.	Enduring
F5b	Repair public or private properties	Crisis may destroy public or private properties which need to be repaired. The system should support the coordination of those repair actions.	Volatile
F5c	Take to hospital	Take victim to nearest hospital, if necessary.	Volatile
F5d	Move to safe place	Take victim to safe location, if necessary.	Volatile
NF1	Response time	The system must react in time in order to handle crisis situations fast enough so that victims can be rescued with efficiency and effectiveness.	Volatile
NF2	Availability	The system must be available in order to be used	Enduring
NF3	Legal issues	Legal issues might be raised to handle responsibilities in mission execution.	Volatile

variations of how rescue missions should be conducted. These variations impose a refactoring operation of the rescue mission concern (F5a1 for car crashes, and F5a2 for floods). We also refactor the repair concern (F5b), so that we can support several different sorts of repair operations, each with their own specialized actors (F5b1 through F5b4). The exact way of transporting victims to the hospital (F5c) or a safe place (F5d) is also bound to change over time (e.g., through the acquisition of new equipments by the rescue teams), so we consider these as volatile concerns.

The response time constraints (NF1) and legal issues (NF3) are two examples of nonfunctional concerns that are typically not controlled by system developers, but have to be dealt with and supported, anyway, so we also consider them as volatile. Table 10.5 presents a summarized overview of the refactored list of concerns.

For the sake of space, we will only present in detail three of the concerns in our model, using the templates discussed in Sect. 10.3.3: *Rescue victim*, *Rescue Victim from car*, and *Take to hospital*.

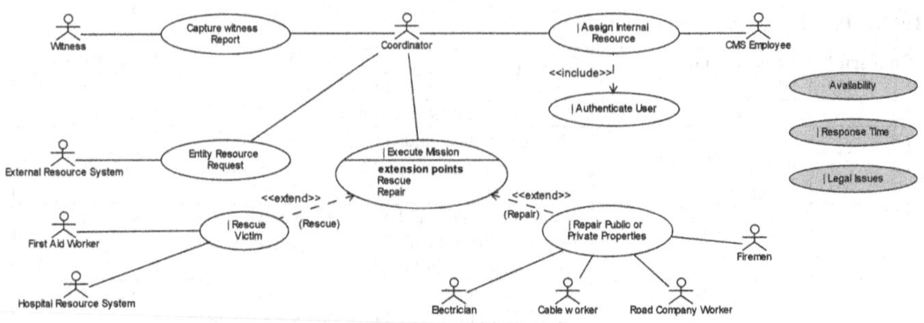

Fig. 10.8 UCPS for the crisis management system (overview)

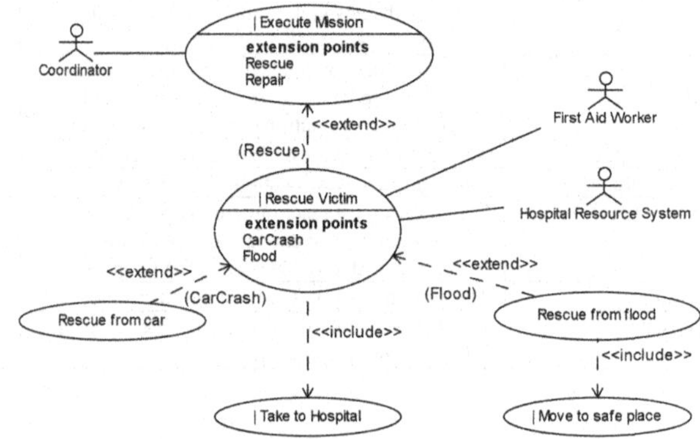

Fig. 10.9 UCPS for Rescue victim from car

10.4.3 Concern Representation

Build the Use Case Models A UCPS is obtained by applying the guidelines offered in Fig. 10.2. The UCPS in Fig. 10.8 illustrates a fragment of the resulting model, including all the concerns expressed in Table 10.5. *Response Time*, *Availability*, and *Legal Issues* are crosscutting concerns that constrain several other use cases, and are therefore represented in gray. The <<*constrain*>> relationships are not represented in the diagram, as it would clutter it. For example, legal issues impose restrictions on how missions should be executed (e.g., which resources should be assigned to a particular mission, or which is the allowable response time for a given crisis—the latter is an example of how a constraint may also constrain other constraints).

In this chapter, we will focus on |`RescueVictim` from a car crash. The fragment of the UCPS for this particular concern is presented in Fig. 10.9.

Build Activity Models Following the rules given in Fig. 10.5, activity diagrams and APSs can be derived from use cases and use case roles. Figure 10.10 includes APSs diagrams for (a) `RescueVictim`, (b) `RemoveFromCar`, and

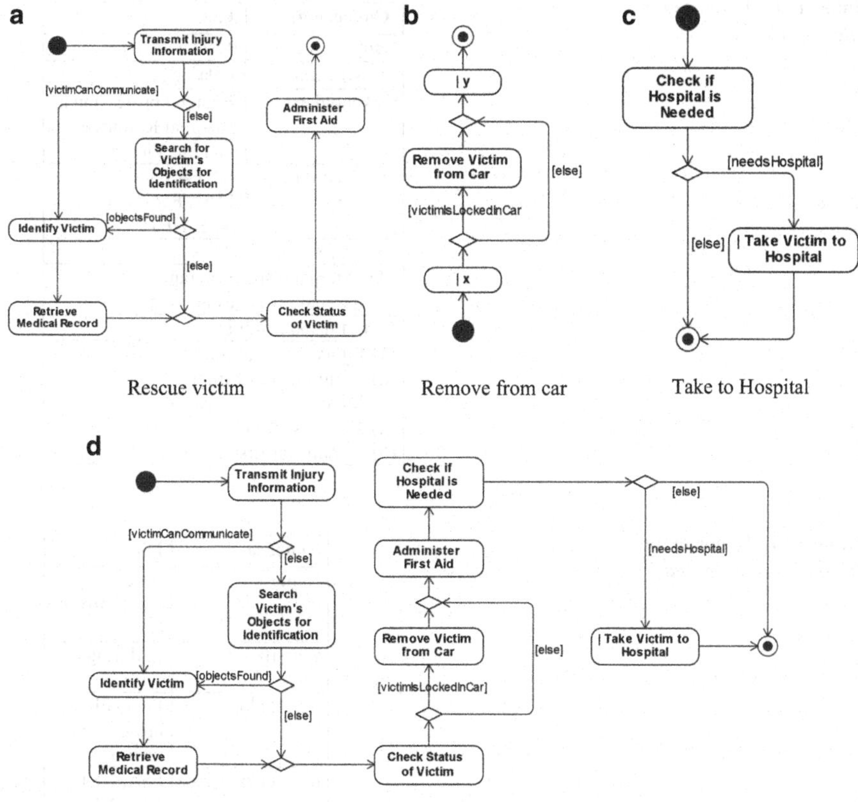

Fig. 10.10 Rescue victim activity diagram and APSs. (**a**) Rescue victim, (**b**) Remove from car, (**c**) Take to Hospital, and (**d**) Composed car crash rescue

(c) `TakeToHospital`. Figure 10.10a–c correspond to the templates defined in Tables 10.6, 10.7, and 10.8, respectively. All the responsibilities listed therein can be directly mapped to activities in these diagrams, with the exception of `Victim Identification`. This activity is broken down into several more fine-grained activities, to support the two alternatives of victim identification: either the victim is able to provide his own identification, or the first aid rescuer can look for the victim's id in the victim's objects.

10.4.4 Instantiation and Composition

At the activity level, composition can be accomplished using the **Replace**, **Insert**, and **Move** operators to bring together APSs and/or activity diagrams. An example

Table 10.6 Template for "*Rescue Victim*"

Concern #	F5a
Name	Rescue victim
Classification	Volatile service
Stakeholders	First aid professional, Hospital Resource system, Victim
Interrelationships	F2, F4, F5, F5a1, F5a2, F5c, NF1, NF2; NF3
List of pre-conditions	
(1) External resources granted (2) Internal resources granted	
List of responsibilities	
(1) Injury information (2) Victim identification (3) Medical record retrieval (4) Victim status check (5) Administer first aid	

Table 10.7 Template for "*Rescue victim from car*"

Concern #	F5a1
Name	Rescue victim from car
Classification	Enduring service
Stakeholder	First aid professional, victim
Interrelationships	F5A, NF1, NF2, NF3
List of pre-conditions	
(1) Car Crash	
List of responsibilities	
(1) Remove victim from car	

of a composition rule joining `RescueVictim` with `RemoveVictimFromCar` is the following:

```
Compose |RescueVictim with RemoveVictimFromCar
 1. Replace |x with CheckStatusOfVictim
 2. Replace |y with AdministerFirstAid
```

A second rule can then be defined to compose `|TakeToHospital` with the result of the previous composition

```
Compose |RescueVictimFromCar with |TakeToHospital
 1. Insert CheckIfHospitalIsNeeded after
      AdministerFirstAid.
```

Table 10.8 Template for *"Take to hospital"*

Concern #	F5c
Concern name	Take to hospital
Classification	Volatile Service
Stakeholder	First aid worker, victim
Interrelationships	F5, NF1, NF2, NF3
List of pre-conditions	
(1) Rescue	
List of responsibilities	
(1) Check if hospital needed (2) Take to hospital	

Figure 10.10d presents the resulting composed model, which can be automatically generated. If needed, the composition process can be applied again to join more models to this resulting model until all models are joined to form a unique model of the full system.

This model can be instantiated in different ways. In particular, the `|TakeVictimToHospital` activity is volatile and can be instantiated so that the victim is transported with an ambulance, using a rule of the type:

```
Replace|TakeVictimToHospital
with TakeWithAmbulance
```

`|TakeVictimToHospital` could also be instantiated so that victims are carried to the hospital by a helicopter.

```
Replace|TakeVictimToHospital
with TakeWithAmbulance
```

Summarizing:

- With externalization, the effort involved in making a change is to identify the volatile concern, to model the concern separately, and to specify the instantiation and composition rules.
- Without externalization, the effort involved is to look at the existing model and decide (perhaps based on existing requirements traceability information) which parts of the model must be changed; then to change those parts and validate the new model.

A key advantage of the externalization approach seems to be that the new model does not need to undergo such extensive validation—of course, one has to be sure that the composition rules are correct and applied correctly, but there is less danger of missing a model element that needs to be changed—because the elements that need to be changed have already been externalized.

The trade-offs seem to be very similar to the trade-offs involved in product line development. Product line development advocates feature modeling whereby commonalities and variations among a family of systems are explicitly modeled. This requires a greater degree of up-front modeling effort, but the payback is in that new members of the product family require less effort to develop. The case is similar for externalizing volatile requirements.

10.5 Method Evaluation

The evaluation criteria used here were proposed in [3]. There four general comparison criteria are defined (evolvability, composability, traceability, and scalability) as well as five other specific criteria (homogeneity concern treatment, trade-off analysis, verification and validation, handling functional and nonfunctional crosscutting requirements, mapping requirements to later stages) for assessing requirements engineering approaches.

General Criteria The main drive to define our method was to offer improved support for *evolution*. Volatile concerns cannot be disregarded as time to market is a major concern of leading companies when developing their systems. Our instantiations and compositions facilitate rapid changes in requirements (see Sect. 10.3.7). By using aspect-oriented concepts combined with role-based models, *composability* is assured at several different levels of abstraction (concern, use case, and activity levels) through the definition of simple composition rules. *Traceability* is supported by concern templates and model derivation guidelines. Finally, the modeler has to specify the instantiations and compositions and these will be, in the worse case, different for each base model crosscut by the aspect. We are now studying how to overcome this *scalability* problem by, for example, reusing instantiations and compositions.

Specific Criteria Core, volatile, or aspectual concerns are all treated homogeneously by using the same set of techniques. While identifying, describing, and classifying concerns, we do not distinguish between *functional requirements*, *nonfunctional requirements*, and crosscutting requirements. The method provides several guidelines that support *mappings* across several models. As we follow a UML-based approach, most of the resulting artifacts have a direct map to the analysis phase. However, we need to invest more on this, maybe basing our research on MDD. *Trade-off analysis* has been addressed in our previous work [19], but not here. *Verification and validation* techniques are not handled in this chapter.

10.6 Related Work

Our pattern specifications are based on [10], where an aspect is defined through role models to be composed into UML diagrams. However, the approach does not allow concrete modeling elements in role models. Interaction pattern specifications with concrete modeling elements and related composition rules were first discussed in [1]. These ideas helped to define UCPS and APS described in [15]. In this paper, we define a model that integrates UCPSs, APSs, and IPSs in a systematic way. We also define similar composition rules with concrete and role elements.

Jacobson agrees that use case extensions are a way to handle aspects during requirements [11]. However, his work does not include broadly scoped properties nor does he handle evolution through volatile concerns.

Theme [2] supports the requirements analysis activity by providing an approach to identify base and crosscutting behaviors from a set of actions. It defines actions as sensible verbs for the domain. An action is a potential theme, which is a collection of structures and behaviors that represent one feature. The results of analysis are mapped to UML models. Compared to our work the definition of themes to express requirements is more structured than our concern definition, but our composition rules using patterns specifications provide more flexibility.

Clarke and Walker [5] describe composition patterns to deal with crosscutting concerns as patterns at the design level. Pattern binding is used, and sequence and class diagrams illustrate compositions. The compositions, however, are rigid as they concentrate on pattern instantiations.

Moreira et al. [16] propose an extension of use case modeling to handle evolution through coordination contracts. The work we present here differs not only on the level of abstraction and the use of aspects, but also the focus on concerns and composition rules. Requirements volatility has also been addressed in the context of coding and testing [14]). The focus is on measuring the impact of requirements changes on defect density which is a measure of software quality used as acceptance criteria for a piece of software. We believe that the early identification, separation, and modularization of volatile requirements, well before the implementation takes place, would reduce the effort to cope with requirements change during coding, where the impact of the change can be easily localized and its side effects better controlled.

The idea to externalize volatile concerns is in some respects similar to the notions of product line architectures [6] and generative programming [7]. They model a family of related applications and then configure particular instances. Our work is similar but focuses on volatility. Although our work is less general, it does not require the huge investment associated with modeling a related family of application.

10.7 Conclusions

In the introduction we stated that volatile concerns and aspects share the need for independency, modular representation, and composition. Throughout the chapter we discussed why those three characteristics were important to support evolution, which is constrained by volatile requirements, and how aspect orientation and pattern specifications can help in handling it. To address this we proposed the externalization and consequent modularization of constraints and volatile services to cope with change on requirements. This is supported by an evolutionary method, where concern classification, requirements refactoring, model instantiation, and model composition play a major role. Composition and instantiation can be applied independently from each other in an incremental manner, where guidelines drive subsequent refinements of abstract requirements models into more concrete analysis models.

For future work we will investigate (1) how graph transformations can be used to offer a more powerful means for composition; (2) how this approach can be adapted in the context of product lines; (3) how to handle possible conflicts resulting from composing pattern specifications; (4) how to address conflicting emergent behavior that may appear when two or more candidate aspects are allowed to coexist, by adapting the approach the authors developed in [19]; (5) how to extend these ideas to the detailed design activity; and (6) develop a tool that supports the identification of concerns, their specification and composition.

References

1. J Araújo, J. Whittle, D.-K. Kim, Modeling and composing scenario-based requirements with aspects, in *Paper presented at the 12th IEEE International Requirements Engineering Conference, 2004 (RE 2004)*, Kyoto, Japan, 2004, pp. 58–67
2. E. Baniassad, S. Clarke, Theme: an approach for aspect-oriented analysis and design, in *Paper presented at the 26th International Conference on Software Engineering (ICSE'04)*, Edinburgh, Scotland, 2004, pp. 158–167
3. R. Chitchyan, A. Rashid, P. Sawyer, A. Garcia, M.P. Alarcon, J. Bakker, B. Tekinerdogan, S. Clarke, A. Jackson, *Survey of Analysis and Design Approaches*, AOSD-Europe, 2005, p. 259
4. L. Chung, B.A. Nixon, E. Yu, *Non-functional Requirements in Software Engineering*, vol. 5 (Kluwer Academic, Boston, MA, 2000)
5. S. Clarke, R.J. Walker, Composition patterns: an approach to designing reusable aspects, in *Paper presented at the 23rd International Conference on Software Engineering (ICSE'2001)*, Toronto, ON, 2001, pp. 5–14
6. P. Clements, L. Northrop, *Software Product Lines: Practices and Patterns*, 3rd edn. (Addison Wesley Professional, New York, NY, 2001)
7. K. Czarnecki, U.W. Eisenecker, *Generative Programming: Methods, Tools and Applications*, 1st edn. (Addison-Wesley, New York, NY, 2000)
8. Å.G. Dahlstedt, A. Persson, Requirements interdependencies – moulding the State of Research into a Research Agenda, in *Paper presented at the 9th International Workshop on Requirements Engineering – Foundation for Software Quality (REFSQ'03)*, Klagenfurt/Velden, Austria, 2003, pp. 55–64

9. D.G. Firesmith, Creating a project-specific requirements engineering process. J. Object Technol. **3**(5), 31–44 (2004)
10. R. France, D.-K. Kim, S. Ghosh, E. Song, A UML-based pattern specification technique. IEEE Trans. Softw. Eng. **30**(3), 193–206 (2004)
11. I. Jacobson, P.-W. Ng, *Aspect-Oriented Software Development with Use Cases* (Addison-Wesley Professional, New York, NY, 2005)
12. G. Kiczales, E. Hilsdale, J. Hugunin, M. Kersten, J. Palm, W.G. Griswold, An overview of AspectJ, in *Paper presented at the 15th European Conference on Object-Oriented Programming (ECOOP 2001)*, Budapest, Hungary, 2001, pp. 327–354
13. J. Kienzle, N. Guelfi, S. Mustafiz, Crisis management systems: a case study for aspect-oriented modeling. Trans. Aspect Oriented Softw. Dev. **6210**(2010), 1–22 (2010)
14. Y.K. Malaiya, J. Denton, Requirements volatility and defect density, in *Paper presented at the 10th International Symposium on Software Reliability Engineering (ISSRE)*, Boca Raton, FL, 1999, pp. 285–294
15. A. Moreira, J. Araújo, Handling unanticipated requirements change with aspects, in *Paper presented at the Software Engineering and Knowledge Engineering Conference (SEKE 2004)*, 2004, pp. 411–415
16. A. Moreira, J.L. Fiadeiro, L. Andrade, Requirements through coordination contracts, in *Paper presented at the Advanced Information Systems Engineering*, 2003, pp. 633–646
17. OMG, *OMG Unified Modeling Language (OMG UML), Infrastructure, version 2.3, formal/2010-05-03* (Object Management Group Inc., 2010a), p. 226
18. OMG, *OMG Unified Modeling Language (OMG UML), Superstructure, formal/2010-05-05* (Object Management Group Inc., 2010b), p. 758
19. A. Rashid, A. Moreira, J. Araújo, Modularisation and composition of aspectual requirements, in *Paper presented at the 2nd International Conference on Aspect-Oriented Software Development (AOSD 2003)*, Boston, MA, 2003, pp. 11–20
20. A. Sampaio, R. Chitchyan, A, Rashid, P. Rayson, EA-Miner: a tool for automating aspect-oriented requirements identification, in *Paper presented at the 20th IEEE/ACM International Conference on Automated Software Engineering (ASE 2005)*, Long Beach, CA, 2005, pp. 352–355
21. I. Sommerville, *Software Engineering*, 8th edn. (Addison-Wesley, New York, NY, 2006)
22. E. Yu, Modelling strategic relationships for process reengineering, PhD Thesis, University of Toronto, 1995

Part IV
Aspect Interactions

Chapter 11
Conflict Identification with EA-Analyzer

Alberto Sardinha, Ruzanna Chitchyan, João Araújo, Ana Moreira, and Awais Rashid

Abstract Conflict identification in Aspect-Oriented Requirements Engineering (AORE) is an integral step toward resolving conflicting dependencies between requirements at an early stage of the software development. However, to date there has been no work supporting detection of conflicts in a large set of textual requirements without converting texts into an alternative representation (such as models or formal specification) or direct stakeholder involvement. Here, we present EA-Analyzer, an automated tool for identifying conflicts directly in aspect-oriented requirements specified in natural language text. This chapter is centered on a case study-based discussion of the accuracy of the tool. EA-Analyzer is applied to the Crisis Management System, a case study used as an established benchmark in several areas of aspect-oriented research.

A. Sardinha (✉)
INESC-ID and Instituto Superior Técnico, UTL, Lisbon, Portugal
e-mail: jose.alberto.sardinha@ist.utl.pt

R. Chitchyan
Department of Computer Science, University of Leicester, Leicester, UK
e-mail: rc256@leicester.ac.uk

J. Araújo • A. Moreira
Departamento de Informática, Universidade Nova de Lisboa, Caparica, Portugal
e-mail: joao.araujo@fct.unl.pt; amm@fct.unl.pt

A. Rashid
Computing Department, Lancaster University, Lancaster, UK
e-mail: marash@comp.lancs.ac.uk

A. Moreira et al. (eds.), *Aspect-Oriented Requirements Engineering*, DOI 10.1007/978-3-642-38640-4_11,

11.1 Introduction to Conflict Identification in Aspect-Oriented Requirements

Aspect-Oriented Requirements Engineering (AORE) [1] aims at addressing the identification, representation, modularization, composition, and subsequent analysis of crosscutting requirements. Identification and resolution of conflicts between concerns is often an essential part of the analysis activity. Since in AORE most concern inter-relationships can be defined via compositions, composition specifications are also a natural focus for conflict identification work. Thus, it is not surprising that a number of studies have been focusing on conflict detection and resolution via composition definitions [2–4].

As discussed in previous chapters, although most requirements documents tend to be written in natural language, research on conflict detection in aspect-oriented (AO) textual requirements tends to reformat the textual artifacts before starting the conflict identification process. For instance, some researchers tackle the conflict identification by first carrying out formalization of requirements and compositions [4–6]; others represent requirements and compositions via models, then undertake model-based analysis [7, 8]; and, finally, others involve stakeholders to help in conflict identification and resolution based on the priorities explicitly expressed by the stakeholders [2]. Prior to our work discussed below, there has been no research on text-only-based conflict identification in AORE.

This chapter presents EA-Analyzer, a tool for identifying conflicts in textual AO requirements, without needing to convert the textual artifacts into an alternative format, or engaging stakeholders directly. The tool operates on annotated natural language text and compositions defined using the RDL annotations [9]. The annotations do not alter or reduce the textual requirements, but only decorate text with syntactic and semantic linguistics tags [10]. A Bayesian learning method, called Naive Bayes [11], is utilized by EA-Analyzer to learn the nature of the composed concerns and to detect conflicts within the textual specifications.

This chapter is centered on a case study-based discussion of the accuracy of the tool, where EA-Analyzer is applied to the Crisis Management System, a case study used as an established benchmark in several areas of aspect-oriented research. The initial evaluation of the tool suggests that this is a promising direction for text-based conflict identification.

The rest of this chapter is organized as follows. Section 11.2 presents the related work and discusses the advantages and disadvantages of aspect-oriented approaches when compared to EA-Analyzer. Section 11.3 details the approach and the EA-Analyzer tool developed to address the problems discussed in the previous section. Section 11.4 presents the case study demonstrating the evaluation of the tool. Section 11.5 concludes the chapter.

11.2 Related Work

The most popular approaches that deal with conflicts in requirements are the goal-oriented and aspect-oriented ones; hence, Sect. 11.2.1 presents some related work on goal-oriented approaches and Sect. 11.2.2 discusses the related approaches of aspect-oriented requirements engineering, where EA-Analyzer is a novel approach within this research area.

11.2.1 Goal-Oriented Approaches

In the NFR framework [12], the focus is on the identification of conflicts of non-functional requirements—it does not explicitly deal with functional concerns, but establishes a link to them. The analysis starts with softgoals, i.e., quality attributes of a system. The system's softgoals may be security, usability, performance, and availability. In the NFR framework, softgoals are normally decomposed and refined into more solution space model elements, captured by a softgoal graph structure. By analyzing the graph, interfering softgoals can be found, e.g., security goals interfere with usability in general. Resolution of such conflicts is achieved by selecting the most appropriate softgoals after some trade-off analysis.

*i** [13] was developed for modeling and reasoning about organizational environments and their information systems. It focuses on the concept of intentional actor. *i** has two main modeling components: the Strategic Dependency (SD) model and the Strategic Rationale (SR) model. The SD model describes the dependency relationships among the actors in an organizational context. The SR model provides a more detailed level of modeling than the SD model, since it focuses on the modeling of intentional elements (goals, softgoals, tasks, and resources) and relationships internal to actors. Intentional elements are related by means-end or decomposition links. Means-end links are used to specify alternative ways to achieve goals. Decomposition links are used to decompose tasks. Apart from these two links, there are the contribution links, which can be positive or negative. These are the basis for the conflict identification, which is specified in a similar way to the NFR framework. In both approaches, the conflict degree is specified and alternatives are used to solve conflicts.

KAOS [14] is a systematic approach for discovering and structuring system-level requirements. In KAOS, goals can be divided into requirements (a type of goal to be achieved by a software agent), expectations (a type of goal to be achieved by an environment agent) and softgoals (e.g., quality attributes). In KAOS, goals can be refined into subgoals through and/or decompositions. There is also the possibility of identifying conflicts between nonfunctional goals and represent it in the goal models.

11.2.2 Aspect-Oriented Requirements Engineering Approaches

Aspect-Oriented Requirement Engineering (AORE) approaches have enabled the early identification of candidate crosscutting concerns within problem domains. Such strategies enable requirements engineers to specify how requirements compose with one another to explicitly externalize their interdependencies.

This has significant advantages for reasoning about requirements, as their mutual influences and tradeoffs can be identified before architecture is derived. As well as this, the transition to an aspect-oriented architecture can be eased by the explicit recognition of early aspects within the domain.

However, this benefit also brings with it a significant challenge—namely, the accurate detection of conflicts between requirements. The increased modularity and advanced composition mechanisms which AORE approaches tend to employ can complicate the task of discerning where requirements interact with one another and whether a given interaction constitutes a potential conflict. This issue has received a great deal of research attention within the AO community when the conflict is expressed at the code level; but research at the requirements level is much less mature. In this section we discuss the existing AORE approaches that support conflict detection and highlight the open issues in this area. We group the available AORE approaches on basis of their overall conflict identification strategy into the following three groups:

11.2.2.1 Formalization-Based Approaches

Within the AO conflict detection research area, many current approaches require some formal specification of requirements in order to detect conflicts among requirements. In other words, these approaches require precise expression of the properties of requirements and decide whether the compositions specified over these requirements invalidate these properties.

Examples of this strand of work are the AO Composition Frames [5]; Composition Frames model the semantics of requirements (in the form of Problem Frames) being composed with one another. The requirements of this composition—that is, the formal properties of its satisfaction—can be validated against the state machine expressed in the Composition Frame and thus conflicts detected. Here the validity of the conflict detection depends on the sound construction of the Problem Frames and their compositions.

In [6], AO models are specified in Aspect-UML, which includes formal annotations of aspects and joinpoints. These Aspect-UML models are transformed into Alloy, a structural modeling language based on first-order logic. Alloy includes an analyzer that can check the validity of assertions over a model, and so the Aspect-UML model of an AO system can be checked for aspects introducing properties to the system that render other aspect assumptions invalid and thus determine conflicts.

Similarly, the work in [4] presents a conflict detection technique based on transformation of textual compositions into temporal logic formulae based on a catalogue of formalizations of natural language operators. The semantics of the compositions can thus be compared with one another for temporal overlap and violation of system properties, which implies a conflict between requirements.

The major disadvantage of these approaches is that the transformation of requirements into specific formal representations will require substantial time and effort, which may outweigh the advantages of precisely detecting conflicts. Moreover, the formalized representations become less accessible to broader audiences. For instance, in order to understand implications of the Alloy analyzer results, the analyst has to be familiar with the formalization framework. Moreover, if there are any errors introduced in the formalization process, the detected conflicts may not be truly representative of those present in the requirements themselves.

11.2.2.2 Model-Based Approaches

A number of AORE approaches take a (design-level) model-based view on conflict detection; that is, they expect the requirements to be (at least initially) structured into specific models before conflicts can be detected.

For instance, the work in [7] models requirements as use cases in UML notation, and the crosscutting concerns are activities which refine the use cases. The approach then translates these UML diagrams into type graphs, with activities being modeled as graph transformations. Applying these graph transformations sequentially can thus reveal conflicts between requirements. A similar technique based on statechart weaving on UML models was proposed in [15].

Similarly, the work in [8] adapts the Theme/UML [16] approach to formally model compositions between base and aspect concerns. Certain forms of conflict based on global properties, such as visibility and kind, can then be discerned and automatically resolved. Another similar technique for class diagrams is presented in [17].

The disadvantages of the model-based approaches are twofold. Firstly, the necessity of modeling adds an extra step to the conflict detection process, which may require additional time and effort. Secondly, the structuring of requirements into models may lose information, which means that information encoded in the requirements, including potential conflicts, may be omitted/lost before the interaction analysis commences. Also, similar to formalization-based approaches, a modeling error may invalidate the results of the analysis.

11.2.2.3 Stakeholder Priority-Based Approaches

Finally, the stakeholder priority-based work [1, 18–20] handles conflicts via stakeholder involvement. If interactions can be identified using a technique such as ARCADE [1], the stakeholders can then determine whether such compositions are positive, negative or neutral from their point of view, and refine the requirements accordingly [1]. Alternatively, stakeholders state their preferred nonfunctional requirements up-front, and mathematical reasoning techniques (i.e., a multicriteria decision making method called Analytical Hierarchy Process [21, 22]) are then applied to help conflict resolution [2].

More recently, in the AMPLE project [23], a novel hybrid assessment method, HAM, was proposed and a software tool was developed. HAM combines the best properties of two well known multicriteria decision making methods, the Analytical Hierarchy Process and the Weighted Average [24]; this combination helped to avoid some problematic features of those methods [25].

The main limitations of these approaches are that (1) each concern must be allocated a specific priority; (2) conflict handling is often based on one criterion, the priority (except for [2], where multicriteria analysis is supported); (3) the conflict identification and resolution requires direct involvement of the stakeholders.

In summary, although the above discussed AORE approaches can help in conflict identification for AORE, what is missing from the current state of the art is a tool-supported informal approach which is able to determine potential interactions based on compositions of the requirements themselves, without having to resort to the formalization/modeling or the subjective (and frequently arbitrary) opinions of stakeholders. Such a tool would enable conflicts to be detected quickly from textual specifications themselves and thus provide a cost-effective solution to developers.

11.3 Detecting Conflicts in an Aspect-Oriented Specification

This section presents the EA-Analyzer tool and the process utilized to identify conflicts between requirements in the Crisis Management System. We will start presenting the annotation process of the Crisis Management specification with the Requirements Description Language (RDL). The following sections describe the inner workings of the tool on the annotated specification and an empirical evaluation of the tool.

11.3.1 Annotating Textual Requirements with RDL

The Requirements Description Language (RDL) [10] utilizes XML tags to annotate a natural language specification, in order to express dependencies and interactions between various groups of requirements (such as viewpoints and use cases). A previous chapter of this book presents a detailed description of the RDL and discusses the usability of the approach; hence, we refer the reader to this chapter for a detailed discussion regarding the RDL.

Figures 11.1 and 11.2 show an example of a Nonfunctional Requirement (NFR) in the Crisis Management System that has been annotated with the RDL tags. The

```
<Concern name="Real-time">
...
<Requirement id="3">
    The <Subject>system</Subject>
    <Degree type="modal" semantics="obligation" level="high">shall</Degree>
    be able to
    <Relationship type="Move" semantics="Transfer_Posession">retrieve</Relationship>
    any stored
    <Object>information</Object>
    with a maximum
    <Object>delay</Object>of 500 milliseconds
  </Requirement>
 </Concern>
```

Fig. 11.1 Example of a NFR requirement in the crisis management system

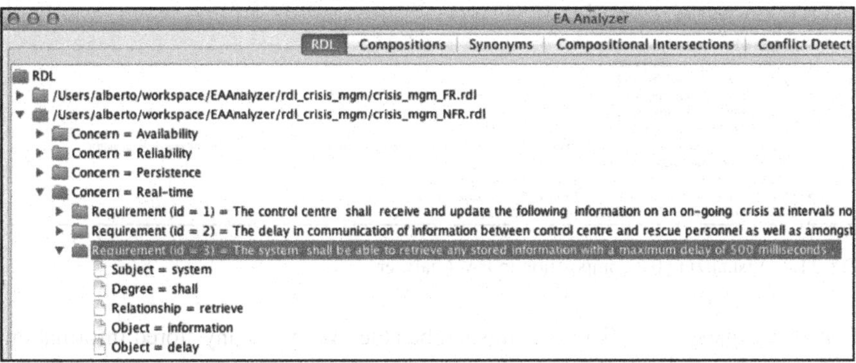

Fig. 11.2 Visualizing the NFR requirement in EA-Analyzer

annotated RDL text is generated with the semiautomated EA-Miner [26] tool, which is based on a general purpose NLP tool, Wmatrix [27].

In addition, the RDL tags also express dependencies and interactions between requirements. Hence, an analyst can define domain relationships (via RDL compositions) using only the natural language text. For instance, RDL compositions can mandate that a requirement must precede another one, such as the real-time requirement in Fig. 11.1 ("The system shall be able to retrieve any stored information with a maximum delay of 500 ms"), which should be satisfied before any other requirement that retrieves information.

An RDL composition consists of three parts, namely *Constraint*, *Base*, and *Outcome*. Each part has a semantic query that selects requirements from the specification with the aim of ensuring a desired interaction. For instance, Fig. 11.3 presents a composition that must ensure that the requirements selected by the *Base* query (e.g., "The system shall have access to detailed maps, terrain data and weather conditions ..." in Fig. 11.4) are constrained by the requirements selected by the

```
<Composition name="Performance (Real-time)">
        <Constraint operator="apply">(subject="system" and relationship="retrieve" and
        object="information" and object="delay")</Constraint>
        <Base operator="before">relationship="handling" or relationship="processing" or
        relationship="request" and relationship="access"</Base>
        <Outcome operator="ensure"/>
</Composition>
```

Fig. 11.3 Example of a composition in the crisis management system

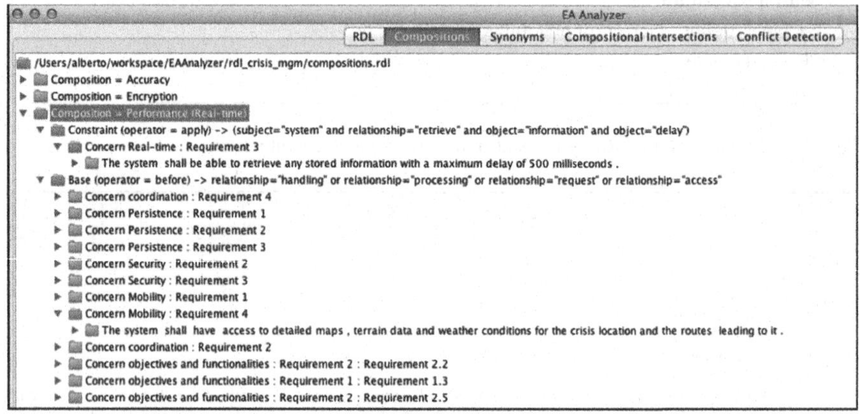

Fig. 11.4 Visualizing the composition in EA-Analyzer

Constraint query (i.e., "The system shall be able to retrieve any stored information with a maximum delay of 500 ms").

11.3.2 Detecting Conflicts in the Crisis Management Specification

The main goal of EA-Analyzer is to detect conflicts within a textual specification that has been previously annotated with RDL tags; recall that RDL tags are added with the help of the EA-Miner tool. In addition, the tool has a Graphical User Interface (GUI) that helps to visualize the annotated specification and the composition, such as the examples in Figs. 11.2 and 11.4.

In EA-Analyzer, the problem of detecting conflicts is formulated as a classification problem, which is a well-studied problem in machine learning [11]. The tool operates on RDL by using its compositions and annotated requirements and utilizes composed requirements to decide whether they have a conflicting dependency.

EA-Analyzer has to go through a learning process before the tool can be utilized for detecting conflicts. The learning process consists of the following steps (1) identifying all the sets of requirements that crosscut one or more base concerns,

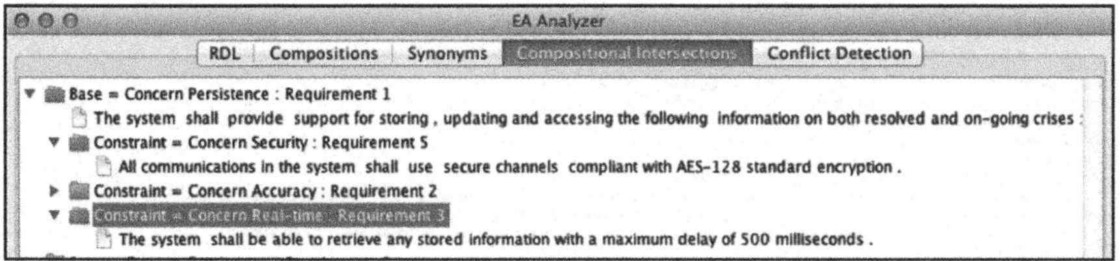

Fig. 11.5 Visualizing the compositional intersections in EA-Analyzer

also known as Compositional Intersections (Sect. 11.3.2.1); (2) generating training examples for the learning method by labeling the Compositional Intersections (Sect. 11.3.2.2); and (3) training the classifier based on the examples generated in step (2) (Sect. 11.3.2.3).

11.3.2.1 Identifying Compositional Intersections

The first step in the learning process is concerned with the identification of the compositional intersections; compositional intersections are used as a basis to detect conflicts among composed concerns, because they explicitly represent the interactions of a requirement with other requirements with reference to a base requirement.

A compositional intersection is the union of all the constraint requirements (i.e., requirements that have been selected by the constraint queries) that crosscut the same base requirement. For instance, the Crisis Management specification has a composition that selects the constraint requirement R_3 of the *Real-time concern* (i.e., "The system shall be able to retrieve any stored information with a maximum delay of 500 ms") and the base requirement R_1 of the *Persistence concern* (i.e., "The system shall provide support for storing, updating and accessing the following information ..."). In addition, the specification has another composition that selects the constraint requirement R_5 of the *Security concern* (i.e., "All communications in the system shall use secure channels compliant with AES-128 standard encryption") and the aforementioned base requirement (i.e., R_1 of the *Persistence concern*). Hence, R_3 of the *Real-time concern* and R_5 of the *Security concern* are part of the compositional intersection of R_1 of the *Persistence concern* as shown in Fig. 11.5.

11.3.2.2 Generating Training Examples

The machine learning technique utilized by EA-Analyzer requires a set of labeled examples to train the tool. This step enables the tool to be trained on a per-organization basis, so that each organization can have their EA-Analyzer tool tailored for detecting conflicts in their requirements documents.

Labeled examples are time consuming to obtain since they normally require a human annotator to examine and label each training example. In order to reduce this burden, we have implemented a module in EA-Analyzer that partially

Fig. 11.6 Generating training examples with EA-Analyzer

automates this step. Figure 11.6 presents the user interface (UI) that helps the human annotator label the composition intersection that has been previously identified (Sect. 11.3.2.1). In the UI, the human annotator is only required to select the conflicting requirements from the top list and the tool automatically performs a brute force procedure that labels each occurrence of the conflicting dependency in the set of examples (i.e., the compositional intersection that have been selected to train the tool). Figure 11.6 shows also that the tool requires not only training examples of conflicting dependencies within a compositional intersection but also examples of requirements within a compositional intersection that are interacting harmoniously.

Figure 11.6 presents a well-known example of a potential conflict between an *Encryption* requirement and a *Performance* requirement [28], since introducing encryption into a system reduces its responsiveness. The *Encryption* requirement is R_5 of the *Security concern* (i.e., “All communications in the system shall use secure channels compliant with AES-128 standard encryption”) and the *Performance* requirement is R_3 of the *Real-time concern* (i.e., “The system shall be able to retrieve any stored information with a maximum delay of 500 ms”). In this example, the human annotator has to select these two conflicting requirements from the top list and the tool automatically labels each occurrence of the conflicting dependency in the compositional intersections below. The labeled examples are then saved to a file so that the tool can train the machine learning technique.

11.3.2.3 Training EA-Analyzer to Identify Conflicts

EA-Analyzer utilizes the Naïve Bayes learning method to train the tool based on the training examples provided in the previous step (Sect. 11.3.2.2). The learning method leads to a bag of words model (BoW); the BoW is a method in Natural Language Processing that models text as an ordered collection of independent words represented in a term-frequency vector, disregarding grammar[1] and even word order.

For instance, one can imagine the BoW of EA-Analyzer with two bags full of words. The first bag is filled with words found in compositional intersections that have a potential conflict, such as the potential conflict presented in Sect. 11.3.2.2 (i.e., the well-known example of a potential conflict between an *Encryption* requirement and a *Performance* requirement). The second bag is filled with words found in compositions that do not have a potential conflict. While some words can appear in both bags, the first bag will contain conflict-related words such as "encryption" and "retrieve" much more frequently. On the other hand, the second bag will contain more words related to the other requirements. Hence, a new compositional intersection that has more words that come from the first bag than the second bag will be classified as a conflict.

11.3.2.4 Advantages and Disadvantages of the Learning Method of EA-Analyzer

This learning method in EA-Analyzer presents two advantages. First, the learning method only requires a small amount of data to train the Naive Bayes classifier [11]. Second, the learning method can be easily trained on a per-organization basis, so that each organization can have their EA-Analyzer tool tailored for detecting conflicts in their requirements documents. Moreover, it has been proven to be very powerful (and with outstanding performance) in NLP problems such as text classification and topic modeling. However, the main disadvantage of this learning method is that it only considers the distribution of the words and loses the relationships between them. To overcome this problem, search engines commonly use vocabularies consisting of combinations of words or expressions, and the same technique is used in EA-Analyzer.

In EA-Analyzer, the binary classification of a compositional intersection as either harmony or conflict could be perceived as an oversimplification of requirements' relationships. The relationship of two quality requirements could be considered conflicting in one system and tolerable in another by a human analyst. However, EA-Analyzer will always pinpoint the potential presence of such conflicts. It is then up to

---

[1]Please note that grammar and semantics are used in RDL composition definitions, as discussed previously. Thus, they are indispensable in the task of collecting the required bags or words. Once such words are collected, in the EA-Analyzer learning phase, the grammar and semantics are not used any further.

the requirements analyst to consider if a given potential conflict can be tolerable in a given context, and so disregard it from the set of real conflicts for that system. Such classifications are not directly supported by the conflict identification support of EA-Analyzer; we consider these to constitute the follow-up step of conflict resolution.

11.4 Empirical Evaluation

This section presents an empirical evaluation of the tool, where the main goal was to assess the ability of EA-Analyzer to detect conflicts using training data gathered from four different documents, each representing a different domain. The documents were selected based on their suitability for this evaluation, with selection criteria including: domain, requirement type, complexity and use in previous studies. In addition, three documents originate from industrial organizations and the fourth document is a case study extensively used in academia to evaluate AO modeling techniques. Furthermore, each of these documents was created prior to the conception of this study by external personnel. The four documents selected were:

- *Health Watcher* (HW) [29] is a web-based health support system which the public can use to register health-related complaints and query disease and symptom information.
- *Smart Home* (SH) [30] is an embedded system which provides functionality to control various sensors and actuators around the home (i.e., lights, blinds, heating, etc.).
- *CAS* [31] is a customer relationship management application (CRM) which utilizes service mash-ups and mobility support in a hosted software-as-a-service environment.
- *Crisis Management System* (CM) [32] is a crisis management system for emergency situations (e.g., natural disasters, accidents, terrorist attacks).

The evaluation consists of four experiments, in which we utilized each requirements document (HW, SH, CAS, and CM) in turn as the training set and evaluated the classification accuracy of the tool with the other three documents. Table 11.1 shows some characteristics of the four documents selected for this study, and the characteristics present two different dimensions of the requirements specifications (1) the size of the documents, by showing the number of words, compositions, and compositional intersections (CI) and (2) the number of compositional intersections that have the *Encryption—Performance* conflict. Each experiment used the *Encryption—Performance* conflict to evaluate the classification accuracy of the tool, because it is the only NFR conflict type that occurs in all four documents.

Table 11.2 presents the classification accuracy of the tool with the four different training sets. The classification accuracy of the HW and CM documents is 93.90 %, while the experiment with SH document achieved 92.05 % and the CAS experiment yielded a classification accuracy of 48.51 %. All the results are compared to

Table 11.1 Characteristics of documents used in experiment

	HW	SH	CAS	CM
Words in RDL	1764	4699	1053	5961
Num. of Compositions	17	9	5	8
Num. of CI	89	71	16	43
Num. of CI with *Encryption* – *Performance* conflict	23	5	3	16

Table 11.2 Results of the classification accuracy in each experiment

	Training Sets			
Validation Data	HW	SH	CAS	CM
HW		88.64%	34.09%	100.00%
SH	94.20%		100.00%	94.20%
CAS	87.50%	87.50%		87.50%
CM	100.00%	100.00%	11.43%	
Weighted Average	93.90%	92.05%	48.51%	93.90%

a baseline accuracy of 50 %, as randomly assigned classes should yield an approximate 50 % accuracy. The results that use HW, SH, and CM as training sets yield classifications results above the baseline accuracy; however, the experiment with the CAS document yields a classification result below the baseline accuracy. This may suggest that the size of the training set (the CAS document has only 16 compositional intersections—see Table 11.1) can significantly influence the classification accuracy of the tool. Despite the poor result with the CAS document, the results with the other three document, when a larger number of examples are utilized to train the tool, present very high classification results. This suggests that the machine learning technique in EA-Analyzer is capable of detecting conflicts in aspect-oriented specifications. A more extensive and detailed evaluation of the tool can be found in [3].

11.5 Conclusions

The AO approach is an effective way to modularize and compose concerns in requirements specifications. In addition, AORE methods help to externalize interactions and interdependencies between concerns by utilizing explicitly dedicated composition specifications. These composed concerns are an excellent starting point for detecting conflicts within the requirements specification. However, detecting conflicts in large natural language specifications can be a burden for requirements engineers, due to the large number and complexity of the interdependencies to be considered. As discussed earlier, the approaches based on formal specifications, models and stakeholder priorities, developed to date in the AORE community, are unable to provide low effort and high precision techniques for conflict identification in large AO specifications.

This chapter presents the EA-Analyzer tool, in which we demonstrate that it is indeed possible to automate the process of detecting conflicts within textual AO requirements specifications. In addition, we present an empirical evaluation of the tool with three industrial-strength requirements documents and a well established academic case study used in the AO research community. The results show that conflicts within requirements specifications can be detected with a high accuracy, as longs as a sufficient number of examples is utilized in the training set.

As future work, we will focus efforts on the empirical evaluation of the tool with other requirements documents from different domains to validate the generalization power of the learning method in EA-Analyzer. In addition, we will also test a number of other classifiers in the tool, such as SVM [33] and nearest neighbor methods [33]. The utilization of different machine learning classifiers may helps us identify the best machine learning approach for detecting conflicts.

EA-Analyzer is the first tool for automated conflict identification in textual AO requirements and compositions, and this work demonstrates that the power of AORE to represent concern interrelationships knowledge can be effectively harvested for conflict detection within natural language specifications. Hence, we see this work as the stepping stone towards effort reduction in AORE conflict identification, and supporting application of advanced modularity and analysis in textual requirements.

References

1. A. Rashid, A. Moreira, J. Araújo, Modularisation and composition of aspectual requirements, in *AOSD'03: Proceedings of the 2nd International Conference on Aspect-Oriented Software Development* (ACM, New York, NY, 2003)
2. I.S. Brito, F. Vieira, A. Moreira, R. Ribeiro, Handling conflicts in aspectual requirements compositions, in *Transactions on Aspect Oriented Software Development (TAOSD)*, 2007
3. A. Sardinha, R. Chitchyan, N. Weston, P. Greenwood, A. Rashid, EA-Analyzer: automating conflict detection in a large set of textual aspect-oriented requirements. Autom. Softw. Eng. **20**(1), 111–135 (2013)
4. N. Weston, R. Chitchyan, A. Rashid, A formal approach to semantic composition of aspect-oriented requirements, in *RE'08: Proceedings of the 16th International Requirements Engineering Conference*, 2008
5. R. Laney, L. Barroca, M. Jackson, B. Nuseibeh, Composing requirements using problem frames, in *RE'04: Proceedings of the Requirements Engineering Conference, 12th IEEE International* (IEEE Computer Society, Washington, DC, 2004)
6. F. Mostefaoui, J. Vachon, Design-level detection of interactions in aspect-UML models using alloy. J. Object Technol. **6**(7), 137–165 (2007)
7. K. Mehner, M. Monga, G. Taentzer, Interaction analysis in aspect-oriented models, in *RE'06: Proceedings of the 14th IEEE International Requirements Engineering Conference* (IEEE Computer Society, Washington, DC, 2006)

8. O. Barais, J. Klein, B. Baudry, A. Jackson, S. Clarke, Composing multi-view aspect models, in *ICCBSS'08: Proceedings of the Seventh International Conference on Composition-Based Software Systems (ICCBSS 2008)* (IEEE Computer Society, Washington, DC, 2008)
9. R. Chitchyan, A. Rashid, P. Rayson, R. Waters, Semantics-based composition for aspect-oriented requirements engineering, in *AOSD'07: Proceedings of the 6th International Conference on Aspect-Oriented Software Development* (ACM, New York, NY, 2007)
10. R. Chitchyan, Semantics-based composition for aspect-oriented requirements engineering, Ph.D. thesis, Computing Department, Lancaster University, 2007
11. T. Mitchell, *Machine Learning* (McGraw-Hill, New York, NY, 1997)
12. L. Chung, B.A. Nixon, E. Yu, J. Mylopoulos, *Non-functional Requirements in Software Engineering* (Kluwer Academic, Dordrecht, 1999)
13. E. Yu, Modelling strategic relationships for process reengineering, Ph.D. Thesis, Department of Computer Science, University of Toronto, 1995
14. A. van Lamsweerde, A. Dardenne, B. Delcourt, F. Dubisy, The KAOS project: knowledge acquisition in automated specification of software, in *Proceedings AAAI Spring Symposium Series, Stanford University* (American Association for Artificial Intelligence, Washington, DC, 1991)
15. P. Shaker, D.K. Peters, Design-level detection of interactions in aspect-oriented systems, in *Proceedings of the Aspects, Dependencies, and Interactions Workshop at ECOOP 2006*, 2006
16. E. Baniassad, S. Clarke, Theme: an approach for aspect-oriented analysis and design, in *ICSE'04: Proceedings of the 26th International Conference on Software Engineering* (IEEE Computer Society, Washington, DC, 2004)
17. Y.R. Reddy, S. Ghosh, R.B. France, G. Straw, J.M. Bieman, N. McEachen, E. Song, G. Georg, Directives for composing aspect-oriented design class models, in *Transactions on Aspect Oriented Software Development I*, ed. by A. Rashid, M. Aksit (Springer, Berlin Heidelberg, 2006), pp. 75–105
18. A. Moreira, J. Araújo, A. Rashid, Multi-dimensional separation of concerns in requirements engineering, in *International Conference on Requirements Engineering (RE)*, Paris, France, 2005
19. I. Brito, A. Moreira, Towards a composition process for aspect-oriented requirements, in *Presented at Early Aspects Workshop at AOSD'03*, Boston, MA, 2003
20. I. Brito, A. Moreira, Integrating the NFR approach in a RE model, in *Presented at Early Aspects Workshop at AOSD'04*, Lancaster, UK, 2004
21. T. Saaty, *The Analytic Hierarchy Process* (McGraw-Hill, New York, NY, 1980)
22. T. Saaty, Decision making with the analytic hierarchy process. Int. J. Serv. Sci. **1**, 83–98 (2008)
23. AMPLE project (2011), http://www.ample-project.net
24. E. Triantaphyllou, *Multi-Criteria Decision Making Methods: A Comparative Study* (Kluwer Academic, Dordrecht, 2000)
25. R. Ribeiro, A. Moreira, P. Broek, A. Pimentel, Hybrid assessment method for software engineering decisions. Decis. Support. Syst. **51**(1), 208–219 (2011)
26. A. Sampaio, R. Chitchyan, A. Rashid, P. Rayson, EA-Miner: a tool for automating aspect-oriented requirements identification, in *ASE'05: Proceedings of the 20th IEEE/ACM International Conference on Automated Software Engineering* (ACM, New York, NY, 2005)
27. P. Rayson, Wmatrix (2010), http://www.comp.lancs.ac.uk/ucrel/wmatrix/
28. A. Sampaio, P. Greenwood, A.F. Garcia, A. Rashid, A comparative study of aspect-oriented requirements engineering approaches, in *ESEM'07: Proceedings of the First International Symposium on Empirical Software Engineering and Measurement* (IEEE Computer Society, Washington, DC, 2007)
29. S. Soares, P. Borba, E. Laureano, Distribution and persistence as aspects. Softw. Pract. Exp. **36**(7), 711–759 (2006)
30. K. Pohl, G. Bockle, F. van der Linden, *Software Product Line Engineering: Foundations, Principles, and Techniques* (Springer, New York, NY, 2005)
31. D. Ayed, T. Genssler, Dynamic variability in complex, adaptive systems. Deliverable D6.1 of DiVA EC project (2009)

Chapter 12
Handling Conflicts in Aspect-Oriented Requirements Engineering

Isabel Sofia Brito, Ana Moreira, Rita A. Ribeiro, and João Araújo

Abstract Identification and resolution of aspectual conflicts should be handled at the requirements level, before major design decisions are made. Treating conflicting situations this early facilitates negotiation among stakeholders. The Aspect-Oriented Requirements Analysis (AORA) approach offers HAM (Hybrid Assessment Method), a technique for the resolution of conflicts between concerns that contribute negatively to each other and have the same importance. HAM uses a multi-criteria decision method to support the resolution of these conflicts and extends this treatment to conflicts between concerns triggered by stakeholders with contradictory interests on a set of concerns. An example taken from the Crisis Management System case study is used to illustrate HAM's potential support for treating concerns during composition.

12.1 Introduction

This chapter discusses HAM, a technique for requirements conflict resolution. This technique has been developed in the context of AORA (Aspect-Oriented Requirements Analysis approach), although it can be used in the general context of AORE.

I.S. Brito (✉)
Escola Superior de Tecnologia e Gestão, Instituto Politécnico de Beja, Beja, Portugal
e-mail: isabel.sofia@ipbeja.pt

A. Moreira • J. Araújo
Departamento de Informática, Universidade Nova de Lisboa, Caparica, Portugal
e-mail: amm@fct.unl.pt; joao.araujo@fct.unl.pt

R.A. Ribeiro
UNINOVA, Caparica, Portugal
e-mail: rar@uninova.pt

A. Moreira et al. (eds.), *Aspect-Oriented Requirements Engineering*, DOI 10.1007/978-3-642-38640-4_12, © Springer-Verlag Berlin Heidelberg 2013

In AORA, conflict management is handled during the composition activity, where conflicts may emerge at given *match point* [1]. A match point identifies specific locations in base concerns at which other concerns' (crosscutting or non-crosscutting) should be composed or satisfied. A *concern* refers to a matter of interest that addresses a certain problem that is important to one or more stakeholders. AORA indicates a conflict any time two or more concerns that contribute negatively to each other, and have the same priority,[1] need to be composed at the same match point. The identification of such a conflict might lead to a revision of the aspectual and non-aspectual specifications, as well as of the composition specifications. In the context of this work, we generalize the AORA's definition of conflict to include situations where stakeholders have different interests with respect to the same set of concerns, independently from the concerns' contributions.[2] The advantage of treating both types of conflicting situations during requirements analysis is to facilitate negotiation and decision-making among stakeholders.

In previous works, AORA used Analytic Hierarchy Process (AHP) [2], a multi-criteria decision method (MCDM) to obtain the raking of a set of concerns. MCDMs help choosing the best choice from a set of alternatives, given a set of decision criteria. Despite the well-known advantages of AHP, such as helping guaranteeing the logical consistency of many human-based judgments, as well as synthesizing a wide range of data in a single solution, the inconsistencies introduced by the scale, associated with the large number of pairwise comparisons, result in low efficiency and cumbersome usability. For these reasons, in this chapter AORA substitutes AHP for HAM, a hybrid MCDM method [3–5] and discusses its suitability and versatility as a decision support tool for handling the two types of aspectual conflicts mentioned above.

HAM's process is simpler than AHP's and its integration in AORA is straightforward. HAM uses a simple two-phase process, which combines one pairwise comparison decision matrix and one classical weighted decision matrix, and then prioritizes alternatives using a weighted average method. These changes, required to handle the new type of conflict, introduce no added complexity to the process (as discussed in Sect. 12.4).

This chapter is organized as follows: Sect. 12.2 gives a general outline of the AORA approach, giving context to HAM. Section 12.3 offers a broad overview on multi-criteria decision methods and finishes by summarizing HAM. Section 12.4 focuses on the composition part of AORA, uses an example from the case study to illustrate the conflict management activity and discusses the obtained results. Section 12.5 presents the related work and Sect. 12.6 concludes pointing directions for future work.

---

[1] If the priority allocated to each concern is different, the problem is not too difficult to solve.

[2] Concern's contributions represent how this concern affects others concerns. This contribution can be positive(+) or negative (−).

12.2 Aspect-Oriented Requirements Analysis

The AORA (Aspect-Oriented Requirements Analysis) approach collects all the required requirements for composition, allowing the application of MCDM techniques for conflict resolution. AORA defines three primary tasks: identify concerns, specify concerns and compose concerns.

The task "identify concerns" can be accomplished by using traditional requirements elicitation techniques, such as ethnographic studies, analysis of the initial requirements, transcripts of stakeholders' interviews, etc. Other good sources for concern identification are existing catalogues, such as the non-functional requirements catalogue offered by Chung et al. [6].

The task "specify concerns" aims at describing each concern while collecting and storing in a template various types of data about the concern [1]. An example template is shown in Table 12.2. For example, the *contributions* element of the template, which offers a list of positive and negative contributions among concerns, is a basic piece of information to detect a conflict (denoted via negative contributions). While s*takeholders' importance* element assigns priorities to concerns from the stakeholders' perspective, in an attempt to help in the conflict resolution process, the r*equired concerns* element acts as a dependency reference to other concerns in the system and is used to identify crosscutting concerns (i.e., concerns that are required by more than one other concern).

The task "compose concerns" allows an incremental analysis of impact of possible concern configurations. A composition is configured according to a composition specification. Each composition specification is analysed for each match point, by taking into account the information in Required Concerns element in the match point concern template [1]. A composition rule shows how a set of concerns can be composed together using pre-defined operators. At this stage, conflicting situations may be detected when concerns contributing negatively to each other (contribution element in template [1]) have the same importance (row stakeholders' importance) and need to be composed in the same match point. Having identified a conflict, the HAM technique is used to rank the concerns under analysis and, where needed, conduct negotiations among stakeholders. HAM, as we said before, guarantees the logical consistency of many human-based judgments, as well as synthesizing a wide range of data in a single solution. The end result is a list of concerns ranked according to a set of criteria. This list of ranked concerns will lead the choice of the system's architecture design.

12.3 Supporting Conflict Resolution with Multi-criteria Decision Methods

12.3.1 Multi-criteria Decision Methods

Multiple Criteria Decision Making (MCDM) methods support decision makers resolving conflicting situations [7–9]. MCDM methods use mathematical techniques to help decision makers to choose among a discrete set of alternative decisions. These methods do not try to compute an optimal solution, but to determine, via rating and ranking procedures, either a ranking of the "the best options" with respect to several criteria, or the "best" actions amongst the existing solutions [7].

Two phases are usually needed to rank the alternatives or to select the most desirable one (1) the aggregation of the degree of satisfaction for all criteria, per decision alternative (rating) and (2) the ranking of the alternatives with respect to the global aggregated degree of satisfaction.

Triantaphyllou [7] warns that there may never be a single MCDM method that guarantees that a derived ranking of alternatives is the correct one because of the subjective assignment of alternative classifications and weights for criteria. Even within the fuzzy MCDM domain [10] this type of problem remains ill-defined. Therefore, MCDM methods can only guarantee the "best possible" solution and not "the optimal" one. Nonetheless, in our view MCDM methods are helpful at negotiating a solution for conflicting concerns because they allow trade-offs and reaching a consensus from different stakeholders.

There are many MCDM methods proposed in the literature [7, 8, 10]: direct scoring and outranking methods, trade-off schemes, distance-based methods, value and utility functions, and interactive methods. Direct scoring techniques are widely used, particularly the weighted average method (WA) [11]. WA calculates the final score of alternatives with the weighted sum of each criteria value. WA is popular due to its simplicity, its compensatory trade-offs among criteria with their weights, and because any spreadsheet can act as tool support as it only requires one decision matrix. However, it does not offer pairwise comparisons or logical consistency measures (hence no dependencies/relationships between criteria can be expressed), which are useful to perform the trade-offs between alternatives, or, in our case, conflicting aspectual requirements. The Analytical Hierarchy Process (AHP) method [2, 7] is a pairwise comparison method that relies on expert judgments to derive priority scales (ranking of alternatives). The comparisons are made using a scale of judgments that represent how much more, one element is important than another with respect to a given criteria. AHP also provides a measure for detecting logical inconsistencies for these judgments.

Comparative studies for such methods [3] concluded that the best option is to combine the pairwise judgment of AHP with the decision matrix simplicity of WA. The combination of both methods and the usage of a geometric scale (Table 12.1

Table 12.1 Scale summary

Index	Interpretation	Scale	Comparative AHP scale
8	Extremely High importance	9	9
6	Very High importance	9/3	7
4	High importance	9/5	5
2	Medium High importance	9/7	3
0	Equal importance	1	1
-2	Medium Low importance	7/9	1/3
-4	Low importance	5/9	1/5
-6	Very Low importance	3/9	1/7
-8	Extremely Low importance	1/9	1/9
Other	Intermediate values		

shows the scale and its semantic interpretation) and aggregation process resulted in the Hybrid Assessment Method (HAM) [4, 5]. From AHP, HAM uses just one pairwise comparison matrix to perform the trade-off analysis between criteria and obtain their weights, while ensuring logical consistency for the trade-off. From WA, HAM uses the decision matrix logic with weights obtained from the AHP pairwise comparisons to determine the final ratings and ranking for the alternatives.

12.3.2 The Hybrid Assessment Method

HAM includes two main tasks, one to determine the importance (weights) of criteria and another one to obtain the prioritization of alternatives [3–5]. As mentioned before, HAM also avoids the two main AHP problems: its computational inefficiency and understandability for large problems and its problematic linear scale and prioritization calculation process [5]. Steps 1–3 below constitute the first task, while steps 4 and 5 form the second task. Each step, and the associated calculations, is explained in detail in [5].

Step 1: Identify the set of stakeholders and concerns. Here the concerns correspond to alternatives in the MCDM methods and criteria are the stakeholder's preferences. Figure 12.1c displays an example.

Step 2: Elicit trade-offs among stakeholders using pairwise comparisons. We use a geometric scale (see in Table 12.1 the scale and its semantic interpretation) to rate the relative importance/preference of one stakeholder over another and then construct a matrix of the pairwise comparison ratings. This scale was used because, according to [7] and [12], it is the most appropriate for MCDM. Figure 12.1a shows an example.

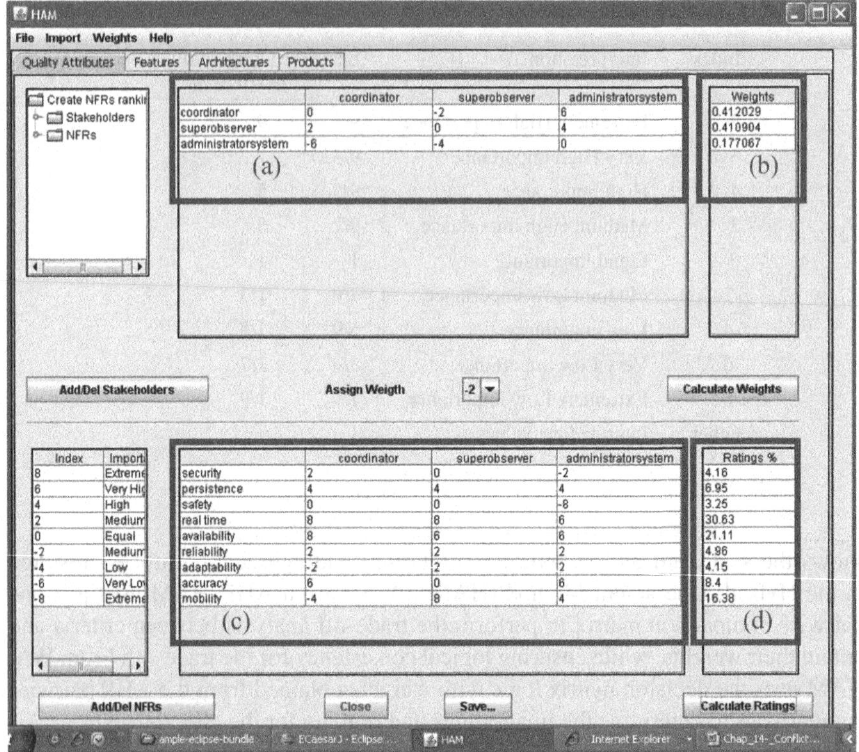

Fig. 12.1 (**a**) Pairwise comparison matrix for stakeholder's criterion and (**b**) respective priority vector (calculated). (**c**) WA matrix for required concerns and (**d**) respective ratings

Step 3: Calculate the stakeholder's priority vector, normalize the respective weights and calculate the consistency ratio. To calculate the priority vector for criteria (stakeholders), which will represent the weights for the second task of HAM, we normalize the pairwise comparison matrix by dividing each column cell by the sum of that column. Then, the weights/importance criteria are calculated by using the geometric mean of the normalized pairwise comparison matrix, for all criteria. Next we calculate the consistency of the pairwise matrix to reduce any logical error that might have been introduced during the judgement process. If the consistency ratio is under 10 %, logical consistency is guaranteed. However, if there is any logical inconsistency the trade-off values in the pairwise matrix are re-checked and a new iteration is performed until consistency is low. Figure 12.1b displays the resulting value for the example.

These 3 steps result in a vector with the importance (weights) for criteria (in our case the stakeholders). The next task (steps 4 and 5) deals with the prioritization of the alternative concerns.

Step 4: Identify contributions of each concern, by eliciting the contributions of each alternative (concern) with respect to each criterion (stakeholders), using a decision matrix. Figure 12.1c shows an example.

Step 5: Calculate the concerns' ratings, includes the aggregation of the criteria values, with the geometric average, per alternative, using as weights the values obtained in step 3. This final step concludes our process by providing the prioritizations for each concern Fig. 12.1d displays the final result of using HAM tool.

To improve the tool usability (see Fig. 12.1), we also introduced an index system to facilitate the interaction among the decision makers involved in the conflict resolution (see Fig. 12.1 bottom-left box). Table 12.1 summarizes the scale, its semantic interpretation and respective index. Moreover, Table 12.1 also depicts the AHP scale for comparative purposes (see Sect. 12.4.4). Details about the advantages of using the HAM scale are discussed in [5].

12.4 A Step Forward in Aspectual Conflict Management

As mentioned previously, a conflict occurs when two or more concerns contributing negatively to each other and having the same priority need to be composed together. For example, consider the case where a module conceived to model or implement a given functionality of the system needs to be secure and to react in a very short period of time. It is well known that security and response time contribute negatively to each other, that is, the more secure we want our module to be, the slower it will become, and vice versa. This means that the system may not be able to satisfy both quality requirements with the same degree of importance. Therefore, this also means that different combinations of each of these concerns may lead to a number of architecture choices that will serve the stakeholder needs with varying levels of satisfaction.

In this chapter, we will use the information collected by AORA and the flexibility of the multi-criteria concepts and techniques and also consider conflicts triggered by contradictory priorities different stakeholders may declare on one or more concerns. This means that even concerns that contribute positively to each other may be involved in a conflict if they need to compete for their satisfaction, for instance, due to scarce resources or where stakeholders' priorities on concerns vary.

Considering that MCDM techniques offer the possibility to find, given a set of alternatives and a set of decision criteria, the best alternative, AORA used AHP method to support conflict management resolution [1, 13]. This list of ranked concerns should drive the choice of the system's architecture design, as mentioned above.

Although being one of the most used methods, AHP has some liabilities that drove us looking for a different solution. In particular, AHP scale introduces inconsistencies, the number of pairwise comparisons can become too large, and it is difficult to analyse results for each single matrix. Therefore, in addition to its scale inconsistency problems, AHP is low in efficiency and in usability [5, 7, 12].

To overcome these liabilities, this chapter changes the AORA conflict management process by using HAM in the following two usage cases (1) to rank required concerns in a match point according to the Stakeholders' opinion, where the one with the highest value is the most important one; (2) to perform "what-if" analysis, achieving system behaviour analysis by simulating changes to it (e.g., "what happens if a new Stakeholder is added to the system?" or "what happens if the weight of a criteria changes?").

12.4.1 Identification and Description of Concerns

Here we will demonstrate the usage of HAM for concerns conflict management.

The concerns are the use cases, identified in Sect. 4.1 of the crisis management stem case study document [14], and the NFRs listed in Sect. 2.3 of the same document. The composition specifications are defined for the various identified match points, and several crosscutting concerns are indicated, some are non-functional (e.g. availability, security and mobility) and others are functional (such as user authentication).

For this section we have chosen the example from the crisis management system pertaining the execution of the mission observed by the SuperObserver actor. The corresponding AORA template is summarized in Table 12.2, where the "responsibilities" entry details its functionality.

The composition specification for the SuperObserver Mission match point would require the construction of an equivalent template for each of the required concerns, but for our goal, it is enough to build the contribution matrix among these required concerns. Based on the developers' expertise and some existing work (e.g. [6] and [15]), the positive and negative contributions between concerns are listed in Table 12.3.[3]

The contribution matrix helps identifying some potential problems. For example, accuracy contributes negatively to real time (the system shall provide up-to-date information to rescue resources quickly), while real time contributes positively to availability (the faster the system is, the longer it is free to handle more SuperObserver).

If we were to consider only conflicts triggered by concerns contributing negatively to each other, we could remove from our subsequent analysis "mobility" and "adaptability". However, given that we also want to consider situations where different stakeholders may have contradictory interests in those concerns, i.e. those concerns have different stakeholders' priorities, the conflict analysis will consider all the required concerns and will take into consideration the stakeholder priorities allocated to each concern.

[3]Note that the contributions specified here are asymmetric.

Table 12.2 Execute SuperObserver mission template

Concern Elements	Definition
Name	Execute SuperObserver Mission.
Stakeholders	Coordinator, SuperObserver and AdministratorSystem; NationalCrisisCenter (needed when the mission cannot be created and replacement missions are possible).
Description	Its aim is to support the SuperObserver to order appropriate missions.
Classification	Functional
Type	Non-Crosscutting
Responsibilities	1. System sends a crisis-specific checklist to SuperObserver. 2. System suggests crisis-specific missions to SuperObserver. 3. System sends a mission-specific information request to SuperObserver. 4. System acknowledges the mission creation to SuperObserver. 5. System informs SuperObserver that mission was completed successfully. Extensions: 1. Mission cannot be created and replacement missions are possible. 1a.1 System suggests replacement missions to SuperObserver. 1b. Mission cannot be created and no replacement missions are possible. 1b.1 System suggests notifying the NationalCrisisCenter. 2a. Mission failed. 2a.1 System informs SuperObserver and Coordinator about mission failure.
Stakeholder Importance	SuperObserver: Very Important Coordinator Very Important AdministratorSystem: Very Important NationalCrisisCenter Very Important
Required Concerns	Real-time, Accuracy, Persistence, Availability, Adaptability, Safety, Reliability Security, Mobility

Table 12.3 Contributions between the concerns required by Execute SuperObserver Mission

	Availability	Reliability	Persistence	Real-time	Security	Mobility	Adaptability	Accuracy
Availability						+		
Reliability	+							-
Persistence								
Real-time	+		-		-			-
Security		+		-				
Mobility	+							
Adaptability	+							
Accuracy	-		+	-				

12.4.2 Composition and Conflict Management

In the AORA context, HAM is going to be used for two cases:

- Case 1: "Prioritize Required Concerns" is used to rank Required Concerns in a match point according to the opinion of Stakeholders'. The result is a ranking of Required Concerns where the one with the highest value is the most important.
- Case 2: "What-if analysis" to perform system behaviour analysis by simulating changes to it. For example, does the Required Concerns ranking change if a new stakeholder, or a new concern, is added to the system?

Case 1: Prioritize Required Concerns

Step 1: Identify criteria and alternatives. The goal is the identification of a finite set of criteria and alternatives to rank the concerns required in a given match point. For our "Execute SuperObserver Mission" example, the alternatives are the required concerns identified in the template. The criteria also referred to as decision criteria, represent the different dimensions from which the alternatives can be analysed, which, in our example, are the identified stakeholders (SuperObserver, Coordinator and AdministratorSystem).

Step 2: Elicit trade-offs among criteria. As mentioned, HAM uses a pairwise comparison matrix to determine the ratings for the stakeholders. In our example, the pairwise matrix is shown in Fig. 12.1a.

Step 3: Calculate the criteria priority vector, normalize the respective weights and calculate the consistency ratio. HAM calculates the normalized priority vector (or stakeholders weights). In our example, the pairwise matrix is shown in Fig. 12.1a and the normalized priority vector in Fig. 12.1b. Notice that pairwise matrix uses illustrative judgements, because the case study's documentation does not have this information. The stakeholder Coordinator is the most important stakeholder according to the values in priority vector (0.412029).

The next step is to calculate the value of the logical consistency ratio to ensure the analyst consistently elicited the stakeholders' priorities. In this case the ratio is 3.93 %. Since this value is under 10 %, the logical consistency is guaranteed.

Step 4: Identify contributions of each alternative. We elicit the contributions of each required concern with respect to each stakeholder, using a regular decision matrix (see Fig. 12.1c). The contributions are illustrative values because the case study's documentation does not have this information.

Step 5: Calculate the alternatives ratings. Figure 12.1 shows the results obtained using the HAM Tool. Figure 12.1d shows the rating of each required concern, using a geometric average as described in HAM model [5].

Based on required concerns rating obtained using HAM Tool, Table 12.4 shows the required concerns final ranking.

Let us now discuss the final ranking in Table 12.4. Because the control centre receives and updates the location of SuperObserver information on an on-going crisis at intervals not exceeding 30 s, it is not surprising that the real-time concern appears ranked first. Availability comes next in the ranking because the system shall be in operation 24 h a day, every day, without break, throughout the year except

Table 12.4 Required concerns ranking

Required Concerns	Rating %	Ranking
Real-time	30,63	1
Availability	21,11	2
Mobility	16,38	3
Accuracy	8,40	4
Persistence	6,95	5
Reliability	4,96	6
Security	4,16	7
Adaptability	4,15	8
Safety	3,25	9

for a maximum downtime of 2 h every 30 days, for maintenance. Furthermore, availability needs to be accomplished before accuracy and persistence to guarantee that the system is accessible for the passengers.

Mobility is ranked third because it is important to guarantee the access to detailed maps, terrain data and weather conditions for the crisis location and the routes leading to it. Also, mobility helps availability, as its contribution is positive.

Accuracy appears in fourth place. Given that it contributes negatively to real time and availability, which have higher preferences for the stakeholders, its ranking makes sense, as its priority needs to be lower in order to help guaranteeing the stakeholders preferences.

A similar intuitive reasoning can be done for the concerns ranked in the last positions. But in general, we can say that despite their importance in the system, accuracy, persistence and security have lower priorities because these concerns contribute negatively to real time and availability, which have higher preferences for the stakeholders.

Case 2: Perform "what-if" analysis "What-if" analysis may be useful to study the impact of adding new concerns and stakeholders, removing them or review the weights allocated to different criteria. Let us consider the simple situation mentioned in the case study, where the new stakeholder NationalCrisisCenter comes into play when a Mission cannot be created and no replacement missions are possible. (We expect that this actor would appear when the crisis is so serious that requires the orchestration of several national services.) We simply add this new stakeholder and perform the five steps of HAM, which the HAM tool will execute in a blink-of-an-eye.

Step 1: Identify criteria and alternatives. The criteria include now also the new stakeholder NationalCrisisCenter.

Step 2: Elicit trade-offs among criteria. Based on the previous step, National-CrisisCenterstakeholder was added to the matrix (originally depicted in Fig. 12.1) with very low importance when compared with Coordinator, SuperObserver and AdministratorSystem because NationalCrisisCenter stakeholder substitutes the system under study and does not use the system, unlike the others stakeholders.

Table 12.5 Required concerns ranking for case 1 and 2

Required Concerns	Rating % Case 2	Ranking Case 2	Ranking Case 1
Real-time	29,07	1	1
Availability	20,34	2	2
Mobility	15,18	3	3
Accuracy	8,45	4	4
Persistence	6,52	6	5
Reliability	5,20	7	6
Security	4,31	8	7
Adaptability	3,93	9	8
Safety	7,01	5	9

Step 3: Calculate the criteria priority vector, normalize the respective weights and calculate the consistency ratio. We start by calculating the priority vector, or stakeholders weights, and normalize them. SuperObserver is the most important stakeholder and NationalCrisisCenter is the less important stakeholder according to the values in the priority vector. Since the consistency ratio value is 3.79 % (lower than 10 %), the logical consistency is guaranteed.

Step 4: Identify contributions of each alternative. We elicit the contributions of each required concern with respect to each stakeholder, using a WA's decision matrix. In this case, we elicit the contributions of each required concern with respect to NationalCrisisCenter, which were: availability: 4; reliability: 2; persistence: −8; real time: 4; security: 0; adaptability: −8; accuracy: 2; mobility: −8; safety: 8.

Step 5: Calculate the alternatives ratings. Table 12.5 represents the rating of each required concern, using the WA formula for both cases.

Real time, availability, mobility and accuracy have the same ranking in the two cases. Safety "jumps" from ninth place to fifth place. This intuitively makes some sense, because despite NationalCrisisCenter having the lowest weight in the system (when it enters in action, it basically substitutes the system under study), safety concern has "Extremely High importance". Consequently, the other concerns decrease one place in the ranking of case 2.

If, in a different case, we were simply to change the importance allocated to NationalCrisisCenter to high, the resulting ranking would be the same for real time (first) and adaptability (ninth). The other concerns decrease and increase by one place. Safety, on the other hand, "jumps" from fifth to second. This makes sense as NationalCrisisCenter, being highly important in the system, has allocated safety a high degree of importance. On the other hand, real time is still in the first place as NationalCrisisCenter's weight is not enough to override the other stakeholders' wishes.

12.4.3 Discussion of Results

Having the concerns ranked by order of importance allows one to select the architectural design that will optimize the attainment of various objectives by their order of importance. Based on the obtained rankings, decisions can be taken to handle unresolved conflicts. Notice that, a crosscutting concern can have different importance in different match points. This information is also supporting useful in supporting architectural design decisions.

To ensure that the method is applied correctly we must guarantee that the questions below are answered during the initial activities of the AORA approach: have all the concerns been identified? Were all the stakeholders considered? How correct is the stakeholder knowledge about the problem? In what concerns of the HAM method we should remember that human judgements are not error free, even if the consistency level is below 10 %, judgements are always subjective. Consistency only tells that the judgements are valid from a logical perspective. However, the reasoning used to achieve those values is subjective and may not reflect the best alternatives.

Another useful result was the what-if analysis. The inclusion of a new stakeholder, even when he is allocated with the lowest importance, can impact the final ranking.

Analysing the results of the application of HAM, the advantages are:

1. It is a robust and flexible method.
2. It allows resolution of trade-offs between concerns.
3. It provides prioritization of criteria (stakeholders) to be used as weights in the ranking process.
4. Provides ranking of alternatives (required concerns).
5. It enables the addition of new criteria and/or alternatives at anytime, obviously at the expense of having to perform new calculations.
6. It allows a what-if analysis, i.e. what happens if we add a new requirement to the system? Will it change the architectural decisions?

Nevertheless, HAM is not a perfect method and its disadvantages are:

1. As all other scoring MCDM methods, judgments made by experts (values assigned) always include opinions (subjective) and HAM can only ensure logical consistency for the judgments.
2. As all other MCDM methods it is a decision support model and not a decision making model (i.e., it does not substitute decision makers, it just supports them in making informed decisions).
3. It does not support group decision making.
4. It requires some technical knowledge from the stakeholders, such as which criteria to use which contributions alternatives make towards the criteria.

Thus, in summary, HAM is a simple, versatile method that seems well suited to helping in analysing potential conflicts in the AOSD context.

Table 12.6 Stakeholders pairwise matrix

Stakeholder	Coordinator	SuperObserver	Administrator
Coordinator	Equal importance	Medium low importance	Very high importance
SuperObserver	Medium high importance	Equal importance	High importance
Administrator	Very low importance	Low importance	Equal importance

Table 12.7 Stakeholders ratings

Stakeholder	AHP	HAM (Figure 1 (b)
Coordinator	0.446	0.412
SuperObserver	0.482	0.410
Administrator	0.072	0.177

12.4.4 HAM Versus AHP

Let us now compare HAM with AHP, for the same illustrative example. Here we only compare the results for phase 1 (determination of stakeholders relative importance) because it is the phase that uses pairwise matrices. As mentioned before, the scales of HAM versus AHP and respective semantic interpretation are shown in Table 12.1.

Table 12.6 shows stakeholders pairwise matrix with the semantic evaluations (Table 12.1). Note that the semantic evaluation is identical for HAM and AHP.

Table 12.7 includes the resulting rating for stakeholders using HAM (Fig. 12.1b) and AHP with arithmetic aggregation.

Even with this small comparison it is obvious that the rankings are different in both methods. For HAM the most important stakeholder is the Coordinator, while with AHP it is the SuperObserver. Now let us observe the semantic evaluations to understand the results. Note that the "equal importance" is not taken in consideration because it is a pairwise matrix. From Table 12.6, the corresponding semantic Coordinator evaluations were: (SuperObserver: medium low importance, Administrator: very high importance) and SuperObserver evaluations were (Coordinator: medium high importance, Administrator: high importance). Clearly from these semantic evaluations we can observe that AHP takes a more "averaging" perspective and benefits (selects) the candidate with both "average" classifications, while with HAM the candidate that stands out (Coordinator) is selected because he has a "very high" grade and only a "medium low" one. These small comparison shows that HAM distinguishes more outstanding alternatives while AHP always takes a classic average perspective, which can lead to select "mediocre" solutions.

More details about comparison of HAM with other methods can be seen in [5].

12.5 Related Work

Several AORE approaches [16–19] handle conflicts mostly based on intuitive and very simple reasoning methods that are error prone and do not allow a rigorous engineering approach to the problem. For example, while Brito et al. [16] propose allocating different priorities to conflicting concerns, in [17] conflict solving is based on the principle of iteratively identifying the dominant candidate aspect, or crosscutting concern, with respect to a set of stakeholders' requirements. This requires extensive negation between stakeholders.

Moreira et al. [18] and Rashid et al. [19] use a similar idea, by assigning weights to those aspects that contribute negatively to each other. Weighting allows them to describe the extent to which an aspect may constrain a base module. The scales used are based on ideas from fuzzy logic. Again, concerns contributing negatively to each other and with the same weight with respect to a given base module require explicit, but informal, negotiations with the stakeholders.

The main limitations of these approaches are:

1. Each concern must be allocated one single different importance using intuition.
2. Conflict handling is based on one criterion, the importance, not considering other parameters that may have an impact on the decision.
3. Different stakeholders may have different interests on the same concern, and the relative importance/power of each one might be different (so their relative position might have to be taken into account).
4. Trade-offs must be negotiated informally with the stakeholders without any rigorous and systematic analysis technique or tool.

It was with these limitations in mind that we started exploring rigorous alternatives take used effectively without having to rely so strongly on a single criterion (importance), taking into consideration other possible useful information collected during the application of the methods.

Multi-Criteria Decision Making (MCDM) methods have been used to solve different types of problems, in particular to identify and prioritize conflicting Non-Functional Requirements (NFRs) [16, 19, 20]. Until recently, efforts have been focused on solving conflicts between aspects for stakeholders, using more formal ways to deal with the issues at hand, and incipient usage of MCDM methods was also proposed to create rankings of concerns, be they aspectual or non-aspectual [13]. The focus was on identifying conflicts between two or more concerns that contribute negatively to each other but have to be included in the same system. This meant that it is not possible to equally satisfy both conflicting concerns. This situation forces a trade-off analysis to establish importance, or priorities, for concerns. According to what is shown in [18], these decisions have a significant influence on the choice of system's architecture, as well as the future stages of the development life cycle. For the latter work, the MCDM method chosen was Analytical Hierarchy Process (AHP) [2, 7, 21].

More recently, in the AMPLE project [22], a novel hybrid assessment method, HAM, was proposed and a software tool was developed. HAM combines the best properties of two well-known MCDM scoring methods, the Analytical Hierarchy Process [2, 21] and the Weighted Average [7, 8], while avoiding some problematic features of those methods [5]. HAM suitability for handling concerns is based on four main points (1) handle conflicting situations between stakeholders objectives (many of these correspond to qualities the system should provide); (2) study which features are affected by those qualities; (3) use these qualities to support architects in their job; (4) use adequate qualities (usually different from those handled until now), to decide which product of the Software Product Lines should be developed first. In this chapter, HAM is applied to AORE instead features or SPL.

12.6 Conclusions

In this chapter an approach that helps to support conflict management at the AORE level has been presented. This approach (HAM) uses AORA to collect the necessary information and to identify potential conflicting situations, and uses a hybrid multi-criteria analysis technique to perform trade-offs and obtain a ranking of concerns. The technique used looks very promising as a tool to support architectural choices during the software architecture design.

We showed that HAM is a versatile technique to help analysing different situations one may wish to explore before design or architectural decisions are made. HAM provides, in a timely and user-friendly way, more robust and logical results, while avoiding scale and prioritization problems faced by other MCDM methods such as AHP.

References

1. I. Brito, Aspect-oriented requirements analysis, PhD Thesis, Universidade Nova de Lisboa, Portugal, 2008
2. T.L. Saaty, *The Analytic Hierarchy Process* (McGraw-Hill, New York, NY, 1980)
3. A. Pimentel, Multi-criteria analysis for architectural choices in software product lines, Master Thesis, Universidade Nova de Lisboa, Portugal, 2009
4. A. Pimentel, R. Ribeiro, A. Moreira, J. Araújo, J. Santos, A. Costa, M. Alférez, U. Kulesza, Hybrid assessment method for SPL aspect-oriented, in *Model-Driven Software Product Lines: The AMPLE Way*, ed. by A. Rashid, J.-C. Royer, A. Rummler (Cambridge University Press, Cambridge, 2011), pp. 125–158
5. R. Ribeiro, A. Moreira, P. Broek, A. Pimentel, Hybrid assessment method for software engineering decisions. Decis. Support Syst. **51**(1), 208–219 (2011)
6. L. Chung, B. Nixon, E. Yu, J. Mylopoulos, *Non-Functional Requirements in Software Engineering* (Kluwer Academic, Dordrecht, 2000)
7. E. Triantaphyllou, *Multi-Criteria Decision Making Methods: A Comparative Study* (Kluwer Academic, Dordrecht, 2000)

8. K.P. Yoon, C.-L. Hwang, Multiple attribute decision making, in *Quantitative Applications in the Social Sciences*, ed. by M.S. Lewis-Beck, vol. 07-104 (Sage, London, 1995)
9. H.J. Zimmerman, L. Gutsche, *Multi-Criteria Analysis* (Springer, Berlin, 1991)
10. S. Chen, C. Hwang, *Fuzzy Multiple Attribute Decision Making: Methods and Application*. LNEMS, vol. 375 (Springer, Heidelberg, 1993)
11. W. Dong, F. Wong, Fuzzy weighted averages and implementation of the extension principle. Fuzzy Sets Syst. **21**(2), 183–199 (1987)
12. Y. Dong, Y. Xu, M. Dai, H. Li, A comparative study of the numerical scales and the prioritization methods in AHP. Eur. J. Oper. Res. **186**, 229–242 (2008)
13. I. Brito, F. Vieira, A. Moreira, R. Ribeiro, Handling conflicts in aspectual requirements compositions in Lecture Notes in Computer Science (LNCS), in *Transactions on Aspect-Oriented Software Development*, ed. by J. Araujo, E. Baniassad. Special issue on "Early Aspects", 2007
14. CMS – Crisis Management Systems, A case study for aspect-oriented modeling (2011), http://www.cs.mcgill.ca/~joerg/taosd/TAOSD/TAOSD_files/AOM_Case_Study.pdf. Accessed July 2011
15. K.E. Wiegers, *Software Requirements*, 2nd edn. (Microsoft Press, Redmond, WA, 2003)
16. I. Brito, A. Moreira, Towards a composition process for aspect-oriented requirements, in *Early Aspects Workshop at AOSD Conference*, Boston, MA, 2003
17. I. Brito, A. Moreira, Integrating the NFR approach in a RE model, in *Early Aspects Workshop at AOSD Conference*, Lancaster, UK, 2004
18. A. Moreira, A. Rashid, J. Araújo, Multi-dimensional separation of concerns in requirements engineering, in *13th IEEE International Conference on RE*, France, 2005
19. A. Rashid, A. Moreira, J. Araújo, Modularization and composition of aspectual requirements, in *International Conference on AOSD, USA* (ACM Press, 2003)
20. R. Wieringa, N. Maiden, N. Mead et al., Requirements engineering paper classification and evaluation criteria: a proposal and a discussion. Require. Eng. **11**, 102–107 (2005)
21. T.L. Saaty, Decision making with the analytic hierarchy process. Int. J. Serv. Sci. **1**, 83–98 (2008)
22. AMPLE project (2011), http://www.ample-project.net/. Accessed July 2011

Chapter 13
Analysis of Aspect-Oriented Models Using Graph Transformation Systems

Katharina Mehner-Heindl, Mattia Monga, and Gabriele Taentzer

Abstract Aspect-oriented concepts are currently exploited to model systems from the beginning of their development. Aspects capture potentially cross-cutting concerns and make it easier to formulate desirable properties and to understand analysis results than in a tangled system. However, the complexity of interactions among different aspectualized entities may reduce the benefit of aspect-oriented separation of cross-cutting concerns. It is therefore desirable to detect inconsistencies as early as possible.

We propose an approach for analyzing consistency at the level of requirements modeling. We use a variant of UML to model requirements in a use-case driven approach. Activities that are used to refine use cases are the joinpoints to compose cross-cutting concerns. Activities are combined with a specification of pre- and post-conditions into an integrated behavior model. This model is formalized using the theory of graph transformation systems to effectively reason about its consistency. The analysis of an integrated behavior model is performed with the tool ACTIGRA.

K. Mehner-Heindl (✉)
Department of Media and Information Engineering, University of Applied Sciences Offenburg, Offenburg, Germany
e-mail: katharina.mehner@gmail.com

M. Monga
Department of Computer Science, Università degli Studi di Milano, Milan, Italy
e-mail: mattia.monga@unimi.it

G. Taentzer
Department of Computer Science and Mathematics, Philipps-Universität Marburg, Marburg, Germany
e-mail: taentzer@mathematik.uni-marburg.de

A. Moreira et al. (eds.), *Aspect-Oriented Requirements Engineering*,
DOI 10.1007/978-3-642-38640-4_13,

13.1 Introduction

Aspect-oriented programming promises to provide better separation and integration of cross-cutting concerns than plain object-oriented programming. Aspect-oriented concepts have been introduced in all phases of the software development life cycle with the aim of reducing complexity and enhancing maintainability already early on.

On the requirements level, cross-cutting concerns, i.e., concerns that affect many other requirements, cannot be cleanly modularized using object-oriented and viewpoint-based techniques. Several approaches have been proposed to identify cross-cutting concerns already at the requirements level and to provide means to modularize, represent, and compose them using aspect-oriented techniques, e.g., for use-case-driven modeling in [2, 8, 19, 20]. A key challenge is to analyze the interaction and consistency of cross-cutting concerns with each other and with affected requirements. It is in particular the quantifying nature [6] of aspect-oriented composition that makes the detection of interactions and inconsistencies difficult.

Until now, approaches to analyzing the aspectual composition of requirements have been informal [19, 20, 23]. Formal approaches for detecting inconsistencies have been proposed only for the level of aspect-oriented programming, e.g., model checking [10], static analysis [21], and slicing [3, 28]. At the programming level, however, the meta-model considered is pretty different and it takes into account many low-level details. Requirements abstract from these implementation-related details, and weaving occurs among the high-level activities which describe the intended behavior of the system.

A commonly used but often informal technique on the requirements level is to describe behavior with pre- and postconditions, e.g., using intentionally defined states or attributes of a domain entity model. This technique is, for example, used for defining UML [18] use cases, activities, and methods. In order to allow a more rigorous analysis of behavior, this approach has to be formalized and also extended to aspect-oriented units of behavior.

We propose a use-case-driven approach with a domain class model. Activity models are used to refine use cases. Object models are used for describing pre- and postconditions of activities. This integration between structural and functional view is called an *integrated behavior model*. Furthermore, we propose an *aspect-oriented extension*. We model the so-called base with use cases and an integrated behavior model. We model aspects as use cases and refine them with an integrated behavior model. During the aspect-oriented composition, we use activities as joinpoints and follow the composition operations suggested by AspectJ [12, 25] and similar languages. An integrated behavior model can be formalized using the theory of graph transformations: Graph transformation rules are used to formalize pre- and postconditions of activities. Graph transformation sequences are used to capture the semantics of the activity models. A formal analysis can be carried out on integrated behavior models computing favorable and critical signs concerning causalities and conflicts between activities. This analysis can be carried out before and after the aspect-oriented composition in order to understand the behavior of use cases and of aspectual use cases separately and in order to understand the effects of aspects. The new tool ACTIGRA [5,26] which itself is based on the well-known AGG engine for graph transformations [4,27], provides this kind of modeling and analysis support. Throughout the chapter we use a UML variant that is directly supported by this tool.

The idea of formalizing pre- and postconditions by graph transformation was presented in [7] first and extended to aspect-oriented models in [15]. The aspect-oriented composition itself was formalized by meta-level graph transformations in [16]. Since then, the theory and the tools for integrated behavior models have been advanced and improved. We demonstrate how they can be used in aspect-oriented modeling.

This chapter is organized as follows. In Sect. 13.2 we present our aspect-oriented modeling approach and sketch the weaving process. Section 13.3 presents the theory of algebraic graph transformations first, including conflict and causality analysis between transformations. Secondly, we give the formal semantics of activity diagrams augmented by graph transformation rules by means of sequences of graph transformations. Section 13.4 presents the plausibility checks based on the formal semantics. These analysis facilities are applied to our example in Sect. 13.5. In Sect. 13.6 we discuss related work. In Sect. 13.7 we conclude and give an outlook.

13.2 Aspect-Oriented Modeling with Integrated Behavior Models

Our approach uses *integrated behavior models* and extends them by aspect-oriented features. An integrated behavior model consists of a *domain model* and a set of *activity models*. The domain model provides the types of the domain objects. Each activity is refined by *pre-* and *postconditions* describing the effect of the activity in terms of domain objects. Typically, an *initial configuration* of the system is provided in terms of domain objects and their relations.

The benefit of an integrated behavior model is an early and better integration of the structural domain model with the functional activity model. Pre- and postconditions are formalized by the theory of graph transformation systems. This formalization can then be used for a rigorous analysis of integrated behavior models.

In addition to the integrated behavior model, a use-case diagram provides a system overview. Each use case is at least specified by a trigger, its actors, pre- and postconditions and its key scenarios. Scenarios are specified using activity diagrams and use cases are the starting point for the aspect-oriented modeling. We model the so-called *base* of the system with use cases and an integrated behavior model. An *aspect* is modeled as a use case. The *joinpoint* for an aspect is an activity of the base. The *pointcut* of an aspect is specified in terms of the activities of the base. During the aspect-oriented composition process, also called *weaving*, aspect activities are inserted into the base according to a composition specification, resulting again in an integrated behavior model.

While up to now proposed for modeling techniques like UML, an integrated behavior model is also *suitable* and *beneficial* for aspect-oriented modeling:

- It is well suited for modeling the base of a system at an early stage.
- It can naturally capture the functional and structural description of each aspect. An aspect may share the base domain model or add its own concepts.

Using the formal analysis of integrated behavior models for aspect-oriented modeling is beneficial as well. Each aspect can be analyzed for consistency, and the consistency of the entire system consisting of the base and aspects can be analyzed as well. Analysis is even more crucial for aspect-oriented models:

- Firstly, because of the separated specification of functionality in base and aspects. (Note that separate specification of functionality also exists in complex modular systems.)
- Furthermore, an aspect is specified once but can be used in many different places of the system. (Note that this also bears similarity with modular systems, where a module can be explicitly used by many other modules.)
- Lastly, an aspect is specified on top of and added to modules later on, with modules not necessarily being aware of the aspect. (Note that this is not the case in object orientation, but is unique to aspect-oriented techniques and similar techniques.)

Because of these three properties, it is difficult to understand and manually analyze functional and data dependencies between base and aspects and also between aspects. On the other hand, there are well-known benefits of this kind of separation of concern, namely for maintenance, reuse, organization of work, etc.

We use ACTIGRA to model the running example before and after the composition, which is carried out manually following the formalization described in [16]. Apart from the use-case diagram, all figures have been generated with ACTIGRA.

13.2.1 The Crisis Management System Example

We present our modeling approach using an example from the Crisis Management Systems (CMS) Case Study [13]. A crisis management system helps in identifying, assessing, and handling a crisis such as a fire, a flood, or an accident. It orchestrates the communication among all parties, thus handling the crisis by managing resources and access to data. Besides informal requirements, the case study contains a wide range of models related to software development. We have adapted a coherent subset of use cases, classes, and activities for the sake of the case study to illustrate our approach. Figure 13.1 gives an overview of the chosen use cases. We are using an ≪ *aspect* ≫ stereotype for an aspect use case and a ≪ *crosscuts* ≫ stereotype for the relation of an aspect to the base. Analogous stereotypes have been proposed in [24]. The ≪ *crosscuts* ≫ relation means that the behavior of the aspect is added to a base without referring to the aspect in the base explicitly. It is called

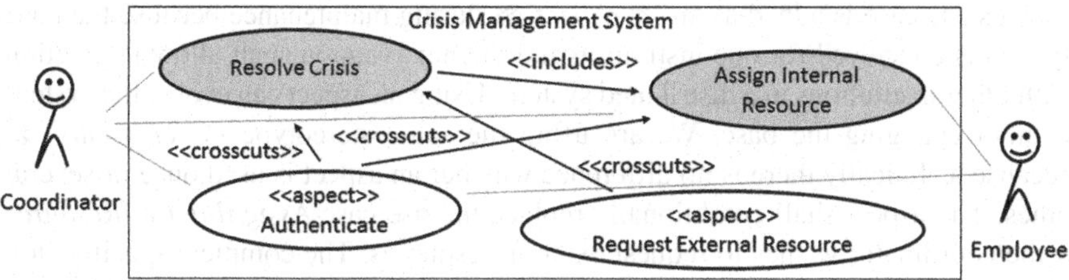

Fig. 13.1 Crisis management use cases

≪ *crosscuts* ≫ because often aspects capture concerns that are broadly scattered. However, it can also be used for adding any other concern without changing the base.

Use-Case *ResolveCrisis*. The intention of this use case is to resolve a crisis by requesting employees and external resources to execute appropriate missions. An available employee is chosen as the coordinator who has to capture the witness' report. With the help of the system, he or she creates the corresponding mission(s). Next, the coordinator assigns missions to resources and controls their completion.

This use case includes the use-case *AssignInternalResource*, as indicated by the ≪ *includes* ≫ relationship. Thus, when the use-case *ResolveCrisis* is refined by an activity diagram it will contain a so-called complex activity named *AssignInternal-Resource*.

Use-Case *AssignInternalResource*. The intention of this use case is to find, contact, and assign a mission to the most appropriate available employee. Here, appropriateness simply means availability. An available employee is chosen. The employee receives the mission information which has to be accepted to be assigned to the mission.

When this use case is refined, the refining activity diagram serves as the refinement of the corresponding complex activity *AssignInternalResource*.

Use-Case *Authenticate*. The actor involved is either a coordinator or an employee. The intention of this use case is to authenticate the actor to the system since authentication is required to use the functions of the system. If the actor is not yet logged on, login id and password are prompted, entered, and validated.

This use case is designed into the system upfront as an ≪ *aspect* ≫. It ≪ *crosscuts* ≫ *ResolveCrisis*, where the coordinating employee has to log on, and *AssignInternalResource*, where all chosen employees have to log on, both, before further activities take place. In a real system, this use case would affect a lot of further use cases. Since the pointcut of this aspect is specified in terms of activities, the complete specification of the composition is given later.

Use-Case *RequestExternalResource*. The intention of this use case is to request help for a mission from an external resource such as an ambulance service. A request is sent to an external resource. The request is either served or denied.

This use case is added as an ≪ *aspect* ≫ during maintenance because the base system is conceived for one institution and the next version shall allow interaction with other institutions in a distributed system. Using an aspect can evolve the system without changing the base. We are using the same stereotype ≪ *crosscuts* ≫ because technically there is no difference whether an aspect is used once or several times. The aspect shall conditionally replace the use-case *AssignInternalResource* if the coordinator wishes to request external resources. The complete specification of the aspectual composition is given later.

13.2.2 Integrated Behavior Models for the Base

A subset of the domain model of the crisis management system is given in Fig. 13.2 using the type graph of ACTIGRA. A "Crisis" "requires" the fulfillment of some "Missions". A "CMSEmployee" "coordinates" a crisis or is "chosen" or "informed" or "assigned" to a mission. The "status" attribute of the employee is either set to "logged on" or "logged off." For a mission that cannot be assigned to an employee, a "Request" "needs" to be generated. Its "status" is either "sent" or "served."

For the subsequent analysis we need an *initial configuration* of our system (cf. Fig. 13.2, middle). It contains the object instances of the classes defined in the type graph. A valid initial configuration is always needed. If the system contains graph transformation rules that create the corresponding objects, then the initial configuration can be the empty one.

Our well-formed activity models (cf. Sect. 13.3) consist of simple and complex activities, start and end nodes, decisions followed by a merge (a decision is depicted as a D in a diamond node, a merge as an M in a diamond node), and loop nodes (a loop is depicted as an L in a diamond node). Directed arcs can be labeled by structural constraints ([. . .]) or interactively evaluated user constraints (¡. . .¿) (compare Fig. 13.3).

The use-case *ResolveCrisis* is refined by the topmost activity diagram in Fig. 13.3. Firstly, the coordinating employee is determined who has to capture the witness report then. The first loop generates the required missions. The next loop assigns an employee to each mission using the complex activity *AssignInternal-Resource*. The last loop controls the success of the missions. We have omitted constraints on the loops, since this use case is not presented in more detail. It is used only to illustrate the composition of several aspects.

The use-case *AssignInternalResource* is refined by the activity diagram in the middle of Fig. 13.3. The first decision node checks whether the innermost activity *DetermineMostAppropriateEmployee* is applicable. The constraint *[AvailableEm-ployeeExists]*(cf. Fig. 13.4) checks whether an employee has not yet been chosen for any mission. The positive pattern "existence of employee" describes parts of a graph that have to exist. The "not chosen" negative application condition (NAC) states that the constraint does not allow this pattern. A constraint can have zero or any number of NACs. This constraint also has NACs "not informed" and "not

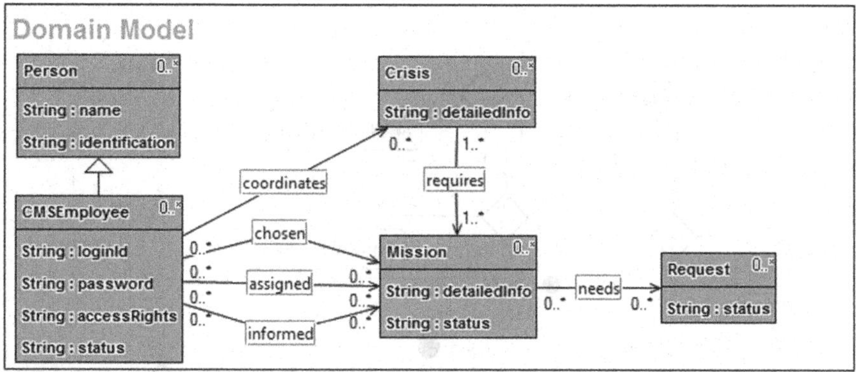

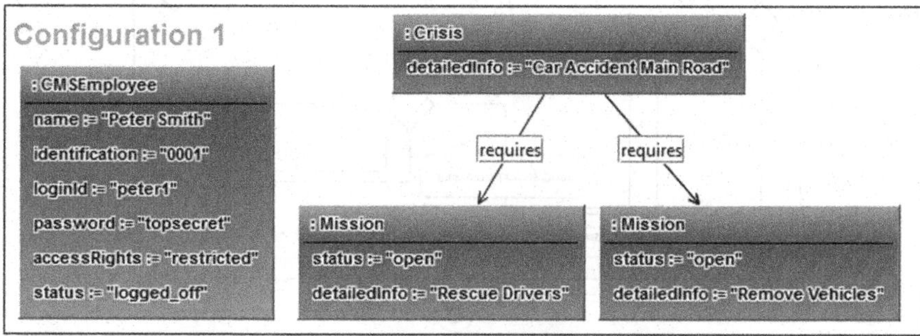

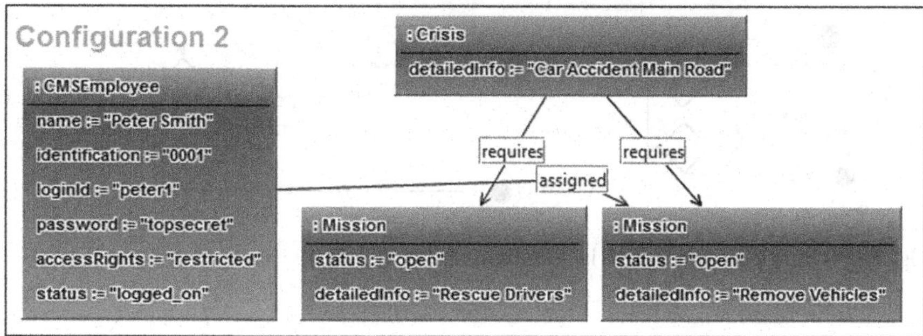

Fig. 13.2 Type graph (*top*), initial configuration (*middle*), simulation result (*bottom*)

assigned" not being depicted. They express that an employee must not be involved in a mission anyhow. Only if the constraint is satisfied, the arc labeled with it can be executed. Each of the following loops are applied until a constraint is satisfied. The innermost loop chooses an employee. Only if the employee is logged on, captured by *[ChosenEmployeeLoggedIn]*(cf. Fig. 13.4), the enclosing loop is executed which sends mission details to the employee. Only if that is successful, captured by *[Stopped]*(cf. Fig. 13.4), the system waits for acceptance, in which case, captured by *[MissionAccept]*(cf. Fig. 13.4), the use case terminates successfully.

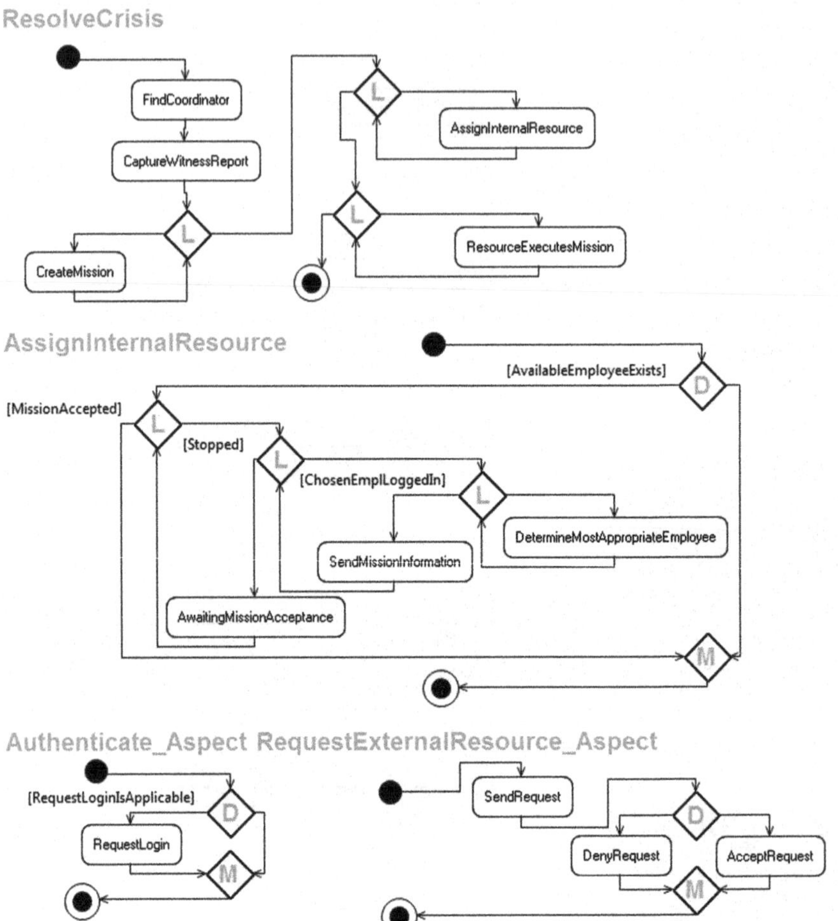

Fig. 13.3 Crisis management activity diagrams

In an integrated behavioral model, each activity is refined by a pre- and a postcondition, describing the situation in which the activity can be applied, and the effect. The precondition consists of a positive pattern for a graph that has to exist, optionally equipped with NACs capturing negative patterns preventing the application. Conditions are presented for the activity model of use-case *AssignInternalResource* in Fig. 13.5. For each activity, the left column presents a NAC, the middle column the positive precondition, and the right column presents the effect of each activity, i.e., the postcondition. The identity of a node is preserved throughout the three columns by assigning the same instance number to it. The first row states that an employee can be assigned once to an open mission. The second row states that a chosen employee who is logged on can be informed about the mission once. The last row states that an informed employee can be assigned to a mission.

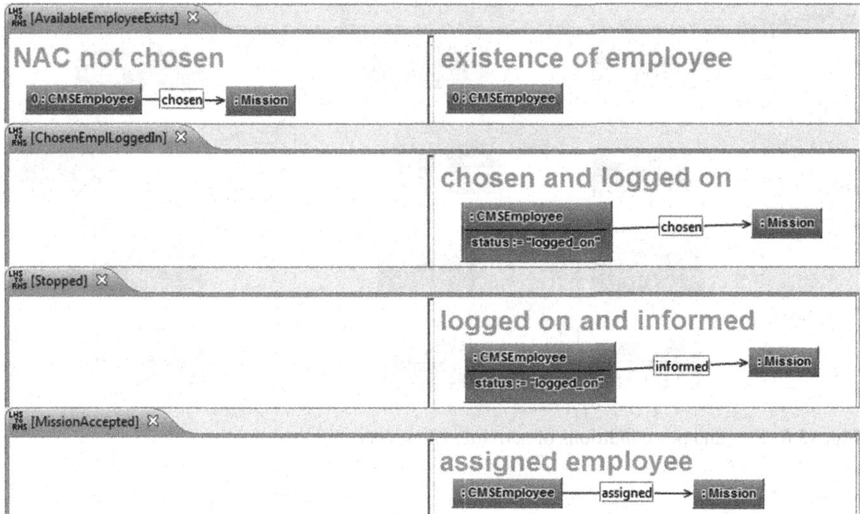

Fig. 13.4 Structural constraints for activity model *AssignInternalResource*

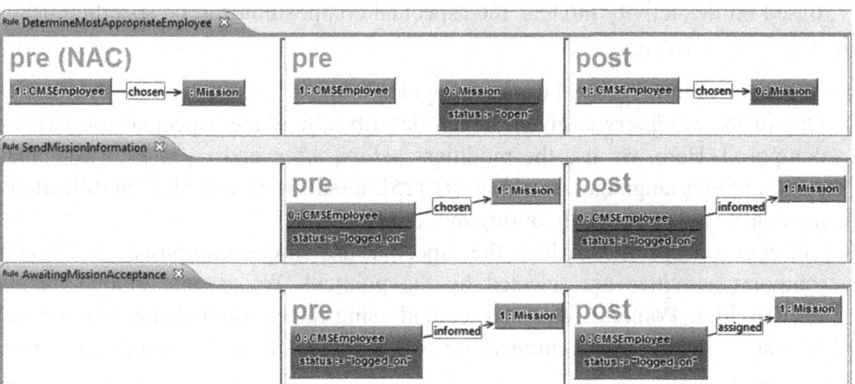

Fig. 13.5 Pre- and postconditions of activities of use-case *AssignInternalResource*

13.2.3 Aspect Modeling

An aspect is identified on the use-case level and subsequently refined with an activity diagram. The use-case *Authenticate* is refined by the corresponding activity diagram in Fig. 13.3 (bottom left). If an employee is not yet logged in, the execution of *RequestLogin* changes the status of the employee from "logged_off" to "logged_on", (cf. also Fig. 13.6, top).

The use-case *RequestExternalResource* is refined by the corresponding activity diagram in Fig. 13.3 (bottom right). A request is sent to an external resource (cf. Fig. 13.6, second row). Either the request is accepted (cf. Fig. 13.6, third row) or

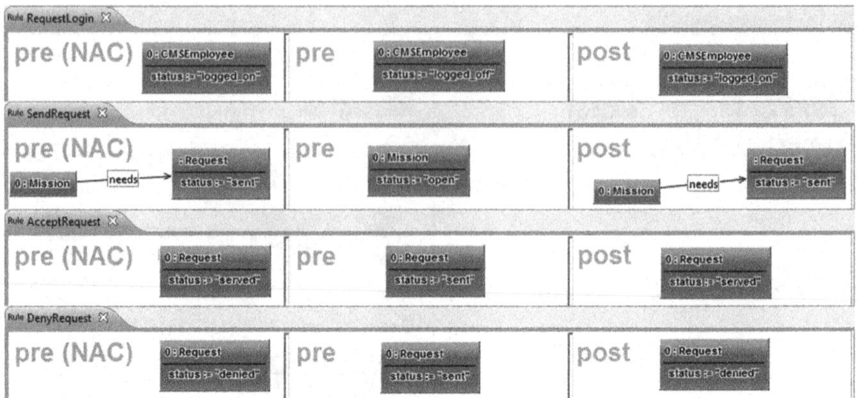

Fig. 13.6 Pre- and postconditions of activities of aspects

denied (cf. Fig. 13.6, last row). In our example, the decision is not specified further since it comes from an external system. During simulation, an arbitrary arc is chosen and during analysis, both arcs are analyzed.

Based on the activity models, the aspectual composition can be specified using the following elements:

- The *name* of the aspectual use case is given.
- One of the *modifiers* is given, which describes, how the aspectual use case is composed. Here, we use the modifiers *before*, *after*, and *replace* of aspectual programming languages like AspectJ [25], albeit more complex modifications are conceivable, especially during modeling.
- The *pointcut* specifies, where the aspectual use case is composed, i.e., which joinpoint activities are selected by the pointcut. We assume unique names for activities. Pointcuts can be specified using rather sophisticated intensional languages or by mere enumeration of activities. Here we adopt the latter approach.
- A *condition* specifies under which circumstances the aspect becomes effective. This allows for a flexible composition with the base. If the condition is fulfilled, the aspect is executing. If no condition is given, the aspect will always execute. As conditions we use structural constraints or interactively evaluated conditions.

An aspect is woven in each single joinpoint which matches the pointcut definition. Here, an aspect has only one pointcut, but more complex weaving technologies exist. Regarding the order of composition, we simply follow the order of specifications. After a replace composition without a condition, further aspects might not be applicable. Furthermore, we do not consider aspects of aspects in our model. Note that aspects without conditions can simulate aspects with conditions by integrating the condition into the normal control flow of the aspect at the beginning of the aspect.

Table 13.1 Aspect-oriented composition

Use Case	Modifier	Pointcut (Activity)	Condition
Authenticate	`after`	FindCoordinator, DetermineMost-AppropriateEmployee	—
RequestExternal-Resource	`replace`	AssignInternalResource	<Request External Resource?>

The composition specification for each ≪ *crosscuts* ≫ relationship is given in Table 13.1. The *Authenticate* aspect is composed once after the activity *FindCoordinator* (of the use case *ResolveCrisis*) and once after the activity *DetermineMostAppropriateEmployee* (of the use-case *AssignInternalResource*). The *Authenticate* aspect has no condition since it shall always be carried out. In addition, this aspect checks by itself whether an employee is already logged on. Aspect *RequestExternalResource* conditionally replaces the activity *AssignInternalResource* (of the use case *ResolveCrisis*) if the coordinator decides to do so.

Finally, ACTIGRA can be used to execute an activity diagram with its pre- and postconditions. When applying use-case *AssignInternalResource* to the initial *Configuration 1* (Fig. 13.2, middle), the simulation is animated on the activity diagram. The execution starts with the innermost loop and executes *DetermineMostAppropriateEmployee* as often as possible but it cannot proceed because the condition *[ChosenEmplLoggedIn]* is never fulfilled. This is due to the absence of an aspect which will be analyzed in more depth later.

13.2.4 Aspect Weaving

Since its coining, the term aspect-oriented programming has always been a synonym for implementing aspects using *weaving*, i.e., for a transformation of the source code which inserts the aspect code in all places specified by a pointcut. We apply the same concept to the activity model of the aspect-oriented use case, i.e., we weave the aspect activity model into activity models of the base. Weaving is controlled by the composition specifications illustrated in the previous section. The modeling of pre- and postconditions does not play a specific role during weaving which is also feasible without, albeit for the subsequent analysis they are mandatory. In [16], we proposed and formalized the model weaving within our approach. Here, we present it informally only and demonstrate the result for the example. The weaving process is as follows. Firstly, the joinpoints have to be determined using the pointcut specifications, i.e., all places where weaving has to take place. The two cases, weaving with conditions and without conditions, have to be combined with the modifiers *before*, *after*, and *replace*.

Weaving without conditions:

- *before*: The aspect activity diagram replaces all incoming arcs to the joinpoint activity specified in the pointcut.
- *after*: The aspect activity diagram replaces the outgoing arcs from the joinpoint activity specified in the pointcut.
- *replace*: The aspect activity diagram replaces the activity. The incoming and outgoing arcs are glued to the first rsp. last activities of the aspect activity.

Weaving with conditions:

- *before*: The condition is inserted as a decision node into the aspect diagram, after the start node with the positive arc linked to the first activity and with the negative arc linked to the end node. A merge node is inserted before the end node and all the incoming arcs become incoming arcs of the merge node. The augmented aspect activity diagram replaces all the incoming arcs to the joinpoint activity specified in the pointcut.
- *after*: The condition is inserted as a decision node into the aspect diagram after the start node with the positive arc linked to the first activity and with the negative arc linked to the end node. A merge node is inserted before the end node and all incoming arcs become incoming arcs of the merge node. The augmented aspect activity diagram replaces all the outgoing arcs from the joinpoint activity specified in the pointcut.
- *replace*: The condition is inserted as a decision node before (see *before* above) the joinpoint activity specified in the pointcut. The positive arc of the branch is linked to the first activity of the aspect. The negative arc is linked to the joinpoint activity. A merge node is inserted after (see *after* above) the joinpoint activity. All incoming arcs of the end node of the aspect become incoming arcs of the merge node.

In all cases, the start and end nodes of the aspect activity diagram are removed and the dangling arcs are glued correspondingly. The weaving results of the example are depicted in Fig. 13.7. Following the order of specification, firstly the aspect *Authenticate* is woven into the use-case *ResolveCrisis* after the joinpoint activity *FindCoordinator*. It is also woven into the use-case *AssignInternalResource* after the joinpoint activity *DetermineMostAppropriateEmployee*. Secondly, the aspect *RequestExternalResource* is woven into the use-case *ResolveCrisis*. It is linked via a new decision node to the joinpoint activity *AssignInternalResource*. Note that after weaving, the complex activity *AssignInternalResource* is changed but this is not visualized in the activity model *ResolveCrisis_woven* for use-case *ResolveCrisis*.

Again, ACTIGRA can be used to execute an activity diagram with its pre- and postconditions. When applying *AssignInternalResource_woven* to the initial configuration in the middle of Fig. 13.2, the simulation is animated on the activity diagram. It starts with the innermost loop and executes each loop and activity once, terminating successfully and resulting in *Configuration 2* of Fig. 13.2 (bottom).

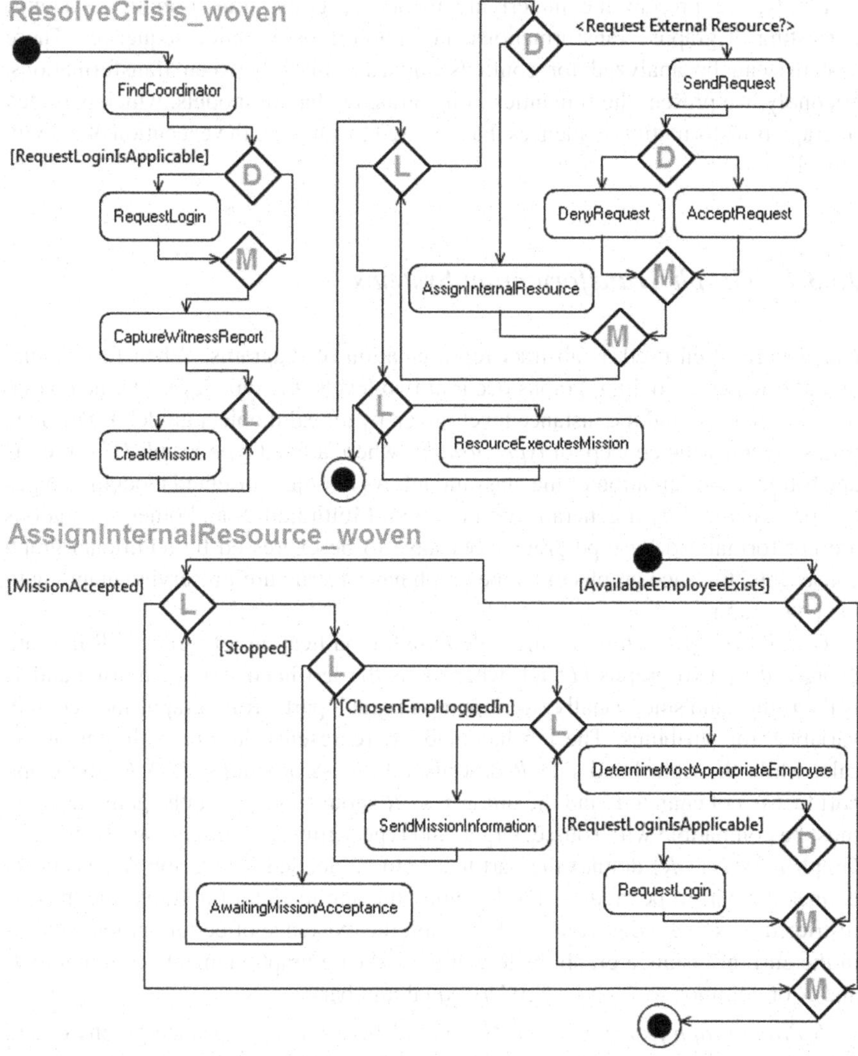

Fig. 13.7 Use cases with aspects woven

13.3 Formalization of Integrated Behavior Models

Integrated behavior models can be formalized by graph transformation systems. Domain models are formalized by type graphs, while configurations are specified by their instance graphs. Pre- and postconditions of activities as well as constraints are expressed by graph transformation rules. The control flow of activity models is defined by graph transformation sequences.

Firstly, we present the underlying theory of graph transformation systems, consisting of graphs, transformations, and graph transformation sequences. These systems can be analyzed for conflicts and causalities between transformations. Secondly, we present the semantics of integrated behavior models, which is rooted in graph transformation sequences that are used to simulate the execution of activity models.

13.3.1 Graph Transformation Systems

Graphs are often used as abstract representation of diagrams. When formalizing object-oriented modeling, graphs occur at two levels: the type level (defined based on class models) and the instance level (given by all valid object models). This idea is described by the concept of *typed graphs*, where a fixed *type graph TG* serves as an abstract representation of the class model. As in object-oriented modeling, types can be structured by a generalization relation. Multiplicities and other annotations are not formalized by type graphs, but have to be expressed by additional graph constraints. Instance graphs of a type graph have a structure-preserving mapping to the type graph.

Graph transformation is the rule-based modification of graphs. Rules are expressed by two graphs (L, R), where L is the left-hand side of the rule and R is the right-hand side, usually overlapping in graph parts. Rule graphs may contain variables for attributes. The left-hand side L represents the preconditions of the rule, while the right-hand side R describes the postconditions. $L \cap R$ (the graph part that is not changed) and the union $L \cup R$ should form a graph again, i.e., they must be compatible with source, target, and type settings, in order to apply the rule. Graph $L \setminus (L \cap R)$ defines the part that is to be deleted, and graph $R \setminus (L \cap R)$ defines the part to be created. Furthermore, the application of a graph rule may be restricted by so-called NACs which prohibit the existence of certain graph patterns in the current instance graph. Note that we indicate graph elements common to L and R or common to L and a NAC by equal numbers.

A *direct graph transformation* $G \overset{r,m}{\Longrightarrow} H$ between two instance graphs G and H is defined by first finding a match m of the left-hand side L of rule r in the current instance graph G such that m is structure-preserving and type-compatible and satisfies the NACs (i.e., the forbidden graph patterns are not found in G). We use injective matches only. Attribute variables used in graph object $o \in L$ are bound to concrete attribute values of graph object $m(o)$ in G. The resulting graph H is constructed by (1) deleting all graph items from G that are in L but not also in R; (2) adding all those new graph items that are in R but not also in L; and (3) setting attribute values of preserved and created elements.

A *graph transformation (sequence)* consists of zero or more direct graph transformations. A set of graph rules, together with a type graph, is called a *graph transformation system* (GTS). A GTS may show two kinds of non-determinism:

(1) For each rule several matches may exist. (2) Several rules might be applicable to the same instance graph. There are techniques to restrict both kinds of choices. The choice of matches can be restricted by object flow, while the choice of rules can be explicitly defined by control flow on activities.

13.3.2 Conflicts and Causalities Between Transformation Rules

If two rules are applicable to the same instance graph, they might be applicable in any order with the same result. In this case the rule applications are said to be *parallel independent* otherwise they are in conflict.

Conflict Types. One rule application *may disable* the second rule application. In this case, the application of rule r_1 is also said to be causing a *conflict* with the application of rule r_2. The following types of conflicts can occur:

delete/use: Applying r_1 deletes an element used by the application of r_2.
produce/forbid: Applying r_1 produces an element that a NAC of r_2 forbids.
change/use: Applying r_1 changes an attribute value used by the application of r_2.

Causality Types. Conversely, one rule application *may trigger* the application of another rule. In this case, this sequence of two rule applications is said to be *causally dependent*. The following types of causalities can occur where the application of rule r_1 *triggers* the application of r_2:

produce/use: Applying r_1 produces an element needed by the application of r_2.
delete/forbid: Applying r_1 deletes an element that a NAC of r_2 forbids.
change/use: Applying r_1 changes an attribute value used by the application of r_2.

Example 1. Figure 13.8 shows an example of a produce–use dependency occurring when first rule *DetermineMostAppropriateEmployee* and then rule *SendMissionInformation* are applied. While the first rule creates a new relation of type "chosen" between a "CMSEmployee" and a mission, the second rule uses this relation and deletes it.

13.3.3 Semantics of Integrated Behavior Models

As in [9], we define integrated behavior models by *well-structured activity models* consisting of a start activity s, an activity block B, and an end activity e such that there is a transition between s and B and another one between B and e. An *activity block* can be a simple activity, a sequence of blocks, a fork-join structure, decision-merge structure, or loop. In addition, we allow complex activities which stand for nested well-structured activity models. In this hierarchy, we forbid nesting

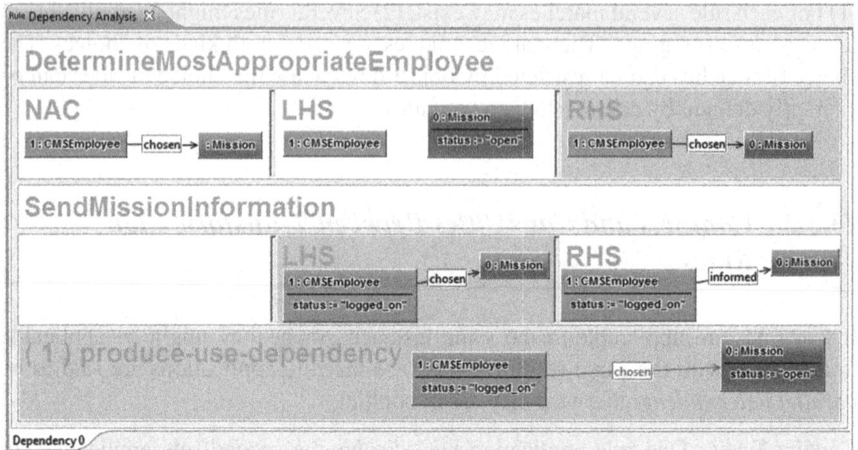

Fig. 13.8 Produce–use causality example between two transformation rules

cycles. Activity blocks are connected by transitions (directed arcs). Decisions have an explicit *if*-guard and an implicit *else*-guard which equals the negated *if*-guard. Loops have a *loop*-guard with corresponding implicit *else*-guard. Guards can be user defined, i.e., independent of system configurations, or graph constraints checking certain conditions on system configurations.

The semantics of an integrated behavior model is defined by a set of graph transformation rules sequences. Considering the formalization of activities with pre- and postconditions by graph transformation rules, the sequences represent all possible control flow paths defined by well-structured activity models. In this context, each graph constraint is translated to a rule containing the constraint as left-hand side and an identical right-hand side. The semantics of a simple activity *Sem*(A) is a set consisting of one sequence with only one rule. The semantics of two subsequent activity blocks A and B contains all sequences beginning with a sequence of *Sem*(A) and ending with a sequence of *Sem*(B). For decision blocks, we construct the union of sequences of both branches (preceded by the guard rule or its negation, respectively). For loop blocks, we construct sequences containing the body of the loop $0 \leq i \leq n$ times (where each body sequence is preceded by the loop guard rule in case that the loop guard is not user defined). The semantics of a complex activity is the semantics of the largest block of its contained integrated behavior model.

Example 2. Considering the integrated behavior model of use-case *AssignInternalResource* (without aspects, cf. Fig. 13.3), its semantics contains the sequence *AvailableEmployeeExists*, *NotMissionAccepted*, *NotStopped*, *NotChosenEmplLoggedIn*, *DetermineMostAppropriateEmployee*, *NotChosenEmplLoggedIn*, *DetermineMostAppropriateEmployee*, *ChosenEmpLoggedIn*, *SendMission Information*, *Stopped*, *AwaitingMissionAcceptance*, *MissionAccepted*.

13.4 Using Plausibility Checks for Integrated Behavior Models with Aspects

Given the formal semantics of integrated behavioral models as simulation runs, these sequences can be formally analyzed for favorable and critical causalities and conflicts between the rules in those sequences. The results are captured in different sets of *relations*.

After introducing the checks from [5], we discuss how they can be used specifically in aspect-oriented modeling. The checks are supported by ACTIGRA.

13.4.1 Plausibility Checks for Integrated Behavior Models

Integrated behavior models combine control flow models with functional behavior specifications. Since two kinds of models are used for this purpose, static analysis of integrated behavior models helps to argue about their consistency. In [5], a variety of so-called plausibility checks are presented that can be used for argumentation. For each check, favorable and critical signs can be determined that support or are opposed to behavior consistency.

1. *Initialization:* The applicability of the first rule in the specified control flow to the initial configuration forms a favorable sign.
2. *Trigger causality along control flow:* This plausibility check computes for each rule in a given control flow which of its predecessor rules may trigger this rule. It is favorable that at least one predecessor exists for each rule.
3. *Conflicts along control flow:* This plausibility check computes for each rule in a given control flow which of its successor rules may be disabled by this rule. It is favorable that there do not exist such successors for any rule.
4. *Trigger causality against control flow:* This plausibility check computes for each rule in a given control flow which of its successor rules may trigger this rule. It is favorable that there do not exist such successors for any rule. In case that such a successor exists, the modeler should inspect if it should be shifted before the rule it triggers.

Note that guards are reformulated as nonchanging rules and integrated into the plausibility check then.

13.4.2 Analysis of Aspects with Plausibility Checks

In our modeling approach, plausibility checks are computed for base and aspect separately and for the entire woven model. The analysis is therefore applied incrementally in two stages:

1. The consistency of the base and the aspects is checked separately. It is desirable that consistency is achieved separately where feasible.
2. The consistency of the composition of aspects and the base is checked. It suffices to analyze the control flow that contains the woven aspect activities. This can be deduced from the pointcut specification (but this inference is not yet implemented in ACTIGRA, and the resulting weaving has to be computed by hand). The problems revealed are directly related to this composition if consistency was achieved beforehand. This stage includes checking the consistency between aspects, since their effects on each other cannot be generally checked on the stage before. Instead, their specific effect on each other when composed with a base system is considered.

In woven control flows in stage 2, triggers and conflicts between activities of the base may change compared to stage 1 if use cases are replaced during the weaving. Conflicts between base activities (including conflicts of an activity with itself) may disappear because an aspect added to a control flow changes the sequence such that a conflict is no longer effective. Newly arising triggers and conflicts at stage 2 have different sources. They may occur between base and aspect or between different aspects. They may also occur between activities of one aspect due to the following reason. After weaving, an aspect becomes part of new control flows. These control flows can have the effect that an aspect is potentially executed several times in a loop. Then its activities are potentially in conflict with themselves and also with each other. If the activities were not part of such loops before weaving, there are new conflicts and triggers after the weaving.

Conflicts and causalities may occur between individual activities rsp. corresponding transformation rules. In general, a potential conflict need not lead to a concrete conflict; this is especially true in the case of change/use conflicts which often indicate that activities use attributes changed by other activities.

- *Conflict between base and aspect:* If a conflict exists between a base activity rsp. its rule r_1 and an aspect activity rsp. its rule r_2, the aspect is disabled by the basis, and vice versa. This is not desirable for before- and after-aspects. For replace aspects it is no problem if the rule r_1 of the basis is completely replaced by the aspect.
- *Conflicts between aspects:* A conflict can exist between two activities rsp. rules stemming from two different aspects. If one aspect disables another aspect and is woven into an activity diagram in the control flow before the other aspect, the conflict is not desirable and has to be examined further.
- *Trigger causality between base and aspect:* If a trigger from base to aspect exists, this is not a problem. If no trigger exists this is also not a problem but then it should be ensured that the aspect still can work.
- *Trigger causality between aspects:* If causalities exist they should be along the control flow of the entire system including aspects. If no trigger causalities between aspects exist, it should be ensured that each aspect can work.

The plausibility checks can be used at *stage 1* as follows:

- Initialization is checked for base and aspects separately. At least one base activity model should be applicable to the initial configuration. If an aspect is applicable to the initial configuration this means that it is orthogonal to the base or perhaps conflicting with the base. It is not required that an aspect is applicable to the initial configuration.
- Triggers along control flow inside an activity model are beneficial. Absence has to be checked for consistency.
- Triggers against control flow have to be checked for consistency.
- Conflicts inside an activity model have to be checked for consistency.

At *stage 2*, plausibility checks can be used as follows:

- An aspect must be applicable to the initial state or needs trigger causalities.
- Trigger causalities along the control flow may stem from the base or from other aspects.
- The check for triggers against control flow can be used to identify problematic cases. It may be the case that a joinpoint is not well chosen, i.e., too late or too early in a given use case or even in the wrong use case.
- There must not be conflicts newly introduced, i.e., of aspect activities with the (remaining) base or with each other.
- If the base was not consistent without aspect(s), one should check if the entire system becomes consistent after aspect composition.

13.5 Analysis of the Example

Here we present the plausibility analysis of the use-case *AssignInternalResource*, the aspect use cases *Authenticate* and *RequestExternalResource*, and the woven use cases *AssignInternalResource* and *ResolveCrisis* using ACTIGRA.

Analyzing the use-case *AssignInternalResource*. ACTIGRA visualizes the results of each plausibility check separately in the activity model. For reasons of space, we can not include the figures for all checks.

1. *Initialization*(not depicted): The first reachable activity *DetermineMostAppropriateEmployee* is applicable to the initial *Configuration 1*.
2. *Triggers along control flow* (cf. Fig. 13.9, top): All activities and conditions have triggers. Because of the loops, these triggers are along the control flow.

   SendMissionInformation triggers *DetermineMostAppropriateEmployee*. Here the first activity deletes the "chosen" arc which is forbidden by the second activity. The condition *[Stopped]*, however, avoids this path. Since there is no other trigger for *DetermineMostAppropriateEmployee* and since it is applicable to the initial configuration, there is no problem.

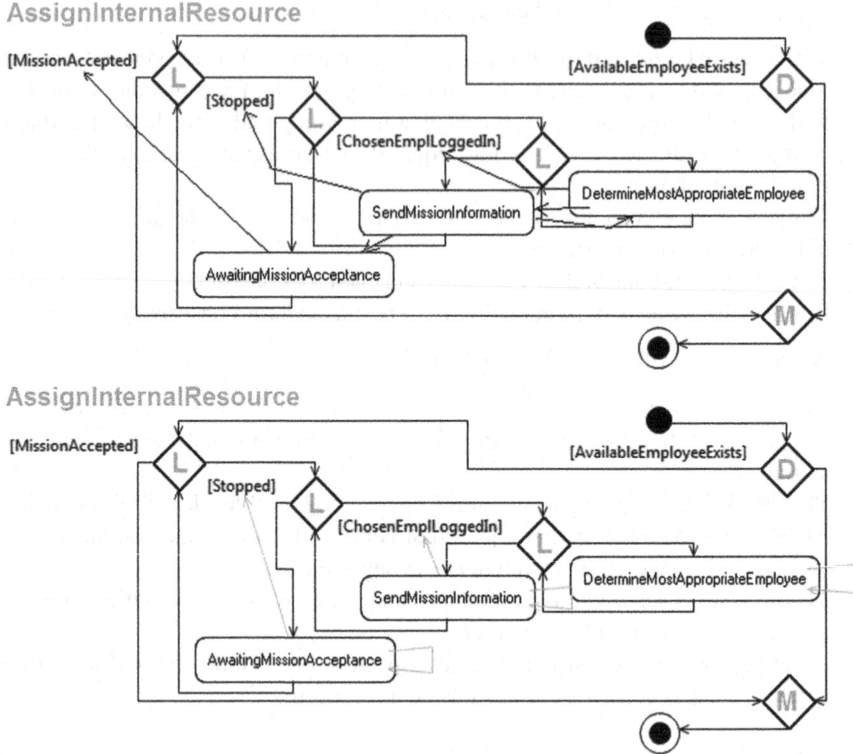

Fig. 13.9 Trigger and conflict checks for *AssignInternalResource*

DetermineMostAppropriateEmployee triggers *SendMissionInformation* by producing a "chosen" arc which is used by *SendMissionInformation*. However, Fig. 13.8 reveals that *SendMissionInformation* is not fully enabled by this trigger, since the employee status is not changed. Moreover, there is no other trigger that would change the status. As the employee status in *Configuration 1* (cf. Fig. 13.2) is "logged_off," the activity model is not executable on this configuration. *SendMissionInformation* triggers *AwaitingMissionAcceptance* by producing the "informed" arc used. More triggers are not needed.

The three triggers for the conditions are producing something used by the conditions and are therefore plausible.

3. *Triggers against control flow*(not depicted): The triggers are the same as above, only now they are categorized differently. The triggering of conditions is still along the control flow. The mutual triggers between *DetermineMostAppropriateEmployee* and *SendMissionInformation* and the trigger from *SendMissionInformation* to *AwaitingMissionAcceptance* are now considered against the control flow. However, their effects on the entire diagram as discussed above remain the same.

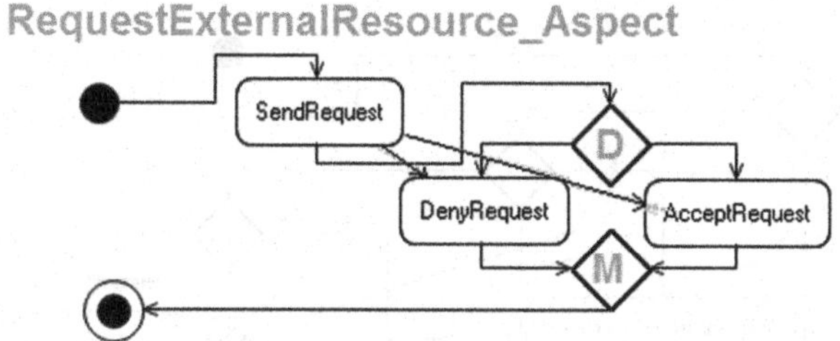

Fig. 13.10 Triggers *along* the control flow for aspect *RequestExternalResource*

4. *Conflicts along control flow* (cf. Fig. 13.9, bottom): There are conflicts of each activity with itself. That means that if an activity can occur in the control flow after itself it cannot be applied a second time because it deletes something that is needed or it produces something that is forbidden. This is no problem here.

   Also there is a conflict between *SendMissionInformation* and the condition *[ChosenEmplLoggedIn]* which means that the loop will not be executed a second time which is desirable. The same holds for *[AwaitingMissionAcceptance]* and *[Stopped]*.

Analyzing the aspect *Authenticate*. Since this aspect contains only one activity and only a condition that checks the applicability of this activity, only two checks are interesting. We explain them shortly without another figure. Please compare Fig. 13.3. The checks for conflicts and triggers against control flow do not make sense in absence of further activities.

1. *Initialization* (not depicted): Activity *RequestLogin* is applicable to the initial configuration.
2. *Triggers along control flow* (not depicted): Obviously the activity *RequestLogin* has no trigger but can be applied to the initial configuration.

Analysing the aspect *RequestExternalResource*. In Fig. 13.10, we visualize the analysis results of the check for triggers. The complete results are as follows:

1. *Initialization* (not depicted): Activity *SendRequest* is applicable to the initial configuration.
2. *Triggers along control flow* (cf. Fig. 13.10): The activity *SendRequest* is never triggered but applicable to the initial configuration. This activity triggers the activity *AcceptRequest* and *DenyRequest* which is consistent.
3. *Triggers against control flow* (not depicted): There are no triggers against the control flow.
4. *Conflicts along control flow* (not depicted): There are no conflicts.

Analyzing the *woven* use-case *AssignInternalResource*. For the use-case *Assign-InternalResource_woven*, the results are as follows (cf. Fig. 13.11.)

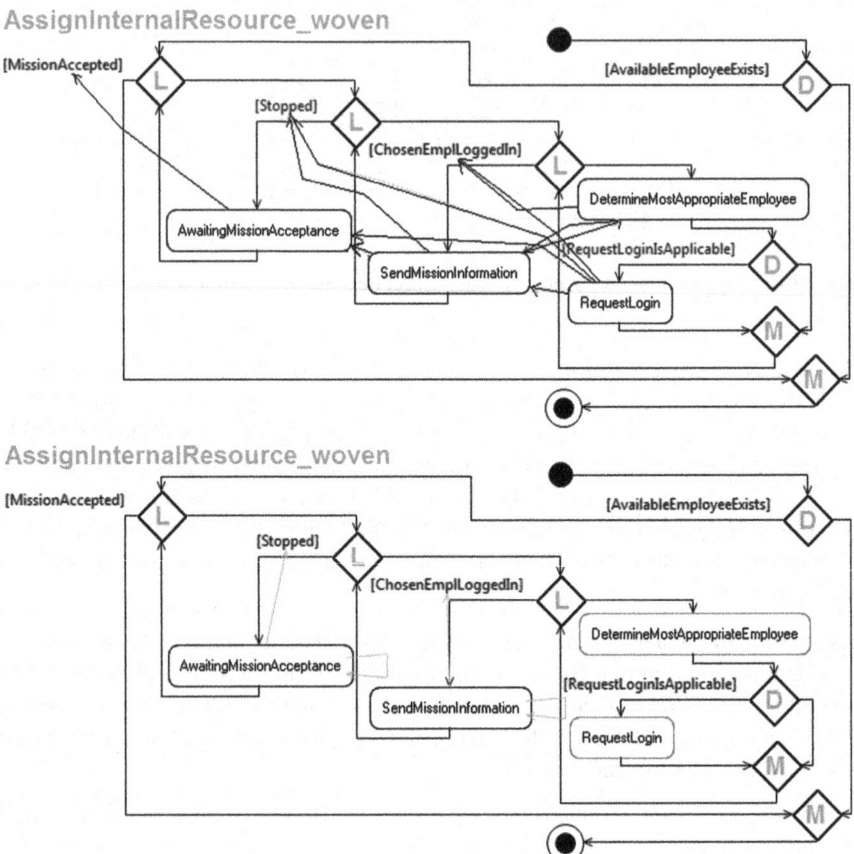

Fig. 13.11 Trigger and conflict checks for *AssignInternalResource_woven*

1. *Initialization* (not depicted): *DetermineMostAppropriateEmployee* is still applicable.
2. *Triggers along control flow* (cf. Fig. 13.11, top): Firstly, there are the same triggers as in the unwoven use-case *AssignInternalResource*. Secondly, *RequestLogin* triggers the conditions *[ChosenEmplLoggedIn]* and *[Stopped]* and the two activities *SendMissionInformation* and *AwaitingMissionAcceptance*. This is because *RequestLogin* changes the *status* to "logged_on" which is needed by all of the aforementioned elements.
3. *Triggers against control flow* (not depicted): Firstly, there are the same triggers as before. Secondly, *RequestLogin* triggers the two activities *SendMissionInformation* and *AwaitingMissionAcceptance*. This is because *RequestLogin* changes the *status* to "logged_on" which is needed by all of the aforementioned elements. Again, because of the loops there are the same triggers along the control flow as against the control flow.

4. *Conflicts along control flow* (cf. Fig. 13.11, bottom): Now there is one less conflict than in the unwoven use case. The conflict of activity *DetermineMostAppropriateEmployee* with itself does not exist any longer because the overall control flow changed.

The insertion of the aspect into the base makes the woven activity model executable for the given *Configuration 1*. The reason is that the activity *RequestLogin* of the aspect provides the missing trigger for the activity *SendMissionInformation* of the base. Executing *AssignInternalResource_woven* on *Configuration 1* with ACTIGRA also terminated.

Analyzing the *woven* use-case *ResolveCrisis*. We cannot present the complete analysis of *ResolveCrisis_woven* for reasons of space since this would also require to illustrate all pre- and postconditions of the involved activities. The interesting question from the aspect-oriented modeling point of view is the analysis of the conflicts and causalities between the aspects involved. This use case has two aspects woven at the top level and one nested aspect woven into its complex activity *AssignInternalResource*. We have to take into account the complete control flow including also all activities of the woven complex activity. There are some noteworthy analysis results (cf. Fig. 13.12):

- Between the two top level aspects *Authenticate* and *RequestExternalResource* there are no conflicts and causalities. This means that the two aspects are independent of each other. This is desirable, especially since the execution of *RequestExternalResource* is conditional.
- The aspect *Authenticate* is also woven into the complex activity *AssignInternalResource*. Here again, *Authenticate* does not create conflicts and causalities with the top level aspect *RequestExternalResource*.
- The top level *Authenticate* aspect is the first in the control flow, the nested *Authenticate* aspect is the second in the control flow. The analysis reveals a conflict between the two, since the first occurrence of the activity *RequestLogin* changes an attribute used by the second occurrence. This is, however, only a potential conflict, since the first *RequestLogin* takes place for the coordinator and the second takes place for an employee.
- The activities of aspect *RequestExternalResource* are each in conflict with itself, because the aspect is now contained in a loop. Also, *DenyRequest* and *AcceptRequest* are in mutual conflicts since they are now contained in a loop. The same happens with the activity *RequestLogin* nested in the complex activity *AssignInternalResource* after the weaving. It is now in conflict with itself due to the outermost loop in which it is now contained.
- In the analysis of *AssignInternalResource* we identified triggers from *RequestLogin* to other elements. The first occurrence of *RequestLogin* triggers now the same activities that are already triggered by the second occurrence in the nested aspect. However, these are potential triggers, since the first *RequestLogin* takes place for the coordinator and the second takes place for an employee.

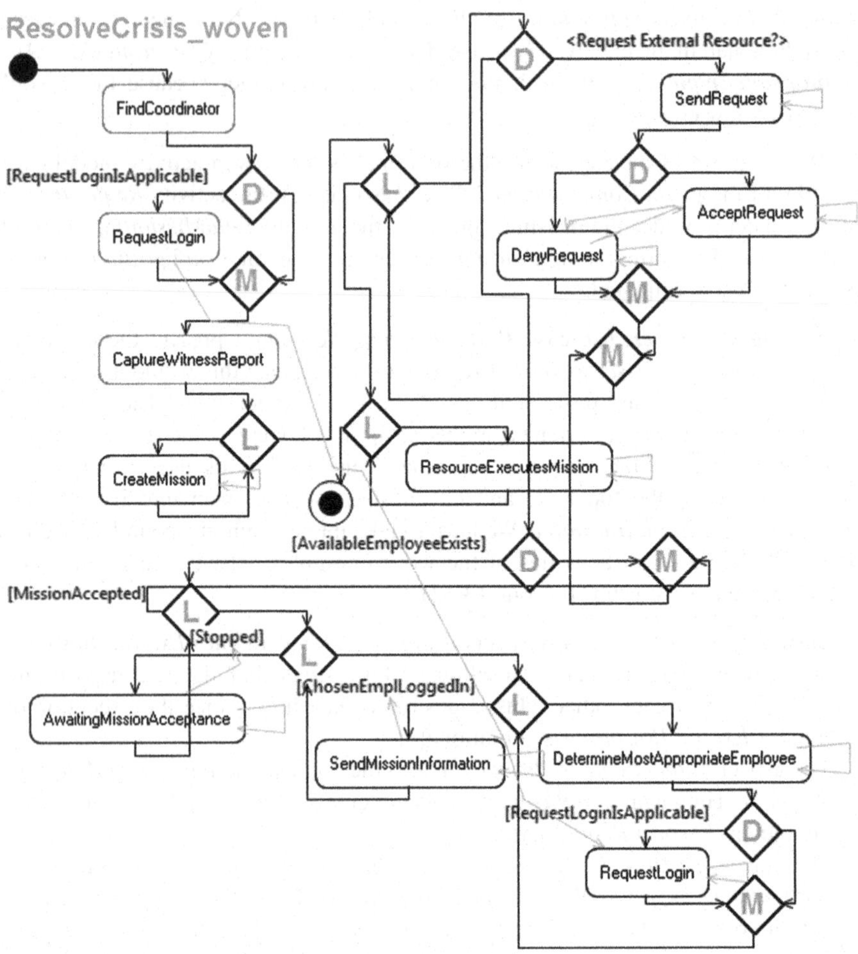

Fig. 13.12 Conflict checks for *ResolveCrisis_woven*

13.6 Related Work

The CMS case study was proposed in [13] as a benchmark example for comparing aspect-oriented modeling approaches. The chapter presents the requirements for a generic CMS informally and details the use cases for a "Car Crash CMS," a system for dealing with car accidents. A non-functional requirement of "Security" states that the CMS shall define access policies for various classes of users. Our analysis introduces an integrated behavior model of the generic CMS and it formalizes the aspects of authentication (a part of the Security requirement that can be described functionally) and the request of external resources (a functionality which crosscuts several parts of the system in our modeling). Our approach is functional in its nature since it requires that everything relevant in the system is modeled as model elements being created and removed by activities.

In our previous work [16] we have used the same conflict and causality (formerly called dependency) definition as here. However, the control flow as given by the activity models was not taken into account, since at that time we could only use AGG [27] to perform the analysis. AGG computes a conflict and dependency matrix and for each two rules all potential conflicts and dependencies. Each conflict is given by graph and two rules applied to it, while each dependency is given by a rule application sequence of length 2 with its intermediate graph. Given a control flow, the relevant conflicts and dependencies have to be manually determined in AGG. With ACTIGRA [5], this step is automatized by integrating activity models.

As recalled in the introduction, several researchers have studied the problem of interference among aspects at the coding level. Sihman and Katz [22] classifies interactions of aspects with a base: an aspect can be considered spectative, regulative, or invasive with respect to the system to which is applied; in [11] the categories are formally described by temporal logic predicates on program states. This classification is useful also at the modeling level we adopted: a *spectative* aspect only gathers information about the system to which it is woven but does not influence the computations of the base otherwise; a *regulative* aspect changes the activation of activities under certain conditions but does not change the base computation further; an *invasive* aspect does change the base system arbitrarily. However, we focus on potential conflicts (and triggers) that may arise when given control flows are woven together.

Other tools for graph transformation systems also allow for their specification and controlled simulation according to given activity flows: see for example Fujaba [17], VMTS [14], and GReAT [1]. These tools, however, do not provide support for analyzing conflicts and causalities: ACTIGRA [5] leverages the critical pair analysis implemented by AGG [27] to detect possibly unwanted interactions. This kind of static analysis is only available in the theory underlying AGG and ACTIGRA, since these tools are based on the algebraic graph transformation approach that uses a specific notion called double-pushout to specify the effect of a graph transformation rule. All graph transformation rules with or without NACs can be analyzed. The graphs may be attributed and typed with node type inheritance.

In [2], Araujo et al. describe nonaspectual requirements as sequence diagrams and aspectual requirements with interaction pattern specifications, which are both woven together in state machines that can be simulated; no support for static conflict detection is provided.

13.7 Conclusion and Outlook

Activity diagrams are a widely used modeling language for describing the functional behavior of a system at different level of abstractions, ranging from requirements models and work flow descriptions to more coding-oriented specifications like flowcharts. Their semantics, however, are often described in a semiformal way and vary a lot. Integrated behavior models are one way to give formal semantics to activity models. Integrated with a domain model, moreover, the formal semantics can be given in a broader context by a refined specification of each activity in terms of the domain model. Such a semantics becomes even more useful when supported by a tool. Integrated behavior models are particularly apt for specifying requirements in a use-case-driven approach using UML.

We use integrated behavior models which are supported by the ACTIGRA tool. We model aspect-oriented separation of concern at the use-case level. Since aspects typically also bear functional behavior, they are straightforward to model as graph transformation rules together with weaving among activities diagrams. Activity diagrams play a key role in the analysis, similar to that of data in dynamic program analysis: in a static program analysis one considers all the possible paths of execution (in fact also several unfeasible ones), while in dynamic analyses the input data is used to narrow the search space. Similarly, activities are used to drive the analysis to a concrete set of interactions, instead of considering all the conceivable ones for a given a set of aspects and a base. At the programming level, this reduction is mostly provided by the base which gives the control flow in which aspects are intertwined. In our models, aspects and base are described as transformation rules on the domain model, thus the activity is the key to reduce the indeterminacy of all the possible weaving actions. By integrating the critical pair analysis (being a "static" analysis) performed by AGG, with the ACTIGRA support for control flow analysis, one has the possibility to see how dependencies might cause problems in the activities of a complex system.

It is an advantage that the analysis is not different across the different modeling concerns, i.e, the base, the aspects, and also the woven system. In the small example presented, we can reveal simple dependencies between base and aspects by using the analysis. The tool also helps in making the example sound and complete by analyzing the base and the aspects separately for flaws. This is an often made observation that models become more sound as soon as a tool for executing or analyzing them is deployed, which is one reason for using tools.

Until now, there is no tool that supports the transformation of integrated behavior models on a meta level which could be used, e.g., for specifying aspect weaving. Using such a tool would even allow to go beyond a set of predefined weaving operations since new activities could be added and tested by the experienced user. Moreover, no dedicated tools for aspect-oriented modeling on top of integrated behavior models exist either, allowing stereotypes and weaving as just mentioned.

In the example, it can be studied how causalities and conflicts established during the separate analysis for base and aspect change after aspect weaving has been carried out. It is up to future work to generalize and formally show such effects.

The example is too small to reveal benefits of the modeling approach and its tooling such as discovering major modeling mistakes like overlapping or missing domain concepts or functionalities. Here, a more comprehensive case study would be useful. It also remains to implement the example in order to study whether the identified aspects persist in the code at all and whether the analysis has a positive effect on the quality of the code. To this end, empirical studies have to be carried out comparing implementation with and without this particular modeling approach as well as with and without the tooling support.

References

1. A. Agrawal, Graph rewriting and transformation (GReAT): A solution for the model integrated computing (MIC) bottleneck, in *Proceedings of the 18th IEEE International Conference on Automated Software Engineering* (2003), pp. 364–368. doi:10.1109/ASE.2003.1240339
2. J. Araújo, J. Whittle, D.-K. Kim, Modeling and composing scenario-based requirements with aspects, in *Proceedings of the Requirements Engineering Conference, 12th IEEE International (RE '04)* (2004), IEEE Computer Society, Washington, DC, pp. 58–67. doi:10.1109/RE.2004.32. http://dx.doi.org/10.1109/RE.2004.32
3. D. Balzarotti, A. Castaldo D'Ursi, L. Cavallaro, M. Monga, Slicing AspectJ woven code, in *Proceedings of the Foundations of Aspect-Oriented Languages Workshop (FOAL2005)*, Chicago, 2005
4. H. Ehrig, K. Ehrig, U. Prange, G. Taentzer, *Fundamentals of Algebraic Graph Transformation* (Monographs in Theoretical Computer Science: an EATCS Series) (Springer, New York, Inc., Secaucus, 2006)
5. C. Ermel, J. Gall, L. Lambers, G. Taentzer, Modeling with plausibility checking: Inspecting favorable and critical signs for consistency between control flow and functional behavior, in *Proceedings of the Fundamental Aspects of Software Engineering (FASE'11)*. Lecture Notes in Computer Science, vol. 6603 (Springer, Berlin, 2011), pp. 156–170. Long version as technical report 2011/2, TU Berlin
6. R.E. Filman, D.P. Friedman, Aspect-oriented programming is quantification and obliviousness, in *Workshop on Advanced Separation of Concerns, OOPSLA 2000* (October 2000), Minneapolis. http://ic-www.arc.nasa.gov/ic/darwin/oif/leo/filman/text/oif/aop-is.pdf
7. J. Hausmann, R. Heckel, G. Taentzer, Detection of conflicting functional requirements in a use case-driven approach, in *Proceedings of International Conference on Software Engineering 2002*, Orlando, 2002
8. I. Jacobson, P.W. Ng, *Aspect-Oriented Software Development with Use Cases* (Addison Wesley, Reading, 2005)
9. S. Jurack, L. Lambers, K. Mehner, G. Taentzer, G. Wierse, Object flow definition for refined activity diagrams, in *Proceedings of the Fundamental Approaches to Software Engineering (FASE'09)*, ed. by M. Chechik, M. Wirsing. Lecture Notes in Computer Science, vol. 5503 (Springer, Berlin, 2009), pp. 49–63
10. S. Katz, Aspect categories and classes of temporal properties, in *Transactions on Aspect-Oriented Software Development I*, ed. by, A. Rashid, M. Aksit (Springer, Berlin Heidelberg, 2006), pp. 106–134
11. S. Katz, Aspect categories and classes of temporal properties, in *Transactions on Aspect-Oriented Software Development I*, ed. by A. Rashid, M. Aksit. Lecture Notes in Computer Science, vol. 3880 (Springer, Berlin, 2006), pp. 106–134
12. G. Kiczales, E. Hilsdale, J. Hugunin, M. Kersten, J. Palm, W. Griswold, An overview of AspectJ, in *ECOOP 2001—Object-Oriented Programming*, ed. by J. Knudsen. Lecture Notes in Computer Science, vol. 2072 (Springer, Berlin, 2001), pp. 327–354
13. J. Kienzle, N. Guelfi, S. Mustafiz, Crisis management systems—A case study for aspect-oriented Modeling. Technical Report SOCS-TR-2009.3, McGill University (2009). Version 1.0.1
14. T. Levendovszky, L. Lengyel, G. Mezei, H. Charaf, A Systematic Approach to Metamodeling Environments and Model Transformation Systems in VMTS. Electron. Notes Theor. Comput.

Sci. **127**(1), 65–75 (2005). Proceedings of the International Workshop on Graph-Based Tools (GraBaTs 2004)

15. K. Mehner, M. Monga, G. Taentzer, Interaction analysis in aspect-oriented models, in *14th IEEE International Conference on Requirements Engineering RE 06* (2006), pp. 69–78. doi:10.1109/RE.2006.35
16. K. Mehner, M. Monga, G. Taentzer, Analysis of aspect-oriented model weaving, in *Transactions on Aspect-Oriented Software Development V*. Lecture Notes in Computer Science, vol. 5490 (Springer, Berlin, 2009), pp. 235–263
17. U.A. Nickel, J. Niere, J.P. Wadsack, A. Zündorf, Roundtrip engineering with FUJABA, in *Proceedings of 2nd Workshop on Software-Reengineering (WSR)*, Bad Honnef, 2000
18. Object Management Group, UML Specification Version 2.0 (2005), Object Management Group, http://www.omg.org
19. A. Rashid, P. Sawyer, A. Moreira, J. Araújo, Early aspects: A model for aspect-oriented requirements engineering, in *Proceedings of the IEEE Joint International Conference on Requirements Engineering* (IEEE Computer Society Press, Silver Spring, 2002), pp. 199–202
20. A. Rashid, A. Moreira, J. Araújo, Modularisation and composition of aspectual requirements. in *Proceedings of the 2nd International Conference on Aspect-Oriented Software Development (AOSD '03)* (2003), ACM, New York, NY, pp. 11–20. doi:10.1145/643603.643605
21. M. Rinard, A. Sălcianu, S. Bugrara, A classification system and analysis for aspect-oriented programs, in *Proceedings of the 2nd International Conference on Aspect-Oriented Software Development (AOSD '03)* (2003), ACM, New York, NY, pp. 11–20. doi:10.1145/643603.643605
22. M. Sihman, S. Katz, Superimpositions and aspect-oriented programming. Comput. J. **46**(5), 529–541 (2003)
23. J. Sillito, C. Dutchyn, A. Eisenberg, K. DeVolder, Use case level pointcuts, in *Proceedings of the ECOOP 2004*, Oslo, 2004
24. D. Stein, S. Hanenberg, R. Unland, A UML-based aspect-oriented design notation for AspectJ, in *Proceedings of the 1st International Conference on Aspect-Oriented Software Development* (2002), ACM, New York, NY, pp. 106–112. doi:10.1145/508386.508399
25. The Eclipse Foundation (2011), AspectJ Homepage, http://www.eclipse.org/aspectj/
26. Technische Universität Berlin (2013), ActiGra Homepage, http://www.tfs.tu-berlin.de/actigra
27. Technische Universität Berlin (2013), AGG Homepage, http://www.tfs.tu-berlin.de/agg
28. J. Zhao, Slicing aspect-oriented software, in *Proceedings of the 10th International Workshop on Program Comprehension (IWPC '02)* (2002), IEEE Computer Society, Washington, DC, p. 251

Chapter 14
Aspect Interactions: A Requirements Engineering Perspective

Thein Than Tun, Yijun Yu, Michael Jackson, Robin Laney, and Bashar Nuseibeh

Abstract The principle of Separation of Concerns encourages developers to divide complex problems into simpler ones and solve them individually. Aspect-Oriented Programming (AOP) languages provide mechanisms to modularise concerns that affect several software components, by means of joinpoints, advice and aspect weaving. In a software system with multiple aspects, a joinpoint can often be matched with advice from several aspects, thus giving rise to emergent behaviours that may be unwanted. This issue is often known as the aspect interaction problem. AOP languages provide various composition operators: the *precedence* operator of AspectJ, for instance, instructs the aspect weaver about the ordering of aspects when advice from several of them match one joinpoint. This ordering of conflicting aspects is usually done at compile-time. This chapter discusses a type of problem where conflicting aspects need to be ordered according to runtime conditions. Extending previous work on Composition Frames, this chapter illustrates an AOP technique to compose aspects in a non-intrusive way so that precedence can be decided at runtime.

14.1 Introduction

Software systems are typically required to satisfy multiple concerns of several stakeholders. Users may want a software system to be responsive and the computer interface to be intuitive. Sponsors of the software system may want the information

T.T. Tun (✉) · Y. Yu · M. Jackson · R. Laney
Department of Computing, The Open University, UK
e-mail: t.t.tun@open.ac.uk; y.yu@open.ac.uk; m.jackson@open.ac.uk; r.c.laney@open.ac.uk

B. Nuseibeh
Department of Computing, The Open University, UK
e-mail: b.nuseibeh@open.ac.uk

Lero, Irish Software Engineering Research Centre, Limerick, Ireland

A. Moreira et al. (eds.), *Aspect-Oriented Requirements Engineering*,
DOI 10.1007/978-3-642-38640-4_14,

to be handled securely. Programmers who maintain the software system may want to work with a program design that is easy to modify. The principle of Separation of Concerns encourages developers to address these concerns of performance, usability, security and maintainability individually. Yet, when composed together, these concerns make different and often conflicting demands on the system architecture, the program design, and other software artefacts. Aspect-Oriented Programming (AOP) languages provide mechanisms for implementing, in a modular fashion, concerns that cut across several components. Towards this end, AOP languages provide mechanisms for joinpoints, advice and aspect weaving, which have been explained and illustrated in [13].

The issue of feature interaction is well known in telecommunication and other software systems [1, 4, 7]. Generally, software features are thought to interact when features that individually satisfy the user requirements, when composed together, produce unwanted behaviour. The interactions are often due to conditions such as non-determinism, divergence and interference. When resolving such feature interactions, compile-time mechanisms are often over-restrictive in the sense that the composition has to be decided at compile-time and it cannot respond to runtime conditions.

For instance, in a smart home application [7], the security and climate control features may interact when the security feature shuts the window because the home owners are away but the climate control feature opens the window to allow fresh air in. This condition is known as divergence.

A similar issue can be observed in aspect composition. A program that has to satisfy multiple concerns may have a joinpoint that could be matched with advice from several aspects, corresponding with the concerns the component has to satisfy. When these aspects are composed, the weaver is free to choose the ordering of the aspects if the developer does not specify the desired ordering. Divergence here can be illustrated by the following main program and the two aspects in the syntax of AspectJ 6 (simply AspectJ henceforth).

```
// The main program Window.java
public class Window {
    public static void main(String[] args) {
        System.out.println("Window has now started.");
    }
}

// SecurityFeature.aj
public aspect SecurityFeature {
    after() returning: execution(* main(..)) {
        System.out.println("SecurityFeature: Window is now
                            shut because it is night now.");
    }
}

// ClimateFeature.aj
public aspect ClimateFeature {
    after() returning: execution(* main(..)) {
```

```
            System.out.println("ClimateFeature: Window is now
                              opened because it is hot indoors.");
    }
}
```

Running the program could produce a seemingly random ordering of the two aspects. In one run of the program, the following output is produced, although another valid ordering of aspects is also possible. Such uncontrolled behaviour may be unwanted and therefore can be seen as a form of aspect interaction.

```
Window has now started.
SecurityFeature: Window is now shut because it is night now.
ClimateFeature: Window is now opened because it is hot indoors.
```

If a particular ordering of these aspects is desired, for instance, if the climate feature is always more important than the security feature, then the precedence of these aspects has to be declared. Since the advice of these aspects are applied after the execution of the main method, the so-called after advice, they need to be listed in ascending order of priority.

```
// ComposeAspects.aj
public aspect ComposeAspects {
    declare precedence: SecurityFeature, ClimateFeature;
}
```

The program now resolves the aspect interaction and always produce the desired ordering of the aspects, namely that the climate control aspect is always executed before the security aspect:

```
Window has now started.
ClimateFeature: Window is now opened because it is hot indoors.
SecurityFeature: Window is now shut because it is night now.
```

This style of resolving aspect interactions is over-restrictive because once the precedence is defined at compile-time, it cannot be changed easily in order to respond to runtime conditions. The ordering of the security and climate control features in the example above cannot be changed at runtime, for instance.

In our previous work on feature composition, we have formalised the notion of Composition Frames which monitor the features being composed, and depending on the requirements and runtime conditions, determine the ordering of features [9]. This style of composition is more flexible and can be extended to aspect composition.

In this chapter, we show that features can be treated as aspects and feature composition as aspect composition. We then discuss how Composition Frames can be used to compose aspects and resolve aspect interactions at runtime. We present a way to implement the aspect composition as a distinct crosscutting concern that can be treated as a separate aspect. We show that this approach to composing aspects at runtime is generic and non-intrusive.

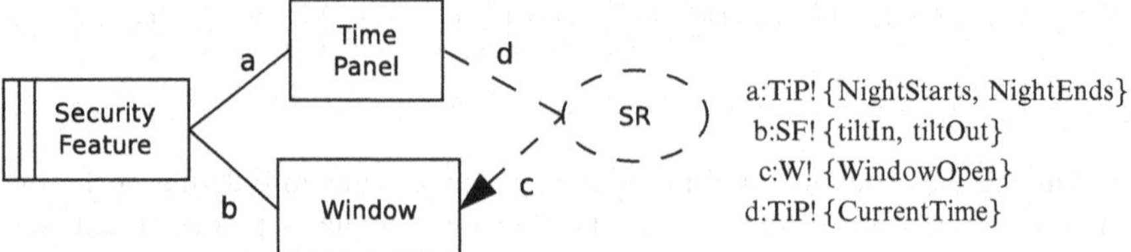

Fig. 14.1 Problem diagram for the security feature

14.2 Preliminaries

This section illustrates the notion of feature interaction using a simple problem from a smart home application [7] before discussing how Composition Frames can be used to resolve the feature interaction problem.

14.2.1 Feature Interaction: An Example

Let us consider again a simple smart home application with two features, both of which control a motorised window that can be opened and shut. The security feature has a requirement for keeping the window shut at night. The requirement for the temperature feature is to keep the window opened when it is hot, meaning when the indoor temperature is higher than the required temperature and at the same time, the outdoor temperature is lower than the indoor temperature. An important characteristic of smart home applications is that their features may be developed independently by manufacturers. Therefore, conflicts between features may have to be detected and resolved at runtime.

When analysing the requirements for these two features, we use problem diagrams [5] to show the relationship between three descriptions: (a) user requirements, (b) problem world domains which make up the context of the software and (c) specifications of the behaviour of the running software. The relationship between these descriptions is intended to indicate that the specifications, in the described context, will satisfy the requirements.

Figure 14.1 shows the problem diagram for the security feature, where the requirement is denoted by a dotted oval, problem world domains are denoted by plain rectangles and the specification is denoted by a rectangle with two vertical stripes. The requirement SR says that the window should be kept shut at night.

The problem world domains are entities in the world that the program must interact with, such as Time Panel and Window, in satisfying the requirement SR. The solid lines (a and b) are domain interfaces representing shared variables and events between the domains and the machine involved. At the interface a, the variables NightStarts and NightEnds are controlled by Time Panel (as denoted by TiP!),

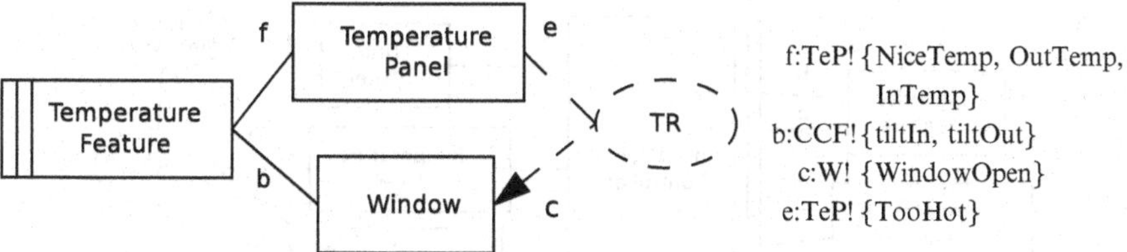

Fig. 14.2 Problem diagram for the temperature feature

and can be observed by the security feature. Descriptions of other interface labels can be read in the same way.

Assuming that NightStarts and NightEnds are variables for non-negative integers between 0 and 2400, when *NightStarts* < *CurrentTime* and *CurrentTime* < *NightEnds*, it is night; otherwise, it is day. At the interface b, the security feature can fire two events tiltIn and tiltOut, and these events can be observed by the window. The property of Window is such that when tiltOut is observed, the window is open, meaning that WindowOpen is true. Likewise, when tiltIn is observed, the window is shut (WindowOpen is false). Dotted lines (c and d) denote requirement phenomena. The requirement is a desired relationship between the current time and the state variable of the window, namely that when *NightStarts* < *CurrentTime* and *CurrentTime* < *NightEnds* is true, WindowOpen should be false.

One description of the specification Security Feature is to fire the event tiltIn whenever it is night and to ensure that tiltOut is not fired until the night ends. The relationship between the three descriptions is as follows: If the behaviour of the window and the time panel is as stated, the specification Security Feature satisfies the requirement SR. This simple specification, of course, ignores a number of issues: for instance, it does not check whether the window is already shut when night starts or how long it takes for the window to fully open. Let us ignore such issues in our discussion.

The problem diagram for the temperature feature, shown in Fig. 14.2 is similar to the diagram in Fig. 14.1. The requirement here is that if it is too hot indoors, meaning that the desired temperature (NiceTemp) and the indoors and outdoors temperatures (OutTemp and InTemp) are in a certain relationship, the window should be kept open. The temperature readings are controlled by the temperature panel, and the temperature feature can observe them. One description of the specification Temperature Feature is to fire the tileOut event whenever the conditions *NiceTemp* < *InTemp* and *OutTemp* < *InTemp* hold and to ensure that the tiltIn is not fired as long as that relation remains true.

Notice that the two requirements above do not say anything about what to do during the daytime, and when it is not hot indoors. However, if the inside temperature is higher than the desired temperature, and the outside temperature is lower than the inside temperature, the window should be opened even if the outside temperature is higher than the desire temperature (thus not possible to achieve the required temperature just by opening the window).

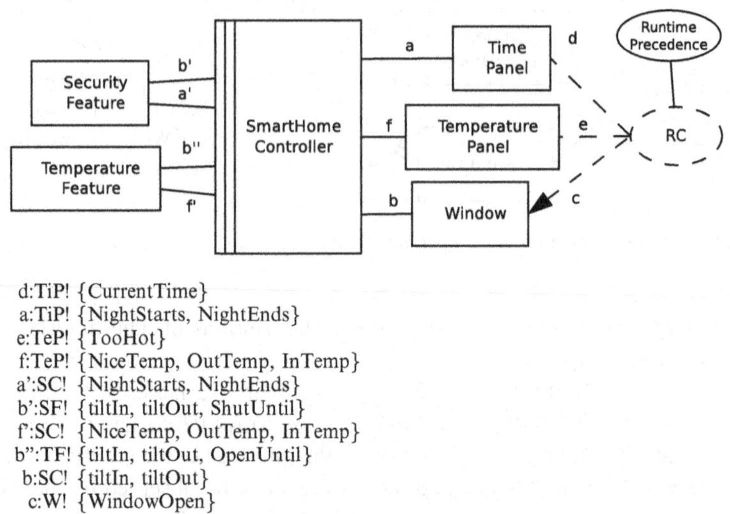

Fig. 14.3 Composition of the security and temperature features

Composing these two features can lead to a divergent behaviour under certain conditions. During a hot night, according to the temperature feature, the window should be open, but according to the security feature, the window should be shut. It is important to note that although the temperature feature will not close the window by firing the tiltIn event, it cannot stop the security feature from firing the same event during the hot night. Likewise, although the security feature will not open the window by firing the tiltOut event, it cannot stop the temperature feature from firing the same event during the hot night. In other words, an individual feature cannot have an exclusive control of the window over a length of time.

Furthermore, if a precedence operator is applied in the composition of these two features, one of the two features will always have priority over the other. This might be over-restrictive. It is sometimes desirable for the system to allow the user to indicate at runtime how the features should be ordered. Finally, in order to separate the concerns of individual features from the concern of composition, the two specifications should not be modified in order that they find out what the other feature is doing before carrying out their own actions. Our previous work on feature interaction shows that Composition Frames are suitable for such feature composition.

14.2.2 Resolving Feature Interaction Using Composition Frames

As shown in Fig. 14.3, the two features can be composed by introducing the new software component SmartHome Controller, which is obtained by merging two wrappers that sit at the interfaces a and b of the security feature in Fig. 14.1 and the interfaces d and b of the temperature feature in Fig. 14.2 (see [15] for wrapper transformation rules). In effect, SmartHome Controller intercepts the information and events going in and coming out of the two features.

The variable ShutUntil is used by the security feature to indicate the time point until which it does not want other features to open the window. In principle, the value of ShutUntil is be determined by the value of NightEnds. The variable OpenUntil is used by the temperature feature to indicate the time point until which it does not want other features to shut the window. In principle, this is the first time point when InTemp is equal to NiceTemp. However, the temperature feature cannot know in advance how long the room will remain too hot. Therefore, it may have to set this time on a periodic basis.

Again, notice that each of the features does not prevent another feature from opening or shutting the window. Each feature only declares what it wants other features not to do within a certain duration. ShutUntil and OpenUntil will then be used by the SmartHome Controller to mediate when conflicts arise. Broadly speaking, a conflict occurs when two features attempt to maintain two contradictory properties. As discussed in [9], the values of ShutUntil and OpenUntil can be derived as part of the specification of the two features by means of the *Prohibit* predicate.

Runtime Precedence defines several ways in which conflicts can be resolved: we will call them the semantics of the composition operator. Although they can be defined more generally and precisely [9], we will focus on the specific example here.

- *No Control:* In this composition, the requirements for the security and temperature features should each be met at times when they are not in conflict; but when conflicts occur, any emergent behaviour is acceptable. It allows, for example, the window to oscillate in a partly open position. None of the requirements of the two features may be satisfied.
- *Exclusion:* In this composition, the requirements for the security and temperature features should each be met at times when they are not in conflict; but when conflicts occur, the requirement of the feature that started first should have priority. For example, if the security feature shuts the window before the temperature feature needs to open it, the temperature feature will not be able to shut the window until the security requirement has been satisfied. This exclusion is symmetrical.
- *Exclusion with Priority.* In this composition, the exclusion is asymmetrical, for instance, in favour of the security requirement. It means that the security feature can shut the window during the time in which the temperature feature wants the window open. The temperature feature, however, cannot open the window if the security feature wants it shut.

Other possible semantics include exclusion with event-level priority [9]. The requirement RC in Fig. 14.3 says that the window should be opened and shut according to the Runtime Precedence option the user of the smart home application has selected.

If the security and the temperature features are implemented as aspects, and if there is no definition of the ordering of these aspects using the precedence operator, the weaver will produce the "no control" behaviour defined above. The precedence operator of AspectJ can produce the composition similar to the behaviour defined by the "exclusion with priority" option. We now show how the "exclusion" option can be implemented using the aspect-oriented technique.

14.3 The Proposed Approach: Runtime Composition of Aspects

In this proposed approach, the problem world domains are implemented first as Java components, forming the base system. Features are then implemented as aspects which weave into the base system of the problem world domains. This separation of aspects from the base system fits well with the separation of specifications from the problem world domains because like aspects, specifications can interface with multiple components, as highlighted in Fig. 14.3. Composition of the features is regarded as a separate concern that is implemented as an aspect in its own right.

14.3.1 Implementing the Problem World Domains

The problem world domains such as Window can be implemented in a straightforward way. We can simply define a singleton class for each of the domains and their variables as class variables and events as methods. (Full listings of all programs in this section are provided in [14].)

```
class Window {
        static boolean WindowOpen;
        Window(){
                // code for initializing the window
                WindowOpen = false;
        }

        public void tiltOut() {
                // code for opening the window
                WindowOpen = true;
        }

        public void tiltIn(){
                // code for shutting the window
                WindowOpen = false;
        }
}
```

Other problem world domains are implemented in a similar fashion, but they are omitted here for space reasons. In the main method of the ProblemWorldDomains class, classes for window, time panel, temperature panel and runtime precedence are instantiated and initialised, as shown below.

```
public class ProblemWorldDomains {
    static Window win = new Window();
    static TemperaturePanel TeP = new TemperaturePanel();
    static TimePanel TiP = new TimePanel();
    static RuntimePrecedence rp = new RuntimePrecedence();

    public static void main(String args[]) {
        win.showStatus();
        TiP.NightStarts=2000;
        TiP.NightEnds=600;
        TeP.NiceTemp = 15;
        rp.Options = 1;
    }
}
```

14.3.2 Implementing the Features

At runtime, features such as the security and temperature features will be long-running and concurrent processes. Therefore, these features are implemented as threads. In principle, some features could be implemented without using aspects. However, to illustrate the problem of aspect interaction, both features for example are implemented using aspects.

```
public aspect SecurityFeature {
  static long shutUntil;
  class Spec implements Runnable {
    Thread runner;
    Window win;
    TimePanel tiPanel;

    public Spec(String threadName, Window w1, TimePanel tp1) {
      runner = new Thread(this, threadName);
      win = w1;
      tiPanel=tp1;
      // -1 indicates that no need to keep the window shut
      shutUntil=-1;
      runner.start();
    }

    public void run() {
      while (true){
        if (currentTime > tiPanel.NightStarts &&
            currentTime < tiPanel.NightEnds) {
          // It is night now, so the window should be shut
```

```
                // and should not be opened until tiPanel.NightEnds
                win.tiltIn();
                shutUntil=tiPanel.NightEnds;
                // do nothing until tiPanel.NightEnds
            }
            shutUntil =-1;
        }
    }
  }

  pointcut getWinRefs(): execution(* main(..));
  after(): getWinRefs() {
    Spec SF =new Spec("Security Feature",
                                  ProblemWorldDomains.win,
                                  ProblemWorldDomains.TiP);
  }
}
```

The aspect above implements the security feature by instantiating a new thread as soon as the main method has been executed. The program then gets hold of the references to the window object `win` and the time panel object `TiP` from the main method. The aspect also declares the variable `shutUntil` to indicate the time point until which the program wants the window to be shut. When the thread starts running, it continuously checks whether the current time is between `NightStarts` and `NightEnds`. Notice that the variable `currentTime` has to be declared and assigned appropriate values in a format compatible with `NightStarts` and `NightEnds`. If the current time is within the range, then the tiltIn method is called and the value of `shutUntil` is set to `NightEnds`.

It is worth emphasising that the security feature does not stop the temperature feature calling the tiltOut method during the night. The temperature feature is implemented likewise: it opens the window when it is too hot and indicates the length of time it wishes to keep the window open by setting the value of `openUntil`. Since the two features are largely independent, they do not communicate with each other about what they do not want the other feature to do. This is in line with the principle of separation of concerns: individual features are not concerned with how they will be composed together.

Notice if the security and temperatures are implemented as singleton classes, then the variables `shutUntil` and `openUntil` are to be treated as class variables.

This completes the implementation of the temperature and security features. If these programs are run, the ordering of the two features is entirely random and will satisfy the "no control" option discussed above.

14.3.3 Implementing Composition Frames

The composition controller SmartHomeController is implemented by a separate aspect. This new aspect monitors the method calls made by the security and temperature features and examines the `openUntil` and `shutUntil` to see whether calls to the `tiltOut` and `tiltIn` methods should proceed. As indicated in Fig. 14.3, the controller will rely on the runtime precedence option selected by the user. If the user wants the "exclusion" option, for instance, the `tiltOut` method call will be delayed until the time point `shutUntil` has passed, and the `tiltIn` method call will be delayed until the time point `openUntil` has passed. These delays could be achieved by putting the threads to sleep. implementation of the mutual exclusion option.

```
public aspect SmartHomeController {
  pointcut delayTiltIn() : call (void tiltIn(..));
  before(): delayTiltIn() {
    // the window is about to tiltIn
    if (TemperatureFeature.openUntil > 0) {
      // but the window should remain open
      if (ProblemWorldDomains.rp.Options == 1)  {
        // the user has selected the exclusion option
        // wait until TemperatureFeature.openUntil has passed
      }
    }
  }

  pointcut delayTiltOut() : call (void tiltOut(..));
  before(): delayTiltOut() {
    // the window is about to tiltOut
    if (SecurityFeature.shutUntil > 0) {
      // but the window should remain shut
      if (ProblemWorldDomains.rp.Options == 1)  {
        // the user has selected the exclusion option
        // wait until SecurityFeature.shutUntil has passed
      }
    }
  }
}
```

The above program also provides a template for the implementation of the exclusion with priority option. For instance, if we want to give priority to the security feature over the temperature feature, there is no need to delay calls to tiltIn, and only calls to tiltOut should be examined for a possible delay.

14.3.4 Comparing Precedence Operator with Composition Frames

The precedence operator of AspectJ is, in a sense, similar to Composition Frames, in particular to the exclusion with priority option. The similarity lies in the fact that they both provide mechanisms for ordering aspects. There are, however, notable differences.

First, the precedence operator has only one semantic, and the operator is applied at compile-time. Composition Frames provide a multitude of possible semantics, of which we have discussed three in this chapter but there are more [9]. Operators of Composition Frames are applied mostly at runtime, although they can also achieve the effect of compile-time composition. In this sense, Composition Frames can be seen as an extension of the precedence operator.

Second, the precedence operator is applicable only when there is a joinpoint matching with advice from multiple aspects. The pointcuts in our composition operator can be defined on multiple joinpoints. In the smart home example, pointcuts are defined on tiltOut and tiltIn, and they are matched with different aspects for delaying the events involved. In order for the precedence operator to work in the smart home example, tiltOut and tiltIn have to be covered by a single pointcut definition, while providing two aspects for dealing with different events. Such a design is feasible but introduces unnecessary complications. When used judiciously, the precedence operator works well as a simple compile-time operator, whilst Composition Frames provide a richer set of runtime composition operators.

14.3.5 Fairness in Exclusion

In our implementation of the temperature and security specifications, we have used the Java thread mechanism to design them as long-running and concurrent processes. The thread mechanism offers an added advantage when delaying method calls: the thread can simply be put to sleep for a certain duration. For example, the temperature thread wanting to open the window can be put to sleep until the night ends. However, the sleep mechanism of Java cannot guarantee that once the night finishes, the temperature feature will definitely open the window: in fact, it is quite possible that the security feature requests to keep the window shut again before the temperature feature closes it and that the request is successful, thus effectively blocking the temperature feature. If fairness of access is important in the application, then the thread synchronisation facility of Java may have to be used.

14.4 Common Case Study: Discussion

Our approach is applicable when there are interacting aspects and features and the software system needs to resolve them at runtime in order to continue to satisfy the requirements as far as possible. In the Crisis Management System (CMS) [6], there are several requirements, which under certain runtime conditions will make conflicting demands on the system.

For instance, although it may be possible to satisfy the statistic logging requirement and the real-time requirement individually and their composition most of the time, there may be runtime conditions when it is not possible to log all data access and provide information about an on-going crisis at intervals not exceeding 30 s. In such cases, the users may want to give priority to one requirement over another in order to maintain a satisfactory level of requirement satisfaction.

Likewise, one requirement for multi-access in CMS states that the system should support management of at least 100 crises at a time. Perhaps not all crises are equally important at all times: some could be more important than others in terms of the level of security they require. Again, in such cases, requirements for certain crises may have higher priority over others.

Our approach for resolving interactions between aspects at runtime could be helpful in such cases.

14.5 Related Work

The ideas presented in this chapter are related to several strands of research work. However, giving a systematic review of all related work is beyond the scope of the chapter. Instead, the following discussions provide a brief overview of some of the work.

Composition Frames: Jackson [5] introduces the conceptual framework of Problem Frames. Laney et al. [8] first use Composition Frames to compose requirements and resolve conflicts before formalising the composition in [9]. We deploy Composition Frames as a kind of architectural wrapper in order to evolve a feature-rich software system [15]. This chapter discusses the synergy between Composition Frames and aspect-oriented programming with respect to managing feature interaction and managing aspect interaction. Both approaches are based on the principle of separation of concerns, but offer different ways of composing features and aspects.

Feature Interaction: The problem of feature interactions is a long-standing problem in software engineering. Although they were first observed in telecommunication software systems [2], they are now considered to be a more general problem affecting many modern software systems [1,4,7]. Sanen et al. [12] highlight the issue of aspect interaction and contribute a scheme to classify and record aspect interactions. This chapter provides a general mechanism to resolve aspect interactions at runtime.

Aspect Interaction: Mussbacher et al. [10] propose an approach for detecting aspect interactions, in which aspects are first annotated with domain-specific markers. These markers are then mapped to a goal model showing how markers influence each other before conflicting markers and their associated aspects are detected. Other approaches to detecting feature interactions, as well as the difficulties faced by these approaches, are discussed by Velthuijsen [16]. The approach presented in this chapter focuses on resolving, rather than detecting, aspect interactions.

Requirement Interaction: Similar to our approach, Chitchyan et al. [3] consider the problems with using syntactic operators when composing requirements written in a natural language. They propose a new language for documenting textual requirements and their composition. Various formulations of the temporal composition operators in their work are similar to the three semantics of the composition operator given in this chapter. Weston et al. [17] present a formalisation of a similar semantics-based approach to resolving requirements conflicts. However, our approach is aimed at resolving conflicting aspects at runtime, rather than resolving conflicting requirements at design time.

Dynamic Aspect Weaving: There are a number of approaches to weaving aspects at runtime. Popovici et al. [11] suggest that they can be divided into compile-time, load time and runtime approaches, and provide a framework for runtime aspect weaving. Although the problems addressed by their approach and ours are similar, their work requires modification of the Java Virtual Machine in order to load and unload aspects at runtime, and there is a performance penalty every time an aspect is weaved or unweaved. Our implementation uses only the standard AspectJ constructs. While their approach offers a way to resolve aspect interactions by weaving and unweaving aspects at runtime, the variety of composition semantics in our approach is more flexible. For instance, exclusion can be achieved without unweaving and weaving aspects at runtime. However in our approach, aspects have to be known at compile time: their approach does not have this limitation.

Locking Access to Shared Variable: There is a long history of research on controlling access to shared variables by concurrent programs. Hoare-style monitors are a case in point. Typically in such cases, a lock has to be introduced in order to indicate when a given program can or cannot access the shared variable. The variables `openUntil` and `shutUntil` in our example are similar to locks, but these locks cannot be observed, let alone be enforced, by the window. Composition Frames make use of these locks, together with runtime conditions and user preference to resolve the conflicts. This mechanism provides a neat way to separate concerns of the individual aspects from the concern of their composition.

14.6 Conclusion

In this chapter, we have described that aspect-oriented software systems that are designed to satisfy multiple requirements may have joinpoints, each of which can be matched with advice from several aspects. In such cases, aspect weavers, such as the one in AspectJ, are free to choose the ordering of aspects. If a particular ordering of aspects is needed, the developer can specify the ordering using the precedence operator, which is used by the weaver to determine the ordering at compile-time. Since the ordering specified by the precedence operator cannot be changed at runtime, the composition of aspects can be over-restrictive and unresponsive to runtime conditions.

In previous work on detection and resolution of feature interactions, Composition Frames have been proposed and formalised as a way to compose features and resolve feature interactions at runtime. Extending the work, we have now proposed that Composition Frames can be used to compose aspects and resolve aspect interactions at runtime. The proposed approach has been illustrated with an aspect-oriented implementation of a simple example from the smart home application.

In our implementation, the problem world domains are first implemented as classes in the base system. Features are implemented as aspects that access class variables and call methods of classes. When aspects access shared variables, perhaps implicitly through method calls, they indicate the length of time for which they want exclusive access to the shared variables. The length of time can often be derived as part of the feature specifications. Respecting the principle of separation of concerns, aspects do not communicate with each other about their intention for exclusive access. Composition Frames are implemented as distinct aspects that monitor method calls by other aspects and when an interaction is detected, attempt to resolve the interaction. Composition Frames provide a number of semantics by which the aspects can be composed at runtime and in a way responsive to runtime conditions. This gives developers additional mechanisms for composing aspects.

Acknowledgements Feedback from the anonymous review process has helped improve this chapter. This work is partially funded by a Microsoft Software Engineering Innovation Foundation (SEIF) Award, by Science Foundation Ireland grant 10/CE/I1855 and by the European Research Council.

References

1. M. Calder, M. Kolberg, E.H. Magill, S. Reiff-Marganiec, Feature interaction: A critical review and considered forecast. Comput. Network. **41**, 115–141 (2003). doi: 10.1016/S1389-1286(02)00352-3
2. E. Cameron, N. Griffeth, Y.J. Lin, M. Nilson, W. Schnure, H. Velthuijsen, A feature-interaction benchmark for in and beyond. IEEE Comm. Mag. **31**(3), 64–69 (1993). doi 10.1109/35.199613
3. R. Chitchyan, A. Rashid, P. Rayson, R. Waters, Semantics-based composition for aspect-oriented requirements engineering, in *Proceedings of the 6th International Conference on Aspect-Oriented Software Development* (ACM, NY, 2007), pp. 36–48
4. R.J. Hall, Fundamental nonmodularity in electronic mail. Automat. Software Eng. **12**(1), 41–79 (2005)
5. M. Jackson, *Problem Frames: Analyzing and Structuring Software Development Problems.* (ACM Press & Addison Wesley, New York, 2001)
6. J. Kienzle, N. Guelfi, S. Mustafiz, Crisis management systems: a case study for aspect-oriented modeling. Trans. Aspect-oriented Software Develop. **7**, 1–22 (2010)
7. M. Kolberg, E.H. Magill, M. Wilson, Compatibility issues between services supporting networked appliances. IEEE Comm. Mag. **41**(11), 136–147 (2003)
8. R. Laney, L. Barroca, M. Jackson, B. Nuseibeh, Composing requirements using problem frames, in *Proceedings of 12th IEEE International Conference Requirements Engineering (RE'04)* (IEEE Computer Society, Silver Spring, MD, 2004), pp. 122–131
9. R.C. Laney, T.T. Tun, M. Jackson, B. Nuseibeh, in *Composing Features by Managing Inconsistent Requirements*, ed. by L. du Bousquet, J.L. Richier. ICFI (IOS Press, Amsterdam, 2007), pp. 129–144
10. G. Mussbacher, J. Whittle, D. Amyot, Semantic-based interaction detection in aspect-oriented scenarios, in *RE* (IEEE Computer Society, Silver Spring, MD, 2009), pp. 203–212

11. A. Popovici, T. Gross, G. Alonso, Dynamic weaving for aspect-oriented programming, in *Proceedings of the 1st International Conference on Aspect-Oriented Software Development, AOSD '02* (ACM, New York, 2002), pp. 141–147
12. F. Sanen, E. Truyen, W. Joosen, A. Jackson, A. Nedos, S. Clarke, N. Loughran, A. Rashid, Classifying and documenting aspect interactions, in *Proceedings of the Fifth AOSD Workshop on Aspect, Components, and Patterns for Infrastructure Software*, ed. by Y. Coady, D.H. Lorenz, O. Spinczyk, E. Wohlstadter (Technical Report No. 33. Hasso-Plattner-Instituts für Softwaresystemtechnik an der Universität Potsdam, 2006), pp. 23–26
13. The AspectJ Team: The AspectJ Programming Guide. Xerox Corporation (2001) URL http://www.eclipse.org/aspectj/doc/next/progguide/index.html. Accessed 15 Dec 2012
14. T.T. Tun, Aspect compoistion using composition frames: Java program listings. Tech. Rep. TR2012/09, The Open University (2012)
15. T.T. Tun, T. Trew, M. Jackson, R.C. Laney, B. Nuseibeh, Specifying features of an evolving software system. Software Pract. Ex. **39**(11), 973–1002 (2009)
16. H. Velthuijsen, Issues of non-monotonicity in feature-interaction detection, in *FIW*, ed. by K.E. Cheng, T. Ohta (IOS Press, 1995), pp. 31–42
17. N. Weston, R. Chitchyan, A. Rashid, A formal approach to semantic composition of aspect-oriented requirements, in *Proceedings of the 2008 16th IEEE International Requirements Engineering Conference* (IEEE Computer Society, Washington, DC, 2008), pp. 173–182

Part V
AORE in Industry

Chapter 15
Implementing Aspect-Oriented Requirements Analysis for Investment Banking Applications

Yuri Chernak

Abstract Aspect-oriented requirements engineering (AORE) introduced an artifact called *Requirements Composition Table* (RCT). RCT presents a holistic view of an application's functionality structured by core features and crosscutting concerns. As AORE remains little known to most practitioners in the software development field, the purpose of this chapter is to explain the RCT concept to practitioners and discuss its benefits.

The RCT technique has been implemented for a number of Wall Street applications at various investment banks. RCT can serve as a common frame of reference for all parties on a project team and it has proven to be one of the most valuable artifacts of a software project. This chapter discusses the steps to develop an RCT and provides RCT examples of two financial applications.

RCT can effectively support various project tasks. This chapter illustrates how RCT can help us (a) perform change impact analysis for releases and (b) assess test coverage of existing regression test suites. The chapter concludes with describing experiences using RCTs in practice and discussing lessons learned on projects implementing the RCT technique.

15.1 Introduction

A number of software project tasks require a holistic and structured view of an application's functionality, for example, performing change impact analysis for new releases as discussed in this chapter. Aspect-Oriented Requirements Engineering is focused on improving requirements modularization and structure, and it introduces a requirements analysis artifact called *Requirements Composition Table* (RCT) [1–4]. An RCT captures a complete inventory of an application's features, structured by

Y. Chernak (✉)
Valley Forge Consulting, Inc., Berwyn, USA
e-mail: ychernak@yahoo.com

A. Moreira et al. (eds.), *Aspect-Oriented Requirements Engineering*,
DOI 10.1007/978-3-642-38640-4_15, © Springer-Verlag Berlin Heidelberg 2013

core functionality and crosscutting concerns. In addition to the inventory of features, an RCT captures the impact of crosscutting concerns on core features and presents their composition as a binary decision, thereby providing a complete and structured view of an application's functionality. This RCT concept and the steps to produce an RCT are discussed in detail in this chapter.

The RCT technique has been implemented for a number of applications on Wall Street and has proven to be an effective solution to various practical problems. The main purpose of this chapter is to explain to practitioners the RCT concept, as well as its benefits provided to all project parties—the product owner, the developers, and the testers. We illustrate the RCT benefits by discussing two important tasks:

(a) Performing change impact analysis for releases
(b) Assessing coverage and identifying gaps in existing regression test suites

15.2 Requirements Composition Table Explained

15.2.1 The Concept and Benefits of RCT

The functionality of any business application can be logically decomposed into two categories of software requirements—core features and supplementary features. Core features capture basic application functionality and, when executed, produce a tangible and distinct business result. For example, use cases can be classified as core features. In contrast, supplementary features do not produce business results by themselves, but rather complement core features and add necessary details to a core feature context. For example, if we book a hotel room or rental car online, performing such a booking can be qualified as a core feature of an online reservation system. However, to complete the booking, the system will invoke various supplementary features such as data entry validation, calculations of the sales tax and reservation cost, interfacing with a credit card vendor for payment processing, etc. Such supplementary features can be invoked in the context of various core features of a given application and impact their behavior.

To improve requirements analysis, modularization, and structure, AORE methods specifically address the fact that supplementary features can be scattered across the application and can impact core features. In AORE, such supplementary features are called *crosscutting concerns* [1, 5, 6]. Characteristics of crosscutting concerns are discussed in the next section. Analyzing the impact of crosscutting concerns on core features is an important requirements analysis task in AORE, where the results of this task are captured in the form of an RCT [1–4]. The steps to produce an RCT are discussed later in this chapter.

Thus, an RCT presents a holistic and structured view of the application functionality that becomes a common frame of reference providing a common language for all parties on a software project—the product owner, the developers, and the testers. The RCT includes an inventory of all application features structured by two

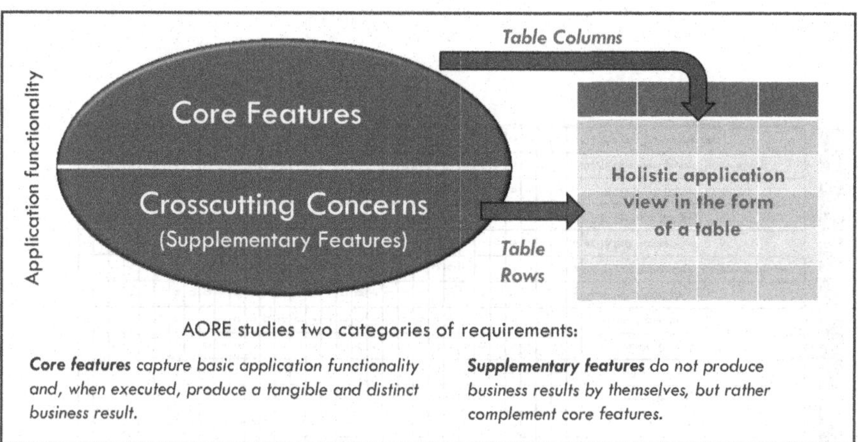

Fig. 15.1 Two dimensions of an RCT

categories, i.e., core features captured in table columns and crosscutting concerns captured in table rows (see Fig. 15.1). At the intersection of each core feature and crosscutting concern, the RCT captures the impact of crosscutting concerns on core functionality as a binary decision, in which 0 means "no impact" and 1 means "the context of the core feature is impacted by the crosscutting concern".

To illustrate the RCT concept, this section provides two RCT examples developed for investment banking applications. Both project teams needed to improve effectiveness of change impact analysis and considered the RCT technique as a solution to the issue. The first example shown in Fig. 15.2 is a partial RCT developed for a prime brokerage application. In this example, we see two of ten modules of which this application functionality was comprised. Figure 15.3 shows another example of an RCT developed for an FX trading application. In this RCT example, we also see two of six application modules. In these tables, columns represent core features grouped by application modules. The table rows, except for the first and second items in the list of concerns, represent crosscutting concerns. The central part of each table captures the composition of concerns as a binary decision represented as 0 or 1.

The first two items in the list of concerns are not crosscutting concerns and require explanation. In an RCT each table column represents a core feature context that includes not only crosscutting concerns but also core functionality as well. In addition, a core feature context can include GUI features. Hence, these two items are standard additions to any RCT and we can see them included in each RCT example in Figs. 15.2 and 15.3. Section 15.2.3 discusses in detail the steps to develop a complete RCT.

Finally, the RCT technique can complement and benefit any existing requirements methodology, and it can be easily adopted on projects that follow, for example, the traditional, use-case-driven, or agile approaches.

RCT Example: Prime Brokerage Application

01. Trade Processing

List of Concerns	01.01 New Instruction	01.02 Trade Correction	01.03 Repo Close	01.04 Trade Cancellation	01.05 Correction Filtering	01.06 Correction Allocation - External	01.07 Correction Allocation - Flip Action	01.08 In-flight Trade Processing	01.09 Manual Price Input	01.10 Finalize Pricing	01.11 Repo Offleg Publishing	01.12 Hide Errors	01.13 Missing Products Repair	01.14 Accrued Interest Batch	01.15 Override Errors	01.16 Account Resolution	01.17 Summarize Trade Counts	01.18 Missing Accrued Interest Repair	01.19 Rebalance Trade File
Core Functionality	1	1	1	1	1	1	1	1	1	1	1	1	1	1	1	1	1	1	1
GUI Features	1	1	1	1	0	1	1	0	1	1	0	1	0	0	1	0	1	1	0
Crosscutting Concerns																			
ET-In - Internal Entitlements	1	1	1	1	0	1	1	0	1	1	0	1	0	0	1	0	0	1	0
ET-Ex - External Entitlements	1	1	1	1	0	1	0	0	0	0	0	0	0	0	0	0	0	0	0
STY - Security	1	1	1	1	0	1	0	0	1	1	0	0	0	0	1	0	0	0	0
CS - Client Setup	1	1	1	1	1	1	1	1	0	0	0	0	0	0	0	1	0	0	1
PT - Product Type	1	1	1	1	1	1	1	1	0	0	1	0	0	0	0	0	0	1	1
CST - Cash Status	0	0	0	0	0	0	0	0	0	0	0	0	0	0	0	0	0	0	0
TST - Trade Status	1	1	1	1	1	1	1	1	0	0	1	1	0	0	0	0	0	0	1
FXST - FX Status	1	1	1	1	0	0	0	0	0	0	0	0	0	0	0	0	0	0	0
TPST - Template Status	0	0	0	0	0	0	0	0	0	0	0	0	0	0	0	0	0	0	0
FS - File Status	1	1	1	1	1	1	1	0	0	0	0	0	0	0	0	0	0	0	0
FV - Field Validation	1	1	1	1	1	1	1	1	0	0	0	1	1	0	1	0	0	1	0
DDV - Data-Dependency Validation	1	1	1	1	0	0	0	0	0	0	0	0	0	0	0	0	0	0	0
DDD - Data-Driven Defaults	1	1	1	1	0	0	0	0	0	0	0	0	0	0	0	0	0	0	0
CL - Calculations	1	1	1	1	1	1	1	1	0	0	0	1	1	0	1	0	0	1	1
ER - Enrichment	1	1	1	1	1	1	1	1	0	0	0	1	1	0	1	0	0	1	1
MP - Mapping	1	1	1	1	0	0	0	0	0	0	0	0	0	0	0	0	0	0	0
CC - Concurrency	1	1	1	1	1	1	1	1	0	0	0	1	0	0	1	0	0	0	0
CN - Connectivity	1	1	1	1	0	1	1	0	0	0	0	0	0	0	0	0	0	0	0
RG - Region	1	1	1	1	1	1	1	0	0	0	1	0	0	0	0	0	0	0	1
DF-In - Data Flow In	1	1	1	1	1	1	1	1	0	1	1	1	1	0	1	1	1	1	0
DF-Out - Data Flow Out	1	1	1	1	1	1	1	1	1	0	1	1	1	1	1	1	0	1	0
SI-In - System Interface In	1	1	1	1	0	0	1	0	0	0	0	0	0	1	0	0	0	1	0
SI-Out - System Interface Out	1	1	1	1	0	0	0	0	0	1	0	0	0	0	0	0	0	0	0
EML-In - Email In	1	0	0	0	0	0	0	0	0	0	0	0	0	0	0	0	0	0	0
EML-Out - Email Out	1	1	1	1	1	0	0	0	0	0	0	0	0	0	0	1	0	0	0
ADT-In - Internal User Audit	1	1	1	1	0	1	1	0	0	0	0	0	0	0	0	0	0	0	0
ADT-Ex - External User Audit	0	0	0	0	0	0	0	0	0	0	0	0	0	0	0	0	0	0	0
CA - Cache	1	1	1	1	1	1	1	1	0	0	0	0	0	0	0	0	0	0	0
ExH - Exception Handling	1	1	1	1	1	1	1	1	0	0	0	0	0	0	0	0	0	0	1
PF - Performance	1	1	1	1	1	1	1	1	0	0	0	0	0	0	0	0	0	0	0

02. Trade Flow

List of Concerns	02.01 Account Mapping, Non-repo	02.02 Account Mapping, Repo	02.03 Account Type Mapping	02.04 Action Mapping	02.05 Buy, Sell Nature Mapping	02.06 Product Type Mapping	02.07 Broker Mapping	02.08 Reporting Only	02.09 Street-side Publishing	02.10 Client-side Publishing	02.11 Swift Account Flag Overrides	02.12 Treasury Breakdown	02.13 Asset Transfer	02.14 Prime Custody	02.15 Bulk Across Client Reference Number	02.16 Bulk Across Price	02.17 Blocking, Merging	02.18 Done-with Broker Processing	02.19 Done-with Broker Trade Filtering	02.20 Repo Trade Figuration
Core Functionality	1	1	1	1	1	1	1	1	1	1	1	1	1	1	1	1	1	1	1	1
GUI Features	1	1	1	1	1	1	1	1	1	1	0	1	1	1	0	0	1	1	1	1
Crosscutting Concerns																				
ET-In - Internal Entitlements	1	1	1	1	1	1	1	1	1	1	0	1	1	1	0	0	1	1	1	1
ET-Ex - External Entitlements	0	0	0	0	0	0	0	0	0	0	0	0	0	0	0	0	0	0	0	0
STY - Security	0	0	0	0	0	0	0	0	0	0	0	0	0	0	0	0	0	0	0	0
CS - Client Setup	1	1	1	1	1	1	1	1	0	0	1	0	1	0	1	1	1	1	1	1
PT - Product Type	0	0	0	0	0	1	0	0	1	1	0	1	1	1	0	0	1	1	0	1
CST - Cash Status	0	0	0	0	0	0	0	0	0	0	0	0	0	0	0	0	0	0	0	0
TST - Trade Status	0	0	0	0	0	0	0	0	0	0	0	0	0	0	0	0	0	0	0	0
FXST - FX Status	0	0	0	0	0	0	0	0	0	0	0	0	0	0	0	0	0	0	0	0
TPST - Template Status	0	0	0	0	0	0	0	0	0	0	0	0	0	0	0	0	0	0	0	0
FS - File Status	0	0	0	0	0	0	0	0	0	0	0	0	0	0	0	0	0	0	0	0
FV - Field Validation	0	0	0	0	1	1	1	0	0	0	1	0	1	1	0	0	0	0	0	1
DDV - Data-Dependency Validation	0	0	0	0	0	0	0	0	0	0	0	0	0	0	0	0	0	0	0	0
DDD - Data-Driven Defaults	0	0	0	0	0	0	0	0	0	0	0	0	0	0	0	0	0	0	0	0
CL - Calculations	0	0	0	0	1	1	1	0	0	0	1	0	1	1	0	0	0	0	0	1
ER - Enrichment	0	0	0	0	1	1	1	0	0	0	1	0	1	1	0	0	0	0	0	1
MP - Mapping	1	1	1	1	1	1	1	0	0	0	0	0	0	0	0	0	0	0	0	0
CC - Concurrency	0	0	0	0	0	0	0	0	0	0	0	0	0	0	0	0	0	0	0	0
CN - Connectivity	0	0	0	0	0	0	0	0	0	0	0	0	0	0	0	0	0	0	0	0
RG - Region	0	0	1	0	0	0	0	0	0	0	0	0	0	0	0	0	0	0	0	0
DF-In - Data Flow In	1	1	1	1	1	1	1	1	1	1	1	1	0	0	1	1	1	1	1	1
DF-Out - Data Flow Out	1	1	1	1	1	1	1	1	0	0	1	1	1	1	1	1	1	1	1	1
SI-In - System Interface In	0	0	1	0	0	0	0	0	0	0	0	0	0	0	0	0	0	0	0	0
SI-Out - System Interface Out	0	0	0	0	0	0	0	0	1	1	0	0	0	0	0	0	0	0	0	0
EML-In - Email In	0	0	0	0	0	0	0	0	0	0	0	0	0	0	0	0	0	0	0	0
EML-Out - Email Out	0	0	0	0	0	0	0	0	0	0	0	0	0	0	0	0	0	0	0	0
ADT-In - Internal User Audit	0	0	0	0	0	0	0	0	0	0	0	0	0	0	0	0	0	0	0	0
ADT-Ex - External User Audit	0	0	0	0	0	0	0	0	0	0	0	0	0	0	0	0	0	0	0	0
CA - Cache	1	1	1	1	1	1	0	0	0	0	0	0	0	0	0	0	0	1	1	0
ExH - Exception Handling	0	0	0	0	0	0	1	0	0	0	0	0	0	0	0	0	0	0	0	0
PF - Performance	0	0	0	0	0	0	0	0	0	0	0	0	0	0	0	0	0	0	0	0

Fig. 15.2 RCT example—prime brokerage application

RCT Example: FX Trading Application

List of Concerns	01. Trade Capture													
	01.01 New Trade	01.02 Modify Trade	01.03 Cancel Trade	01.04 New Order	01.05 Modify Order	01.06 Accept Order	01.07 Cancel Order	01.08 Execute Order	01.09 Book Order	01.10 Complete Order	01.11 Book Sales Credit	01.12 Modify Sales Credit	01.13 Update FX Rates	01.14 Update Interest Rates
Core Functionality	1	1	1	1	1	1	1	1	1	1	1	1	1	1
GUI Features	1	1	1	1	1	1	1	1	1	1	1	1	1	1
Crosscuting Concerns														
ET - Entitlements	1	1	1	1	1	1	1	1	1	1	1	1	0	0
PT - Product Type	1	1	1	0	0	0	0	0	0	0	0	0	0	0
ST-O - Order Status	0	0	0	0	1	1	1	1	1	1	0	0	0	0
ST-T - Trade Status	0	1	1	1	0	0	0	0	0	0	1	1	0	0
FV - Field Validation	1	1	0	1	1	0	0	0	0	0	1	1	1	1
DDV - Data-Dependency Validation	1	1	0	1	1	0	0	0	0	0	1	1	0	0
DDD - Data-Driven Defaults	1	1	0	0	0	0	0	0	0	0	1	1	0	0
CC - Concurrency	0	1	1	0	1	1	1	1	1	1	0	1	0	0
CN - Connectivity	1	1	1	1	1	1	1	1	1	1	1	1	1	1
CA - Cache	1	1	0	1	1	0	0	0	0	0	1	1	1	1
DF-In - Data Flow In	1	1	1	1	1	1	1	1	1	1	1	1	1	1
DF-Out - Data Flow Out	1	1	1	1	1	1	1	1	1	1	1	1	1	1
SI-In - System Interface In	1	1	1	0	0	0	0	0	0	0	0	0	0	0
SI-Out - System Interface Out	0	0	0	0	0	0	0	0	0	0	1	1	1	1
PF - Performance	1	1	1	1	1	1	1	1	1	1	0	0	0	0

List of Concerns	02. Data View															
	02.01 View Trade Blotter	02.02 View Trade Inquiry Request	02.03 View Order Blotter	02.04 View Order Inquiry	02.05 View Mark-To-Market Blotter	02.06 View Sales Blotter	02.07 View Sales Sign Off Blotter	02.08 View Wash Trades	02.09 View Currency Summary	02.10 View Real Time Summary	02.11 View Customer Inquiry	02.12 View Credit Exposure Inquiry	02.13 View Currency Prices	02.14 View Interest Rates	02.15 View Linked Trades	02.16 View FX Reports
Core Functionality	1	1	1	1	1	1	1	1	1	1	1	1	1	1	1	1
GUI Features	1	1	1	1	1	1	1	1	1	1	1	1	1	1	1	1
Crosscuting Concerns																
ET - Entitlements	1	1	1	1	1	1	1	1	1	1	0	0	0	0	1	1
PT - Product Type	1	1	0	0	1	1	1	1	0	0	0	0	0	0	1	1
ST-O - Order Status	0	0	1	1	0	0	0	0	0	0	0	0	0	0	0	0
ST-T - Trade Status	0	0	0	0	0	0	0	0	0	0	0	0	0	0	0	0
FV - Field Validation	0	0	0	0	0	0	0	0	0	0	0	0	0	0	0	0
DDV - Data-Dependency Validation	0	0	0	0	0	0	0	0	0	0	0	0	0	0	0	0
DDD - Data-Driven Defaults	0	0	0	0	0	0	0	0	0	0	0	0	0	0	0	0
CC - Concurrency	0	0	0	0	0	0	0	0	0	0	0	0	0	0	0	0
CN - Connectivity	1	1	1	1	1	1	1	1	1	1	1	1	1	1	1	1
CA - Cache	0	0	0	0	0	0	0	0	0	0	0	0	0	0	0	0
DF-In - Data Flow In	1	1	1	1	1	1	1	1	1	1	1	1	1	1	1	1
DF-Out - Data Flow Out	0	0	0	0	0	0	0	0	0	0	0	0	0	0	0	0
SI-In - System Interface In	0	0	0	0	0	0	0	0	0	0	0	0	0	0	0	0
SI-Out - System Interface Out	0	0	0	0	0	0	0	0	0	0	0	0	0	0	0	0
PF - Performance	1	1	1	1	1	0	0	0	0	1	1	0	1	0	0	0

Fig. 15.3 RCT example—front-office FX trading application

An RCT has been implemented for many software development projects in the investment banking sector and has proven to be one of the most important project artifacts. It can help solve common practical issues and effectively support various tasks:

- Performing software change impact analysis for new releases
- Assessing test coverage and identifying gaps in existing regression test suites
- Planning functional and regression testing
- Supporting renovation projects to replace legacy applications
- Planning iterative and incremental development
- Planning sprints on Agile projects
- Performing effective exploratory testing
- Supporting knowledge transfer

The first and the second tasks in the above list are discussed in this chapter.

15.2.2 Characteristics and Examples of Crosscutting Concerns

In practice, in any business application we can find features that comply with two characteristics—they are (a) *scattered*, i.e., are invoked across an application at different functional areas and (b) *tangled* with other features thereby impacting their context. The extent to which some features can be scattered and tangled with other features can be illustrated by the numbers from the prime brokerage application for which we provided the RCT example (Fig. 15.2) in the previous section. In this application, each of the core features is impacted, on average, by ten crosscutting concerns. On the other hand, most of the application's crosscutting concerns impact at least 20 % of core features, whereas some of them impact from 60 % to 80 % of core features.

Thus, supplementary features that can be analyzed and modeled as crosscutting concerns are those that [2, 3]:

- Cannot be invoked directly by end-users, i.e., to be executed, a crosscutting concern needs a context of core features
- When invoked, a crosscutting concern impacts a core feature's behavior in one of the following ways:
  - It constrains a core feature execution (example: user entitlements)
  - It interrupts a core feature flow (examples: field validation, concurrency)
  - It adds detail to a core feature (example: calculations)
- Are sufficiently scattered, i.e., each crosscutting concern impacts at least three to four core features

Table 15.1 shows examples of crosscutting concerns common to investment banking applications and grouped by seven categories. The Appendix section includes Table A.1 that shows descriptions of these crosscutting concerns. Typically,

Table 15.1 Crosscutting concerns common to investment banking applications

Categories of Crosscutting Concerns for Investment Banking Applications			
Access & Entitlements	**Client Setup & System Configuration**	**Product Type & Transaction Status**	**Data Validation & Manipulation**
ET-In - Internal Entitlements	CS - Client Setup	PT - Product Type	FV - Field Validation
ET-Ex - External Entitlements	SC - System Configuration	CLT - Collateral Type	DDV - Data-Dependency Validation
AUT - Authorization	RG - Region	TRC - Trade Category	DDD - Data-Driven Defaults
STY - Security	LE - Legal Entity	TIF - Time-In-Force	DER - Data Enrichment
		OST - Order Status	DMP - Data Mapping
Audits & Alerts	**Data & Transaction Flow**	TRST - Trade Status	CL - Calculations
ADT-In - Internal User Audit	MB - Message Broadcasting	CST - Cash Status	CC - Concurrency
ADT-Ex - External User Audit	CN - Connectivity	SST - Settlement Status	
ALR - Alerts	SDF - Static Data Flow	FXST - FX Status	
ExH - Exception Handling	TDF-In - Transaction Data Flow In	TPST - Template Status	
	TDF-Out - Transaction Data Flow Out	FST - File Status	
Non-functional Concerns	SI-In System Interface In (inbound)	DST - Deal Status	
CA - Cache	SI-Out - System Interface Out (outbound)	TST - Transaction Status	
PF - Performance	NOT - Notifications	AST - Agreement Status	
	EML-In - Email In		
	EML-Out - Email Out		
	FAX-Out - FAX Out		

a list of crosscutting concerns for a given application can include from 20 to 40 items; however, this number depends primarily on the application complexity and level of abstraction to identify crosscutting concerns. For example, some project teams defined *Entitlements* as a single category of concern, whereas other teams needed more visibility and defined this concern as two subcategories—*Internal Entitlements* (for internal users) and *External Entitlements* (for external users). Another example can be the *System Interface (SI)* concern. Many financial applications exchange transactions with upstream and downstream applications. To differentiate between the inbound and outbound transactions and their impact on core features, we can represent the system interface concern as two subcategories—*SI-In (Inbound)* and *SI-Out (Outbound)*, respectively.

Another point about crosscutting concerns is that they can be associated with both functional and non-functional requirements [1, 6]. In Table 15.1, we see most of the crosscutting concerns representing a functional category; however, two concerns, *Cache* (i.e. memory cache) and *Performance*, represent a non-functional category.

Finally, we frequently find that many items in the list of crosscutting concerns are generic and repeat across many other applications in the same business domain, e.g., financial applications. This can be explained by the fact that supplementary requirements are often not application-domain-specific, but rather reflect some common software engineering principles that we use to design business applications.

15.2.3 Steps to Produce an RCT

Developing an RCT is a relatively small effort. Based on the author's experience, it takes about 10–12 h for medium-to-large size applications (include 100–200 core features). This procedure can be conducted as a series of 1 h working sessions with

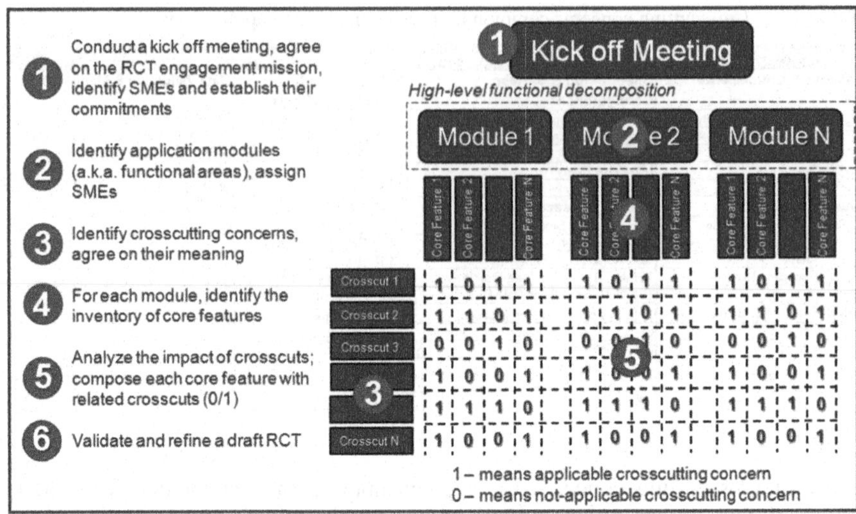

Fig. 15.4 Steps to produce an RCT

application subject matter experts (SME) and it includes the following six steps also illustrated in Fig. 15.4:

Step 1: Identify SMEs. Conduct a kickoff meeting with the engagement's key stakeholders; discuss and agree on the engagement mission, i.e., what issue we are trying to solve with RCT, how the RCT will be used by the team, etc. Developing an RCT is the process of extracting knowledge about the application functionality from available sources and presenting it in a specific structured view. So, at the kickoff meeting, we need to identify SMEs who will be the source of knowledge and establish their commitments.

Step 2: Identify Application Modules. Conduct a working session with SMEs to analyze the application functionality at a high level and break it into modules, a.k.a. functional areas. Assign one or more SMEs to each module and schedule additional working sessions that will focus on one module at a time.

Step 3: Identify Crosscutting Concerns. Identify crosscutting concerns, agree on each, and capture their meaning. Guidelines to identify crosscutting concerns can be found in published sources, for example [2, 3, 8]. As most categories of crosscutting concerns are reusable, a good starting point would be to review the list from a previous engagement and see which crosscut categories from the existing list can be applied to a given application. Further, if the project has specifications of existing product requirements, they can be analyzed to identify crosscutting concerns as well [6].

Step 4: Identify Core Features. Conduct the working sessions with the assigned SMEs, as scheduled in Step 2, to identify the inventory of core features for each application module. Be mindful about the level of abstraction at which you want

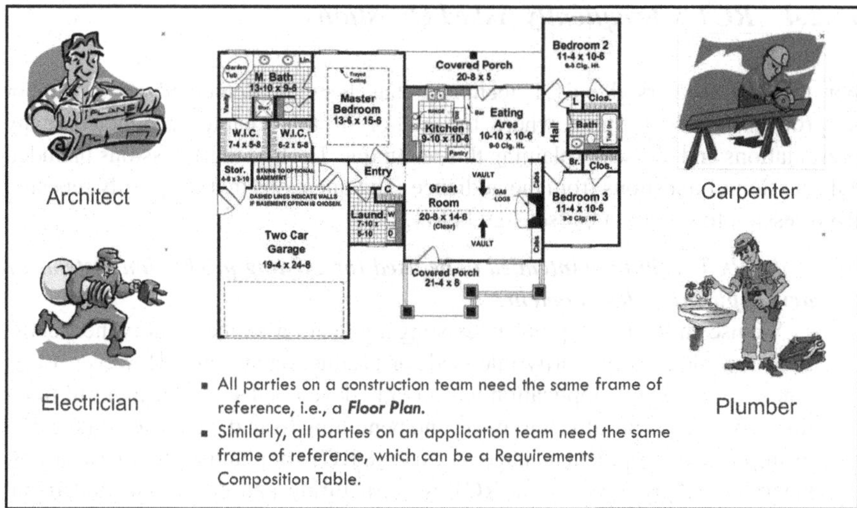

Fig. 15.5 RCT as an "application's floor plan"

to identify core features. Each core feature should be identified as producing some tangible and distinct end-result that the user can achieve by executing this feature.

Step 5: Compose Concerns. Compose core features with crosscutting concerns. To do that, select each core feature in turn, one at a time, and go down the list of crosscutting concerns to decide which of them will or will not be applicable to its context. Capture results in the RCT as a binary decision (0 = No, 1 = Yes).

Step 6: Validate RCT. When all core features are composed with related crosscutting concerns, perform some basic RCT validation. First, determine the degree of scattering of crosscutting concerns by building a distribution of occurrences in the table. A crosscutting concern is considered to be sufficiently scattered if it is used (occurs) in the table at least three to four times. Eliminate categories of crosscuts that you did not use in the table (no occurrences). Identify any concerns that have fewer than three occurrences and discuss whether you want to keep them on the list. Second, review and validate a draft RCT with the product owner and testers, solicit their feedback, and ensure that they understand the RCT and feel comfortable to use it going forward. Doing this ensures that the RCT can effectively serve as a common language for all parties on the project team.

As a result of these steps, we capture a complete and structured view of an application's functionality in the form of an RCT that can serve as a common frame of reference for all members of a project team. In this regard, RCT can be compared to a floor plan used by all members of a construction team (see Fig. 15.5), e.g., an architect, a plumber, an electrician, etc. Because of this similarity, project teams frequently refer to an RCT as an "application's floor plan."

15.2.4 RCT's Frequently Asked Questions

For the last 6 years the RCT technique has been implemented on a number of projects on Wall Street where the author of this chapter conducted many presentations and classes explaining this technique. Each of these sessions included a discussion of questions from the audience. The questions that frequently repeated from session to session are discussed below.

1. ***Is the RCT technique intended to be used for existing production systems or new application development?***

   We use an RCT to capture an existing application's functionality; hence, the RCT technique is primarily intended for production systems. However, when a new development application has already developed some meaningful functionality, a team can also start using and benefiting from the RCT technique. For example, a development manager can use an RCT for planning future iterations, business analysts can use an RCT for structuring and developing functional requirements, and testers can use an RCT for structuring their test repository and developing tests, etc.
2. ***Creating an RCT is conceptually the same as performing functionality reverse-engineering, which is typically a time-consuming task for any business application. What is different about the RCT technique that allows it to perform the same task with a relatively small effort?***

   This is a very common question. Yes, to develop an RCT, we essentially perform functionality reverse-engineering. However, the main difference with the conventional reverse-engineering is that the RCT captures just the inventory of functional features and presents it in a specific structured view. This requires much less effort and time as compared to rewriting functional specifications, which is what people commonly think of functionality reverse-engineering.
3. ***Who are the more common SMEs involved in the development of an RCT, e.g., end-users, business analysts, developers, or testers?***

   In general, any project team member who has good knowledge of the application functionality can effectively contribute to the development of RCT. From the author's experience, most commonly such SMEs were lead developers and business analysts. One benefit of engaging developers is that they can check the source code, for example, when we are not sure about the impact of some crosscuts on core features. However, when a draft RCT is produced, it needs to be reviewed by all parties on the project team to ensure that they all have agreed to this artifact and it can serve as a common language and can be used as a common frame of reference by the entire project team.
4. ***How do you know whether a newly developed RCT is complete?***

   This is a valid and important question. A draft RCT should be reviewed, validated, and agreed to by all project parties before we start using it. A consensus among the parties is a good sign that the RCT is fairly complete and ready to be used. However, it is expected that during the first few releases, when we will be using an RCT, some discrepancies with the actual application functionality will be noticed. When this happens, the RCT should be updated and a new version approved and baselined.

5. ***Can we automate the RCT development?***
   This is a very frequent question. Unfortunately, the short answer is NO. Most commonly, the sources of application functionality are application SMEs, and the process of developing an RCT is based on the interviews of these SMEs, which cannot be automated. Second, the method of structuring the application by modules and then breaking it down by core features is subjective, and the RCT is frequently adjusted and revised as we proceed with its development. The list of crosscutting concerns and the level of their abstraction are also subjective. These factors make it difficult to automate the RCT development. However, the good news is that the "manual" effort to develop an RCT is relatively small and provides flexibility to tailor the level of the RCT abstraction during the working sessions to make it more meaningful to the team members who will be using the RCT.
6. ***Is the composition of concerns always "black & white" (i.e., 0 or 1)?***
   Yes, the concept of RCT requires that the impact of crosscuts is captured as a binary decision. This is consistent with the implementation of crosscuts in the application's source code, where the code related to a given crosscutting concern either exists or does not exist in the context of a core feature.
7. ***What can you do if you are not sure whether a crosscutting concern impacts a particular core feature or not?***
   The answer to this question was briefly discussed above. The best way to resolve the uncertainty is to ask a developer to review the source code related to the feature in question. Seeing how the actual functionality is implemented will be the most accurate reference. Consulting other application SMEs can be another useful resource.
8. ***What if a given crosscutting concern does not impact any core features?***
   By definition, a crosscutting concern is a supplementary feature that impacts multiple other features. However, when we develop a new RCT, it is not uncommon that we see some crosscuts not mapped yet to any of the core features. Such candidate crosscuts should be investigated as part of the draft RCT validation. First, we need to confirm whether a candidate crosscut is really needed and can fully comply with the characteristics of crosscutting concerns. Then we should review the inventory of core features, where we will most likely find some features to which the crosscut in question can be mapped. If these steps do not produce a result, then such a crosscutting concern should be removed from the list of crosscuts and possibly reclassified as a core feature in an RCT.
9. ***If two crosscutting concerns have the same composition pattern (0/1), i.e., they impact the same core features in the same way, can we merge them?***
   Not necessarily. Two crosscutting concerns can have the same composition pattern but completely different meanings. Thus, we should keep them as two separate items in the RCT.

10. ***What is a practical number of crosscutting concerns for a business application? What if the list of crosscuts grows too long?***

    The longer the list of crosscuts, the larger the RCT becomes, which makes it more difficult to develop, use, and maintain. Based on experience, a practical maximum number of crosscuts in the RCT is about 30 or 40 items. If the list grows much longer, we should look for possibilities to reduce it by collapsing some of the crosscuts with similar purposes and replacing them with a single and more general crosscut category.
11. ***Can crosscutting concerns impact each other? If so, how can we reflect it in the RCT?***

    In general, crosscutting concerns can impact not only core features but also each other as well. However, for the purposes of RCT, where we analyze and capture the impact of crosscuts on core features, we disregard their possible mutual impact.
12. ***Can a core feature be tangled with other core features? If so, how can we reflect it in the RCT?***

    Yes, core features can impact each other in the way that one core feature can be a part of others. This fact was recognized long ago and addressed by the use-case modeling. In particular, UML defines *include* and *extend* relationships among use cases (i.e., core features from the RCT perspective) that we can use to model their mutual impact. However, the RCT is intended for analyzing how crosscuts impact core features, which is a different view from the use-case modeling. Hence, the RCT disregards the mutual impact of core features and captures each core feature context independently from other core features.
13. ***What is the difference between a Requirements Composition Table (RCT) and a Requirements Traceability Matrix (RTM)?***

    The short answer is that RCT and RTM are two completely different artifacts. What sometimes confuses people who ask this question is the fact that both artifacts capture relationships among requirements. However, the type of relationship is different in each case. The RCT captures the relationship between related features where a given crosscutting concern is a part of other requirements, i.e., core features. In contrast, an RTM captures links between pairs of related project artifacts produced at different phases of a project. For example, we can capture in the RTM links between user requirements and related functional requirements and also links between functional requirements and related tests. These links provide the ability to follow the life of a requirement in both forward and backward directions to support development tasks [7].

15.3 RCTs for Performing Change Impact Analysis

15.3.1 Capturing CIA Results in an RCT

Most business applications in a typical IT department are existing production systems that go through regular cycles of production releases. The scope of a new release is usually defined by reviewing a backlog of user (a.k.a. business or stakeholder) requirements and requests to fix bugs, then selecting higher priority items to be implemented in the next release.

User requirements are usually captured as short descriptions of stakeholder needs. Although these descriptions may not be sufficient to describe how the requested changes impact the application's existing functionality, it is not uncommon that a team would not produce any more detailed product (a.k.a. functional) requirements. This creates challenges for (a) developers to accurately estimate the release effort and (b) testers to understand and define the scope of functional testing based on only the high-level user requirements. Performing change impact analysis can be a solution to this issue. This task is a part of the general requirements engineering discipline [9]; guidelines to perform it can be found, for example, in [10–12].

However, performing change impact analysis based on an RCT can provide more granular and complete results. Commonly for production systems, most new user requirements typically overlap with the application's existing functionality. Hence, to better understand their impact, we can use an RCT as a frame of reference. The RCT presents a holistic and structured view of the application's functionality and has proven to be effective to perform change impact analysis.

Using the RCT, we can analyze user requests one at a time, and decide whether each request overlaps with some of the existing application features or if it requires adding a new feature. The detailed workflow of this activity is shown in Fig. 15.6. Once we have identified impacted features in the RCT, we enter the related user request ID in the respective RCT cells (see Fig. 15.7) to establish traceability [7] between a given user request and related product requirements. Commonly, a given user request can impact multiple product features, and a given product feature in an RCT can be impacted by multiple user requests.

When performing change impact analysis, it is important to differentiate between two types of impact—*direct* (a.k.a. primary) and *indirect* (a.k.a. secondary) [11]. Direct impact means that we need to change the source code of some features or add new features, and they will require functional testing. Indirect impact means that we do not change code, but because of side or ripple effects of directly impacted features, we still have some quality concerns about other features that would require regression testing [13]. To differentiate between the two types of impact in an RCT, we use the impact type indicators (D) or (I), where (D) means "direct impact" and (I) means "indirect impact" of a given user requirement. We place these indicators after each user requirement ID, e.g. 31896 (D) (see Fig. 15.7), in the RCT cells that

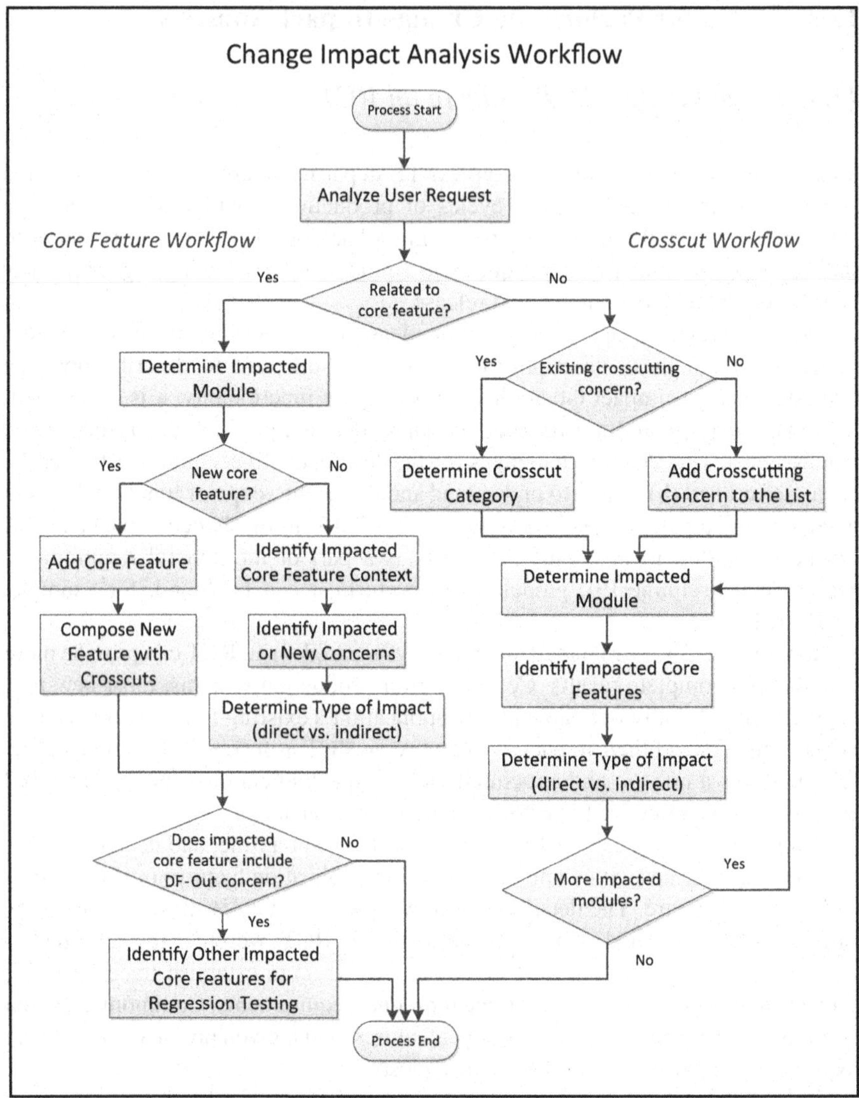

Fig. 15.6 Change impact analysis workflow

represent impacted concerns. The highlighted RCT columns show the entire context of impacted core features.

Now, we will illustrate in more detail the change impact analysis procedure and discuss two examples of user requirements that were implemented in a release of the prime brokerage application. The first user requirement 31896 stated "The user should be able to rebalance a trade file on demand". After reviewing the existing features, the team realized that this capability did not exist in the application and

List of Concerns	Requirements Composition Table																		
	01. Trade Processing																		
	01.01 New Instruction	01.02 Trade Correction	01.03 Repo Close	01.04 Trade Cancellation	01.05 Correction Filtering	01.06 Correction Allocation - External	01.07 Correction Allocation - Flip Action	01.08 In-flight Trade Processing	01.09 Manual Price Input	01.10 Finalize Pricing	01.11 Repo Offleg Publishing	01.12 Hide Errors	01.13 Missing Products Repair	01.14 Accrued Interest Batch	01.15 Override Errors	01.16 Account Resolution	01.17 Summarize Trade Counts	01.18 Missing Accrued Interest Repair	01.19 Rebalance Trade File
Core Functionality	1	1	1	31897 (I)	1	1	1	1	1	1	1	1	1	1	1	1	1	1	31896 (D)
GUI Features	1	1	1	31897 (D)	0	1	1	0	1	1	0	1	0	0	1	0	0	1	0
Crosscuting Concerns																			
ET-In - Internal Entitlements	1	1	1	31897 (I)	0	1	1	0	1	1	0	1	0	0	1	0	0	1	0
ET-Ex - External Entitlements	1	1	1	1	0	1	0	0	0	0	0	0	0	0	0	0	0	0	0
STY - Security	1	1	1	1	0	1	0	0	1	1	0	0	0	0	1	0	0	0	0
CS - Client Setup	1	1	1	1	1	1	1	1	0	0	0	0	0	0	0	1	0	0	31896 (D)
PT - Product Type	1	1	1	31897(I)	1	1	1	1	0	0	1	0	0	0	0	0	0	1	31896 (D)
CST - Cash Status	0	0	0	0	0	0	0	0	0	0	0	0	0	0	0	0	0	0	0
TST - Trade Status	1	1	1	31897 (D)	1	1	1	1	0	0	1	1	0	0	0	0	0	0	31896 (D)
FXST - FX Status	1	1	1	1	0	0	0	0	0	0	0	0	0	0	0	0	0	0	0
TPST - Template Status	0	0	0	0	0	0	0	0	0	0	0	0	0	0	0	0	0	0	0
FS - File Status	1	1	1	1	1	1	1	0	0	0	0	0	0	0	0	0	0	0	0
FV - Field Validation	1	1	1	31897 (D)	1	1	1	1	0	0	0	1	1	0	1	0	0	1	0
DDV - Data-Dependency Validation	1	1	1	1	0	0	0	0	0	0	0	0	0	0	0	0	0	0	0
DDD - Data-Driven Defaults	1	1	1	31897 (D)	0	0	0	0	0	0	0	0	0	0	0	0	0	0	0
CL - Calculations	1	1	1	1	1	1	1	1	0	0	0	1	1	0	1	0	0	1	31896 (D)
ER - Enrichment	1	1	1	1	1	1	1	1	0	0	0	1	1	0	1	0	0	1	31896 (D)
MP - Mapping	1	1	1	1	0	0	0	0	0	0	0	0	0	0	0	0	0	0	0
CC - Concurrency	1	1	1	31897 (D)	1	1	1	1	0	0	0	1	0	0	1	0	0	0	0
CN - Connectivity	1	1	1	31897 (D)	0	1	1	0	0	0	0	0	0	0	0	0	0	0	0
RG - Region	1	1	1	31897 (I)	1	1	1	0	0	0	1	0	0	0	0	0	0	0	31896 (D)
DF-In - Data Flow In	1	1	1	1	1	1	1	1	1	1	1	1	1	1	1	1	1	1	0
DF-Out - Data Flow Out	1	1	1	31897 (D)	1	1	1	1	1	1	1	1	1	1	1	1	1	1	0
SI-In - System Interface In	1	1	1	1	1	1	1	0	0	0	1	0	0	1	0	0	0	0	0
SI-Out - System Interface Out	1	1	1	31897 (I)	1	1	1	1	0	0	0	0	0	0	0	0	0	0	0
EML-In - Email In	0	0	0	0	0	0	0	0	0	0	0	0	0	0	0	0	0	0	0
EML-Out - Email Out	1	1	1	1	1	0	0	0	0	0	0	0	0	0	0	1	0	0	0
ADT-In - Internal User Audit	1	1	1	31897 (I)	0	1	1	0	0	0	0	0	0	0	0	0	0	0	0
ADT-Ex - External User Audit	0	0	0	0	0	0	0	0	0	0	0	0	0	0	0	0	0	0	0
CA - Cache	1	1	1	1	1	1	1	1	0	0	0	0	0	0	0	0	0	0	0
ExH - Exception Handling	1	1	1	31897 (I)	1	1	1	1	0	0	0	0	0	0	0	0	0	0	31896 (D)
PF - Performance	1	1	1	31897 (I)	1	1	1	1	0	0	0	0	0	0	0	0	0	0	0

Fig. 15.7 Change impact analysis results captured in an RCT

they needed to add a new core feature. They also agreed that the new feature should be added to the module "01. Trade Processing." After they added a new column "01.19 Rebalance Trade File" to the RCT (see Fig. 15.7) they then went down the list of crosscutting concerns and identified other supplementary features that should also be part of the newly added core feature. To mark the impacted features, they entered the user requirement ID in the related RCT cells. As a result, not only did the team agree on a new core feature to be added, but they also agreed on additional concerns to be implemented and tested in the context of the new core feature.

The second user requirement 31897 stated "The system should allow the user cancellation of multiple trades." The application already had a core feature "01.04 Trade Cancellation," although it allowed only a single trade cancellation. The team decided that modification of the existing core feature 01.04 would be sufficient to implement this user requirement. They then reviewed the list of the crosscutting concerns applicable to this core feature context to decide which of them were impacted by the requested change 31897 and whether the impact was *direct* or *indirect*.

As we can see in Fig. 15.7, the context of the core feature 01.04 included various crosscuts directly and indirectly impacted by the change. As crosscutting concerns

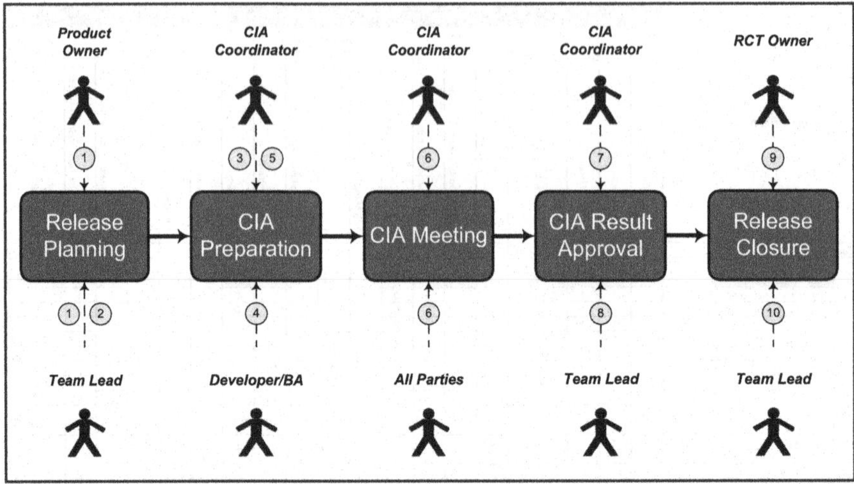

Fig. 15.8 Change impact analysis (CIA) process—roles and responsibilities

are scattered across other core features, investigation of their ripple effects was required. We analyzed ripple effects for each impacted crosscutting concern one at a time and following the steps defined in the crosscut branch of the CIA workflow shown in Fig. 15.6. For example, one of the directly impacted crosscutting concerns was DF-Out—Data Flow Out (see Fig. 15.7), which means that the output of this feature 01.04, i.e., cancelled trades, will be inputs to and used by other core features. As a result of the DF-Out ripple effect investigation, the team identified additional core features in two other modules, where all of them were qualified as indirectly impacted. Finally, the directly impacted features were then included in the scope of functional testing, and the indirectly impacted features were included in the scope of regression testing.

15.3.2 Change Impact Analysis Procedure: Roles and Responsibilities

Change impact analysis can be more effective when it is defined and performed as a formal procedure with all parties participating—the product owner, who decides on and approves the release scope, the developers, who are assigned to implement changes, and the testers, who will test the release. In this procedure the CIA process can be defined as five phases (see Fig. 15.8):

- Release Planning
- CIA Preparation
- CIA Meeting

- CIA Result Approval
- Release Closure

The formal CIA meeting is the central activity in this process. As a result of the formal session, all parties can reach a consensus on the feature-level scope of release implementation, as well the scope of functional and regression testing as it is defined and captured in the RCT. A complete step-by-step CIA procedure is shown in Fig. 15.8, and the responsibilities of various parties are defined below:

1. **Product Owner** and **Team Lead**: Finalize the release scope, i.e., a list of user requests (a.k.a. business or user requirements) to be implemented in the release.
2. **Team Lead**: Assigns user requests to developers to analyze and implement.
3. **CIA Coordinator**: Schedules a CIA meeting.
4. **Assigned Developers/BA**: Prepare a CIA case for each user request.
5. **CIA Coordinator**: Reconciles inputs from Developers/BA, prepares the meeting materials.
6. **CIA Coordinator**: Conducts a CIA meeting (Business Owner, Developers, QA parties are invited):

   (a) **Developers/BA**: Present a CIA case for each user request.
   (b) **All Parties**: Examine and validate the presented results.
   (c) **CIA Coordinator**: Facilitates a discussion, takes notes.

7. **CIA Coordinator**: Publishes the final CIA results after the meetings.
8. **Team Lead**: Approves the CIA results for the release.
9. **RCT Owner**: At the end of a release, updates the RCT and produces a new version to be approved and baselined.
10. **Team Lead**: Approves the latest RCT version.

This procedure has proven to be effective on the author's projects and can be recommended to other project teams who look to improve effectiveness of their change impact analysis for releases. Finally, it is worth noting that different roles discussed above can be assigned to the same person to make the procedure more practical. For example, the CIA Coordinator and RCT Owner can be the same project team member.

15.4 RCTs for Assessing Coverage and Identifying Gaps in a Regression Test Suite

15.4.1 Steps to Perform an Assessment

For critical applications, a QA team commonly develops a sizable suite of regression tests over time and uses it for testing new releases. However, the project team frequently does not have an adequate view into the test coverage provided by the regression suite and, specifically, cannot identify where the coverage gaps are. This issue stems from the common fact that a project team does not develop and maintain a complete set of product requirements, which is necessary to assess and measure regression suite coverage.

An RCT presents a complete inventory of functional features and can be used as a point of reference to assess coverage gaps. In fact, the RCT technique has proven to be quite effective in solving this issue on the author's projects [4]. The RCT-based assessment can be performed as the following ten steps:

1. Produce a requirements composition table.
2. Review and refine the inventory of regression tests (each test should have a defined objective).
3. Populate the RCT features in a test management tool (e.g., HP Quality Center).
4. Create a new test repository structure consistent with the structure of requirements (breakdown by modules, core features).
5. Populate existing tests in the new repository.
6. Establish traceability between requirements and tests.
7. Identify gaps and measure test coverage.
8. Review and validate the assessment results with the QA team.
9. Refine the assessment results based on the review feedback.
10. Produce and present the assessment report to the stakeholders.

To better manage regression tests, a common practice is to store them in a commercial test management tool, for example, HP Quality Center (HP QC). This tool also includes a Requirements module that is intended to be a repository of features that can be traced to tests and will allow us to measure test coverage. Hence, assuming that we already have regression tests in HP QC and have developed an RCT (Step 1), we follow other steps to assess coverage and identify gaps.

In Step 2 we review and analyze the descriptions of regression tests, in particular, we need to make sure that the test objective is clearly stated for each test, so we could better decide to which core feature and its applicable crosscutting concerns this test should be mapped.

In Step 3 we need to populate the inventory of RCT features in HP QC's Requirements module. We create a folder structure reflecting the application's breakdown by modules (defined in an RCT). Then in each module's folder, we create a list of requirements, both core features and crosscutting concerns, comprising that application module.

To better establish traceability between requirements and tests and better maintain the regression suite going forward, its structure in the test management tool should be exactly the same as the structure of requirements. Hence, before we start mapping tests to requirements, we perform refactoring of the existing regression suite structure as two steps. In Step 4 we create a new test repository structure in the Test Plan module of HP QC to be consistent with the structure of requirements. Then in Step 5 we populate it with the existing tests.

In Step 6 we establish traceability between tests and the features that they designed to validate. Most commercial test management tools provide this

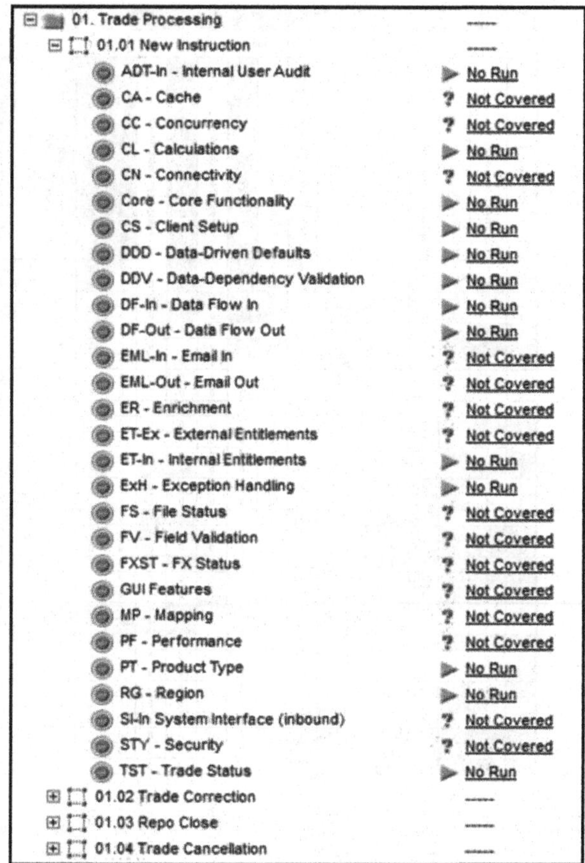

Fig. 15.9 Test coverage gaps shown in HP QC

capability. Note that a given test could be traced to several requirements (RCT features), and any RCT feature could be traced to more than one test. Because the accuracy of the traceability is critical to determining the assessment results, we need to engage the QA team members at the end of this step to carefully review the mapping.

When all tests are traced to their related requirements in HP QC, we can clearly see coverage gaps. As illustrated in Fig. 15.9, requirements that do not have any representation in the regression suite are listed as "Not Covered" and represent coverage gaps. Once we have identified gaps, we can perform Step 7 to measure test coverage. We begin this step by marking with a different color those RCT cells (see Fig. 15.10) that represent the gaps identified in HP QC and then calculate coverage measurements, first, for each core feature context (an RCT column) and, second, the average coverage for each module.

Requirements Composition Table

List of Concerns	01.01 New Instruction	01.02 Trade Correction	01.03 Repo Close	01.04 Trade Cancellation	01.05 Correction Filtering	01.06 Correction Allocation - External	01.07 Correction Allocation - Flip Action	01.08 In-flight Trade Processing	01.09 Manual Price Input	01.10 Finalize Pricing	01.11 Repo Offleg Publishing	01.12 Hide Errors	01.13 Missing Products Repair	01.14 Accrued Interest Batch	01.15 Override Errors	01.16 Account Resolution	01.17 Summarize Trade Counts	01.18 Missing Accrued Interest Repair	01.19 Rebalance Trade File	Core functionality only:
	01. Trade Processing																			
Core Functionality	1	1	1	1	1	1	1	1	1	1	1	1	1	1	1	1	1	1	1	57.9%
GUI Features	1	1	1	1	0	1	1	0	1	1	0	1	0	0	1	0	1	1	0	
Crosscuting Concerns																				
ET-In - Internal Entitlements	1	1	1	1	0	1	1	0	1	1	0	1	0	0	1	0	0	1	0	
ET-Ex - External Entitlements	1	1	1	1	0	1	0	0	0	0	0	0	0	0	0	0	0	0	0	
STY - Security	1	1	1	1	0	1	0	0	1	1	0	0	0	0	1	0	0	0	0	
CS - Client Setup	1	1	1	1	1	1	1	1	0	0	0	0	0	0	0	1	0	0	1	
PT - Product Type	1	1	1	1	1	1	1	1	0	0	1	0	0	0	0	0	0	1	1	
CST - Cash Status	0	0	0	0	0	0	0	0	0	0	0	0	0	0	0	0	0	0	0	
TST - Trade Status	1	1	1	1	1	1	1	1	0	0	1	1	0	0	0	0	0	0	1	
FXST - FX Status	1	1	1	1	0	0	0	0	0	0	0	0	0	0	0	0	0	0	0	
TPST - Template Status	0	0	0	0	0	0	0	0	0	0	0	0	0	0	0	0	0	0	0	
FS - File Status	1	1	1	1	1	1	1	0	0	0	0	0	0	0	0	0	0	0	0	
FV - Field Validation	1	1	1	1	1	1	1	1	0	0	0	1	1	0	1	0	0	1	0	
DDV - Data-Dependency Validation	1	1	1	1	0	0	0	0	0	0	0	0	0	0	0	0	0	0	0	
DDD - Data-Driven Defaults	1	1	1	1	0	0	0	0	0	0	0	0	0	0	0	0	0	0	0	
CL - Calculations	1	1	1	1	1	1	1	1	0	0	0	1	1	0	1	0	0	1	1	
ER - Enrichment	1	1	1	1	1	1	1	1	0	0	0	1	1	0	1	0	0	1	1	
MP - Mapping	1	1	1	1	0	0	0	0	0	0	0	0	0	0	0	0	0	0	0	
CC - Concurrency	1	1	1	1	1	1	1	1	0	0	0	1	0	0	1	0	0	0	0	
CN - Connectivity	1	1	1	1	0	1	1	0	0	0	0	0	0	0	0	0	0	0	0	
RG - Region	1	1	1	1	1	1	1	0	0	0	1	0	0	0	0	0	0	0	1	
DF-In - Data Flow In	1	1	1	1	1	1	1	1	0	1	1	1	1	0	1	1	1	1	0	
DF-Out - Data Flow Out	1	1	1	1	1	1	1	1	1	0	1	1	1	1	1	1	0	1	0	
SI-In System Interface In	1	1	1	1	0	0	1	0	0	0	0	0	0	1	0	0	0	1	0	
SI-Out - System Interface Out	0	0	0	0	0	0	0	0	0	1	0	0	0	0	0	0	0	0	0	
EML-In - Email In	1	0	0	0	0	0	0	0	0	0	0	0	0	0	0	0	0	0	0	
EML-Out - Email Out	1	1	1	1	1	0	0	0	0	0	0	0	0	0	0	1	0	0	0	
ADT-In - Internal User Audit	1	1	1	1	0	1	1	0	0	0	0	0	0	0	0	0	0	0	0	
ADT-Ex - External User Audit	0	0	0	0	0	0	0	0	0	0	0	0	0	0	0	0	0	0	0	
CA - Cache	1	1	1	1	1	1	1	1	0	0	0	0	0	0	0	0	0	0	0	
ExH - Exception Handling	1	1	1	1	1	1	1	1	0	0	0	0	0	0	0	0	0	0	1	
PF - Performance	1	1	1	1	1	1	1	1	0	0	0	0	0	0	0	0	0	0	0	
Covered Concerns:	13	14	6	9	3	5	2	0	1	0	3	0	2	0	0	0	2	0	0	Module average:
Total Concerns:	28	27	27	27	16	21	20	13	5	6	6	10	6	3	10	5	3	10	8	
Coverage %	46%	52%	22%	33%	19%	24%	10%	0%	20%	0%	50%	0%	33%	0%	0%	0%	67%	0%	0%	19.8%

Fig. 15.10 Presenting coverage gaps in an RCT

The benefit of capturing coverage results in an Excel document is that it allows us to easily calculate coverage as a ratio between the covered concerns and the total number of concerns in the context of a given core feature. After we calculate coverage for all core features, we can derive the average number for the entire module as illustrated in Fig. 15.10. Hence, to measure test coverage, we follow four steps:

(a) Calculate the sum of all applicable concerns for a given use case context. This number represents 100 % of concerns to be covered by tests.
(b) Subtract from the sum the number of colored cells—i.e., concerns not covered by tests. This will give us the number of covered concerns in each core feature context.
(c) Calculate for each core feature the ratio of covered concerns to the total number of concerns and present it as a core feature coverage percentage.

(d) Once test coverage is calculated for all core features in a given module, we can derive the average number for the entire model.

In Steps 8 and 9 the first assessment results should be reviewed, refined, and agreed with the QA team before we produce a final assessment report in Step 10. This step is discussed in detail in the next section.

Performing coverage assessment of existing regression tests can be a time-consuming task, where the effort is proportional to the size of the regression suite. An important factor is the clarity of the test specifications. Sometimes it is not immediately clear which feature a tester intended to validate when he/she designed a given test. Mapping such a test to its related features will require more time and effort. However, once all tests are analyzed and traced, the end-result will pay off—the team will have excellent visibility into the coverage gaps and can better decide on the strategy to close the gaps and evolve their regression suite further.

Finally, it is important to clarify that assessment of test coverage is not the same as evaluation of test-design completeness for individual requirements. For example, 100 % test coverage can be achieved by designing at least one test case for each of an application's features, yet most of the individual requirements, to be sufficiently validated, could still require additional test cases. Hence, this RCT technique is primarily intended to support our analysis from three perspectives:

1. Identifying test coverage gaps.
2. Providing testers with visibility into which requirements have more and which ones have less test coverage.
3. Helping testers understand which types of concerns they commonly miss in test designs.

Based on the results of this analysis, testers can make better decisions about how to evolve their regression suite further.

15.4.2 Presenting Assessment Results

The assessment results should be captured in an assessment report, which is an important deliverable of the RCT-based assessment and should be presented to the engagement stakeholders. The assessment report should include:

- Executive summary providing the engagement sponsors, objectives, and summarizing the assessment findings.
- Identified coverage gaps highlighted in the RCT cells (see Fig. 15.10).
- Charts representing the assessment results from different perspectives. Some examples are discussed in this section.
- Recommendations for a strategy to close the coverage gaps and the steps to implement it.

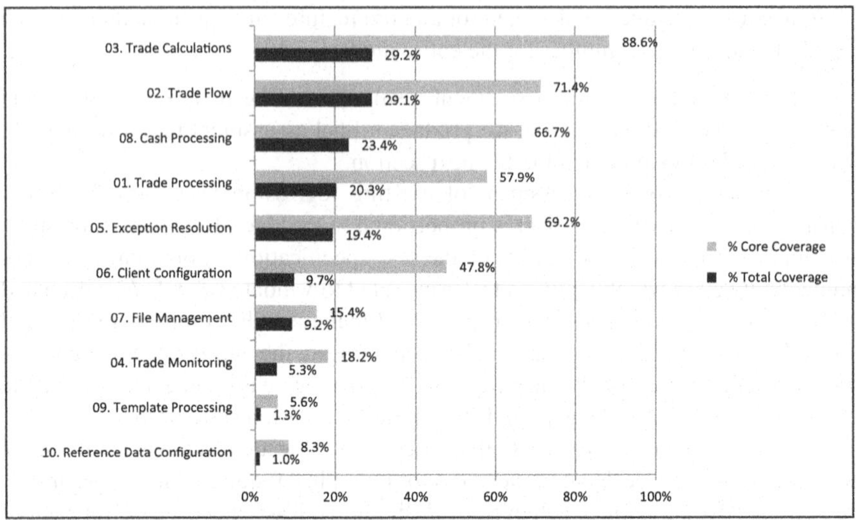

Fig. 15.11 Distribution of test coverage results by application modules

The charts representing the coverage measurements can be presented at two levels of detail—(a) at a module level for the entire application (Fig. 15.11) and (b) at a core feature level for individual modules (Fig. 15.12). In addition, a chart showing the coverage distribution by crosscuts (Fig. 15.13) can be produced as well. This chart can help testers understand which categories of crosscutting concerns they covered more and which ones they commonly overlook in testing. The charts we discuss below illustrate the assessment results for one of our example applications—the prime brokerage application.

As Fig. 15.11 shows, the results for each module are presented as a range between the core functionality coverage and the total coverage, i.e., the coverage provided for the entire set of requirements that includes both core functionality and crosscutting concerns. For example, the test coverage results for the module "01. Trade Processing" are shown as a range between 19.8 % representing the result for all concerns in the context of core features and 57.9 % representing the result for core functionality only, where both numbers are derived from the RCT as shown in Fig. 15.10. This is useful for the following reason. When we execute regression testing we always have limited time. This means that a project team should decide which of the software requirements are most important to validate; such a decision will determine the regression test scope. Commonly, validating core functionality is a minimal requirement for regression test coverage. In addition, the team might decide that some of the identified crosscutting concerns should also be included in the regression test scope. Thus, when assessing test coverage, we can present the results as a range between covering only the core functionality and covering a complete inventory of requirements, including all crosscutting concerns

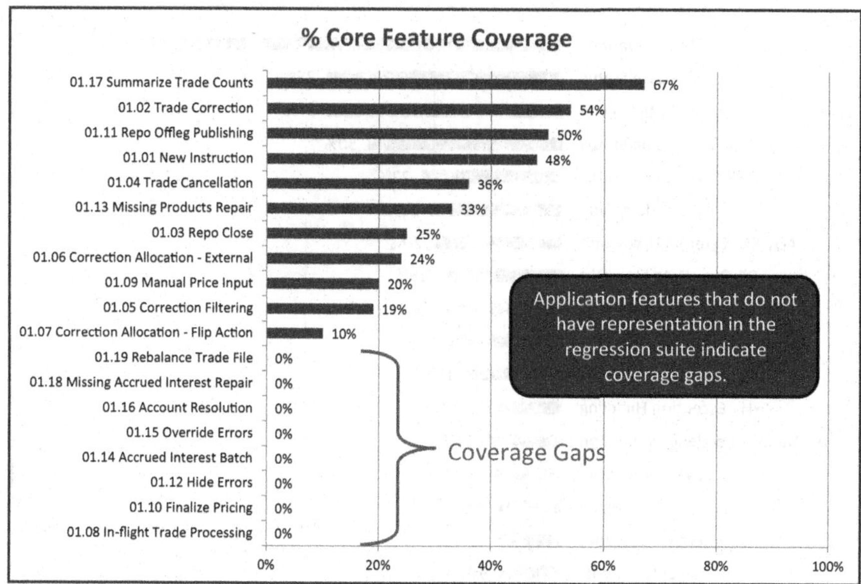

Fig. 15.12 Module "01. Trade Processing": distribution of coverage results by core features

(see Fig. 15.11). Then it will be up to the project team to decide how much regression test coverage is really necessary for their application.

Next, we present assessment results for individual application modules, which is a lower level of detail compared with the previous chart. It can provide better visibility and the project team can clearly see which core features are covered more and which ones represent coverage gaps in individual modules. Figure 15.12 shows such an example for the module "01. Trade Processing" of the prime brokerage application.

Finally, we can present the assessment results for the entire application from the crosscut perspective. This view can provide visibility into which categories of crosscuts are covered more and which ones represent coverage gaps as shown in Fig. 15.13. This finding can be especially interesting for testers, and it can help them understand what they commonly miss in testing when they do not use a list of crosscuts as a reference for designing tests and achieving better test coverage.

15.5 Lessons Learned

For the last 6 years the RCT technique has been implemented for over a dozen Wall Street projects at three global investment banks. These projects included equity, fixed income, and prime brokerage trading applications. There were three categories of sponsors of these engagements:

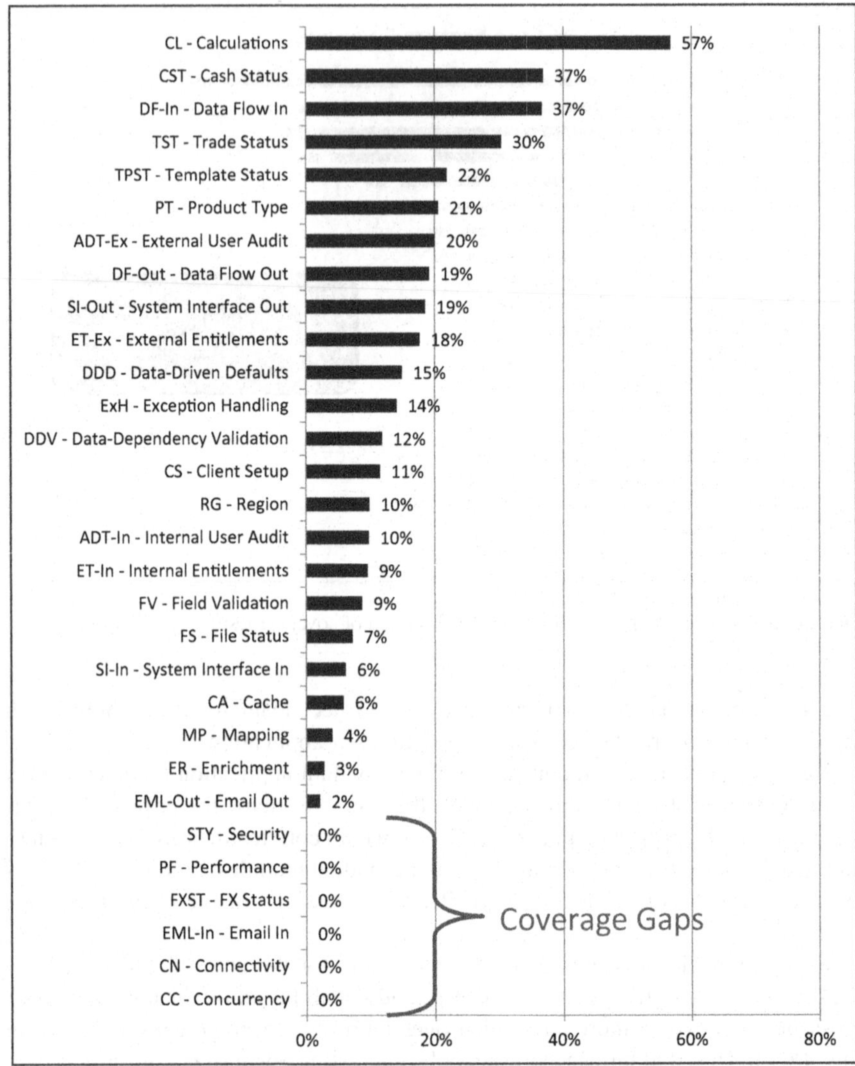

Fig. 15.13 Distribution of test coverage results by crosscutting concerns

1. **Developers** who needed to improve change impact analysis and better plan new releases
2. **Testers** who needed to assess coverage and identify gaps in their existing regression suites
3. **Business analysts**, hired for renovation projects, who needed a holistic view of the legacy system to be replaced with the new application

Although these engagements had different objectives, each needed a holistic view of an application's functionality and building an RCT proved to be an effective solution as indicated by testimonials from the team members who used the RCT technique:

- Scott, business product owner: "An RCT allows all project parties, from requirements analysis to delivery, to speak the same language."
- Chris, lead developer: "An RCT allows us to more comprehensively analyze the impact of system changes to improve our development estimates and test coverage."
- Mihir, QA lead: "An RCT provides a much more complete and structured view of the application functionality. It is very effective to analyze gaps in the existing regression suite and helps both developers and testers agree on and prioritize the scope of testing for new releases."

When an RCT is developed for a given application and first introduced to the entire project team, it usually presents some surprises; a few most common are the following:

Knowledge gaps. Commonly for complex applications, any particular team member may not have a complete knowledge and holistic view of the application functionality. Once an RCT has been developed, each developer or tester can clearly see the gaps in his or her knowledge of the application functionality. The discovery of these gaps sometimes comes as a big surprise.

Regression suite gaps. For critical applications, a QA team commonly develops over time a sizable suite of regression tests and uses it for testing new releases. However, the project team frequently does not have a complete understanding of the test coverage provided by the regression suite and, specifically, where the coverage gaps are. This is another issue of the knowledge gaps discussed above. Using an RCT to assess coverage and identify gaps in existing regression suites proved to be an effective solution [4]. In the projects observed by this author, the actual coverage was in the range from 20 % to 30 %, which was surprising to the teams and much below their prior estimates of the regression suite coverage.

Understanding the impact of changes. Commonly, prior to using an RCT to perform change impact analysis the first time, the author asks developers and testers to perform this task the way that they have always done it and compile a list of impacted application features. The team then conducts a formal change impact analysis session using the RCT. The team compares the result of the formal RCT-driven analysis with the initial list of impacted features. The RCT-driven analysis frequently shows a much more complete (up to 50 %) picture of the impact than does the initial list. Commonly, the initial list includes only core features and overlooks crosscutting concerns impacted by changes. Such a comparison is a good illustration of the RCT technique's effectiveness and can help the team to see its benefits.

However, the RCT benefits do not come for free. Even though developing an RCT is a relatively small effort, it still requires obtaining commitments from and the involvement of application SMEs, which can be challenging when, for example, a project is under delivery time pressure or SMEs do not believe in RCT benefits.

Second, once an RCT has been developed, it must be kept consistent with the application functionality and be maintained through releases. This presents a small but necessary overhead for a project team. To better maintain an RCT, this task should be discussed and agreed to at an engagement kick off meeting where a future RCT owner should also be assigned. In the author's projects, this role was usually given either to a lead business analyst or, in the absence of such a party within the project team, to a lead QA analyst.

15.6 Conclusion and Future Work

Despite the fact that AORE methods have been around for at least a decade, they remain little known to most practitioners in the software industry. This chapter describes an analysis artifact introduced in AORE called the *Requirements Composition Table*. An RCT captures a holistic and structured view of an application's functionality which provides an effective common frame of reference for all project team parties—the product owner, the developers, and the testers. This chapter explained the RCT concept and discussed the steps to produce an RCT.

RCT can support a number of project tasks and can help us resolve some important practical issues. Two of them, very common to software projects, were discussed in this chapter. We showed how to use RCT to perform change impact analysis for new releases and how it can help us assess test coverage and identify gaps in existing regression test suites.

The future work will focus on developing an RCT at multiple levels of detail. The RCT view described in this chapter can be qualified as the main floor plan. In this view, crosscutting concerns represent generic categories, for example, Product Type, Transaction Data Flow, System Interface, etc. To support more detailed analysis, such categories of concerns can be elaborated and lower level views, I call them "second floor plans", can be produced separately for each generic crosscutting concern to complement the main view.

For example, we can elaborate the System Interfaces concern in RCT's second floor plan and replace it with a list of the actual external systems. Then each interface to external systems can be analyzed as a crosscutting concern and its impact on core features of a given application can be captured in the second floor plan. Such a second floor plan can benefit, in particular, testers when they need to plan end-to-end testing for a release. Once we performed change impact analysis and captured results in both levels of the RCT, the main floor plan will show us the scope of functional testing of a given application, and the second floor plan will show us the scope of end-to-end testing from the perspective of external applications.

A.1 Descriptions of Common Crosscutting Concerns (Table A.1)

Table A.1 Descriptions of crosscutting concerns

Crosscutting Concerns Common to Investment Banking Applications	
Concern Category	**Concern Description**
ET - Entitlements	This concern relates to different user access privileges (roles) and how they impact the behavior of core features. Examples of User Roles: Front Office Trader, Trade Support, Sales, Controllers
STY - Security	This concern relates to requirements to control user access to various client accounts.
CS - Client Setup	This concern is used to model the dependency of core feature behavior on the client profile, client rules, etc.
PT - Product Type	This concern relates to different product types being processed by core features. A list of products can include: Equity, Treasuries, Options, Repo, FX Products, CDS, MBS, etc.
TST - Trade Status	This concern relates to the trade statuses comprising the trade lifecycle. Examples: New, Validated, Sent, Received, Canceled, etc.
OST - Order Status	This concern relates to the order statuses comprising the order lifecycle. Examples: New, Accepted, Executed, Booked, Completed, etc.
FV - Field Validation	This concern relates to validating individual data entry fields.
DDV - Data-Dependency Validation	This concern relates to validating field value combinations. It also includes validation of constrains, for example, a currency cannot be make inactive if it has outstanding orders/trades.
DDD - Data-Driven Defaults	This concern relates to populating field default values based on another field value.
CL - Calculations	This concern represents various "behind-the-screen" calculations that are executed in the context of core features.
ER - Enrichment	This concern is commonly used in prime brokerage applications and relates to any data enrichment rules being applied to data coming from external clients, e.g., hedge funds.
CC - Concurrency	This concern relates to simultaneous data manipulation by more than one user. For example, both users see the same order. User 1 tries to modify this order, whereas User 2 tries to execute this order.
CN - Connectivity	This concern relates to the broken architecture of an application where the front-end can be disconnected from the back-end and that might change the behavior of the impacted core features. Commonly, front-office trading systems implement this functionality.
RG - Region	This concern relates to global financial applications that are used in different regions. Some core features may behave differently depending on the region where they are used. Regions can include: Europe, Americas, Asia.
DF-In - Data Flow In	This concern addresses the core feature behavior when it takes data in from another core feature of the same application.
DF-Out - Data Flow Out	This concern addresses the core feature behavior when it generates data used by other core features of the same application.
SI-In - System Interface In	This concern relates to receiving [transaction] data from external applications and is used to indicate which of the core features of a given application consume such data. Using this concern category can help a team to better analyze the impact of changes and better plan E2E testing.
SI-Out - System Interface Out	This concern relates to sending [transaction] data from core features of a given application to external applications. Using this concern category can help a team to better analyze the impact of changes and better plan E2E testing.
TVH - Trade Version History	Commonly, trading applications capture trade version history and allow users to audit and see what actions were applied to a given trade to date.
CA - Cache	Some static data on the back end can change during a day and may not be stored in the memory cash and immediately available for the front-end users. To retrieve this data, the user should explicitly refresh cache; after this action core features could process the latest values of static data.
PF - Performance	This concern relates to performance requirements applied to some core features.

References

1. A. Rashid, A. Moreira, J. Araújo, Modularization and composition of aspectual requirements, in *Proceedings of 2nd International Conference on Aspect-Oriented Software Development (AOSD)* (ACM, 2003), pp. 11–20
2. Y. Chernak, Requirements composition table explained, in *Proceedings of the 20th IEEE International Requirements Engineering Conference* (IEEE Computer Society, 2012), pp. 273–278
3. Y. Chernak, Building a foundation for structured requirements. Part 1, in *Better Software*, Jan 2009, pp. 90–96
4. Y. Chernak, Mind the gap: using a requirements composition table to assess test coverage, in *Better Software*, Mar 2008, pp. 38–44
5. A. Rashid, P. Sawyer, A. Moreira, J. Araújo, Early aspects: a model for aspect-oriented requirements engineering, in *Proceedings of IEEE Joint International Conference on Requirements Engineering (RE)* (IEEE Computer Society, 2002), pp. 199–202
6. L. Rosenhainer, Identifying crosscutting concerns in requirements specifications, in *Proceedings of the Aspect-Oriented Requirements Engineering and Architecture Design Workshop*, Vancouver, Canada, 24–28 Oct 2004
7. O. Gotel, A. Finkelstein, An analysis of the requirements traceability problem, in *Proceedings of the First International Conference on Requirements Engineering*, 1994, pp. 94–101
8. E. Baniassad, P. Clements, J. Araújo et al., Discovering early aspects. IEEE Softw. **23**(1), 61–69 (2006)
9. G. Kotonya, I. Sommerville, *Requirements Engineering* (Wiley, New York, NY, 2003)
10. K. Wiegers, *Software Requirements* (Microsoft Press, Redmond, WA, 2003)
11. A. Aurum, C. Wohlin, *Engineering and Managing Software Requirements* (Springer, Heidelberg, 2005)
12. B. Berenbach, D. Paulish, J. Kazmeier, A. Rudorfer, *Software & Systems Requirements Engineering: In Practice* (McGraw Hill, New York, NY, 2009)
13. H. Kabaili, R.K. Keller, R.A. Lustman, Change impact model encompassing ripple effect and regression testing, in *Proceedings of the Fifth International Workshop on Quantitative Approaches in Object-Oriented Software Engineering*, Budapest, Hungary, 2001, pp. 25–33

Chapter 16
Experience Report: AORE in Slot Machines

Arturo Zambrano, Johan Fabry, and Silvia Gordillo

Abstract In the context of an industrial project in the domain of slot machines, we needed to perform Aspect-Oriented Requirements Engineering, with a special emphasis on dependencies and interactions among concerns. The critical importance of interactions in this domain demanded explicit and detailed documentation of all interactions. We evaluated two AORE approaches: Theme/Doc and MDSOCRE, to establish their applicability in our setting. In this work we report on our experience, showing successful uses of both approaches and also where they fall short. To address these limitations, we have proposed some enhancements for both approaches and we present them here as well.

16.1 Introduction

To have Aspect-Oriented Requirements Engineering (AORE) gain the acceptance of the software development industry and become a mainstream practice for requirement engineering, it is necessary to demonstrate its power against industrial problems. This work is intended to be a contribution in that direction.

In the context of an industrial project we are re-implementing the software that runs on the casino gambling device best known as a slot machine (SM). Due to previous experience with this software, we know that there are an important amount of crosscutting concerns in slot machine applications. Moreover, many of these

A. Zambrano (✉) · S. Gordillo
LIFIA, Facultad de Informática, Universidad Nacional de Plata, 50 y 115 La Plata, Argentina
e-mail: arturo@lifia.info.unlp.edu.ar; gordillo@lifia.info.unlp.edu.ar

J. Fabry
Pleiad Lab, DCC, Universidad de Chile, Blanco Encalada 2120, Santiago,
Chile. Partially funded by FONDECYT project 1090083
e-mail: jfabry@dcc.uchile.cl

A. Moreira et al. (eds.), *Aspect-Oriented Requirements Engineering*, 317
DOI 10.1007/978-3-642-38640-4_16, © Springer-Verlag Berlin Heidelberg 2013

concerns interact with each other. We therefore have opted to use Aspect-Oriented Software Development in our new implementation.

Being aware of the critical importance of interactions in this domain, we have focused early in the development cycle, i.e., in the AORE phase, on interaction modeling. Our specific objective for this step is to document all interactions explicitly. This information would then be used later in the design and implementation phases. We therefore require the result of the modeling process to be a consistent model of the requirements, containing detailed and explicit interactions. To accomplish this, we needed to be able to rely on expressive mechanisms in the selected modeling techniques for this phase. To establish their suitability to our needs, we therefore performed an evaluation of two existing AORE approaches.

We elected to evaluate performing requirements engineering using both the Theme/Doc approach [2] and Multidimensional Separation of Concerns for Requirements Engineering (MDSOCRE) [7], focusing on how these allow us to express and document aspectual dependencies and interactions. The choice of these two approaches was mainly based on our perception of their maturity and of their acceptance in the AORE community, the latter as reflected by their publication record.

In this text we report on our experiences evaluating the above two approaches, and include proposals for extending them where they fall short. Our evaluation has been reported in more detail in [13]. In this chapter, we focus on the more salient points of the evaluation and add our proposals for extension. Briefly put, our evaluation has shown that both of the approaches we evaluated enable us to express the requirements, but neither of them satisfies our needs with regard to the specifications of interactions. We were however able to extend both approaches such that these limitations were overcome.

This chapter is organized as follows: Sect. 16.2 characterizes the slot machine domain, its concerns, and requirements. In Sect. 16.3 we present the results of applying the two AORE approaches to the SM domain, including report of their shortcomings and proposals for extensions. Section 16.4 presents the conclusions for our work.

16.2 Requirements for Slots Machines

A slot machine (SM) is a gambling device. It has five reels that spin when a *play* button is pressed. A SM includes some means for entering money, which is mapped to credits. The player bets an amount of credits on each play, the SM randomly selects the displayed symbol for each reel, and pays the corresponding prize, if any. Credits can be extracted (called a *cashout*) as coins, tickets, or electronic transfers.

Requirements for the SM domain are defined in different documents: Regulations (for each jurisdiction), standards (documents released by certification laboratories) and protocol specifications (technical documents for interoperability). These are written by different stakeholders, with diverse interests and backgrounds. This results in a large set of documents using multiple terms for describing the same object, action, or event. Furthermore, in some cases it is necessary to complement and normalize different sources referring to the same topic. For instance, consider the case of *Error Conditions*, which are treated by both the Nevada regulations [8] and the GLI standard [6]; some of the conditions are specified by the regulations match, but others are defined by just one of them.

A notable characteristic of communication protocol requirements, which has an impact on requirements modeling, is that they are divided in topics and that part of the communication functionality is optional. As we will see later, these optional requirements are the source of one of the aspectual interactions we need to deal with.

16.2.1 Crosscutting Concerns in the Slot Machine Domain

Based on our experience in the domain, we organized the requirements as follows, where Game is a base concern and the rest are crosscutting concerns.[1] As the domain is complex, there may be other possible concern decompositions. We choose this one because, according to our experience and observations, it properly modularizes the different required features of slot machines and shows the interactions that are at the core of this evaluation.

Game: This is the basic logic of a gambling device at a casino. The user can enter credits into the machine and then play. The output is determined randomly and when the player wins, he is awarded an amount of credits.

Metering: This refers to a set of (hundreds of) counters that are used to audit the activity of the game. For instance, there are meters that count the number of plays, the total amount bet, total won, error condition occurrences, etc.

Program Resumption: Requirements in this concern determine how the machine should behave after a power outage, specifying which data and state need to be recovered.

Game Recall: This refers to the information that must be available about the current and previous plays, in order to solve any dispute with players.

Error Conditions Under certain circumstances, the game should detect error conditions and behave accordingly. This concern defines what are considered error conditions and how the game must react to them.

Communications The SM is connected to a reporting system (RS). This concern defines the kinds of data, the format, and when data must be exchanged between the SM and RS. Several communication protocols with similar functionality exist. In this work we will refer to the most widely used protocols in the SM industry: *Game to Server protocol* (G2S) and *Proprietary Communication Protocol* (PCP[2]).

[1] We use the terms *Base* and *crosscutting concerns* as usual in the AOSD community.

[2] Licensing issues prevent us to use the real protocol name and disclosing implementation details.

Demo The demo concern contains the requirements specifying how the game behaves in this mode. Playing the game in demo allows testing hardware and software works, simulating events such as entering money or winning a prize.

16.2.2 Interactions in the Slot Machine Domain

We based our investigation, and therefore this discussion, on the AOSD-Europe technical report that gives an overview on aspect interactions [11]. In this report, the authors classify aspect interactions into dependency, conflict, mutex (mutual exclusion), and reinforcement. Dependency is the case where one aspect explicitly needs another to work correctly. A conflict between two aspects happens when they work correctly in isolation, but the presence of both at the same time negatively influences the behavior of the system. A mutual exclusion (mutex for short) occurs when two aspects implement the same functionality, but only one of them can be used at a time. Reinforcement is a positive interaction where an aspect influences the correct working of another, allowing it to provide extended functionality. Note that, even though the consequence of mutex and conflict are the same (just one of the conflicting aspects can be active at a time), there is a semantic difference: mutex applies to aspects that implement similar behavior, while conflict is more general and applies to any kind of incompatibility between aspects. We found this classification to match the kinds of interactions we observed in the SM domain.

For example, in the SM domain, there is a conflict between the *Demo* and *Meters* concerns, since *Meters* works correctly without *Demo*, but if *Demo* mode is active, activity in the machine must not be counted by *Meters*. An example of mutex is in the communication protocols: it is forbidden to have two protocols providing the same functionality at the same time. A dependency example is the relationship between *Communications* and *Meters*; the protocol needs to communicate the status of the SM, which is in part represented by the meters. Finally, a reinforcement is a positive interaction, for instance between *Error Conditions* and *Communications* concerns (Proprietary Protocol and G2S Protocol). The existence of error condition detection enables communication protocols to provide "extra" functionality, in this case real time error condition reporting.

Understanding how concerns interact with each other is key information that needs to be passed to designers and programmers. For example, in the case of a dependency the dependent concern will be affected by design decisions on the other concern. On the other hand, if there is a mutex relationship, architectural mechanisms should be provided to ensure that both aspects will not be active at the same time.

Considering the concern division and the associated requirements, we have deduced the relationships between different concerns and identified their

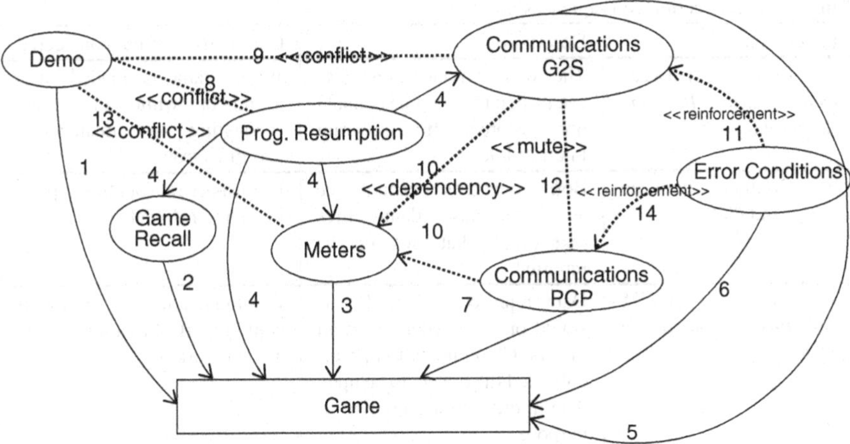

Fig. 16.1 Concern interactions. Regular *arrows* indicate crosscutting; *dashed arrows* indicate interactions between concerns, tagged with UML-like stereotypes

interactions, as shown in Fig. 16.1. The notation in this figure is an ad hoc mechanism to analyze the relationships between concerns that we will try to model in the following sections using well-known AORE approaches. The base concern (Game) is depicted by a box and crosscutting concerns by ovals. Relationships 1–7 are crosscutting (solid arrows). For each, there is a crosscutting concern where one or more requirements cut across several requirements on the base requirement (where the arrow ends). For example, consider the relationship between *Error Conditions* and *Game*, where the behavior associated with error conditions needs to be woven into the game behavior. Requirements in *Game* that could raise an error condition vary: a bill inserted, the printer is out of paper, tilt, a door opened, etc.

In Fig. 16.1, relationships 8–14 are interactions, which are depicted by dotted lines. Dependency and reinforcement are asymmetric, so the arrowhead indicates the direction of the relationship, while mutex and conflict are symmetric, so no arrowhead is used. Table 16.1 describes them and presents potential consequences of not considering interactions during the design/implementation phases. We use an informal notation here and will later evaluate how different AORE approaches perform while trying to model such information more formally.

16.2.3 Selected Requirements

In this text, due to space limitations, we only use three concerns to illustrate our work. We focus on the crosscutting relationship between Meters and Game, and the *dependency* of G2S on Meters. Table 16.2 presents an extract of the requirements for these concerns. We refer to [13] for a more complete treatment.

Table 16.1 Interaction consequences

Interaction	Description	Consequence if not considered
8. Conflict between *Demo* and *Program Resumption*	The demo mode fires *fake* events that must not be counted nor restored after program interruption.	Wrong data is loaded after a reboot while in Demo, accounting mismatches, auditing errors.
9. Conflict between *Demo* and *G2S*	Both concerns cannot be active, because demo fires fake events that must not be reported.	Inconsistent accounting reports including *fake* data.
10. Dependency of *G2S* and *Prop. Protocol* on *Meters*	Data reported to the RS is stored or can be derived from meters. Communication protocols need the meters to be up to date in order to accomplish its purpose.	Communication protocols could report old data if meters are not working.
11. Reinforcement of *G2S* with *Error Conditions*	Parts of the G2S protocol are not mandatory for specific instances. When error conditions are tracked in the game, additional behavior is made available in G2S, such as real time event reporting.	Real time events are not reported when available. Casino operator cannot efficiently react to situations such as coin-tilt, hand-pay, and stacker full.
12. Mutex between *G2S* and *Proprietary Protocol*	There is overlapping functionality defined in the requirements of both protocols. Therefore, they cannot be active at the same time.	Overlapping features of both can interfere. For example, using both to keep the time in sync between the SM and the RS may render the time of the SM inconsistent.
13. Conflict between *Demo* and *Meters*	Data generated during demo mode must not affect meter values.	Demo plays may result in inconsistent accounting information if they are counted by the meters.
14. Reinforcement of *Prop. Protocol* with *Error Conditions*	Similar to 11.	Similar to 11.

16.3 Application of AORE

In order to deal with requirements and concerns in the SM domain, we applied two well-known AORE approaches: Theme/Doc and MDSOCRE. This resulted in the identification of some limitations and proposed extensions. We discuss this here, first focusing on Theme/Doc and then on MDSOCRE.

Table 16.2 Requirements for Game, Meters, and G2S concerns

	Game		
GM-1	Slot machines have 5 reels.	GM-4	A slot machine has one or more devices for entering money.
GM-2	Reels spin when play button is pressed.	GM-5	As money is inserted credits are "assigned" to the player.
GM-3	Prizes are awarded according to a pay table.	GM-6	A slot machine must provide some means for cashing the credits out. It could be a ticket printer or a coin hopper.
	Meters		
M-1	Credit meter: shall at all times indicate all credits or cash available for the player to wager or cashout.	M-3	Accounting Meters: *Coin In*: [...] a meter that accumulates the total value of all wagers [...]. *Gamesplayed*: accumulates the number of games played; since power reset, since door close and since game initialization.
M-2	Credit Meter Incrementing: The value of every prize (at the end of a game) shall be added to the player's credit meter [....]. The credit meter shall also increment with the value of all valid coins, tokens [..].	M-4	Meters should be updated upon occurrence of any event that must be counted, including: play, cashout, bill in, coin in.
M-5	G2S meters are: *gamesSinceInitCn* Number of games since initialization. *WonCnt*: Number of primary games won by the player. *LostCnt*: Number of primary games lost by the player.		
	Communication: G2S		
G2S-1	The G2S protocol is designed to communicate information between an SM and one or more host systems.	G2S-4	The device can generate an event in a unsolicited manner or in response to a host command
G2S-2	Meter information can be queried by a host in real time, or a host may set a periodic subscription to cause the SM to send selected meters[..]	G2S-5	Current time stamp can be set by the host.
G2S-3	Information provided by the SM is used for audit purposes.	G2S-6	Command GetGameRecallLog is used by a host to request the contents of a transaction log of last plays from a SM.

16.3.1 Application of Theme/Doc

Theme/Doc [1] is the requirement analysis part of the Theme approach [2, 5]. In Theme/Doc, requirements are organized into concerns called *themes*. Themes can be defined through an initial set of domain-specific actions or concepts, others may be recurring typical concerns: persistence, logging, etc.

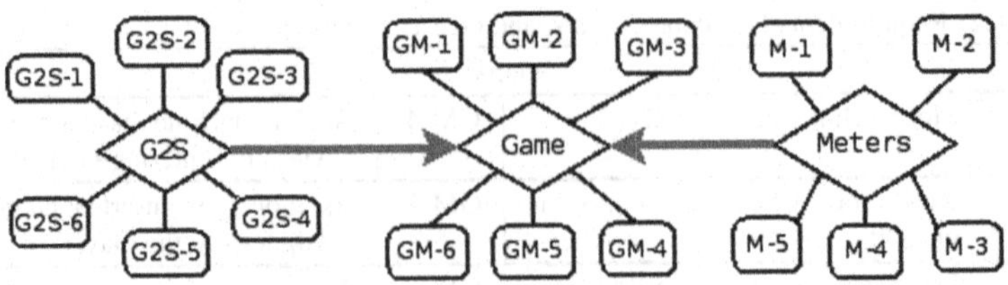

Fig. 16.2 *Game*, *Meters*, and *G2S* concerns expressed using the Theme/Doc notation

In Theme/Doc a requirement is attached to a theme if the name of the theme appears in the requirement. In other words, Theme/Doc relies on the name-based analysis of actions in requirements to relate them to themes. In our study we did not strictly follow this rule, as in our setting it is error prone due to ambiguities (see Sect. 16.3.1.2). Instead, we use the concerns we identified in Sect. 16.2.1 as themes.

Ideally, each requirement should belong to one theme, but chances are that some of them are shared among themes, i.e., crosscutting. In Theme/Doc, a shared requirement is considered crosscutting if: (1) the requirement cannot be split in order to avoid tangling, (2) one of the themes dominates the requirement, (3) the dominant theme is triggered by events in the base theme, and (4) the triggered theme is externally fired in multiple situations [5]. Note that for Theme/Doc, the term *dominant* refers to the potentially crosscutting concern, *i.e.,* which contains the requirement that cuts across other requirements.

An important feature of Theme/Doc is its visual support through diagrams. In Theme/Doc views, requirements are represented by rounded boxes, and they are organized around themes, which are depicted by diamonds. When a crosscutting theme exists, a gray arrow is drawn from the theme that crosscuts (*i.e., the aspect*) to the theme that is being cut across (*i.e., the base*). Consider, for example, Fig. 16.2, where *Game*, *Meters*, and *G2S* concerns are represented along with their requirements and crosscutting relationships.

16.3.1.1 Successful Uses of Theme/Doc

As shown in Fig. 16.2, the graphical approach of Theme/Doc makes it easy to read the relationships between requirements and themes. Each theme can be easily identified along with its associated requirements. The four steps to check for crosscutting helped us to confirm which are the crosscutting concerns. In the resulting diagrams, the crosscutting relationships are reasonably documented, enabling us to easily identify which concern is playing the base and/or the aspectual role. Furthermore, it is possible to express all the crosscutting relationships shown in Fig. 16.1, although we cannot include them here due to space limitations.

16.3.1.2 Limitations of Theme/Doc

In our evaluation, we encountered the following limitations of Theme/Doc.

Granularity: As explained before, gray arrows denote crosscutting. As each concern potentially contains many requirements, it is difficult to discern which specific requirement of the crosscutting theme affects which requirements on the base theme. Consider, for example, Fig. 16.2 and the crosscutting relationship between *Meters* and *Game*; here, it is not possible to know which requirement in *Meters* is crosscutting. Furthermore, it is not possible to know which specific requirements in *Game* are affected as the result of the crosscutting. Where possible, it is desirable to pass that information to the design phase, so that base and aspectual components can be properly designed. In fact, this information is available during the analysis phase—identification of crosscutting themes—of Theme/Doc, but it is not made explicit.

Expressing Interactions: In Fig. 16.1 we show different examples of interactions between aspectual concerns for requirements. If we consider Fig. 16.2 we can however see that the interactions explained in Sect. 16.2.2 are missing. This is because Theme/Doc lacks support for expressing interactions. For instance, missing in Fig. 16.2 is a dependency of *G2S* on *Meters*. This information is however crucial: Multiple perspectives of a system (*themes* in this case) need to be combined to form a system [12]. We require the dependency information to select a sound set of themes for a system. For example, it is not possible to build an SM with *G2S* support but lacking *Meters*. This is because *G2S* requires the existence of *Meters* to provide its own functionality. The same happens with *conflicts*, for instance, between *Demo* and *Meters*. It is critical to know that architectural or design mechanisms need to be included to avoid the activation of both concerns at the same time. The reinforcement from *Error Conditions* to *G2S* is also missing. Documenting it signals that an optional part of G2S is active when *Error Conditions* are available.

Adaptability to our case study requirements: In our case study there is no single requirements specification unifying all the sources, and we are faced with significant ambiguity. This is in contrast to an ideal requirements specification that is complete, unambiguous, verifiable, consistent, modifiable, and traceable [10]. This variety of sources results not only in synonyms being used in different documents, but also in equivalent ideas—full sentences—explained in different ways. There are complete key ideas, concepts, or interactions that are expressed using different vocabulary and style. Although we might consider our case as being exceptional, it is based on requirements from a real-world problem and it is worthwhile to examine the impact of this.

The ambiguity we face affects the mechanism proposed in Theme/Doc to assign requirements to themes, and to identify potential crosscutting themes. In the most ambiguous case, the requirement and the theme could be related by implied actions: actions that are activated as a consequence of other actions [4]. Unfortunately, the ambiguities we found cannot be solved by using a synonym dictionary as proposed in [2].

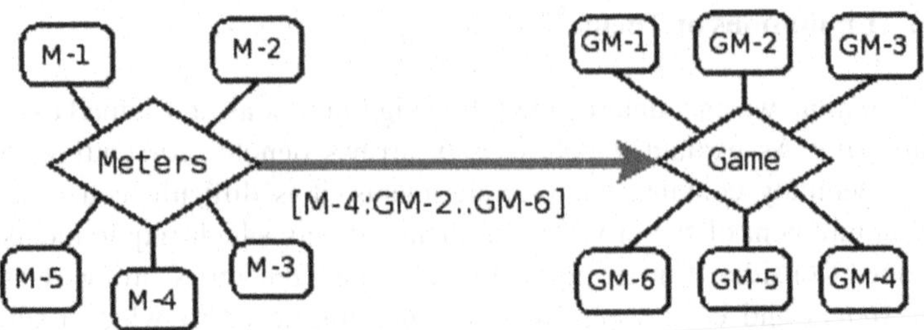

Fig. 16.3 Quantification labels applied to the crosscutting relationship between Meters and Game concerns

We consider two options to resolve ambiguities. The first one is to rewrite all the requirements, normalizing them to use the same vocabulary; the second one is to use domain knowledge to associate requirements to the corresponding themes. Due to the large number of requirements and presence of multiple sources, only the second option is feasible, and moreover is a well-known practice [3, 7].

As a consequence of doing a domain knowledge-based analysis of our requirements, new requirements that are more suitable for understanding concern relationships, may appear. This is similar to the approach proposed by Bar-On et al. [4], where implied actions are used to generate new *derived requirements*.

16.3.1.3 Extensions to Theme/Doc

Quantification Labels for Granularity. In order to tackle the granularity problem, we introduce the concept of *quantification labels*, which are tags that allow us to clearly specify which requirements participate in a crosscutting relationship (and are also permitted in the interaction relationships we introduce below). A quantification label is an expression referring to a *base concern* and a *crosscutting concern*. Figure 16.3 shows an example where the *Meters* concern crosscuts the *Game* concern; we can see here that requirement M-4 crosscuts requirements GM-2 to GM-6.

Quantification labels allow us to specify which requirements are involved in a given crosscutting (and interaction) relationship, from both sides: the crosscutting concern and the base concern. It has two parts separated by a colon:

Crosscutting requirements IDs: This is a list, a range, or the keyword *all* that indicates which requirements are crosscutting in the concern where the arrow has its origin.

Base concern requirements IDs: This is a list, a range, or the keyword *all* that indicates which requirements are the requirements affected by the crosscut concern (the destination of the arrow).

Interaction Relationships. In order to properly express the interactions between concerns, we added a new kind of relationship to Theme/Doc. The new interaction relationship is denoted using a dashed arrow. The arrow also has a label indicating

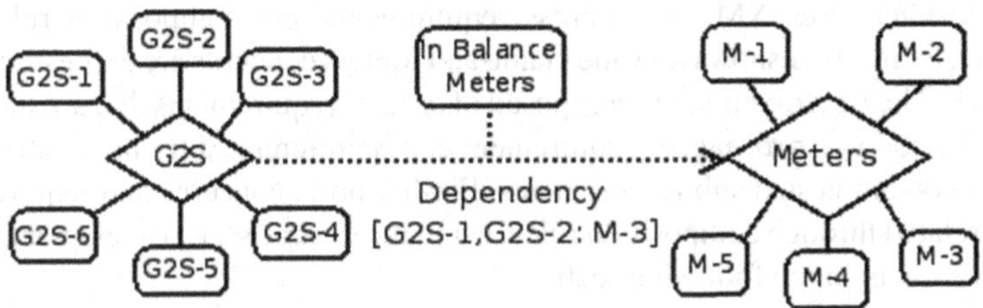

Fig. 16.4 Dependency of G2S concern on Meters concern

the kind of interaction. Quantification labels can be used along with interaction relationships; this allows to clearly state the requirements interacting for each concern. The interaction relationship can be symmetrical (mutex or conflict) or directional (dependency and reinforcement).

Figure 16.4 shows a dependency between the *G2S* concern, which needs the information stored by the *Meters* concern. The dotted line indicates the interaction, which in this case is directional. Quantification labels are also included to indicate the requirements participating in the interaction. The "In Balance Meters" label is a derived requirement, which we explain below.

Ambiguity of Requirements. In our setting, requirements disambiguation needs to be performed by domain experts. The Theme/Doc methodology establishes specific steps for requirements processing (e.g., split, add, and remove) [2]. We propose to add a dedicated step that performs disambiguation before performing the existing processing steps. As a result, during this step new (derived) requirements may arise as shown in Fig. 16.4. In this case the derived requirement states that meters need to be updated in consistent sets, so that they are reported to the accounting reporting system when they are in balance. This derived requirement is represented by the *In Balance Meters* label in Fig. 16.4.

16.3.2 Application of MDSOCRE

MDSOCRE (Multidimensional Separation of Concerns in Requirements Engineering) is the evolution of a line of AORE approaches such as PreView and ARCaDe [9]. MDSOCRE treats the concerns in a uniform fashion, regardless of the nature of the requirement (functional or nonfunctional). It makes it possible for the requirement engineer to choose a subset of requirements to observe the influences on each other and to analyze crosscutting behavior.

In contrast to Theme, MDSOCRE does not provide visualization facilities. Conflicts referring to contradictory concerns are detected and handled using contribution matrices. Conflicts in MDSOCRE differ slightly from our definition in Sect. 16.2.2 (taken from [11]). In our case, concerns are not a subject of negotiation, as all are required by some standard or regulation. We must however check that at runtime, conflicting concerns are not simultaneously active.

MDSOCRE uses XML to express requirements and composition rules. For example, listing 16.1 shows how the Game and Meters concerns are expressed in this approach. The `Concern` tag is composed of several requirements that are indicated by the `Requirement` tag. A requirement can be referenced by its identifier (*id*) and can contain nested sub-requirements. Furthermore, concerns and requirements can be related through composition rules, using the `Composition` element, which we will explain in the following section.

Listing 16.1: Concerns written using MDSOCRE

```
<Concern name="Game">
  <Requirement id="1"> A slot machines has 5 reels. </Requirement>
  <Requirement id="2"> Reels spin when the play button is pressed.</
       Requirement>
  <Requirement id="3"> Prizes are awarded according to a pay table.
  </Requirement>
  <Requirement id="4"> A slot machine has one or more devices for entering
       money. </Requirement>
  <Requirement id="5"> As money is inserted credits are "assigned" to the
       player. </Requirement>
  <Requirement id="6"> A slot machine must provide means for cashing the
       credits out.</Requirement>
</Concern>
<Concern name="Meters">
   <Requirement id="1"> Credit meter: shall at all times indicate all credits
or cash available for the player to wager or cashout
 </Requirement>
  <Requirement id="2"> Credit Meter Incrementing: The value of every
prize [...futher details omitted ... ]
  </Requirement>
  <Requirement id="3"> Accounting Meters: Coin In: a meter that
accumulates the total value of all wagers [... omitted ...]. </Requirement>
   <Requirement id="4"> Meters should be updated upon occurrence of any event
        that must be counted, including: play, cashout, bill in, coin in.
 </Requirement>
</Concern>
```

16.3.2.1 Successful Uses of MDSOCRE

Listing 16.2: Compositions written using MDSOCRE

```
<Composition>
 <Requirement concern="Meters" id="4">
   <Constraint action="enforce" operator="on">
         <Requirement concern="Game" id="3,4,5,6" />
   </Constraint>
   <Outcome action="fulfilled"/>
 </Requirement>
</Composition>
```

Composition rules are used to express crosscutting relationships. Listing 16.2 shows a composition rule, consisting of a `Constraint` tag that defines how the base requirements are constrained by aspectual requirements. The `Constraint` tag has *actions*, *operators*, and *outcome* elements used to express in detail how the base is affected. The action and operator tags informally describe how the base concern is constrained, imposing conditions in the composition. We shall use these in Sects. 16.3.2.2 and 16.3.2.3, for more detailed information about them we refer to [7].

The composition rule in Listing. 16.2 shows how the *Meters* concern crosscuts the *Game* concern. In this example we have used the outcome action "fulfilled," because there is no other set of requirements to be satisfied.

The granularity of the approach is adequate for our case study, since it is possible to clearly state which requirements are affected. The flexibility provided by the parametrized `Constraint` tag helps to express different variants of crosscutting relationships. For example, we combine actions and operators to document the interactions. We use the action *ensure* and the operator *with* to represent a *Dependency* interaction. This follows the informal definition by Moreira et al. [7] that says that a certain condition for a requirement that is needed actually exists. We use the action *provide* and the operator *for* for *Reinforcement*, as it specifies additional features to a set of concern requirements.

16.3.2.2 Limitations of MDSOCRE

No Support for Interactions. The actions and operators included in the composition rules only describe relationships between the crosscutting concern and the selected base concern. As we explained in Sect. 16.2.2, interactions occur even between concerns without a crosscutting relationship. In our case we need to express somehow that *G2S* depends on the existence of *Meters* to report this information and also that having *Error Conditions* could reinforce the functionality of *G2S* enabling it to report a new set of events (errors). These interactions as well as mutex (see Sect. 16.2.2) are not explicitly supported by this approach. Note that conflict is not supported in anyway, as they are supposed to be removed through negotiation. As a workaround we have combined pairs of actions and operators, for example: the action *ensure* and the operator *with* to represent a *Dependency* in the case of *Meters* and *G2S*, and the action *provide* with the operator *for* to represent *reinforcement* of *Error Conditions* and *G2S*.

This solution however has two downsides:

1. It forces the use of composition rules even when no crosscutting is present, which seems contradictory with the original purpose of composition rules expressed by the authors: "they describe how a concern cuts across other concerns..." [7]
2. The expressiveness of our combinations is not optimal, as it is not easy to map the different interaction types with pairs of actions and operator. Consider for instance *provide for* compared to the word "*reinforce*." *Reinforce* makes it explicit that the interact on is a positive influence to the other aspect, but we have to use *provide for* to represent this idea.

No Support for Unification As mentioned before in Sect. 16.3.1.2, in our setting there are multiple and ambiguous requirement documents and, as in Theme/Doc, this raises unification issues. Some concerns, such as *Meters*, are defined in many requirements in several of these documents. This makes it difficult to trace the complete definition of meters (which is necessary for the design and implementation). Rewriting all the requirements referring to meters, to condense them into one piece of requirements is not feasible due to the large number of requirements. Besides this, it is difficult to maintain the merged version of the requirements once one of the sources evolves. We conclude that for MDSOCRE we need a way of keeping related requirements linked without coupling them, so that they can evolve at their own pace.

16.3.2.3 Extensions of MDSOCRE

Explicit Interaction Compositions In order to provide explicit support for interactions, we extended MDSOCRE. After evaluating several possible extensions that are not included here due to space limitations, we decided to extend the `Composition` element with a new `Interaction` element. It can be parametrized with the specific interaction type. The `Interaction` element is contained in a `Requirement` element, and itself includes at least another `Requirement` element, as can be seen in Listing 16.3. The interaction direction goes from the outer element to the inner one. For example, Listing 16.3 is read as follows: *requirements 1 and 2 from the G2S communication protocol depend on requirement 3 from the Meters concern.* Note that this order only applies to the directional interactions *dependency* and *reinforcement.*

Listing 16.3: Explicit interaction support for MDSOCRE

```
<Composition>
  <Requirement concern="G2S" id="1,2">
    <Interaction type="dependency">
      <Requirement concern="Meters" id="3"/>
    </Interaction>
  </Requirement>
</Composition>
```

Cross-references for Linked Requirements The different requirement sources complement each other. Hence, there is no unique and complete piece of text that allows us to produce a full design for certain requirements. Therefore, to enable an unabridged description of these requirements, we extended MSDOCRE with cross-references. We added a new attribute, called `seeAlso`, to the `Requirement` element. The value associated with this attribute is a list of requirements IDs where additional information is present. The `seeAlso` allows to relate all the requirements defining one concept (see Listing 16.4). These references are intended to be used in a single concern. As we mentioned before, this issue also manifests itself in Theme, but have not been able to solve it without overly cluttering the diagrams.

Listing 16.4: Cross references extension

```
<Concern name="Meters">
 <Requirement id="1" seeAlso="3,4,5"> Credit meter: shall at all times
      indicate all credits or cash available for the player to wager or
      cashout. </Requirement>
 <Requirement id="2"> Credit Meter Incrementing: The value of every prize
      [...] </Requirement>
 <Requirement id="3" seeAlso="1,4,5"> Accounting Meters: Coin In: a meter that
       accumulates the total value of all wagers . Games-played: [...]
 </Requirement>
 <Requirement id="4" seeAlso="1,3,5"> Meters should be updated upon occurrence
       of any event that must be counted, including: play, [...].
</Requirement>
<!-- From G2S Docs-->
 <Requirement id="5" seeAlso="1,3,4"> Some G2S meters are: gamesSinceInitCn
      Number of games since initialisation. [...]
 </Requirement>
</Concern>
```

16.4 Conclusions

In our work, we evaluated two well-known AORE approaches in an industrial setting—the slot machines (SM) domain—where many functional crosscutting concerns are present. This domain is furthermore characterized by aspectual interactions, and the legal applicability of several large requirement documents that have ambiguity issues. In our previous experience, developing this software and not considering aspectual interactions led to costly bugs in production.

When re-implementing the SM software we therefore decided for an AOSD approach and evaluated two AORE approaches for the first phase of the development cycle. We found that both of these approaches: Theme/Doc and MDSOCRE however fall short. Theme/Doc showed problems with requirements granularity and lack of aspectual interaction support. MDSOCRE presented a appropriate granularity, but however lacks an explicit way to express interactions.

To address these shortcomings, we developed extensions to both approaches that make Theme/Doc and MDSOCRE more suitable for the industrial problem at hand. The extensions made to Theme/Doc allow us to explicitly document the interaction between concerns as well as the requirements participating in the crosscutting and interaction relationships. The extensions made to MDSOCRE allow us to relate different requirements and explicitly support concern interactions.

It is our opinion that applying existing AORE approaches to industrial software is an important effort, as it may reveal shortcomings in these approaches, which is what we have shown here. Using these approaches in different settings will show avenues for improvement and extension of their applicability.

References

1. E. Baniassad, S. Clarke, Finding aspects in requirements with theme/doc, in *Early Aspects Workshop at AOSD*, Lancaster, March 2004
2. E. Baniassad, S. Clarke, Theme: An approach for aspect-oriented analysis and design, in *ICSE '04: Proceedings of the 26th International Conference on Software Engineering* (IEEE Computer Society, Washington, DC, 2004), pp. 158–167
3. E. Baniassad, P.C. Clements, J. Araujo, A. Moreira, A. Rashid, B. Tekinerdogan, Discovering early aspects. IEEE Software **23**(1), 61–70 (2006)
4. D. Bar-On, S. Tyszberowicz, Derived requirements generation: The DRAS methodology, in *IEEE International Conference on Software Science, Technology and Engineering*, Herzlia, Israel, 30–31 October 2007, pp. 116–126
5. S. Clarke, E. Baniassad, in *Aspect-Oriented Analysis and Design. The Theme Approach*. Object Technology Series (Addison-Wesley, Boston, USA, 2005)
6. Gaming Laboratories International. *Gaming Devices in Casinos*, 2007, http://www.gaminglabs.com/. Accessed June 2011
7. A. Moreira, A. Rashid, J. Araujo, Multi-dimensional separation of concerns in requirements engineering, in *Proceedings of 13th IEEE International Conference on Requirements Engineering*, Paris, 29 August–2 September 2005, pp. 285–296
8. Nevada Gaming Commission. *Technical StandardsForGamingDevices And On-Line Slot Systems*, 2008. http://gaming.nv.gov/stats_regs.htm. Accessed June 2011
9. A. Rashid, A. Moreira, J. Araújo, Modularisation and composition of aspectual requirements, in *AOSD '03: Proceedings of the 2nd International Conference on Aspect-Oriented Software Development* (ACM, New York, 2003), pp. 11–20
10. Recommended practice for software requirements specifications. *IEEE Std 830–1998*, 1998
11. F. Sanen, E. Truyen, B.D. Win, W. Joosen, N. Loughran, G. Coulson, A. Rashid, A. Nedos, A. Jackson, S. Clarke, Study on interaction issues. Technical Report AOSD-Europe Deliverable D44, AOSD-Europe-KUL-7, Katholieke Universiteit Leuven, 28 February 2006
12. P. Tarr, H. Ossher, W. Harrison, S.M. Sutton Jr., N degrees of separation: multi-dimensional separation of concerns, in *ICSE '99: Proceedings of the 21st International Conference on Software Engineering* (IEEE Computer Society, Los Alamitos, CA, 1999), pp. 107–119
13. A. Zambrano, J. Fabry, G. Jacobson, S. Gordillo, Expressing aspectual interactions in requirements engineering: Experiences in the slot machine domain, in *Proceedings of the 2010 ACM Symposium on Applied Computing (SAC 2010)* (ACM, Sierre, Switzerland, 2010), pp. 2161–2168

Chapter 17
Advancing AORE Through Evaluation

Phil Greenwood

Abstract One of the fundamental ways that progress is made in any field is through evaluation and reflection on the observations made. This is no different for Aspect-Oriented Requirements Engineering and the techniques developed to assist this area. However, for effective evaluation to be performed "best-practices" and guidelines need to be established for the observations made to be acceptable by the wider community. There has been little work to consolidate the variety of practices and problems experienced when conducting AORE-based evaluation studies. This chapter draws upon experience from evaluation performed in other phases of development and also the problems that can be experienced when evaluating AORE approaches to establish a series of guidelines to assist AORE practitioners.

17.1 Introduction

Evaluation is one of the most important stages of any research or development task. It not only highlights both the benefits and drawbacks of techniques but also illuminates potential new research or development paths that can be followed. Individually, practitioners recognise the importance of evaluation to their work and expend great amounts of time and effort ensuring their evaluation is rigorous and thorough. However, these evaluation activities are often performed in isolation. A primary reason for this is that practitioners often have very focused goals in mind that require very specific evaluation methods. Although this satisfies the researcher's needs, it does result in only small incremental advancements in very specific areas of research.

In niche domains, such as Aspect-Oriented Requirements Engineering (AORE), this isolation and fragmentation of evaluation activities can be particularly limiting.

P. Greenwood (✉)
Phil Greenwood, School of Computing and Communications, Lancaster University, UK
e-mail: greenwop@comp.lancs.ac.uk

A. Moreira et al. (eds.), *Aspect-Oriented Requirements Engineering*,
DOI 10.1007/978-3-642-38640-4_17,

Furthermore, evaluation of Requirements Engineering (RE) approaches in general and, more specifically AORE approaches, are particularly critical due to their influence on subsequent phases of development [2]. This is due to the key design decisions that can be made during these early phases of development and the significant effect they can have on the final implementation of a system. Therefore, evaluation of these artefacts and activities are critical in order to understand the relationship between phases and allow more informed decisions regarding design choices to be made.

For effective evaluation, and to advance the area through evaluation, certain criteria need to be met, including:

- Common links need to be established between evaluation results to be able to identify causes and effects of different approaches/techniques;
- Accurate and consistent comparisons between approaches need to be made to ensure the accuracy of any conclusions drawn;
- Evaluation results need to be reusable to avoid repetition and duplication; this also enables third-parties to validate and build-upon previous results;
- Benchmarks need to be identified to evaluate approaches against; this will allow third-parties to compare their evaluation results with previous sets;
- Common ways of measuring the properties of the approaches found to allow comparisons of approaches that address the same issues to be made.

These steps allow systematic comparisons and evaluation to be performed across the advancements made within a community. By applying a systematic approach, broader evaluation results can be obtained, highlighting to the entire community the areas of research that require the most attention [3].

For this to be achieved, each community has to establish its own set of "best-practices" and guidelines for evaluation. These can then be followed to ensure that certain standards and criteria are met that will allow other community members to utilise and build upon the results collected. These guidelines should not be in anyway restrictive but instead be applicable to a wide variety of approaches emerging from the community. Of course, new approaches will emerge that do not fit with the current guidelines, so it should be expected that the guidelines evolve as the community evolves.

The AORE community is no different and needs to establish its own set of guidelines to support the evaluation of both established and emerging approaches. The AORE community also has the added problem of aligning itself with the wider RE community to enable comparisons to be performed between AO and non-AO RE approaches. However, the AORE community has the advantage of being a relatively young and emerging community allowing future research to be shaped and driven by "best-practice". However, the use of AO techniques at other phases of development have achieved relatively higher levels of maturity, experiences from these phases can be drawn upon to derive "best-practices" for AORE evaluation.

The purpose of this chapter is to begin the process of establishing a set of best-practices and guidelines for evaluating AORE approaches. This chapter will discuss some of the techniques used to evaluate approaches at other development phases and outline some of the specific problems encountered when evaluating AORE approaches. From this, we will attempt to extract common practices and guidelines.

The rest of the chapter covers the following topics. Section 17.2 discusses the styles of evaluation performed in other stages of evaluation and draws inspiration from them. The difficulties of evaluating requirements engineering approaches and AORE approaches specifically are described in Sect. 17.3. General guidelines extracted from methods described in the previous chapters are detailed in Sect. 17.4. Section 17.5 looks forward to some of the difficulties the AORE community has to face in the future.

17.2 Evaluation in Other Software Engineering Phases

This section discusses evaluation approaches that have been used in other Software Engineering development phases, with a particular focus on AO-based approaches. The purpose of this is to draw inspiration from these other phases that can be applied to AORE evaluation.

Aspect-oriented approaches have been the subject to a large amount of scrutiny from the Software Engineering community. In particular, AO implementation approaches such as AspectJ [15], JBoss AOP [11], and CaesarJ [1] have been the focus of several studies due to their perceived high levels of maturity. Their proponents have undertaken a number of studies [5, 6, 8, 10, 12, 17] in order to demonstrate their benefits to increase uptake and adoption, particularly in industrial development environments. These studies have attempted to assess a variety of attributes associated with software development including: maintainability, comprehensibilty, reusability, stability, and complexity. These quality attributes are relevant to all development phases, including requirements engineering, and so can be taken as a starting point for our discussion.

In terms of implementation level evaluation, a large body of work exists in terms of software metrics to assess the quality attributes mentioned above. The generic definition of some of these metrics allow them to be applied to a wide variety of implementation approaches without requiring any alteration. This is a key factor in the success of any metric as it allows them to be easily reused and measured values can be directly compared to evaluate a number of approaches against each other. Of course, some techniques do require specific metrics to be developed (as discussed further below).

Some metrics are defined for a particular paradigm, for example, Coupling Between Objects (CBC) and Lack of Cohesion of Methods (LCOM) [3] metrics were defined to assess Object-Oriented designs. However, the definition of these measures allows them to be applied to other paradigms, such as AO designs, very easily. This enables AO and non-AO implementations to be compared side-by-side, highlighting both the benefits, draw back and differences between AO and non-AO approaches.

Although a range of pre-existing metrics exist for assessing implementation level artefacts, the AO community soon realised that these alone were insufficient to evaluate all characteristics of AO approaches and so defined additional measures. One of the most notable introductions were metrics that measured Separation of Concerns (SoC) attributes [19]. These metrics are able to measure the degree to which a particular concern is scattered or tangled across the system. Although these metrics were introduced with the specific aim of evaluating AO implementations, these metrics were defined to be paradigm agnostic. This allows the metrics to be applied to a variety of implementation techniques (e.g., OO, procedural, functional, etc.) making it possible to directly compare alternative designs. It is important that any new metrics introduced to specifically assess AORE attributes possess these properties as well.

Other metrics were introduced with an even more generic definition to allow them to be applied across phases of development [7]. This is extremely useful as it enables links between development phases to be established and allows the effects of one phase on others to be determined. These properties can be particularly useful for requirement engineering approaches, and more specifically AORE, where it is often reported that the early design decisions made as a consequence of requirement engineering approaches have a significant effect on subsequent development phases. Having metrics that can be applied across phases will enable these effects to be observed. It is important to keep in mind that metrics alone are insufficient to determine the quality attributes mentioned above (maintainability, comprehensibilty, reusability, etc.). Metric values are only ever indicators that certain phenomenon is occurring, further analysis of underlying artefacts is needed to accurately assess the desired quality attributes.

In order to increase the confidence of quality attributes observed it is often necessary to employ industrial examples. This also helps demonstrate the applicability of the approach undergoing evaluation to real-world scenarios. However, locating an appropriate industrial case study can be problematic due to the reluctance of organisations to share their artefacts (this problem is discussed further in Sect. 17.3).

Instead, a solution frequently employed is to employ academic applications as case studies. These are applications that emerge from a project or other research-led activity. The benefits of these types of applications is that their creators are normally quite willing to provide these applications to other researchers in the community who are conducting further evaluation studies. This begins to establish a common reference point, albeit in an ad hoc manner, that allows results to be directly compared with each other when approaches are evaluated against this reference point. These direct comparisons can be made without the underlying case study obscuring or artificially highlighting any differences between the approaches being evaluated. One of the difficulties when selecting an appropriate common case study is choosing one that is suitable for a wide range of approaches that may emerge from the community. This could involve not only considerations that go beyond the case study's application domain but also other factors such as the artefacts that are available for the case study or, particularly for AO related approaches, the range of concerns present. It may be the case that a single case study is insufficient and a number of case studies are needed to provide adequate coverage.

For AO-related approaches, a number of case studies have begun to emerge to establish themselves as common case studies. HealthWatcher [20] has been used a number of times to compare a variety of attributes of AO and non-AO designs such as design stability, architectural compositions and exception handling. HealthWatcher suffers from certain limitations, most notably that it is not a software product line. As a consequence of this, MobileMedia [9] is now widely used alongside HealthWatcher to assess properties relating to software product lines. Similarly, JHotDraw [16] is frequently used to assess aspect mining techniques as it is well designed but suffers from clear problems due to cross-cutting concerns. The acceptance of these case studies to the AO community has enabled much more effective evaluations to be performed as results obtained can be compared directly against each other. However, niche areas will continue to select a case study that is suited to their needs.

Even with a common case study defined further activities may be required to ensure it possesses the appropriate characteristics to evaluate the desired characteristics. One task that is often required is identifying and applying treatments to the case study to cause certain behaviour to be exhibited and observable. For example, studies that investigate design stability require design changes to be applied to the case study to observe the impact of the change and cause design stability issues to emerge. Designing these treatments can be time consuming and difficulty to ensure that they are unbiased and realistic. Often, experts are recruited to design these treatments to ensure they meet the required standards for the evaluation. If possible, existing treatments should be reused across studies, however, the nature of these treatments means that often they are very specific to a particular study making reuse difficult. However, they can be used as inspiration to derive relevant treatments. For example, a study [4] evaluating the fragility of AORE composition techniques required a series of treatments to exercise the fragility properties. Treatments from a comparable implementation-level study [12] were used as inspiration to define the requirement level treatments.

This section has discussed some of the techniques that have been considered and addressed within other development phases when performing evaluation activities. Although this is not an exhaustive set of factors that need to be considered, they are common and general factors that do affect a variety of studies performed. Furthermore, they are applicable to other development phases, including requirements engineering. Therefore, these techniques applied can be used as inspiration when addressing specific difficulties in AORE evaluation activities.

17.3 Difficulties in Evaluating AORE

The previous section (Sect. 17.2) discussed some of the strategies that have been used in other stages of development for performing effective evaluation. This section discusses some of the difficulties that arise when applying these and other strategies to AORE approaches.

As discussed in the previous section, it is desirable to establish a set of common case studies for which a whole variety of studies can be performed to evaluate a range of approaches. Establishing what these common case studies should be for RE approaches, and AORE approaches more specifically, is particularly difficult. This is mainly due to the lack of suitable examples. For other development phases, open-source or academic projects can contain useful artefacts for studies. However, projects from these sources frequently do not have any associated requirements documents. This is because these projects usually emerge in an ad hoc manner and so have no formal requirements elicitation process. For example, open-source projects can emerge from a communities motivation to create a solution that addresses their own needs and so typically no formal requirements process is applied. Similarly, in academic settings either artefacts emerge from the needs of a specific research project or researcher so, again, no formal elicitation process is performed. This is not to say that no elicitation process is ever performed or that requirements documents never exist, but extensive requirement documentation is less likely to exist for such projects.

As discussed in Sect. 17.2, often researchers turn to industrial partners for their case studies as such case studies offer extra credibility to any evaluation due to their real-world settings. However, finding an industrial partner who is willing to provide the necessary artefacts is extremely challenging. Accessing requirement-related artefacts from industrial partners is particularly difficult due to their sensitive nature. The requirements documents may contain specific customer needs which may be critical for the company to maintain their competitive edge. Furthermore, the requirement artefacts may contain features that have not yet been released yet or features that are part of their long-term plans. Providing such artefacts could jeopardise a company's long-term plans.

These difficulties are further compounded by the lack of AORE techniques used in industry, lowering the number of available AORE-related artefacts. Even AO implementation techniques, which are now relatively mature, are not extensively used. Therefore, finding an organisation or product that used AORE techniques and subsequently finding AORE artefacts that will be the focus of an evaluation study can be a massive challenge.

One way to avoid these problems is for study executors to reverse-engineer the artefacts that are available to them to create the required artefacts. This has frequently be done in other phases of development, for example, generating architecture artefacts or other design artefacts from source code. However, recreating requirements documents is particularly difficult for two main reasons: (1) the different levels of abstraction and (2) the potential for incomplete specifications.

Generating certain artefacts, such as architecture or design diagrams from source code, is relatively straightforward due to the comparable levels of abstraction. Furthermore, tool support is often available to generate certain artefacts source code, such as class diagrams from Java code, and the overall architectural structure can also be derived. Some requirement level artefacts can also be extracted, e.g., sequence diagrams and use cases can be generated from analysing the behaviour specified in code. However, the difference in levels of abstraction for some artefacts can be difficult to overcome. For instance, certain AORE tools require a textual description of system features for them to be successfully evaluated. Recreating such a description from source code or other design artefacts alone can be difficult. The original intentions of the developers and needs of the stakeholders can only be speculated making errors and inaccuracies very likely.

What also needs to be kept in mind when generating requirement documentation in this way is that the artefacts from later developer phases will only contain those features/concerns that were deemed to be implementable at that time. Concerns may have been omitted due to resource or time constraints; relying solely on these later development artefacts will likely result in an incomplete specification. Other concerns may have been omitted due to incompatibilities. This type of information can be critical to certain AORE approaches, particularly those whose purpose is to identify conflicting concerns/requirements. Accurately recreating this information will be virtually impossible as these conflicts will already have been resolved during the natural development process. Furthermore, certain non-functional requirements may not be explicitly observable within later artefacts. For example, requirements relating to response time will be achieved through the use of efficient algorithms and the overall design of the system. Generally, requirement artefacts generated in this way will only be an alternative view of artefacts from later phases of development. In reality, this is not the case due to concerns emerging and disappearing through the development process.

Typically when performing evaluation activities, it is desirable for unambiguous results to be observed. When assessing requirements engineering-related approaches this can be more difficult to achieve due to the subjective and creative nature of the activities. For example when creating feature diagrams, a system can be represented in multiple different ways with each being considered equally valid. Although similar arguments can be made for other phases of development, the number of potential alternatives is much less restrictive at the requirements phase as fewer design decisions will have been made. The potential for equally valid alternatives makes finding a consensus of the best possible design difficult, making evaluation awkward. For example, approaches which automate conflict identification, the evaluation could involve comparing the conflicts identified by the tool with a set of conflicts identified by experts. The experts may not necessarily agree on the complete set of conflicts making it difficult to accurately evaluate the tool. Should the complete set of conflicts be considered or should just the overlapping conflicts where all experts agree be considered?

Further ambiguity can be introduced due to the very nature of the artefacts being examined. Requirements engineering often require processing and analysing artefacts that contains natural language text. These types of artefacts can be inherently ambiguous or vague and open to interpretation that can affect evaluation tasks. For example, a requirements specification could state "The client must receive updates every 500 ms". This requirement is both vague and ambiguous. Does the requirement mean that updates must be received on *average* every 500 ms and some updates being received later is acceptable? Or, must all updates be received within 500 ms of each other? In some cases, ambiguity is desirable as the approach may assist in the identification or modelling of ambiguous requirement. Whereas in other cases, such ambiguity is unhelpful for evaluation activities.

A further compounding factor to these ambiguity issues is the differing levels of granularity that are present in requirement level artefacts. For example, use-case descriptions can be fairly detailed in terms of the concerns that they are describing. In contrast, activity diagrams may be less detailed by providing a more high level overview. This differing level of granularity can cause the emergence (or not) of cross-cutting concerns. For example, approaches that specify requirements to a finer level of granularity may promote Crosscutting Concerns (CCCs) to emerge. Whereas more coarse-grained approaches may cause CCCs to be subsumed by other concerns. For comparable evaluations to be performed across different approaches, the levels of granularity need to be equivalent. This requires alignment of artefact that can be problematic as it requires a single person to possess expertise in a range of approaches.

Other alignment issues can also arise due to the heterogenous nature of AORE approaches and concepts. A variety of approaches may use similar concepts and define comparable process activities, but these relationships may not be immediately apparent due to the different terms used. In order for comparisons to be drawn, these differences need to be overcome and equivalent artefacts/activities need to be identified. Sampaio et al. [18] have defined a common naming scheme to overcome these alignment issues. This common naming scheme can be applied to a variety of approaches to identify equivalent artefacts and activities, allowing comparisons to be drawn.

A lack of dedicated RE metrics also increases the difficulty of performing effective evaluation at this stage. As mentioned in the previous section (Sect. 17.2), a wide range of metrics have been defined for other development phases. One of the most frequently used metrics to assess and compare AORE approaches is time. The assumption is that the approach which allows a certain activity to be performed the quickest is superior as it is the most efficient. However, this has frequently been found to be an unreliable measure [14] and offers only a simplistic view of the activities being performed. Frequently, time is used with other measures to offer a more complete view but the danger is that other measures are more difficult to comprehend and so the measures of time become the predominant factor. Generic metrics have been defined [7] that measure attributes relating to scattering, tangling and crosscutting. The generic definition of these metrics allow them to be applied to any development stage, including AORE. Such measures are useful for evaluating other quality factors, in this case modularity. The added advantage of using metrics that have a generic definition is that they can be easily applied to other phases, allowing correlations to be drawn between the effects of development phases. However, the generic definition of such metrics means that it is difficult to provide tool support for them. Instead this requires certain aspects of the measures to be collected manually. For example, typical scattering/tangling measures requires the manual assignment of each artefact or sub-element to a particular concern for the metrics to be calculated. This causes significant difficulties and can be a source of errors. More well-defined measures, such as those related to coupling and cohesion for source code, can be collected in an automatic manner using tools. This reduces the possibility of errors and also allows studies to be easily and quickly replicated and verified by other members of the community.

This section has discussed a variety of the problems associated with evaluating AORE approaches. Table 17.1 summarises the issues discussed. These problems can cause difficulties when performing evaluation activities and need to be overcome for a successful outcome to be achieved.

17.4 General Guidelines

The previous sections have highlighted some of the problems that can arise when performing evaluation activities and also some the specific problems that can arise when performing AORE evaluation. Also, some of the common techniques that are used in other phases of development to conduct effective evaluation have been discussed. The purpose of this section is to bring these discussion areas together and extract a series of guidelines that can be applied within the AORE domain.

17.4.1 Applications

Our first guideline involves the selection of the application that should be used as the basis of the evaluation activities. Often the exact domain which the application represents is not entirely critical. Instead, and in particular for AO-related evaluations, it is the type, number and variety of concerns that are present which is the critical factor. It is important that the concerns present have differing scopes, whereby some are widely scoped concerns (i.e. affect a wide variety of system behaviour such as security or distribution) and some are narrowly scoped concerns (i.e. some isolated behaviour). This range is necessary regardless of the approach being evaluated to determine how well it can cope with different types of concerns that may cause different types of interactions. In certain cases, the presence of specific concerns, such as exception handling or security may be needed due to the specialised nature of some approaches. The application should be selected with this specifically in mind.

Subsequently, it is important that a number of applications are accessible to the community to ensure that different combinations of concerns are available for evaluation. Furthermore, this range should also require different development styles be applied for development, for example, single system vs. software product lines. Again, having this range will allow the approaches being evaluated to be tested in a variety of ways.

Table 17.1 Summary of the problems encountered when conducting AORE-related evaluation

	Problem description	Difficulty caused
Case studies		
	Academic vs. Industrial applications	Academic applications may not provide the necessary rigour for evaluation but equally finding industrial partners willing to participate may be difficult.
	Lack of requirements	Applications from certain domains may not have accompanying requirements documentation, reducing their suitability.
Artefacts		
	Suitable artefacts	If the necessary artefacts are not present, they may have to be generated that can result in errors.
	Incompleteness	When using generated artefacts, incomplete specifications may occur due to relying on implementation-based artefacts.
	Ambiguity in models	AORE approaches that involve creating models may introduce ambiguity and may allow for multiple equally "correct" solutions.
	Ambiguity in specifications	Equally, the nature of some requirement artefacts (e.g., natural language) causes ambiguity to naturally occur. In such cases, evaluation can become difficult
Approaches		
	Granularity mismatch	Different approaches may have different levels of granularity in terms of the artefacts they use to specify or model concepts. This may cause difficulties when directly comparing approaches.
	Misalignment in definitions	When comparing a number of approaches, artefacts for each approach needs to be created. Ensuring these artefacts are consistent in terms of what they specify needs to be guaranteed.
Metrics		
	Lack of metrics	The number of dedicated AORE metrics is low, meaning that unreliable measures are often applied.
	Lack of tool support	For the metrics that do exist, this is distinct lack of tool support which makes it difficult to accurately collect metrics.

17.4.2 Available Artefacts

As mentioned in the previous section, it is critical that the application has the necessary artefacts, or they can be easily generated for evaluation. Ensuring this is not easy and in some circumstances it may not be possible to avoid having to generate the artefacts manually requiring significant effort. In such cases, it is desirable to collaborate with other members of the community. This maybe industrial practitioners who may be able to provide case study artefacts directly or academic practitioners who may be specialists in relevant techniques. If such collaborations can forged then the likely quality of the evaluation will improve. Another consideration that should be made is the publication of these artefacts after the evaluation activities. Good practice dictates that these artefacts should be publicly available to provide transparency and peer review of the study performed. This also has the added benefit of allowing these artefacts to be used in any subsequent studies, which can only help improve their quality and also assist the area advance.

17.4.3 Participants

As stated above in Sect. 17.4.2, it is desirable to collaborate with other members of community and call upon their expertise to, e.g., recreate missing artefacts. Furthermore, these experts can also play a critical role to overcome other problems that may be experienced when conducting evaluation activities. As discussed in Sect. 17.3, a specific difficulty experienced when performing AORE-related evaluations is the ambiguity that may occur in both the models produced from applying approaches and within the actual requirements specification. Recruiting experts from the community can help clarify these ambiguities and also other evaluation activities.

However, it is critical that these experts are carefully chosen to prevent the study being invalidated. Firstly, experts need to be chosen who have the necessary levels of expertise for the task in hand; this is particularly important if having to include students in the evaluation. If it is necessary to recreate some artefacts, then it is natural to recruit the inventors of the relevant approach or someone who has significant experience using the approach. Second, the experts chosen should not introduce an inherent bias; this is particularly significant when attempting to overcome any type of ambiguity. Finally, external collaborators can play a crucial role when having to align artefacts across a number of approaches being evaluated, however, finding a single person who has the necessary skills can be difficult.

17.4.4 Treatments Applied

Similarly, the treatments that need to be applied to the application, such as maintenance changes should also be generated in a similar way. The original developers should be consulted to ensure the treatments being applied are realistic and fit the original development intentions. If they are no longer available or unwillingly to co-operate then, again, collaborations should be forged within the community to recruit experts with the necessary skills to identify relevant treatments and apply them to a high standard. The same publication guidelines should be applied to the availability of the different versions of the artefacts generated from applying the treatments.

17.4.5 Metric Suites

As discussed throughout this chapter, a variety of metric suites are available for different phases of development and the RE phase is no different. As has been highlighted in the previous section (Sect. 17.3), there is a distinct lack of metric suites that are specifically suited for AORE. Some have been defined with a generic definition [7] that allows them to be applied to a variety of development phases, including AORE. Other measures have begun to emerge such as mobility indices and reachability [4] that relate to AORE development practices. This chapter has also highlighted some generic measures, such as time and precision and recall, that are frequently used in AORE evaluations.

The most important consideration when selecting a metric suite is that it is a suitable measure for the attributes of interest. For example, the AORE measures mentioned above have been used to measure attributes relating to modularity, expressiveness, effort, and information retrieval. These attributes cover a broad range of properties that are relevant to AORE approaches and can be applied to assess a variety of their characteristics. But they are unlikely to be sufficient for all current and future AORE approaches. For example, there are no specific metrics that are able to measure the stability of AORE approaches. The variance observed in the currently defined set of metrics could be one indicator of (in)stability, but is this sufficient?

As discussed in the previous section, openness is one potential key to success. Making the definition of metric suites publicly available will allow the community to determine under what circumstances a set of measures are suitable to be applied and what circumstances they are not. This will allow deficiencies in current metrics to be more quickly identified and so speed up the development of new metrics to fill this void. It should be expected that new metrics emerge over time as knowledge of the domain improves.

17.4.6 Clearly Defined Evaluation Goals

One of the most important underpinning aspects of each of the items discussed above is the necessity to have clearly defined evaluation goals. This requires identifying the evaluation questions that need to be answered and then subsequently defining appropriate hypotheses to test. Only with these defined can the evaluation study be appropriately configured and executed. An appropriate application should be selected that will ensure the validity of the evaluation performed (e.g., is an industrial application needed or is an academic application sufficient). Relevant artefacts need to be available (or generated) to allow the treatments necessary to be applied. The metric suites to be applied need to be carefully chosen so that they answer the defined evaluation questions and hypotheses. Finally, the appropriate participants should be selected based on the activities to be performed. The Goal-Question-Metric (GQM) method [21] is one approach that can be applied to assist this process.

An important point to keep in mind when collecting and analysing results from metric suites is that they are not always direct evidence of a certain characteristic existing and alone do not answer evaluation goals. Instead, they should be considered an indicator to a particular problem, and the artefacts undergoing evaluation need to be thoroughly analysed further to determine if a problem or characteristic does actually exist. For example, size is frequently misused as a measure of productivity; however, this does not take into account the complexity of the problem being solved and can therefore be a misleading measure. Further examination of the artefacts is necessary to determine the causes and solutions to the problems that have been identified by metrics. The metric results do not show these by themselves.

17.4.7 Towards an AORE Test-Bed

A potential solution to ease some of the issues described above is the introduction of an AORE test-bed. The presence of a dedicated AORE test-bed will allow proponents of AO and non-AO-based techniques to compare their approaches in a consistent manner. A proposed design of such a test-bed is shown in Fig. 17.1.

As can be seen in Fig. 17.1, the design consists of a number of common attributes that are used during the course of an evaluation and highlights the relationship between them. The test-bed would provide the AORE community with a set of resources that they can use to conduct a variety of different studies. The idea that the number of resources would grow over time as more studies were conducted and members of the AORE community would donate the resources that were generated as a result of the studies they perform. The boxes highlighted in yellow indicate one possible study configuration from the test-bed resources to compare the modularity and expressiveness of a use case with a RDL-based approach.

Currently, a single AORE test-bed does not exist. However, islands of studies centred on particular applications have begun emerging. For example, a number of AORE specific studies have been conducted that involve the Crisis Management system (as used throughout this book). Other applications, such as HealthWatcher and MobileMedia, have been used in studies for other phases of development, as well as RE. However, there is yet to be any initiatives in the AORE community to bridge these islands of activity to form a consolidated and definitive AORE test-bed. Such a resource would prove to be of great value to the AORE community and potentially allow greater strides to be made in the area.

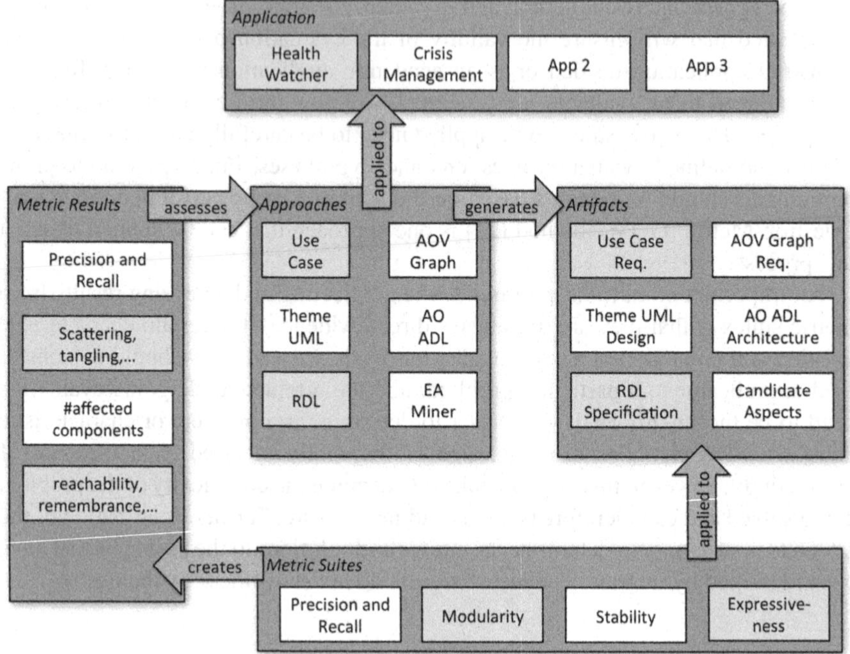

Fig. 17.1 Proposed AORE test-bed design

17.5 Looking Forward

The previous section discussed one possible future development for AORE-based evaluations and advancing the area through the development of an AORE-specific test-bed. This section will examine other emerging AORE techniques and how they may affect future evaluation practices.

17.5.1 Requirements at Run-Time

Requirements at run-time is a radical change to the traditional view of requirements models as static, slowly evolving, and purely design-time entities. Requirements at run-time explores the potential of run-time abstractions to model volatile or poorly understood requirements. This may involve requirements that are subject to dramatic and unforeseen economic conditions or environments that are particularly hostile. Under such conditions it is difficult to establish a set of stable requirements; instead, the requirements will have to be revisited and revised a number of times that would be untenable using current methods. Requirements at run-time seek to avoid this by maintain requirements models that are dynamic run-time entities that support reasoning.

Such a change to the perception of requirements increases the links between the requirements engineering phase and other phases of development. The earlier sections of this chapter have discussed some of the techniques used in other phases of developments and how they can help influence and guide the evaluation techniques applied to RE approaches. With requirements at run-time becoming a significant research area, these links between the requirements phases and, in particular, the implementation phases will become ever stronger. This has a particularly significant impact on evaluation activities and imposes strong constraints on the study's configuration. For example, for requirements at run-time approaches will not only need requirement-related artefacts but also implementation-based artefacts as well. Furthermore, the influences between the phases need to be carefully examined to determine the causes and consequences of any phenomenon observed.

17.5.2 New Requirement Sources

Traditionally, requirements are elicited from a customer or potential user of a system, however, in recent times, the notion of a stakeholder has become increasingly more diverse and broadly scoped due to social action initiatives led by different groups, e.g., government or crowd-sourcing. In these cases the stakeholders of the system become the entire community. Although this can have an effect on requirement approaches due to the increase in scale and the synthesis that is required (new techniques may emerge to accommodate these), the effects on evaluation can also be significant.

Typically, when performing evaluation at any stage of development, and in particularly during requirements evaluation, consultations with stakeholders may have to be performed to check certain information or to clarify some details. With a traditional set of stakeholders this is difficult, as they may move on to different organisations or forget relevant details. However, with community-based stakeholders this becomes even more difficult as being able to trace the same set of stakeholders to perform the necessary consultations maybe impossible. Therefore, evaluation that involves such types of stakeholders may not be as effective. Equally, however, the potential number of people reachable by these social action initiatives is huge, meaning that new participants can be found easily so simplifying additional consultations. The study goals need to be carefully considered to determine if this is a viable option. Social networks could become a prime mechanism for engaging with large numbers of stakeholders in a scaleable way to perform these types of mass-consultations. Early work [13] has begun exploring the role social networks have to play during requirements elicitation and consultation.

17.5.3 Tool Support

One of the most crucial properties of any evaluation is that it is repeatable and can be verified independently. A problem of some of the evaluation approaches, in particular the definition of some AORE specific metrics, is that they are open to interpretation. Furthermore, these types of metrics typically require some form of manual data collection in order for them to be calculated. Both of these factors reduce the potential for a study to be repeatable due to the chances of both the errors being introduced and different interpretations of the measures causing different results to be observed.

One way the repeatability of a study to be increased is through the introduction of a test-bed, as discussed earlier. This will make both the artefacts being evaluated and the metric results that have been collected to be publicly available allowing them to be reused in future evaluation studies. However, this repeatability can be improved further through the introduction of increased tool support to assist the collect of the metrics. This will improve metric collection in two ways: (1) ensures a consistent definition of the metric is applied and (2) removes the need for manual collection and so reduces the chances for error. Currently, the amount of tool support for AORE-related evaluation support is fairly limited. Improvements in this direction would significantly improve the quality of AORE-based studies.

17.5.4 Beyond an AORE Test-Bed

Section 17.4 highlighted the need and benefits that could be obtained through the development of an AORE test-bed. Although this would be significant step to improve AORE-based evaluations, in the future it would be more desirable to develop a test-bed that integrated all stages of development. As we discussed earlier in this section, techniques such as requirements at run-time highlight the need to incorporate other phases of development into the evaluation activities. Furthermore, this integration will form an end-to-end AO-based test-bed that would allow the effects of previous and subsequent development phases to be established. Identifying these effects can play a significant role in the evaluation of approaches as they can potentially highlight problems that may not be immediately observable but instead manifest themselves in other phases of development.

References

1. I. Aracic, V. Gasiunas, M. Mezini, K. Ostermann, An overview of caesarj, in *Transactions on Aspect-Oriented Software Development I*. Lecture Notes in Computer Science, vol. 3880 (Springer, Heidelberg , 2006), pp. 135–173
2. J.C. Chen, S.J. Huang, An empirical analysis of the impact of software development problem factors on software maintainability. J. Syst. Software **82**, 981–992 (2009)
3. S.R. Chidamber, C.F. Kemerer, Towards a metrics suite for object-oriented design, in *Proceedings of OOPSLA'91* (ACM, New York, 1991), pp. 197–211
4. R. Chitchyan, P. Greenwood, A. Sampaio, A. Rashid, A.F. Garcia, L. Fernandes da Silva, Semantic vs. syntactic compositions in aspect-oriented requirements engineering: An empirical

study, in *Proceedings of the 8th International Conference on Aspect-Oriented Software Development* (ACM, New York, 2009), pp. 149–160
5. R. Coelho, A. Rashid, A. Garcia, F. Ferrari, N. Cacho, U. Kulesza, A.V. Staa, C. Lucena, Assessing the impact of aspects on exception flows: An exploratory study, in *ECOOP 2008 Object-Oriented Programming*, ed. by J. Vitek. Lecture Notes in Computer Science, vol. 5142 (Springer, Berlin/Heidelberg, 2008), pp. 207–234
6. J.M. Conejero, E. Figueiredo, A. Garcia, J. Hernendez, E. Jurado, Early crosscutting metrics as predictors of software instability, in *Objects, Components, Models and Patterns*, ed. by M. Oriol, B. Meyer, W. Aalst, J. Mylopoulos, M. Rosemann, M.J. Shaw, C. Szyperski. Lecture Notes in Business Information Processing, vol. 33 (Springer, Berlin/Heidelberg, 2009), pp. 136–156
7. J.M. Conejero, J. Hernández, E. Jurado, K. van den Berg, Analysis of modularity by an aspect-oriented measurement process, in *JISBD* (Gijn, Spain, 2008), pp. 3–14
8. M. Eaddy, T. Zimmermann, K.D. Sherwood, V. Garg, G.C. Murphy, N. Nagappan, A.V. Aho, Do crosscutting concerns cause defects? IEEE Tran. Software Eng. **34**(4), 497–515 (2008)
9. E. Figueiredo, N. Cacho, C. Sant'Anna, M. Monteiro, U. Kulesza, A. Garcia, S. Soares, F. Ferrari, S. Khan, F.C. Filho, F. Dantas, Evolving software product lines with aspects, in *ACM/IEEE 30th International Conference on Software Engineering, 2008. ICSE '08*, ACM, New York, NY, 2008, pp. 261–270
10. E. Figueiredo, I. Galvao, S.S. Khan, A. Garcia, C. Sant'Anna, A. Pimentel, A.L. Medeiros, L. Fernandes, T. Batista, R. Ribeiro, P. van den Broek, M. Aksit, S. Zschaler, A. Moreira, Detecting architecture instabilities with concern traces: An exploratory study, in *WICSA/ECSA 2009. Joint Working IEEE/IFIP Conference on Software Architecture, 2009 European Conference on Software Architecture*, IEEE, Cambridge, 2009, pp. 261–264
11. M. Fleury, F. Reverbel, The JBoss extensible server, in *Proceedings of the ACM/IFIP/USENIX 2003 International Conference on Middleware*, Middleware '03 (Springer, New York, 2003), pp. 344–373
12. P. Greenwood, T.T. Bartolomei, E. Figueiredo, M. Dósea, A.F. Garcia, N. Cacho, C. Sant'Anna, S. Soares, P. Borba, U. Kulesza, A. Rashid, On the impact of aspectual decompositions on design stability: An empirical study, in *ECOOP*, Springer, Berlin, Germany, 2007, pp. 176–200
13. P. Greenwood, A. Rashid, J. Walkerdine, UDesignIt: Towards social media for community-driven design, in *ICSE*, IEEE, Zurich, Switzerland, 2012, pp. 1321–1324
14. C. Jones, Software metrics: Good, bad and missing. Computer **27**(9), 98–100 (1994)
15. G. Kiczales, E. Hilsdale, J. Hugunin, M. Kersten, J. Palm, W. Griswold, Getting started with aspectJ. Comm. ACM **44**, 59–65 (2001)
16. M. Marin, L. Moonen, A. van Deursen. An integrated crosscutting concern migration strategy and its application to jhotdraw, in *SCAM 2007. Seventh IEEE International Working Conference on Source Code Analysis and Manipulation, 2007*, IEEE, Paris, France, September 30–October 1 2007, pp. 101–110
17. A. Molesini, A. Garcia, C.F.G. von Chavez, T. Batista, On the quantitative analysis of architecture stability in aspectual decompositions, in *Seventh Working IEEE/IFIP Conference on Software Architecture, 2008. WICSA 2008* (Vancouver, BC, Canada, 2008), pp. 29–38
18. A. Sampaio, P. Greenwood, A.F. Garcia, A. Rashid, A comparative study of aspect-oriented requirements engineering approaches, in *ESEM 2007* (Madrid, Spain, 2007), pp. 166–175
19. C. Sant'Anna, E. Figueiredo, A.F. Garcia, C. José Pereira de Lucena, On the modularity of software architectures: A concern-driven measurement framework, in *ECSA* (Aranjuez, Spain, 2007), pp. 207–224
20. S. Soares, E. Laureano, P. Borba, Implementing distribution and persistence aspects with aspectJ, in *Proceedings of the 17th ACM SIGPLAN Conference on Object-oriented Programming, Systems, Languages, and Applications*, OOPSLA '02 (ACM, New York, 2002), pp. 174–190
21. R. Van Solingen, E. Berghout, *The Goal/Question/Metric Method: A Practical Guide for Quality Improvement of Software Development* (McGraw-Hill, London, 1999)

Appendix
Crisis Management Systems: A Case Study for Aspect-Oriented Modeling

Jörg Kienzle, Nicolas Guelfi, and Sadaf Mustafiz

Abstract The intent of this document is to define a common case study for the aspect-oriented modeling research community. The domain of the case study is crisis management systems (CMSs), i.e., systems that help in identifying, assessing, and handling a crisis situation by orchestrating the communication between all parties involved in handling the crisis, by allocating and managing resources, and by providing access to relevant crisis-related information to authorized users. This document contains informal requirements of CMSs in general, a feature model for a CMS product line, use case models for a car crash CMS (CCCMS), a domain model for the CCCMS, an informal physical architecture description of the CCCMS, as well as some design models of a possible object-oriented implementation of parts of the CCCMS backend. AOM researchers who want to demonstrate the power of their AOM approach or technique can hence apply the approach at the most appropriate level of abstraction.

A.1 Introduction

The need for crisis management systems (CMSs) has grown significantly over time. A crisis can range from major to catastrophic affecting many segments of society. Natural disasters (e.g., earthquakes, tsunamis, twisters, fire, and floods), terrorist attacks or sabotage (explosions, kidnapping, etc.), accidents (plant explosion, pollution emergency, a car crash, etc.), and technological disruptions are all examples of emergency situations that are unpredictable and can lead to severe after-effects

J. Kienzle (✉) · S. Mustafiz
School of Computer Science, McGill University, Montreal, QC, Canada H3A 0G4
e-mail: Joerg.Kienzle@mcgill.ca; sadaf@cs.mcgill.ca

N. Guelfi
University of Luxembourg, Luxembourg City, Luxembourg
e-mail: Nicolas.Guelfi@uni.lu

A. Moreira et al. (eds.), *Aspect-Oriented Requirements Engineering*,
DOI 10.1007/978-3-642-38640-4, © Springer-Verlag Berlin Heidelberg 2013

unless handled immediately. Crisis management involves identifying, assessing, and handling the crisis situation. A CMS facilitates this process by orchestrating the communication between all parties involved in handling the crisis. The CMS allocates and manages resources, and provides access to relevant crisis-related information to authorized users of the CMS.

Different existing AOM approaches and techniques are meant to be used during different phases of software development. As a result, different AOM approaches work with different kinds of models and modeling notations. In order to make sure that all AOM approaches and techniques are somehow applicable to this case study, we present a collection of models that describe the CMS at different levels of abstraction:

1. Short, *informal requirements* text describing the domain of CMSs in more detail. It also mentions some nonfunctional requirements of a CMS, e.g., security and dependability. This text, presented in Sect. A.2 on page 352, probably contains information that is important to everyone who wants to work on this case study.
2. *Feature diagrams* highlighting the software product line aspect of CMSs. CMSs can be used to handle many types of crises (e.g., natural disasters, epidemics, accidents, and attacks) and may have to interface and interoperate with different types of external services (e.g., military systems, police systems, government, and medical services). The feature diagram models are presented in Sect. A.3 on page 357.
3. *Use cases* describing a particular CMS suitable for dealing with *car crash crises*. The Car Crash CMS (CCCMS) use case model description can be found in Sect. A.4 on page 361.
4. A domain model documenting the key concepts and the domain-vocabulary of the CCCMS is presented in Sect. A.5 on page 368.
5. An informal description of a possible physical architecture for the CCCMS is presented in Sect. A.6 on page 368.
6. Some detailed design models for the CCCMS backend are given in Sect. A.7 on page 370.

A.2 CMS: Requirements

The user requirements outlined in this section are based on a draft of a real requirements document for CMSs created by the company Optimal Security [1]. The general objectives of a CMS include the following:

- To help in the coordination and handling of a crisis;
- To ensure that an abnormal or catastrophic situation does not get out of hand;
- To minimize the crisis by handling the situation using limited resources;
- To allocate and manage resources in an effective manner;

- To identify, create, and execute missions in order to manage the crisis;
- To archive the crisis information to allow future analysis.

A.2.1 Crisis Scenario of a CCCMS

A crisis management scenario is usually triggered by a crisis report from a witness at the scene. A coordinator, who is in charge of organizing all required resources and tasks, initiates the crisis management process. The coordinator has access to the camera surveillance system. The surveillance system is an external system used to monitor traffic on highways or other busy routes. The cameras are installed only in specific locations. If a crisis occurs in locations under surveillance, the CMS can request video feed that allows the coordinator to verify the witness information.

A super observer, an expert in the field (depending on the kind of crisis), is assigned to the scene to observe the emergency situation and identify the tasks necessary to cope with the situation. The tasks are crisis missions defined by the observer. The coordinator is then required to process the missions by allocating suitable resources to each task.

Depending on the type of crisis, human resources could include firemen, doctors, nurses, policemen, and technicians, and hardware resources could include transportation systems, computing resources, communication means (such as PDAs or mobile phones), or other necessities like food or clothes. Animals, for instance police dogs, are also used as resources in some situations. The human and animal resources act as first-aid workers. Each first-aid worker is assigned a specific task which needs to be executed to recover from the abnormal situation. The workers are expected to report on the success or failure in carrying out the missions. The completion of all missions would allow the crisis to be concluded.

A.2.2 Scope of the CMS

A CMS should include the following functionalities:

- Initiating a crisis based on an external input from a witness,
- Processing a crisis by executing the missions defined by a super observer and then assigning internal and/or external resources,
- Wrapping-up and archiving crisis,
- Authenticating users,
- Handling communication between coordinator/system and resources.

A CMS replaces existing CMSs that (a) still manually keep track of important crisis-related information and (b) operate largely without automated support for crisis resolution strategies in order to respond to a crisis.

A.2.3 Nonfunctional Requirements of the CMS

The CMS shall exhibit the following nonfunctional properties:

- **Availability**
  - The system shall be in operation 24 h a day, everyday, without break, throughout the year except for a maximum downtime of 2 h every 30 days for maintenance.
  - The system shall recover in a maximum of 30 s upon failure.
  - Maintenance shall be postponed or interrupted if a crisis is imminent without affecting the systems capabilities.
- **Reliability**
  - The system shall not exceed a maximum failure rate of 0.001 %.
  - The mobile units shall be able to communicate with other units on the crisis site and the control center regardless of location, terrain, and weather conditions.
- **Persistence**
  - The system shall provide support for storing, updating, and accessing the following information on both resolved and ongoing crises: type of crisis; location of crisis; witness report; witness location; witness data; time reported; duration of resolution; resources deployed; civilian casualties; crisis management personnel casualties; strategies used; missions used; location of super observer; crisis perimeter; location of rescue teams on crisis site; level of emissions from crisis site; log of communications; log of decisions; log of problems encountered.
  - The system shall provide support for storing, updating, and accessing the following information on available and deployed resources (both internal and external): type of resource (human or equipment); capability; rescue team; location; estimated time of arrival (ETA) on crisis site.
  - The system shall provide support for storing, updating, and accessing the following information on crisis resolution strategies: type of crisis; step-by-step guide to resolve crisis; configuration of missions required; links to alternate strategies; applications to previous crises; success rate.
- **Real-time**
  - The control center shall receive and update the following information on an ongoing crisis at intervals not exceeding 30 s: resources deployed; civilian casualties; crisis management personnel casualties; location of super observer; crisis perimeter; location of rescue teams on crisis site; level of emissions from crisis site; ETA of rescue teams on crisis site.

- The delay in communication of information between control center and rescue personnel as well as amongst rescue personnel shall not exceed 500 ms.
- The system shall be able to retrieve any stored information with a maximum delay of 500 ms.

– **Security**

- The system shall define access policies for various classes of users. The access policy shall describe the components and information each class may add, access, and update.
- The system shall authenticate users on the basis of the access policies when they first access any components or information. If a user remains idle for 30 min or longer, the system shall require them to reauthenticate.
- All communications in the system shall use secure channels compliant with AES-128 standard encryption.

– **Mobility**

- Rescue resources shall be able to access information on the move.
- The system shall provide location-sensitive information to rescue resources.
- Rescue resources shall communicate their location to the control center.
- The system shall have access to detailed maps, terrain data, and weather conditions for the crisis location and the routes leading to it.

– **Statistic Logging**

- The system shall record the following statistical information on both ongoing and resolved crises: rate of progression; average response time of rescue teams; individual response time of each rescue team; success rate of each rescue team; rate of casualties; success rate of missions.
- The system shall provide statistical analysis tools to analyze individual crisis data and data on multiple crises.

– **Multi-Access**

- The system shall support at least 1,000 witnesses calling in at a time.
- The system shall support communication, coordination, and information access for at least 20,000 rescue resources in deployment at a time.
- The system shall support management of at least 100 crises at a time.
- The system shall support management of at least 200 missions per crisis at a time.

– **Safety**

- The system shall monitor emissions from the crisis site to determine safe operating distances for rescue resources.
- The system shall monitor weather and terrain conditions at crisis site to ensure safe operation and withdrawal of rescue resources, and removal of civilians and casualties.

  - The system shall determine a perimeter for the crisis site to ensure safety of civilians and removal of casualties to a safe distance.
  - The system shall monitor criminal activity to ensure safety of rescue resources, civilians, and casualties.
  - The safety of rescue personnel shall take top priority for the system.

- **Adaptability**
  - The system shall recommend alternate strategies for dealing with a crisis as the crisis conditions (e.g., weather conditions, terrain conditions, civilian or criminal activity) change.
  - The system shall recommend or enlist alternate resources in case of unavailability or shortage of suitable resources.
  - The system shall be able to use alternate communication channels in case of unavailability or shortage of existing channels.
  - The system shall be able to maintain effective communication in areas of high disruption or noise at the crisis site.

- **Accuracy**
  - The system shall have access to map, terrain, and weather data with a 99 % accuracy.
  - The system shall provide up-to-date information to rescue resources.
  - The system shall record data upon receipt without modifications.
  - The communication between the system and rescue resources shall have a maximum deterioration factor of 0.0001 per 1,000 km.

A.2.4 Car Crash CMS

Some of the models presented in this paper focus on one particular CMS: the CCCMS. The CCCMS includes all the functionalities of general CMSs, and some additional features specific to car crashes such as facilitating the rescuing of victims at the crisis scene and the use of tow trucks to remove damaged vehicles.

Scope of the CCCMS A car accident or car crash is an incident in which an automobile collides with anything that causes damage to the automobile, including other automobiles, telephone poles, buildings or trees, or in which the driver loses control of the vehicle and damages it in some other way, such as driving into a ditch or rolling over [2]. Sometimes a car accident may also refer to an automobile striking a human or animal.

Our CCCMS addresses car crashes involving single or multiple vehicles, humans, or other objects. This case study is however limited to management of human victims only and does not provide rescue missions specifically for animals. First-aid animal workers are not included in the scope of this case study either.

Car crash-specific functionalities include the following:

- Facilitating the rescue mission carried out by the police by providing them with detailed information on the location of the crash;
- Managing the dispatch of ambulances or other alternate emergency vehicles to transport victims from the crisis scene to hospitals;
- Facilitating the first-aid missions by providing relevant medical history of identified victims to the first-aid workers by querying databases of local hospitals;
- Facilitating the medical treatment process of victims by providing important information about the crash to the concerned workers, i.e., paramedics, doctors, upon arrival at the hospital;
- Managing the use of tow trucks to remove obstacles and damaged vehicles from the crisis scene.

CCCMS Actors The actors involved in the CCCMS are defined in this section.

- **Coordinator** oversees management of the crisis by coordinating the resources and communicating with all the CMS employees and external workers.
- **Super Observer** is dispatched to the crisis scene to evaluate the situation and define the necessary missions to cope with the crisis.
- **CMS Employee** is an internal human resource who is qualified and capable of performing missions related to his field of expertise. The worker acts as a facilitator actor when he is in charge of or operating local resources (e.g., tow trucks or ambulances).
- **External Worker** is an external resource who is specialized and capable of performing missions related to his field of expertise. The worker acts as a facilitator actor when he is in charge of or operating external resources (e.g., police trucks or fire trucks).
- **System Admin** is the specialist who maintains the system and creates all profiles of workers and resources to feed the crisis management database.
- **Witness** is the person who reports the crisis by calling the crisis management center.
- **Phone Company** is an external entity contacted for verification of witness purposes.
- **Surveillance System** is an external entity which monitors traffic in highways and cities with the use of cameras.

A.3 CMS: Feature Models

Since there are so many different kinds of crises, the domain of CMSs is very broad. However, any CMS has a common set of responsibilities and functionalities. It is therefore natural to build a framework or product line of CMSs, which can be specialized to create CMSs for a particular kind of crisis and a particular context. A feature diagram listing many possible features of a CMS is given in Figs. A.1–A.3. It has been taken from [3].

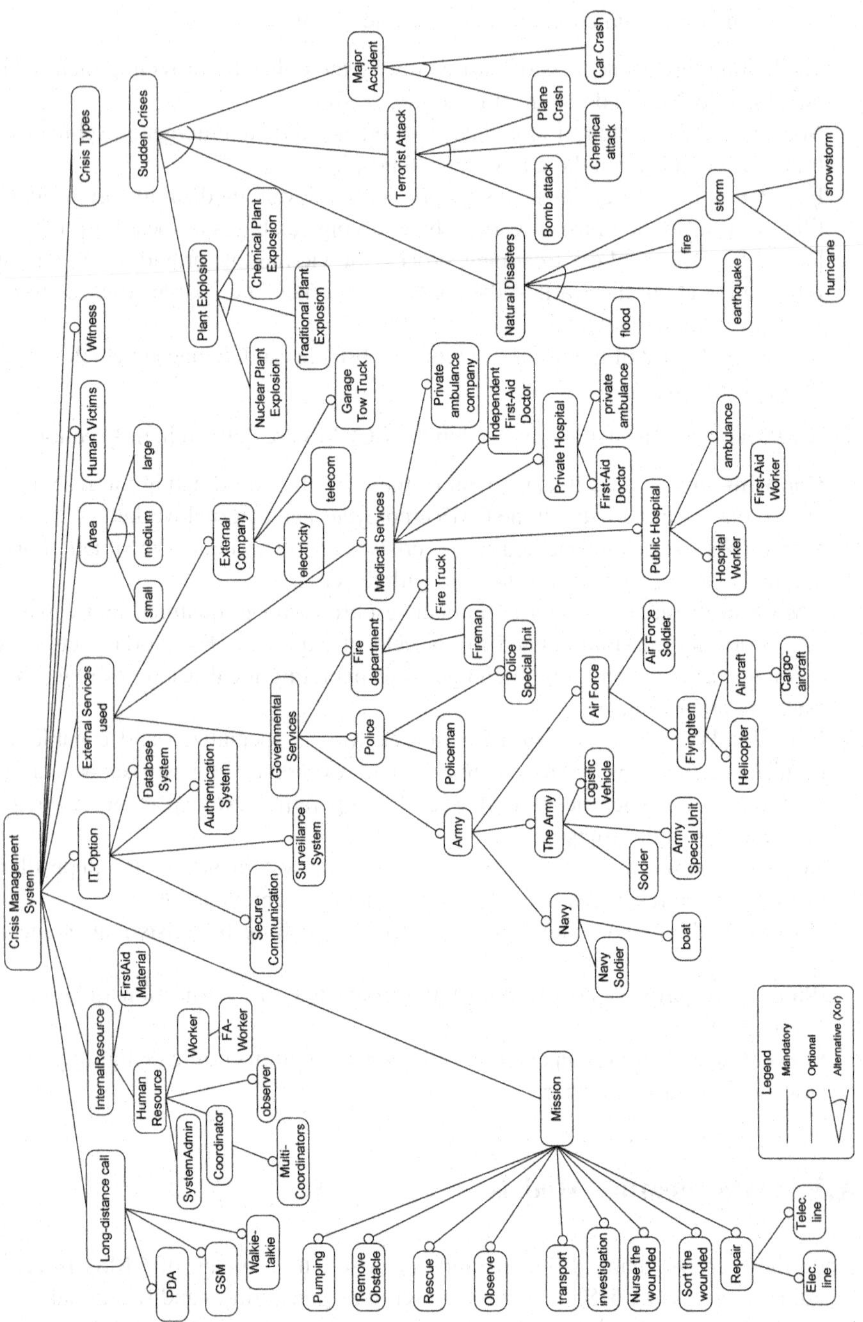

Fig. A.1 CMSs feature diagram—Part 1

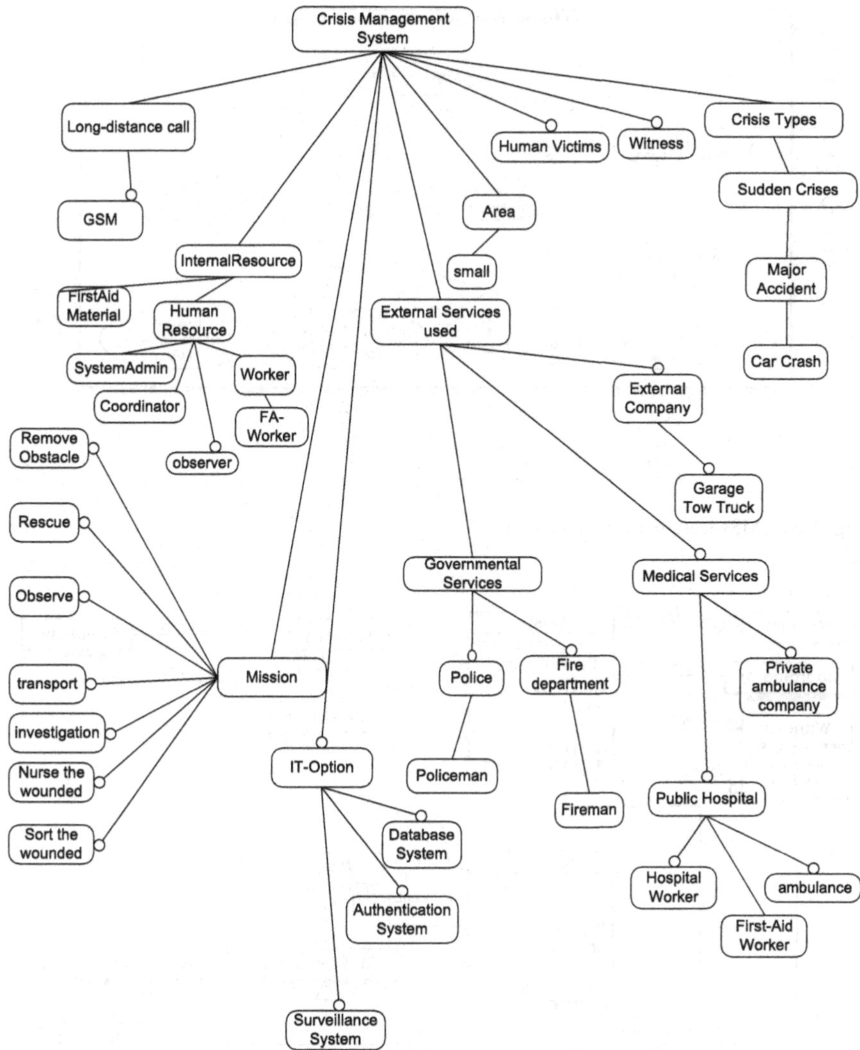

Fig. A.2 CMSs feature diagram—Part 2

Selection of some features requires the selection of other features. Examples of such dependencies are:

- *Natural Disasters* requires *Fire Department* and *External Company*
- *Terrorist Attack* requires *Army Special Unit* and *Police* and *Police Special Unit* and *Public Hospital*
- *Major Accident* requires *Police* and *Fire Department* and *Public Hospital* and *Private Hospital* and *Independent First-Aid Doctor* and *Private Ambulance Company*

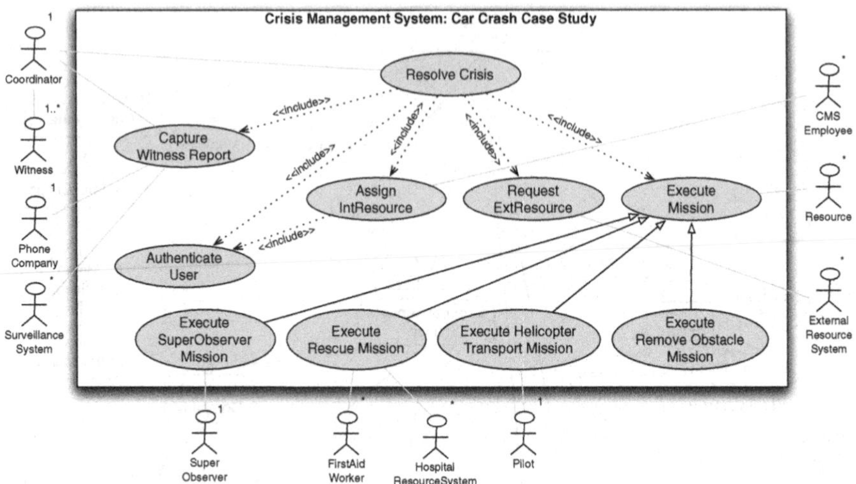

Fig. A.3 CMSs feature diagram—Part 3

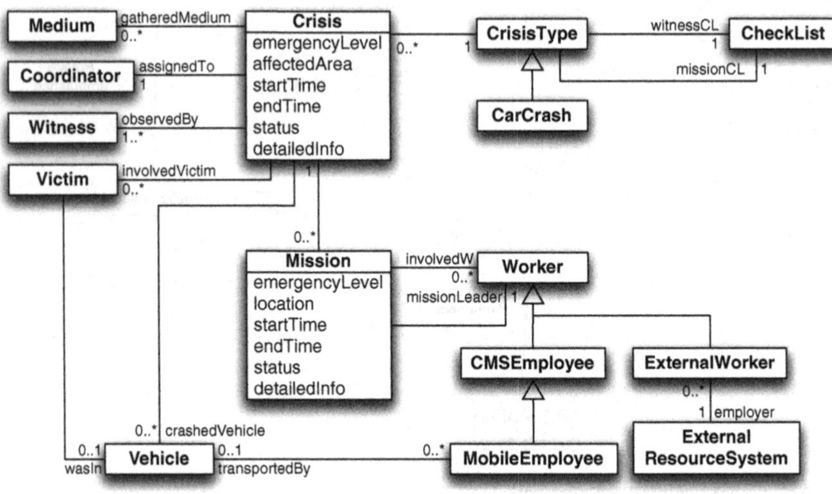

Fig. A.4 CCCMSs feature diagram

- *Plant Explosion* requires *Police* and *Fire Department* and *Public Hospital*
- *Nuclear Plant Explosion* requires *The Army* and *Army Special Unit*

Figure A.4 presents a possible set of features selected for the CCCMS.

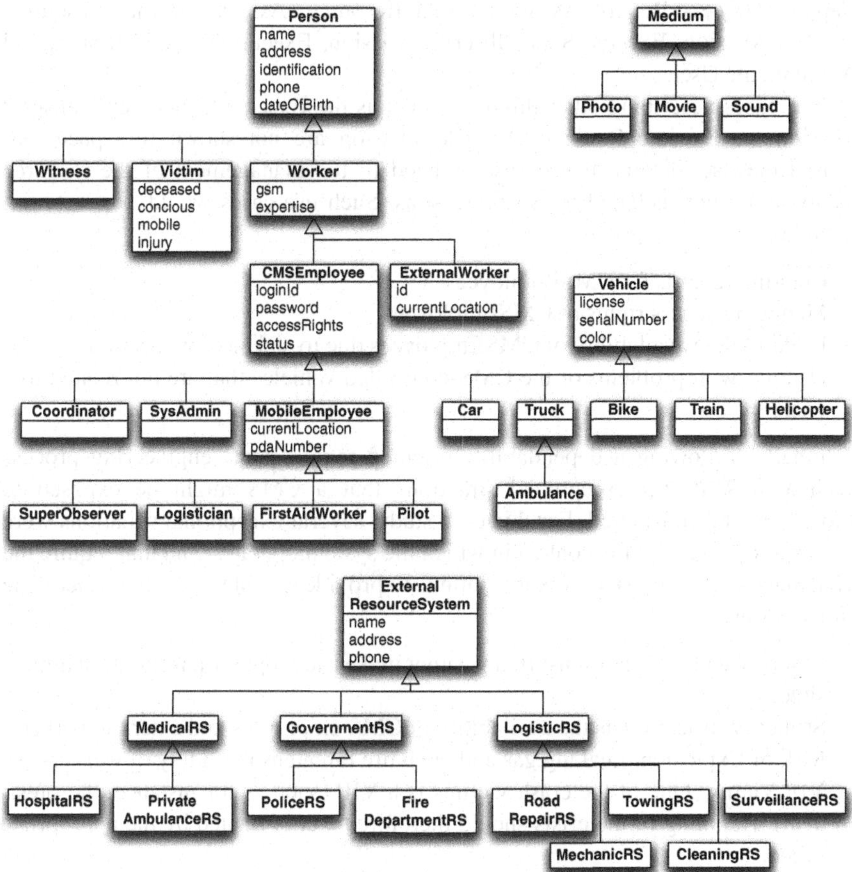

Fig. A.5 CCCMS: standard use case diagram

A.4 CCCMS: Use Cases

Use cases [4, 5] are a widely used formalism for discovering and recording behavioral requirements of software systems, since they can be effectively used as a communication means between technical and nontechnical stakeholders of the software under development. In short, use cases are stories of using a system to meet goals. They are in general text-based, but their strength is that they both scale up or scale down in terms of sophistication and formality, depending on the need and context.

Figure A.5 shows the use cases related to the summary-level goal *Resolve Crisis* in the CCCMS by means of a use case diagram.

Details of all the use cases that directly relate to the summary level use case *Resolve Crisis* are given in Sect. A.4.1. The listed use cases are: Resolve Crisis,

Capture Witness Report, Assign Internal Resource, Assign External Resource, Execute Mission, Execute SuperObserver Mission, Execute Rescue Mission, and Authenticate User.

Use cases describing other missions, such as the Execute Helicopter Transport Mission, or Execute Remove Obstacle Mission are not shown for space reasons. Likewise, details of use cases related to the management of the resource database are not included for space reasons. Such use cases would, for instance, include:

- Creating records for CMSEmployees
- Managing access rights of CMSEmployees
- Updating the availability of CMSEmployees due to sickness or vacation
- Dealing with problems of the CMS-controlled vehicles that are not related to a crisis

Finally, following a dependability-oriented requirements engineering process such as DREP [6], exceptional situations that a CMS might be exposed to should also be considered. For this case study, several exceptional situations were discovered that affect the context in which the system operates, and that require the system to react in a certain way to continue to provide reliable and safe service. The situations are:

- Severe Weather Conditions: Bad weather makes helicopter transportation impossible.
- Strike: A strike affects the availability of CMS employees and external workers.
- Risk of Explosion: Leaking gas and open fire threatens the safety of workers.
- VIP Victim: One of the crash victims is a VIP (such as for instance, the president). Handling of the crisis should therefore be coordinated by the appropriate office.
- Criminal Case: The reason for the crash is of criminal nature, and therefore the rescue missions have to be carried out accordingly.

To detect and to handle the above situations, we added the following exceptional actors: WeatherInformationSystem, NationalCrisisCenter [7]. The detailed handler use cases that describe the functionality that such a reliable CCCMS is to provide are not described in this document for space reasons.

A.4.1 Textual Use Cases

The use cases presented here follow a textual template. The *main success scenario* is a numbered list of lines of text (subsequently named *steps*) that describes the possible interactions between the primary actor, potential secondary actors, and the CCCMS (subsequently named *System*) that occur to reach a particular goal. Alternate ways of achieving a goal, or situations in which the goal cannot be reached, are described in the *extension* part of the template.

Resolve Crisis

Use Case 1: Resolve Crisis
Scope: Car Crash Crisis Management System
Primary Actor: Coordinator
Secondary Actor: Resource
Intention: The intention of the Coordinator is to resolve a car crash crisis by asking employees and external workers to execute appropriate missions.
Main Success Scenario:

Witness places a call to the crisis centre, where it is answered by a Coordinator.
1. *Coordinator* captures witness report (UC 2).
2. *System* recommends to *Coordinator* the missions that are to be executed based on the current information about the crisis and resources.
3. *Coordinator* selects one or more missions recommended by the system.

For each mission in parallel:

4. For each internal resource required by a selected mission, *System* assigns an internal resource (UC 3).
5. For each external resource required by a selected mission, *System* requests an external resource (UC 4).
6. *Resource* notifies *System* of arrival at mission location.
7. *Resource* executes the mission (UC 5).
8. *Resource* notifies *System* of departure from mission location.
9. In parallel to steps 6–8, *Coordinator* receives mission status updates from *System*.
10. In parallel to steps 6–8, *System* informs *Resource* of relevant changes to mission or crisis information.
11. *Resource* submits the final mission report to *System*.

12. In parallel to steps 4–8, *Coordinator* receives new crisis-related information from *System*.
13. *Coordinator* closes the file for the crisis resolution.

Use case ends in success.

Extensions:

1a. *Coordinator* is not logged in.
1a.1 *Coordinator* authenticates with System (UC 10).
1a.2 Use case continues with step 1.

4a. Internal resource is not available after step 4.
4a.1 *System* requests an external resource instead (i.e., use case continues in parallel with step 5).

5a. External resource is not available after step 5.
5a.1 Use case continues in parallel with step 2.

6a. *System* determines that the crisis location is unreachable by standard transportation means, but reachable by helicopter.
6a.1 *System* informs the *Coordinator* about the problem.
6a.2 *Coordinator* instructs *System* to execute a helicopter transport mission (UC 09).
6a.3 Use case continues with step 6.

6b. *Resource* is unable to contact *System*.
6b.1 *SuperObserver* notifies *System* that resource arrived at the mission location.

6c. Although *Resource* should be at mission location by now, *Resource* has not yet notified *System*.
6c.1 *System* requests *Resource* to provide an update of its location.
6c.2 Use case continues at step 6.

7a. One or more further missions are required in step 6.
7a.1 Use case continues in parallel with step 2.

7b. The mission failed.
  7b.1 Use case continues with step 2.

8a. *Resource* is unable to contact *System*.
  8a.1 *SuperObserver* notifies *System* that resource is leaving the mission location.

8b. Although mission should be completed by now, *Resource* has not left mission location.
  8b.1 *System* requests *Resource* to provide the reason for the delay.
  8b.2 Use case continues at step 7.

9a. Changes to mission are required.
  9a.1 Use case continues in parallel with step 2.

11a. *Resource* never files a mission report.
  11a.1 Mission use case ends without mission report.

12a. Changes to mission are required.
  12a.1 Use case continues in parallel with step 2.

Capture Witness Report

Use Case 2: Capture Witness Report
Scope: Car Crash Crisis Management System
Primary Actor: Coordinator
Secondary Actor: PhoneCompany, SurveillanceSystem
Intention: The Coordinator intends to create a crisis record based on the information obtained from witness.
Main Success Scenario:

Coordinator requests Witness to provide his identification.
1. *Coordinator* provides witness information[1] to *System* as reported by the witness.
2. *Coordinator* informs *System* of location and type of crisis as reported by the witness.

In parallel to steps 2–4:
  2a.1 *System* contacts *PhoneCompany* to verify witness information.
  2a.2 *PhoneCompany* sends address/phone information to *System*.
  2a.3 *System* validates information received from the PhoneCompany.

3. *System* provides *Coordinator* with a crisis-focused checklist.
4. *Coordinator* provides crisis information[2] to *System* as reported by the witness.
5. *System* assigns an initial emergency level to the crisis and sets the crisis status to *active*.

Use case ends in success.

Extensions:

1a,2a. The call is disconnected. The base use case terminates.

In parallel to steps 3–4, if the crisis location is covered by camera surveillance:
  3a.1 *System* requests video feed from *SurveillanceSystem*.
  3a.2 *SurveillanceSystem* starts sending video feed to *System*.
  3a.3 *System* starts displaying video feed for *Coordinator*.

4a. The call is disconnected.
  4a.1 Use case continues at step 5 without crisis information.

5a. PhoneCompany information does not match information received from Witness.
  5a.1 The base use case is terminated.

5b. Camera vision of the location is perfect, but *Coordinator* cannot confirm the situation that the witness describes *or* the *Coordinator* determines that the witness is calling in a fake crisis.
  5b.1 The base use case is terminated.

[1]Witness information includes the first name, last name, phone number, and address.
[2]Crisis information includes the details about the crisis, the time witnessed, etc.

Assign Internal Resource

Use Case 3: Assign Internal Resource
Scope: Car Crash Crisis Management System
Primary Actor: None
Secondary Actor: CMSEmployee
Intention: The intention of System is to find, contact, and assign a mission to the most appropriate available CMSEmployee.
Main Success Scenario:

System selects an appropriate CMSEmployee based on the mission type, the emergency level, location and requested expertise. In very urgent cases, steps 1 and 2 can be performed for several CMSEmployees concurrently, until one of the contacted employees accepts the mission.

1. *System* sends *CMSEmployee* mission information.
2. *CMSEmployee* informs *System* that he accepts the mission.

Use case ends in success.

Extensions:

1a. *CMSEmployee* is not logged in.
  1a.1 *System* requests the *CMSEmployee* to login.
  1a.2 *CMSEmployee* authenticates with System (UC 10).
  1a.3 Use case continues at step 1.
1b. *CMSEmployee* is unavailable or unresponsive.
  1b.1 *System* selects the next appropriate *CMSEmployee*.
  1b.2 Use case continues at step 1.
    1b.1a No other *CMSEmployee* is available. Use case ends in failure.
2a. *CMSEmployee* informs *System* that he cannot accept the mission.
  2a.1 *System* selects the next appropriate *CMSEmployee*.
  2a.2 Use case continues at step 1.
    2a.2a No other *CMSEmployee* is available. Use case ends in failure.

Request External Resource

Use Case 4: Request External Resource
Scope: Car Crash Crisis Management System
Primary Actor: Coordinator
Secondary Actor: ExternalResourceSystem (ERS)
Intention: The System requests a mission from an external resource, such as a fire station, police station or external ambulance service.
Main Success Scenario:

1. *System* sends mission request to *ERS*, along with mission-specific information[1].
2. *ERS* informs *System* that request can be processed.

Use case ends in success.

Extensions:

2a. *ERS* notifies *System* that it partially approves request for resources. Use case ends in degraded success.
2b. *ERS* notifies *System* that it can not service the request. Use case ends in failure.

[1]Mission-specific information includes things such as the location and emergency level of the mission, the quantity of vehicles requested, special characteristics of the aid worker or vehicle, etc...

Execute Mission

Use Case 5: Execute Mission
Intention: The Resource executes a mission in order to help resolve a crisis. ExecuteMission is an abstract use case. The details of the interaction for specific missions are presented in child use cases such as ExecuteSuperObserverMission (UC 6), or ExecuteRescueMission (UC 7).

Execute SuperObserver Mission

Use Case 6: Execute SuperObserver Mission
Scope: Car Crash Crisis Management System
Primary Actor: SuperObserver
Secondary Actor: None
Intention: The intention of the SuperObserver is to observe the situation at the crisis site to be able to order appropriate missions.
Main Success Scenario:

SuperObserver is at the crisis location.
1. *System* sends a crisis-specific checklist to *SuperObserver.*
2. *SuperObserver* feeds *System* with crisis information.
3. *System* suggests crisis-specific missions to *SuperObserver.*

Steps 4–8 is repeated as many times as needed.

4. *SuperObserver* notifies *System* of the type of mission he wants to create.
5. *System* sends a mission-specific information request to *SuperObserver.*
6. *SuperObserver* sends mission-specific information[1] to *System.*
7. *System* acknowledges the mission creation to *SuperObserver.*
8. *System* informs *SuperObserver* that mission was completed successfully.
9. *SuperObserver judges that his presence is no longer needed at the crisis location.*

Use case ends in success.

Extensions:

7a. Mission cannot be created and replacement missions are possible.
  7a.1 *System* suggests replacement missions to *SuperObserver.*
  7a.2 Use case continues with step 4.

7b. Mission cannot be created and no replacement missions are possible.
  7b.1 *System* suggests notifying the *NationalCrisisCenter.*
  7b.2 Use case continues with step 4.

8a. Mission failed.
  8a.1 *System* informs *SuperObserver* and *Coordinator* about mission failure.
  8a.2 Use case continues with step 4.

[1]Mission-specific information includes things such as the quantity of vehicles requested, special characteristics of the aid worker or vehicle, etc...

Execute Rescue Mission

Use Case 7: Execute Rescue Mission
Scope: Car Crash Crisis Management System
Primary Actor: FirstAidWorker
Secondary Actor: HospitalRS

Intention: The intention of the FirstAidWorker is to accept and then execute a rescue mission that involves transporting a victim to the most appropriate hospital.
Main Success Scenario:
FirstAidWorker is at the crisis location.
1. *FirstAidWorker* transmits injury information of victim to *System.*
Steps 2 and 3 are optional.
2. *FirstAidWorker* determines victim's identity and communicates it to *System.*
3. *System* requests victim's medical history information from all connected *HospitalResourceSystems.*
FirstAidWorker administers first aid procedures to victim.
4. *System* instructs *FirstAidWorker* to bring the victim to the most appropriate hospital.
5. *FirstAidWorker* notifies *System* that he is leaving the crisis site.
6. *FirstAidWorker* notifies *System* that he has dropped off the victim at the hospital.
7. *FirstAidWorker* informs *System* that he has completed his mission.
Use case ends in success.
Extensions:
4a. *HospitalResourceSystem* transmits victim's medical history information to *System.*
4a.1 *System* notifies *FirstAidWorker* of medical history of the victim relevant to his injury.
4a.2 Use case continues at step 4.

Execute Helicopter Transport Mission

Use Case 8: Execute Helicopter Transport Mission
Scope: Car Crash Crisis Management System
Primary Actor: Pilot
Secondary Actor: None
Intention: The intention of the Pilot is to accept and then execute a transport mission that involves transporting a CMSEmployee to and from a mission location.
Main Success Scenario: To be defined.

Execute Remove Obstacle Mission

Use Case 9: Execute Remove Obstacle Mission
Scope: Car Crash Crisis Management System
Primary Actor: TowTruckDriver
Secondary Actor: None
Intention: The intention of the TowTruckDriver is to accept and then execute a remove obstacle mission that involves removing a crashed car from a mission location.
Main Success Scenario: To be defined.

AuthenticateUser

Use Case 10: AuthenticateUser
Scope: Car Crash Crisis Management System
Primary Actor: None
Secondary Actor: CMSEmployee
Intention: The intention of the System is to authenticate the CMSEmployee to allow access.

Main Success Scenario:

1. *System* prompts *CMSEmployee* for login id and password.
2. *CMSEmployee* enters login id and password into *System*.
3. *System* validates the login information.

Use case ends in success.

Extensions:

2a. *CMSEmployee* cancels the authentication process. Use case ends in failure.
3a. *System* fails to authenticate the *CMSEmployee*.
 3a.1 Use case continues at step 1.
  3a.1a *CMSEmployee* performed three consecutive failed attempts.
   3a.1a.1 Use case ends in failure.

A.5 CCCMS: Domain Model

The domain model offers insight into the problem domain, in our case the CCCMS. Taking the form of a UML class diagram, it provides a description of the concepts of the problem domain relevant to the CCCMS, by representing the concepts as classes, attributes, and associations between classes. Although any domain concept could be added to the domain model, we decided to include here only concepts that must define information that must be recorded for the purpose of fulfilling the system's responsibilities over time. In other words, the domain model presented here only contains concepts that are used to describe the necessary information to fulfill system goals.

Because of size constraints, the domain model is split into two parts. The top part of Fig. A.6 depicts the Crisis and Mission concepts and how they relate to the other concepts, whereas the bottom part shows the generalization/specialization hierarchies inherent in the domain of the CCCMS.

A.6 CCCMS: Informal Physical Architecture Description

A typical architecture for a CMS contains many machines that are connected with different types of networks. Figure A.7 gives an overview of the kinds of machines and communication networks that could be used in an instance of the CCCMS.

The backend of the system is composed of a server or a server cluster that implements most of the business functionality. Local CMS employees, such as the coordinators and the system administrators, use terminals or desktop machines to access the backend through a private network. External services and mobile CMS employees with laptops are connected to the backend by means of virtual private networks on top of public networks. Cell phones, GPS (Global Positioning System) devices, and PDAs (Personal Desktop Assistants) are reached using a GSM (Global System for Mobile Communications) antenna.

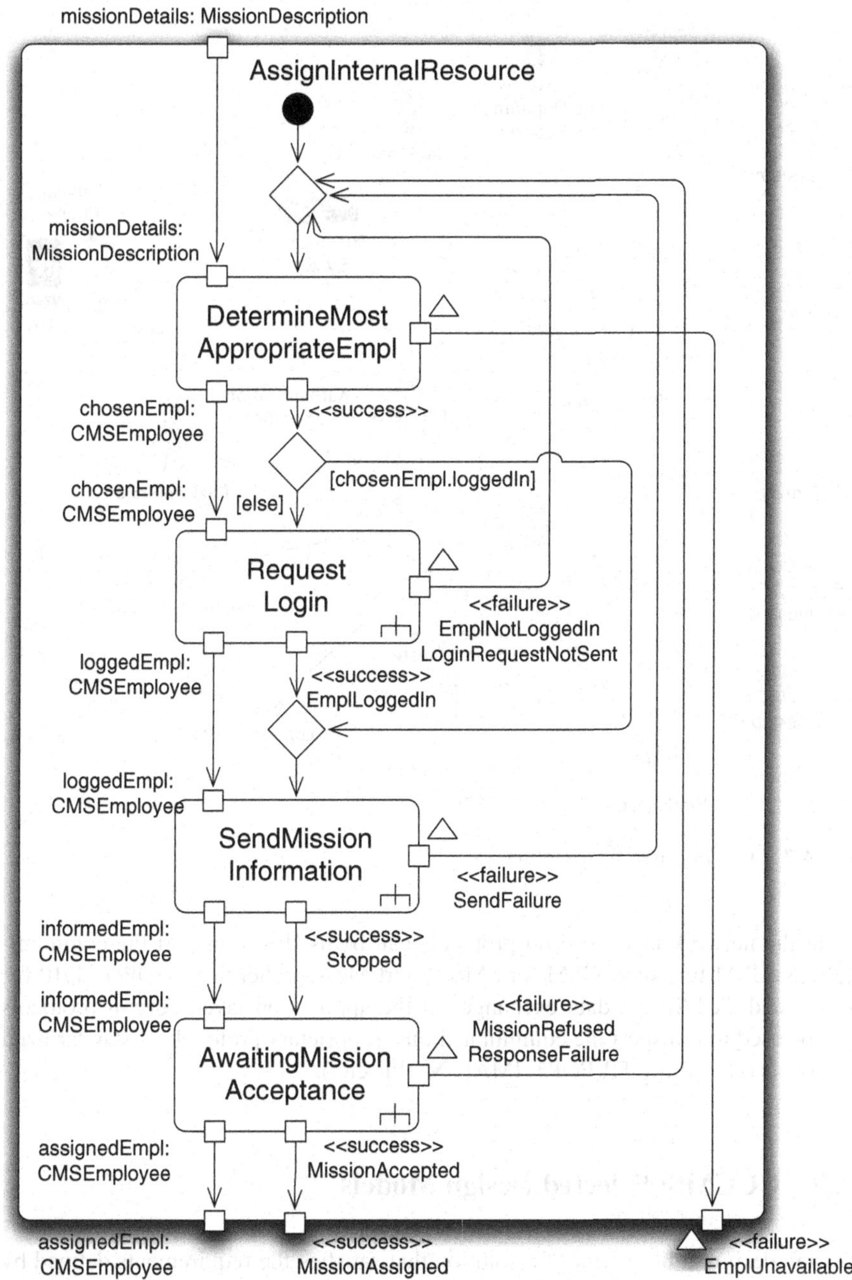

Fig. A.6 CCCMS domain model

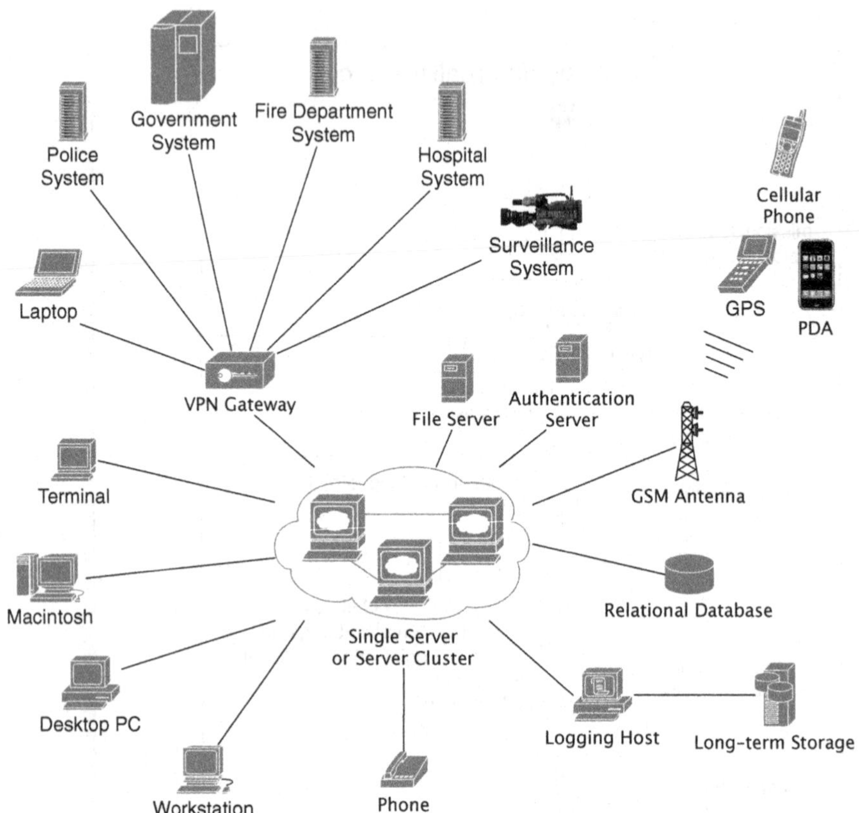

Fig. A.7 CCCMS: physical architecture

In the network layer, several protocols can be used to transport the communications: GSM for voice, GSM for SMS (Short Message Service), UDP/TCP/IP for voice, and TCP/IP for data exchange. In the application layer, several protocols can be used to transport the communications: proprietary protocols or standardized protocols (HTTP, SMTP, POP3, IMAP, XMPP, etc.).

A.7 CCCMS: Selected Design Models

During design, a blue print of a solution that satisfies the requirements defined by the analysis models is devised. In object-oriented design, the conceptual state has to be mapped to objects, and then the developer has to decide how the conceptual state changes specified in every system operation are to be implemented by interacting objects at run-time.

The concepts identified during analysis, in our case, e.g., Crisis, Mission, and CMSEmployee, are initial candidates for becoming design objects that hold the application state. However, some concepts may be implemented using several objects, or, alternatively, some concepts may be implemented as attributes. The granularity of objects affects several aspects of the system under development. Too fine-grained decomposition leads to systems with thousands of objects. Such systems might be hard to understand and maintain due to their high coupling and generate huge communication overhead. On the other hand, a coarse decomposition leads to bulky architectures and objects with unclear responsibilities, which can also be hard to understand and maintain. Good designers try to maximize object coherence while minimizing object coupling.

The idea of this section is to present some design models of a possible object-oriented design of the CCCMS backend. Currently, the only functionality that is designed is the *CreateMission* functionality that is triggered by the SuperObserver when ordering missions to deal with the crash.

A.7.1 Creating Missions

Summary of Functionality The *CreateMission* functionality allows the Super-Observer to inform the CCCMS about a mission that needs to be accomplished in order to deal with the crash. The system has to store the relevant mission information, determine the candidate CMSEmployees that could accomplish the mission, establish contact with at least one of them, and propose the mission to him. The design of *CreateMission* also implements some secondary functionality. For instance, it takes care of gathering statistics on how many potential candidate employees the system was able to choose from when assigning the mission. Also, it makes sure that employees have properly logged into the system (and hence authenticated) before sending them mission-related information.

Interaction Design It is assumed that somehow the user interface on the PDA allows the SuperObserver to select the appropriate mission kind, select the emergency level of the mission, and enter detailed mission information before sending the request to the CCCMS backend. The sequencing of message exchanges between objects that are triggered by this request is shown in a sequence diagram in Fig. A.8.

The initial request is directed to the *CrisisManager*. After instantiating a new mission object and linking it to the crisis, the crisis manager hands the responsibility of assigning the mission to a CMSEmployee to the *ResourceManager*. The resource manager has access to a hash table of employees indexed by expertise, and hence is able to obtain a collection of employees that are qualified to execute the mission. The resource manager then proceeds by looping though this list, and inserting any available employee (i.e., an employee that currently is not affected to other missions or otherwise unavailable) that is close enough to the mission location (i.e., can get to the mission location in a reasonable amount of time) into a priority queue. In the

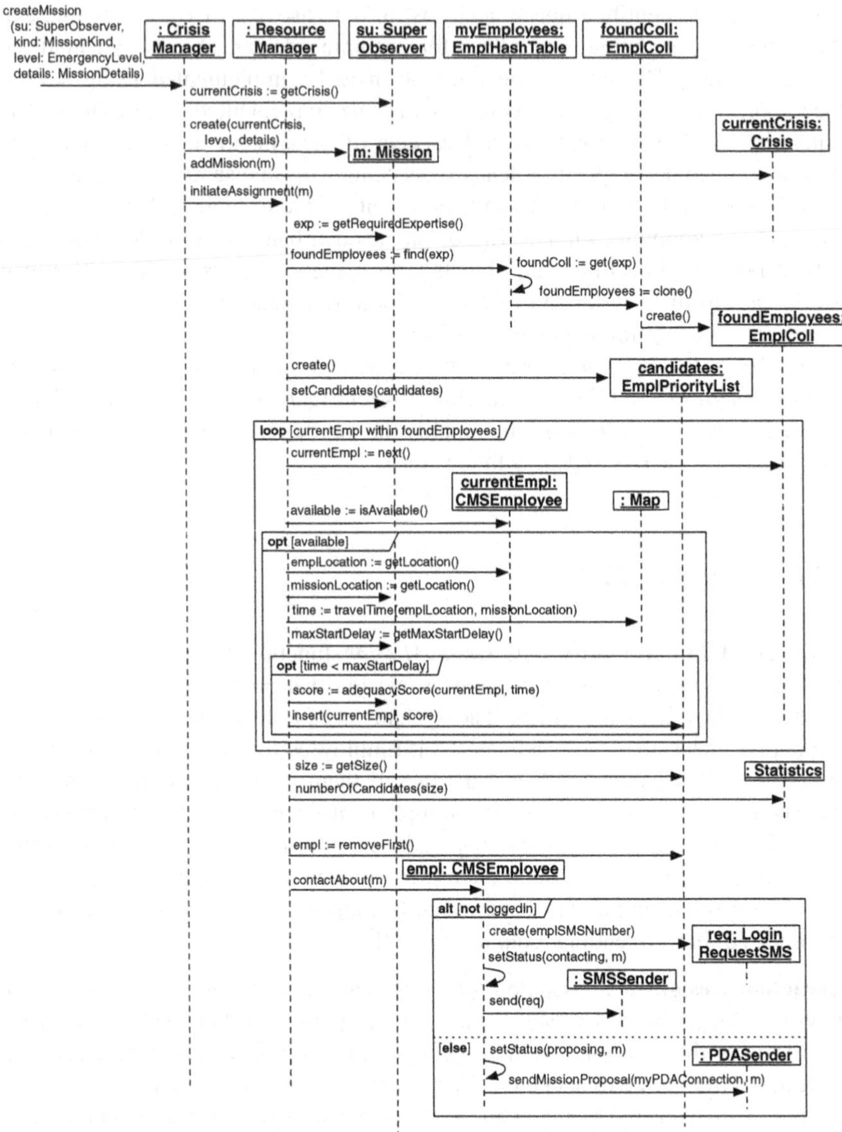

Fig. A.8 CCCMS: CreateMission design sequence diagram

queue, the employees are sorted with respect to their "adequacy" for performing the mission. Once this list is established, the size of the list is remembered for statistical purpose. Finally, the resource manager proceeds by contacting the first employee on the list. If that employee is not currently logged in, then he is requested to do so by sending him an SMS.

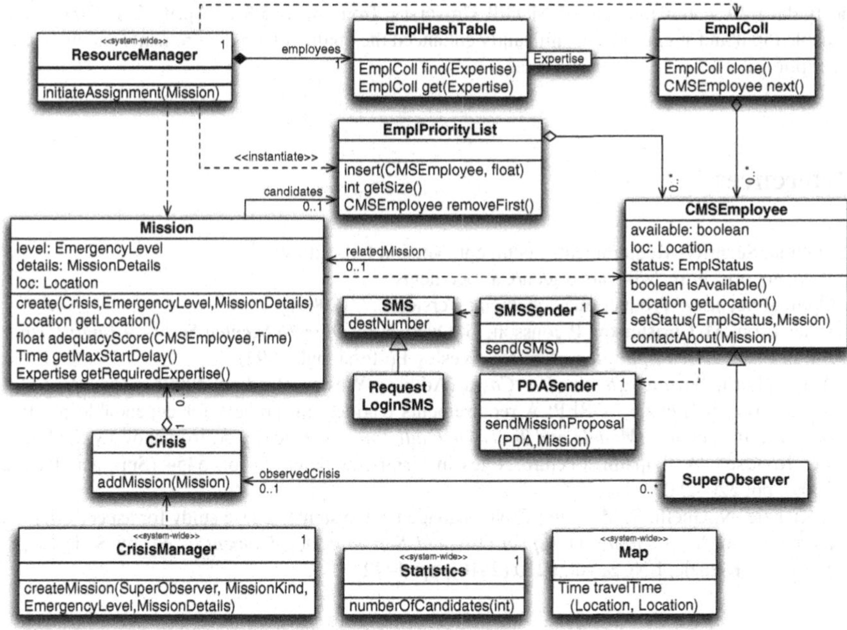

Fig. A.9 CCCMS: partial design class diagram based on CreateMission design

The interaction design ends here, because the system now has to wait for an answer from the employee (which can either be a login request, or a mission acceptance notification).

Structural Design The chosen design solution presented in the sequence diagram has many implications on the design. It assumes, for instance, the existence of many classes with particular fields and method definitions. Also, some permanent associations are assumed to exist. For example, a super observer must be associated with a crisis. This is obvious from the first message in the sequence diagram in Fig. A.8. Another example is the employee hash table that can find employees based on a particular expertise. The *CreateMission* design assumes that this hash table already exists. This means that the functionality that deals with the creation of employees must also take care of building this hash table, establishing permanent references between expertise and groups of employees.

The classes, attributes and methods, and the dependencies and associations between classes created, used and assumed by the *CreateMission* design are shown in Fig. A.9.

Acknowledgments The authors would like to thank Christian Fischer, Damien Garot, Laurent Vuillermoz, Jacques Klein, and Alfredo Capozucca for sharing requirements documents and models of CMSs with us. Their contributions led to the creation of the first draft of this document. Our thanks also extend to Mehmet Aksit, Wisam Al Abed, João Araújo, Florencia Balbastro, Franck Fleurey, Jean-Marc Jézéquel, Gunter Mussbacher, Awais Rachid, Pablo Sánchez, and Jon Whittle, the participants of the first 1-week aspect-oriented modeling workshop held at the Bellairs Research Institute of McGill University from April 5th to April 12th 2009. Their valuable input and suggestions significantly enhanced the quality of the requirements and use cases descriptions.

References

1. Optimal Security: Requirements document: Version 0.8. (2009)
2. Wikicars.org: http://wikicars.org/en/Car_accidents
3. Optimal Security: Product line document: Version 0.7. (2009)
4. I. Jacobson, M. Christerson, P. Jonsson, G. Overgaard, *Object-Oriented Software Engineering: A Use Case Driven Approach* (Addison-Wesley Professional, 1992)
5. A. Cockburn, *Writing Effective Use Cases* (Addison-Wesley, Reading, 2000)
6. S. Mustafiz, J. Kienzle, DREP: A requirements engineering process for dependable reactive systems, in *Methods, Models and Tools for Fault Tolerance*, ed. by A. Romanovsky, C. Jones, J.L. Knudsen, A. Tripathi. Lecture Notes in Computer Science, vol. 5454 (Springer, Berlin, 2009), pp. 220–250
7. J. Kienzle, N. Guelfi, S. Mustafiz, Crisis management systems: a case study for aspect-oriented modeling, in *Transactions on Aspect-Oriented Software Development 7*, ed. by S. Katz, M. Mezini, J. Kienzle. LNCS, vol. 6210 (2010), pp. 1–22

About the Editors

Ana Moreira is an Associate Professor at Universidade Nova de Lisboa where she leads the Software Engineering group. Currently, her main research topics are aspect-oriented requirements engineering and architecture design, model-driven development, variability and trade-off analysis. She is a member of the editorial board of the journals "Transactions on AOSD" and "Software and Systems Modeling". She is, or has been, a member of the Steering Committee for the international conferences MODELS and AOSD. She has been a regular member of the program or organizing committees of several international conferences, including AOSD, ICSE, MODELS, ECOOP, RE, CAiSE and SPLC. She has co-organized over 50 international workshops, including the Early Aspects workshop series, and conferences and published over 100 peer-reviewed journal and conference research papers. She is co-founder or the international movements Early Aspects and precise UML Group. She has been Program Committee Chair of several international conferences, such as AOSD 2009 and MODELS 2013.

Ruzanna Chitchyan is a lecturer in Software Engineering the Department of Computer Science, University of Leicester. Her current research interests are in requirements modelling and analysis in general and aspect-oriented requirements engineering and architecture design in particular. She has worked on several major EC projects on this topic (e.g. AOSD-Europe, AMPLE, and DiVA), and, throughout the years, has actively participated in the Early Aspects workshops.

João Araújo is an Assistant Professor of the Department of Informatics at the Universidade Nova de Lisboa, Portugal. He holds a PhD in Computer Science from Lancaster University, UK, in the area of Requirements Engineering. His principal research interests are in Requirements Engineering in general and Early Aspects in particular, where he has published several papers on this topic in international conferences and workshops. He has been a co-founder of the Early Aspects workshop at AOSD, OOPSLA, SPLC and ICSE conferences since 2002. Additionally, he served on the organization or program committees of MODELS, RE, ECOOP, AOSD, CAiSE and ICSE in the past few years. He served as a guest

A. Moreira et al. (eds.), *Aspect-Oriented Requirements Engineering*,
DOI 10.1007/978-3-642-38640-4, © Springer-Verlag Berlin Heidelberg 2013

editor of the Special issue on Early Aspects at Transactions on AOSD journal in 2007. He has taught several tutorials on Early Aspects.

Awais Rashid is a Professor of Software Engineering at Lancaster University where he leads research on advanced software modularity and composition mechanisms as well as their implications for secure systems in the modern digital world. His relevant research interests are in aspect-oriented software development (AOSD), model-driven engineering and their applications for managing software variability and product lines. He has led a number of European Commission projects on these topics totalling over 10M € in funding. He is the founding co-editor-in-chief of the journal Transactions on AOSD. He was a member of the steering committee of the international conference on aspect-oriented software development (AOSD) from 2006 to 2012 and its executive committee from 2007 to 2012. He has been a regular member of its program and organising committees since its inception in 2002 (including roles as organising chair in 2004 and program co-chair in 2006). He has also severed on the program committee of the European Conference on Object-Oriented Programming (ECOOP) and is currently a member of AITO. He also held a visiting professor position as the Pays de la Loire Chair Regionale at the Ecole des Mines de Nantes, France (2008–2011). He has authored over 100 scholarly articles in software engineering, software modularity and security.

Index

A. Moreira et al. (eds.), *Aspect-Oriented Requirements Engineering*, DOI 10.1007/978-3-642-38640-4, © Springer-Verlag Berlin Heidelberg 2013

Printed in the United States
By Bookmasters